INDIANA BLACKS IN THE TWENTIETH CENTURY

History • Travel

INDIANA BLACKS IN THE TWENTIETH CENTURY

+

Emma Lou Thornbrough

Edited and with a final chapter by Lana Ruegamer

INDIANA UNIVERSITY PRESS

BLOOMINGTON • INDIANAPOLIS

Frontis: Crispus Attucks basketball fans cheer an overtime victory over archrival Indianapolis Technical High School in the 1948 state tournament, only a few years after the black school was permitted to compete in the IHSAA contest. Indianapolis Recorder Collection, Indiana Historical Society.

This book is a publication of

Indiana University Press
601 North Morton Street
Bloomington, IN 47404-3797 USA

http://www.indiana.edu/~iupress

Telephone orders 800-842-6796
Fax orders 812-855-7931
Orders by e-mail iuporder@indiana.edu

Library of Congress Cataloging-in-Publication Data

Thornbrough, Emma Lou.
    Indiana Blacks in the twentieth century / Emma Lou Thornbrough ; edited and with a final chapter by Lana Ruegamer.
        p.   cm.
    Sequel to: Negro in Indiana before 1900 : a study of a minority, 1993.
    Includes index.
    ISBN 0-253-33799-2 (cl: alk. paper)
    1. Afro-Americans–Indiana–History–20th century.
2. Indiana–History–20th century.   3. Afro-Americans–Indiana–Social conditions–20th century. 4. Indiana–Social conditions–20th century. I. Ruegamer, Lana. II. Title.

E185.93.I4 T47   2000
977.2004'96073—dc21   00-039645

1   2   3   4   5   05   04   03   02   01   00

Acknowledgment of Sponsorship

Publication of this book is made possible by the generous
support of Lilly Endowment Inc.

Acknowledgment of Sponsorship

Publication of this book is made possible by the generous
support of Lilly Endowment Inc.

Contents

Editor's Introduction

Emma Lou Thornbrough (1913–1994) was a pioneer in writing Indiana's African American history. Her University of Michigan doctoral dissertation, "Negro Slavery in the North: Its Constitutional and Legal Aspects" (1946), was the basis for her classic *The Negro in Indiana: A Study of a Minority* (1957), and this widely praised work was followed by studies of the Ku Klux Klan in Indianapolis and the movements to "break the barriers" to equal access to public accommodations in Indiana, among many others. Thornbrough's work "set the standard" for studies of northern black populations.

Thornbrough was also a pioneer as a woman in the historical profession and as a white historian whose principal subject was African Americans. Born in Indianapolis into a family interested in history—her younger sister Gayle was also an historian—Thornbrough was appalled by the racial injustice she saw around her. She not only wrote about black history, she also worked to change it, as a longtime member and board member of the Indiana Civil Liberties Union and the Greater Indianapolis National Association for the Advancement of Colored People. Her lifelong engagement with civic affairs in Indianapolis and her interest in the politics of social change in her state meant that she had an unparalleled knowledge of Indiana's twentieth-century black history and a personal acquaintance with many of its protagonists.

These assets emerged clearly in the manuscript she was working on at the time of her death in December 1994, "Indiana Blacks in the Twentieth Century." She had completed a draft of all but the last chapter (which she entitled "The Continuing Search for Identity" in her table of contents), and she had complete footnote citations for all of chapter 1 and most of the material in her chapter 2, which I subsequently divided into chapters 2 and 3. For the remaining seven chapters there were authors' surnames and page numbers but usually no title and certainly no full citations. Hence the manuscript required both copyediting and research to identify and complete the footnotes.

Indiana University Press Senior Editor Joan Catapano and I agreed that the manuscript needed the final chapter Thornbrough had planned, and I undertook the task of researching and writing it. I was invited to work with the manuscript because of my experience as an editor for the Indiana Historical Society (1975–1984) and my own publications in Indiana history. I accepted both because I knew and admired Thornbrough and because I believed that the manuscript makes a major contribution to our understanding of Indiana and American history.

The changes I have made in Thornbrough's text have been minor, smoothing some rough places, clarifying some confusing passages, turning passive sentence constructions into active ones. I have not knowingly altered the meaning of any of her text.

The last chapter that Thornbrough completed was chapter 9, which discusses changes in social and economic conditions since 1970. I have added material to this chapter to bring it up to the present.

The final chapter, for which I am alone responsible, lacks, of course, the deep background of knowledge and experience that Thornbrough would have brought to it. I have attempted to compensate in part for my relative inexperience by drawing on the knowledge of others. I wish to thank the persons who agreed to be interviewed for this chapter, without whom there would have been little upon which to base it, since little has been written on the post-1970 period: Walter Blackburn, Collins and Dorothy Ferguson, Pam Freeman, David Hubbard, Herman Hudson, George Juergens, Phyllis Klotman, Frances Linthecome, Fred McElroy, James Mumford, Shirley Palmer, Alice Brokenburr Ray, William Ray, Kay Rowe, and Janice Wiggins. Constraints of time and other responsibilities have meant that this chapter does not reflect many sources beyond those available in Indianapolis and Bloomington. It must be considered only a first word on a large and more varied subject than this essay suggests.

I would like to thank Martin Ridge, Suellen Hoy, and James H. Madison for their critiques of chapter 10, as well as those of interviewees Pam Freeman, George Juergens, Phyllis Klotman, James Mumford, Alice Ray, Kay Rowe, and Janice Wiggins. The chapter is better than it would have been without these readers and not as good as it would have been had I followed all their recommendations.

Thanks too to Wilma L. Gibbs of the Indiana Historical Society and Chazz Means of the Indianapolis *Star* for help with illustrations.

The entire manuscript was read and critiqued by Frances Linthecome of Indianapolis, long involved in the city's movements for black equality. Without her conviction that I could do this job and her promise to help, I would not have undertaken it. The last chapter is for her.

Thornbrough dedicated her life to researching and teaching history. The manuscript shows her commitment to this final project as her health and handwriting deteriorated. The book is another pioneering state study of a black population, and we are fortunate that she dedicated her last years to writing it.

Lana Ruegamer
Bloomington, Indiana
September 1999

INDIANA BLACKS IN THE TWENTIETH CENTURY

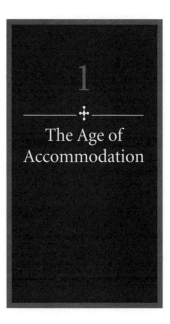

1

✠

The Age of
Accommodation

At the beginning of the twentieth century American citizens of African descent were debating among themselves about the name by which they wished to be called in much the same way they had debated in the closing years of the nineteenth century. Some people preferred "colored," others "Negro." Most leaders chose the latter, and Booker T. Washington in particular carried on a campaign to persuade white publishers and editors to spell the word with a capital "N." A few, among whom T. Thomas Fortune, editor of the New York *Age,* was most conspicuous, called for the use of "Afro-American." (Washington founded the National Negro Business League, while Fortune created the Afro-American League.) A few years later when another group founded an organization with objectives similar to those of the Afro-American League they chose to call it the National Association for the Advancement of Colored People (NAACP). Robert S. Abbott, publisher of the Chicago *Defender,* the newspaper with the largest circulation among blacks, refused to use the word "Negro" because it had derogatory connotations among whites. Instead he used the terms "Race" and "Race Man," a practice that other newspapers and speakers sometimes copied. The term "black," so widely used in later years, was frowned upon because it had been used in the days of slavery.

White publications usually used the terms "colored" or "negro." As late as 1920, compilers of United States census reports tried to differentiate between persons of unmixed African descent and those of mixed ancestry, calling the former "black" or "negro" and the latter "mulatto." But by 1910 they admitted that these classifications were not accurate. They were likely to reflect "perceptibility dependent upon ability of the enumerator" and were abandoned after 1920.[1] The 1900 census showed a Negro population in Indiana of 57,507, or 2.3 percent of the state's total. In the next decade, black population increased only to 60,320, reflecting a smaller rate of growth than that of the white population. At that time slightly less than half the black population had been born in Indiana. Most of the remainder were immigrants from the states of the upper South.[2]

In the years before the First World War, most of the black population of the United States was still concentrated in the South and was largely rural. In Indiana, however, before the end of the nineteenth century blacks from rural communities in the state had already begun to move from farms to towns and cities, where most of the newcomers from out of state also settled. By 1900, 73.5 percent of the black population in the state was classified as urban; by 1910, the percentage had increased to 80.3.[3] The black population within the state also moved northward, from the towns and rural communities in the southern counties to the more industrialized communities in the central and northern parts of the state. In the Ohio River towns of New Albany, Jeffersonville, Madison, Rockport, and Lawrenceburg, the black population declined between 1900 and 1910. In Evansville, where 7,518 African Americans lived in 1900, the total had declined to 6,266 by 1910. Many blacks from Kentucky who had settled in these cities moved northward to communities where employment opportunities were more promising, and native blacks also left after graduating from high school. Black farming communities, such as Lyles Station in Gibson County, declined or disappeared as settlers moved to Indianapolis or Terre Haute in search of jobs.[4]

Elementary school class, Lyles Station, 1900s. Indiana Historical Society Library.

Hopes of better economic opportunities, better schools, and the amenities of town life were the usual reasons for migrating, but white hostility was also sometimes a factor. For example, by 1900 Leavenworth, the county seat of Crawford County, had the reputation of being the most "anti-Negro" town on the Ohio River. Captains of riverboats were said to discipline black crewmen by threatening to put them off the boat at Leavenworth. By 1900 there was only one Negro resident in Crawford County. A little farther north in Washington County, where there had been a few blacks from very early times, a county history boasted that by 1900 there were no blacks. It appears that black farmers had been forced by their white neighbors to sell their land and move out of the county. In 1902, notices were posted in French Lick and West Baden in Orange County "notifying the negroes [*sic*] that if they were on the street after sundown they would be annihilated." Although there were no statutory laws forbidding black settlement, in numerous small towns throughout the state there was a tradition of "sunset" or "sundown laws," enforced not only by public opinion but also by sheriffs and other local officers, that decreed blacks could not settle in the town or stay overnight.[5]

The focal point for most migrants, whether they came from within the state or from outside, was Indianapolis, the state capital, located in the center of the state. By 1900, the capital had the state's largest concentration of African Americans, and it continued to have the largest black population—as well as the largest white population—of any Indiana city throughout the rest of the century. Out of a total city population of 169,164, 9.4 percent, or 15,391, were African Americans, giving Indianapolis one of the highest percentages of blacks of any northern city. By 1910, the number of blacks had reached 21,816 out of a total of 233,650. Of that number, slightly more than one-third had been born in Indiana, while 62.2 percent had been born in other states. Smaller numbers moved to other cities—South Bend, Fort Wayne, Terre Haute, Muncie, and Anderson.[6]

These "city folks" did not forget the small towns and farming communities from which they came. The black newspapers in Indianapolis regularly published columns of news about their readers' former hometowns—weddings, funerals, fraternal organizations, and social events. As blacks moved from "the country" to cities in Indiana as well as outside the state, annual family homecomings gained a special importance in reminding them of their roots. Former residents and their children returned to the places where their ancestors had come as pioneers. They gathered at reunions to commemorate family members who had died and to mingle with living relatives. Some gatherings were so large that railroads and interurbans ran special excursions for them.[7]

Between 1900 and 1910, a spectacular increase in the black population began with the arrival of a few blacks in the Calumet area along Lake Michigan in the extreme northwestern part of the state. By 1910, the town of Gary, which did not even appear in the United States census in 1900, reported a population of 16,802. Of this number, 383 were blacks—2.3 percent of the total. The sudden growth of population resulted from the decision of the United States Steel Corporation to build mills in a hitherto largely unsettled and barren area along the lake where it bought 9,000 acres of land.

The first blacks to arrive were construction workers brought in by the company and housed, along with white workers, in tents and barracks. They helped to lay out the town site and the steel mill complex. Some of them moved on, but by 1910 an African American community was developing. Some of the arrivals were beginning to buy real estate in the area between the Wabash and Pennsylvania railroads, later known as the Patch, which was to remain the center of the growing black settlement. During these early years, blacks mingled with a heterogeneous throng of foreign-born settlers who had been recruited by agents of United States Steel.[8]

Blacks from southern states came northward in hope of escaping not only from poverty but also from racial segregation and discrimination. But, although African Americans in Indiana enjoyed some rights that had been denied them in the South, they found that segregation and discrimination in many aspects of life continued in their new home.

Before the Civil War, although Indiana was a "free state" with a constitution that prohibited slavery, it had the harshest Black Code in the North, with restrictions similar to those imposed by slave states upon free blacks. Most of these legal disabilities were removed after the war, including the notorious Article XIII of the state constitution, which had barred blacks from coming into the state. The Fourteenth Amendment to the United States Constitution gave citizenship to black residents, and the Fifteenth guaranteed the right to vote. The state legislature passed laws to provide for tax-supported schools for black children. In 1885 a state Civil Rights Law prohibited racial discrimination in access to public accommodations. The only racial distinctions remaining in Indiana law by 1900 were an article in the state constitution limiting service in the state militia to white men, a harsh prohibition of interracial marriages, and statutes that permitted but did not require racially segregated public schools. Nevertheless, regardless of laws, Indiana blacks lived in a society in which racial discrimination and segregation were as pervasive in most aspects of life as in the states of the upper South.[9]

In Indianapolis, where there was already a well-established black community before 1900, the largest number lived in an area just northwest of the center of the city, along Indiana Avenue, while others had settled since the Civil War on the near eastside of the city. As new arrivals moved into these neighborhoods, the concentration of blacks increased, often prompting the few white residents to leave. Although the influx of blacks to the capital city in the years from 1900 to the First World War was not great, older black residents viewed it with some apprehension, fearing that the presence of newcomers might intensify white prejudice. One longtime resident observed that Indianapolis, like other northern cities, felt the "increase in its colored population by the increase in racial discrimination." A study by social workers at Indiana University showed that in some eastside neighborhoods, whites and blacks lived side by side without friction. But in another neighborhood, where the closing of a small factory caused its "former white employees to move out and created opportunities for blacks to move in, 'better families' objected" to living in a "colored" district.[10]

In Evansville, where the black population actually declined slightly during the early years of the century, residential segregation lines were clearly drawn by race and were seldom crossed. From early times most blacks had lived in Baptisttown, an area so named because of a Baptist church around which settlers clustered. In the period from 1900 to the First World War, the concentration of blacks in this area increased. The quality of housing was generally deplorable. Several streets lacked connections with sewer systems, and there was little inside plumbing. People continued to live in houses that had been condemned by the fire chief because no other shelter was available. A housing law passed by the city council was not enforced.

When a black couple, both of whom were teachers, tried to escape from ghetto conditions by buying a house in a "white neighborhood," residents tried to prevent them from moving in. Ignoring the fact that little decent housing was available in black neighborhoods, a local newspaper asked: "Why don't they go among Negroes and buy property if they want to own a home?" As early as 1909, restrictive covenants that forbade selling or renting property to blacks were introduced into deed records, and custom and fear of reprisals inhibited blacks from trying to move. As Darrel Bigham has observed, although the number of black residents in Evansville declined, physical separation of the races increased—evidence that migration was not always the reason for the development of black ghettos.[11]

As black families began to arrive in Gary, many of them lived in "row houses" in which several families were crowded together, sharing one pump and one outside toilet. Others lived in shacks built by male family members on lots for which they paid five dollars a month. Housing for blacks was not included in plans for residential areas in the new city, and native-born whites made it clear very early that they were opposed to making real estate available outside the Patch area.[12]

Just as custom and prejudice, rather than law, assigned blacks to certain residential areas, so custom and prejudice decreed that only certain kinds of employment were open to "colored persons"—usually seasonal jobs that whites disdained. United States census reports show that most black men were classified as common laborers. The two largest categories were "servants" and "porters." Others worked at building and resurfacing roads and streets and as janitors, draymen and teamsters, and waiters. A fairly large number were classified as "helpers" in the building trades, but few were carpenters or masons. Others were working in brick and cement factories, where they tended blast furnaces. Some worked in coal yards and as deliverymen. One skilled trade in which black men continued to be numerous was that of barbering, a field they had nearly monopolized in earlier years.[13]

Few black men belonged to labor unions. Except for the American Hod Carriers Union, which they dominated, they were excluded from the building trades affiliated with the American Federation of Labor, the only important unions in Indianapolis. The United Mine Workers provided a notable exception to the usual pattern of excluding blacks or segregating them in separate unions; in the coal mines of southwestern Indiana, a few hundred blacks worked side by side with white miners. There were various attempts, usually short-lived, to organize independent unions of black workers. One of the more successful was the Colored Railroad Men's Benevolent and Industrial Association, organized in Indianapolis in 1915 for men employed by the railroads and the Pullman Company.

Of more than nine thousand black women employed in Indiana in 1910, the United States census showed that over seven thousand were servants or laundresses. Others worked as seamstresses, hairdressers, waitresses, operators in laundries, or kept boardinghouses.[14]

In social life and recreation, as in employment, racial lines were sharply drawn, in spite of the state civil rights law adopted in 1885. That law declared that all persons were "entitled to the full and equal accommodations, advantages, facilities and privileges of inns, restaurants, eating houses, barber shops, public conveyances on land and water, theaters, and all places of public accommodation and amusement, subject only to the conditions and limitations established by law and applying to all citizens." Violations were classed as misdemeanors punishable by a fine of one hundred dollars or imprisonment of thirty days or by the payment of a forfeit of one hundred dollars to the injured party.[15]

Adoption of the civil rights law was not widely publicized. Few whites were aware of it, and those who were ignored it. Blacks rarely challenged violations and won cases even more rarely. They were seldom served in restaurants patronized by whites and were barred completely from white hotels except as servants. Many theaters and places of entertainment simply refused to admit them, while those that did relegated them to "jim crow" (segregated) galleries. Even Booker T. Washington, who was usually exempt from racial restrictions in the South as well as in the North, was summarily refused service in the barbershop of the Union Railway Station in Indianapolis, and when he arrived in Anderson, where he had been invited by local Republicans to give an address, the hotel refused him a room.[16]

None of the private hospitals in the state admitted black patients. The few who were admitted to City Hospital in Indianapolis were assigned to a "jim crow" ward, where, according to a black physician, conditions were "such that many who need hospital treatment will not take advantage of it, but prefer to remain at home." In the late nineteenth century, a few black interns had been accepted for training at City Hospital, but after 1900 they were rarely accepted. There were no facilities, public or private, for training black nurses.[17]

Discrimination and denial of rights were commonplace. In Indianapolis and Gary, for example, blacks were not admitted to the local YMCAs. In Evansville, the most segregated city in the state, where blacks were expected to ride at the back of street-cars, the Carnegie Library served whites only, and a separate branch for "colored" was opened. In all three cities, police sometimes drove black children from public playgrounds, and respectable black adults were sometimes barred from city parks.[18]

By its portrayal of blacks as inherently criminal, the white press encouraged the perception that African Americans were unfit to associate with whites. Accounts of crimes by blacks against whites, particularly against white women, were reported in lurid detail under sensational headlines. This perception that blacks were inherently lawless was apparently shared by law enforcement officers. Police records in Indianapolis and Evansville show that the number of blacks arrested was disproportionately high. In both cities, blacks made up about 10 percent of the population, but samplings of police records for the period 1900 to 1916 show that 25 to 40 percent of the persons arrested were black. Contrary to popular belief, however, the number of blacks arrested for violent crimes was small. Most arrests were for minor crimes—petty larceny, drunkenness, prostitution, vagrancy, and loitering.[19] In all Indiana cities with sizable black populations, police looked with suspicion on unemployed black males. During the winter months, "drifters," who had summer jobs on riverboats, on southern plantations, and in other seasonal employment, flocked into Indiana cities, looking for work or charity or hoping to subsist by thievery. As a preventive measure, police rounded them up, sometimes arresting them for vagrancy and sending them to the workhouse, sometimes simply telling them to leave town and not return.[20]

But in spite of numerous arrests and acts of harassment by the police, black ministers and civic leaders complained that police made no effort to stamp out gambling, prostitution, and other forms of vice that flourished in certain sections of the black communities—sometimes in saloons and taverns owned by whites.

The Indiana constitution, adopted in 1851, said it was the duty of the General Assembly "to provide, by law, for a general and uniform system of Common Schools, wherein tuition shall be without charge, and equally open to all." (Article 8, section

1.) However, the words "equally open to all" were not interpreted by lawmakers or law courts to prevent racial segregation of students. The first state law to fund public schools for blacks, adopted in 1869, required that black and white students be educated separately. This was amended in 1877 to permit local school authorities to maintain segregated schools, but the law also provided that, where there were no separate schools, "colored children shall be allowed to attend the public schools with white children." The law also provided that when a pupil in a colored school had demonstrated that he (or she) had advanced sufficiently to be placed in a higher grade than that offered in the colored school, he (or she) should be permitted to enter the advanced grade in the white school, and no distinction should be made in that school on account of race or color.[21]

With the largest public school system in the state, Indianapolis had established separate schools under the 1869 law and continued the policy of segregated elementary schools after 1877. Soon after the adoption of the 1877 law, the attorney for the school board interpreted the law as meaning that where separate schools were maintained, black children could not be admitted to schools for whites.[22]

By 1908, there were seven elementary schools for blacks in Indianapolis, and as the black population grew, the number of schools increased. The elementary schools were never entirely segregated, however. One reason was that in some of the black elementary schools there were only six grades, and students were transferred to white schools for the seventh and eighth grades. There were also a few pupils living in areas outside the predominantly black neighborhoods who were allowed to attend schools with whites. However, most of these pupils had been transferred to all-black schools by 1915, even though this meant some of them had to travel long distances.

From the beginning, the policy of the Indianapolis Board of School Commissioners was to hire black teachers to staff the colored elementary schools, but black teachers never taught in the few racially mixed schools. Although the length of the terms and the course of study for both races was essentially the same, the buildings used for the colored schools were frequently old and in disrepair in contrast to white schools. In all elementary schools, courses in "domestic science" and "manual training" were introduced in the early years of the century, but in the colored schools more emphasis was placed on such courses. Girls were given training in laundry work and housekeeping as well as in sewing and cooking, because it was expected that they would go into domestic service, while boys were given instruction in such vocational courses as repairing shoes.[23]

Although segregation in elementary schools was the norm, there was no separate high school for blacks. The first black student, a girl, had been admitted to Indianapolis High School (later Shortridge High School) in 1873 and had graduated in 1876. The few black students who entered high school, and the fewer still who remained to graduate, continued to attend either Shortridge or one of the two new high schools that were opened after 1900, Manual and Technical. By 1916, 174 blacks were enrolled at Shortridge, 118 at Manual, and 21 at Technical.[24]

In the southern counties of the state, segregated schools were the rule, and those for blacks were uniformly inferior to those for whites. Segregated elementary schools in Evansville were funded only after state law required that blacks be educated. Children from outlying rural communities were sent to Evansville schools as a method of meeting the requirements of state law without the expense of maintaining separate schools. The schools were conducted in poorly heated frame buildings that lacked equipment available in white schools. One school still had no indoor toilets as late as 1919. One or two black teachers taught all pupils. There were only seven grades in each of the black elementary schools except Clark, where there were eight grades and a high school of sorts. The same teachers taught in both the elementary and high school.[25]

The Evansville high school initially claimed to offer the same courses as were traditional in the white school, including Latin. But in 1902, the school board made it clear that they thought education for blacks should be of a special kind. They reduced the requirement for graduation from four to three years, eliminated some courses in Latin and mathematics, and added manual training, domestic science, and commercial courses. In language Booker T. Washington would have approved, the board minutes said they had tried to take out of the curriculum "the things that are of no practical benefit to the pupils and substitute matters that are very essential . . . [for] the pupils of the school when they come to enter their life work."

The changes met with the approval of black leaders because they thought the vocational courses would lead to "immediate uplift of the race," whereas blacks who had studied foreign languages and mathematics seldom found employment except in the same menial jobs as those at which unschooled blacks worked.[26]

Racial distinctions among teachers were clearly drawn in Evansville. In 1909, the school board ruled that black and white teachers must sit in separate sections at meetings. There were also sharp differences in pay between the two races. In 1914, the maximum annual pay for a black teacher was $900, while a white teacher could earn $1,600. Salaries of black principals were less than half of those paid to whites.[27]

Information about schooling for blacks in most towns and counties in the southern and central parts of the state is meager, but segregated elementary schools were the rule, and in some places there were separate high schools. A 1904 report of the State Superintendent of Public Instruction on colored high schools in Madison, Jeffersonville, New Albany, Rockport, Mount Vernon, Princeton, Corydon, and Evansville throws some light on the general inferiority of educational opportunities for blacks. In Madison, a total of 199 pupils were enrolled in three elementary schools, and a high school was taught in two rooms in one of them. At this school (the only accredited black high school in the state at that time) a staff of five taught the eight elementary grades and the four-year high school course. In Jeffersonville, there were nine teachers for 370 black pupils, 25 of whom were enrolled in high school. There was one full-time teacher for the high school and one who divided her time between elementary and high school classes. In New Albany, there were two black high school teachers. In Rockport, Princeton, Mount Vernon, and Corydon, a single teacher taught all high school subjects.

Administrators in all these schools expressed interest in manual training and domestic science courses to prepare black pupils for employment, but there appears to have been little money to finance them. In Madison, girls were taught sewing and boys learned elementary woodworking and carpentry, but in Corydon, "ladies of the church" trained girls in "needlework." [28]

There were some improvements in later years, but declines in enrollments as more and more blacks moved northward, seeking better jobs (and also better schools), meant that there was little reason for school boards to spend more money in improving the colored schools. In addition to the schools in the towns, there were also one-room (one-teacher) rural colored schools throughout the counties in the southern half of the state. Some were abandoned as enrollments declined, but others continued until well into the twentieth century. [29]

In towns and cities in the northern parts of the state, there were no official policies of separate schools for blacks, but residential patterns sometimes resulted in some schools being designated as "colored." Black teachers usually taught in these schools, but blacks were never employed in schools with racially mixed enrollments. In Muncie, some black citizens urged the establishment of a black elementary school as a means of giving jobs to black teachers, but opposition from other black groups defeated the proposal. [30]

In contrast to the policy of older communities in the northern counties, black children in Gary were placed in separate schools. The burgeoning school population in the Steel City was under the direction of Superintendent William A. Wirt, a man who gained nationwide publicity for innovations geared to what he considered the particular needs of Gary children. While he sought to "Americanize" the large number of white children of foreign parentage, Wirt firmly believed in separate schooling for blacks. "We believe," he said, "that it is only justice to the negro [sic] children that they should be segregated. There is naturally a feeling between negroes [sic] and whites in the lower grades and we are sure the colored children will be better cared for in schools of their own, and they will take a pride in their work and get better grades." [31] About thirty black children were first placed in rented facilities in a Baptist church. The next year they were moved to a new portable school building where they were taught by a black teacher. As enrollment grew, two other teachers soon joined him, and another portable building was added. But these quarters were soon overcrowded, and they obviously lacked the facilities being planned for the schools for white pupils. The Gary *Daily Tribune,* which reflected the thinking of influential whites, said that, while segregation must be continued, black children must not be allowed to remain in inferior buildings. To deal with the problem, Superintendent Wirt devised a novel solution: the portable schools were abandoned, and black pupils were transferred to the newly opened Froebel School, which included all eight elementary grades and a four-year high school and was originally intended for whites only. Although students of both races attended the school, a system of internal segregation was devised under which black elementary pupils attended separate classes taught by black teachers. The few African Americans who enrolled in the high school in the early years attended racially mixed classes taught by whites. However, blacks were not allowed to use all of the school facilities. For example, they were excluded from shop classes. Wirt defended his segregation policy by saying that foreign parents "strenuously object to mixing colored children with the others," although there is little evidence that immigrant parents had in fact asked for segregation.[32]

In spite of inferior schools and other obstacles, educational levels among younger African Americans showed steady improvement, although many older blacks remained illiterate. United States census figures in 1910 showed that 62.5 percent of Indiana blacks between the ages of seven and twenty were enrolled in school. At that date, 13.5 percent of the entire Negro population was reported to be illiterate, but only 2.6 percent of those fifteen to twenty-four years of age were so classified.[33]

Although a compulsory attendance law enacted in 1901 required pupils to remain in school until the age of fourteen, truancy was widespread among blacks, and many of them did not graduate from the eighth grade. Reports of attendance officers in Indianapolis schools showed that economic and social conditions in the black community created educational problems. Many black mothers were forced to do "day work" outside the home, especially in the winter, when men who often had seasonal summer jobs were without employment. When mothers worked outside the home, their older children often stayed away from school in order to care for younger brothers and sisters. Black youths were frequently forced to leave school to find jobs to supplement family income. Parents sometimes defended their children's truancy by pointing out that education rarely increased employment opportunities for blacks; high school graduates often worked at the same menial jobs as members of the race with less education.[34]

A few high school graduates went on to colleges and universities, some to black colleges in the South. Within the state, the largest number attended Indiana University in Bloomington, where Preston Eagleson had played football on the university team and received an A.B. degree in 1896.[35]

But although blacks were admitted to the university and played on athletic teams, they were excluded from student dormitories and social activities. Some of these deficiencies were remedied by Samuel Saul Dargon, who received a law degree in 1909 and was for many years curator of the law library. As owner of "Dargon House" and other houses where black students lived and of a cafeteria where they ate, he became a kind of unofficial black "dean of students." Social life was enlivened by a black fraternity, Kappa Alpha Mu, which later changed its name to Kappa Alpha Psi, a secret order founded in 1911 by Elder Francis Diggs and ten other undergraduates. It adopted as its slogan "Achievement through knowledge, fraternity and fidelity." The fraternity soon spread to other universities and colleges, and many of its members became civic leaders in northern cities. Excluded from such white organizations as Rotary and Lions Clubs, they founded alumni chapters which wielded important social and political influence in black communities.[36]

Some black students at Indiana University came from Bloomington and other small cities in the state, but most of them came from Indianapolis. Some other black graduates of Indianapolis high schools attended Butler College, located in Irvington on the eastern edge of the city, where both white and black student commuters traveled by streetcar. Butler's attractions to black students included the fact that Indianapolis offered more job opportunities than Bloomington as well as the convenience of continuing to live at home while attending college. But there were no opportunities for blacks to participate in the social life of the college. In 1922, seven young black women who were teaching in the public schools after graduating from Butler founded a sorority, Sigma Gamma Rho, with the purpose of furnishing educational opportunities for black female students. From this beginning in Indianapolis, the sorority grew into a national organization with chapters and alumni organizations all over the United States.[37]

African American students in Evansville who were able to continue their education after graduating from Clark High School usually attended black colleges in other states. A few went to Indiana State Teachers College in Terre Haute or to Indiana University.[38]

None of the private denominational colleges in the state had official policies that excluded African Americans, and a few black students attended such institutions as DePauw, Wabash, Hanover, and Franklin, where they were usually the lone members of their race. The experience of Percy Julian as an undergraduate at DePauw was probably typical. Julian, later a renowned chemist, was the only black student on the campus, and he was allowed to live in the attic of the Sigma Chi house in exchange for work he did for the fraternity members. Lonely and isolated in Greencastle, Julian looked for company in Indianapolis, where he spent many hours at the Colored YMCA.[39]

Excluded from full participation in a society dominated by whites, and thrown on their own resources, blacks developed a strong sense of community and created their own separate institutions. Whatever their private feelings, most Indiana African Americans appeared to accept as inevitable a society in which they were relegated to an inferior status. For members of the middle class, Booker T. Washington was the model "race man." Ministers preached his doctrines from the pulpit, and political orators, black and white, exhorted members of the race to follow his example. Some black newspapers like the Chicago *Defender* and the New York *Age* often voiced protests against the existing racial order, but the black press in Indianapolis, which both reflected and helped shape views and attitudes of the black community, was consistently accommodationist in tone.

Most civic leaders, ministers, and writers of editorials were apologetic about the behavior of "lower-class Negroes" and sought to win approval from "better-class whites." A typical editorial from the Indianapolis *Freeman* illustrates the characteristically cautious and conciliatory tone of the press: "The colored people of this city are assured protection in the city parks," it said. "The colored have been enjoying the parks as the white people [do]. That they do not go in large numbers is best under the circumstances. What we wish is our right of enjoyment rather than to be in the parks at all times. If we are careful in not overdoing the matter, . . . the right to go where we wish will not be opposed."[40]

Blacks who admired middle-class values and lifestyle and tried to emulate them and to distance themselves from lower-class members of their race nevertheless found within the black community opportunities denied them outside it. Black newspapers are an obvious example. The color line and the existence of a distinct racial community were the raison d'être for race journalism. In the early years of the century, there were three black weeklies in Indianapolis—the Indianapolis *World,* founded in 1882; the Indianapolis *Freeman,* founded in 1888; and the Indianapolis *Recorder,* which began publication in 1897. The Indianapolis *Ledger* began publication a few years later, but like most black publications it lasted only a few years and only partial files survive.

Except for the *World,* which was often cautiously Democratic in tone, all of the black papers were strongly Republican in politics.[41] But regardless of political affiliation, the views of the Indianapolis papers were much alike on racial questions. In the early years of the century, the *Freeman* enjoyed a wide circulation throughout the United States and was certainly the most influential black newspaper in Indiana. It had been purchased in 1892 by George L. Knox, who had amassed a considerable amount of money as proprietor of a downtown barbershop that catered to an influential white clientele. Through his white patrons he made the acquaintance of leading Republicans and subsequently became the most influential black Republican in the state. The *Freeman*'s circulation outside of Indiana was due in part to its coverage (both as news and advertisements) of black entertainment and entertainers in cities all over the country. The *Freeman* was also one of the first black papers to give extensive coverage to sports. Like most race papers of the era, it was essentially a family business, and it ceased publication after Knox died in 1926.[42]

Like the *Freeman,* the *Recorder* was largely a family enterprise. George Pheldon Stewart, its founder, moved to Indianapolis in 1894 after graduating from high school in Vincennes. Along with Will Porter he began publication of the paper in 1897 and two years later became sole owner. Unlike the *Freeman* and the *World,* which filled their pages with race-related news from all over the country, the *Recorder* emphasized local and state news.[43] Black newspapers, with few exceptions, were marginal business enterprises. Many survived only a few years or even months. Those that lasted longer usually depended upon supplementary income from other sources. Stewart, for example, operated a printing business along with the *Recorder.* As partisan organs all Indianapolis papers were subsidized to a degree by political organizations. This became obvious during political campaigns, when the size of the paper was sometimes increased to include detailed reports of political speeches along with pictures of candidates and pages of paid political advertisements. As already noted, the *Freeman* relied heavily on entertainment ads. The Indianapolis papers also received income from local black-owned businesses and from a few white merchants. Like all papers of the era, they printed advertisements for patent medicines, but unique to the black press were ads for hair-straightening preparations and creams guaranteed to lighten skin color.[44]

A growing black population and a distinct racial community created opportunities for businesses to serve the needs of black patrons. This development was supported by the black press, which strongly endorsed the Washingtonian precept that self-help and economic success would open the way for acceptance of African Americans into the mainstream of American society. In publishing a list of black-owned businesses in Indianapolis the *Recorder* observed, "The thoughtful members of the race have come to the conclusion that progress lies, not in political recognition alone, nor in book learning, but must come along material lines. It is a stern fact that the Negro must represent something tangible before he can hope for any degree of success."[45]

Support for this philosophy was reflected in the support that Indianapolis citizens gave to the National Negro Business League, founded by Washington in 1900. A few men from Indianapolis were among the charter members of the national organization, and the Indianapolis league was one of the earliest local chapters. Knox, of the *Freeman*, who was Washington's close associate, was an early president of the national organization, and George Stewart, the *Recorder*'s publisher, was also a strong supporter. Sumner Furniss and Freeman Ransom were members of the national board. By 1918, local leagues had been founded in Evansville, Marion, and Muncie. Delegations from the Indiana leagues went annually to the national conventions, where they listened to reports of successful black enterprises in all parts of the country and heard speeches invoking Washingtonian principles of self-help and racial self-respect.

Blacks started a variety of small businesses, most of them designed to serve the needs of the black community. They usually began with high hopes and little capital and failed after a few years, to be replaced by similar enterprises, which were also likely to be short-lived. Some survived and enjoyed modest success, but few fulfilled the hopes expressed by the National Negro Business League. In 1902, under the headline "SOME WEALTHY INDIANAPOLITANS," the *Recorder* published a list of local men and women who, it said, were worth $5,000 or more. Most were business owners who had accumulated their wealth by "hard labor, self denial and small earnings," said the paper. A good many of them, it appears, had invested their profits in real estate.[46]

Most black-owned businesses served an almost exclusively black clientele. Among the most prosperous were funeral homes. In Indianapolis, the Willis Funeral Home, founded before 1900, was still in business in the last years of the twentieth century. In Evansville, the most successful African American businessman was W. A. Goins, who also founded funeral homes in Covington and Paducah, Kentucky.[47]

The Walker Manufacturing Company of Indianapolis, by far the most widely known and financially successful black-owned business in Indiana, catered solely to a black clientele. It was founded and owned by Madam C. J. Walker, who had been born in Louisiana, orphaned at the age of six, married at fourteen, and widowed at the age of twenty. For a time she supported herself and her small daughter as a laundress, but her creation of products to stimulate hair growth and to straighten hair quickly led to business success. After peddling her products from door to door in St. Louis, she came to Indianapolis in 1910, where she incorporated her company, listing herself as sole stockholder in 1911. She was advised in the business by Freeman B. Ransom, an able young lawyer who was also a newcomer to Indianapolis. As operating manager and lawyer until his death in 1947, Ransom contributed greatly to the financial success of the company. Between its founding in 1911 and the death of Madam Walker in 1919, the company grossed over $100,000 a year, with peak sales of $119,000 in 1916. Agents all over the United States sold the company's products, and beauty schools that taught the use of Walker products were established in several cities. In an age when most black women worked as domestic servants or laundresses, the Walker Company opened new avenues of employment to some as sales agents and beauty culturists.

With her profits Madam Walker invested in real estate (in Indianapolis and other cities) and carried on a wide range of philanthropic and educational activities. These included funding scholarships at Tuskegee Institute and giving financial support to the NAACP, Flanner House, the Senate Avenue YMCA, and Indianapolis churches.[48]

Other successful enterprises, such as draying and hauling in an era before automobiles, depended upon white as well as black patronage. Some barbers, among whom George L. Knox was the best known, prospered by serving white customers and refusing to serve blacks. Catering businesses and bakeries, often owned by women, also served white customers.[49] In Indianapolis, the businesses clustered on Indiana Avenue and adjacent streets served the physical needs of the black population and were also centers of social life. A recent study shows that in 1916, everything that a person might need could be purchased in an eight-block segment along the avenue. There were 33 restaurants, 33 saloons (including taverns and clubs), 26 grocery stores (including meat and poultry shops), 17 barbershops and hair stylists, 16 tailors and clothing retailers, 14 cobblers, 13 dry goods stores, as well as drugstores, pawnbrokers, pool halls, funeral parlors, and offices of lawyers, physicians, dentists, and real estate agents.[50]

No district in Evansville was as famous as "the Avenue" in Indianapolis, but similar small businesses operated to meet the needs of its black community. Most were only marginally successful; Logan Stewart's insurance and real estate business was an exception. He amassed a small fortune investing in real estate. In Gary, along with the many who arrived seeking work in construction of the steel mills and other buildings in the new city, others came to open rooming houses, restaurants, barbershops, grocery stores, and saloons. As in other cities, these enterprises were often short-lived, but they were soon replaced by similar new businesses.

The survey made by the Indianapolis *Recorder* in 1901 showed a surprising number of black businesses in the smaller cities and towns of the state. Some, like grocery stores and saloons, were clearly for black patrons, but other small businesses and individual black workers clearly depended upon white patronage. These included numerous dressmakers, cateresses, cooks, wallpaper hangers, carpenters, and a few persons with more unusual skills, such as broom makers and horse trainers.[51]

Successful businessmen were admired, but members of the professions—lawyers, physicians, dentists, and teachers—were more often looked upon as leaders and spokesmen for the black community. Lawyers, some of whom were also engaged in other businesses, were especially influential in Indianapolis. By 1901, there were already twelve lawyers in the capital city, among them J. T. V. Hill, Gurley Brewer, W. E. Henderson, and J. H. Lott, who had already established themselves as civic leaders, active in politics. In the years before the World War, they were joined by three young men who were to become leaders for more than a quarter of the century. Freeman B. Ransom, already mentioned as manager of the Walker Company, was born in Grenada, Mississippi, had graduated from the college and law school of Walden University in Nashville, Tennessee, and studied law at Columbia University before coming to Indianapolis in 1910. Robert Lee Brokenburr, the son of a hotel chef, was born in Virginia and educated at Hampton Institute, where he was greatly influenced by the philosophy and personality of President H. B. Frisell, the mentor of Booker T. Washington. After graduating from the law school at Howard University, Brokenburr came to Indianapolis in 1909 and set up an office where he was joined by Ransom. He also served as legal counsel to the Walker Company and eventually succeeded Ransom as general manager. Ransom and Brokenburr were joined by Robert Lee Bailey in 1914. A native of Florence, Alabama, Bailey had worked his way through Talladega College and law school at Indiana University. In later years, all three men became leaders in the NAACP and active in the defense of the civil rights of fellow African Americans. Bailey, in particular, gained a reputation as an able criminal lawyer in cases involving the rights of blacks.[52]

The situation was different in Evansville, where, as in numerous cities in the South, there was for many years only one black representative of the legal profession, John H. Wilson, and he was able to do little in the face of the racial attitudes of local white officials. Several aspiring lawyers were among the early black arrivals in Gary, although some did not remain long. The most influential was Louis Caldwell, a native of Mississippi, who had worked as a Pullman porter and at various other odd jobs to earn money for his education. He came to Gary in 1915 after graduating from Northwestern Law School.[53]

Like lawyers, physicians and dentists were leaders in civic life and sometimes active in politics. One of the most highly respected and influential black citizens in Evansville was Dr. George Washington Buckner. In Indianapolis there were nineteen black physicians and five dentists by 1910. The most prominent among them was Dr. Sumner Furniss, who maintained close ties with the white community. The son of two public school teachers who had migrated from Mississippi, he graduated from Indianapolis High School and the Medical College of Indianapolis and was the first black to be accepted as an intern at the Indianapolis City Hospital.[54] Dr. Henry L. Hummons, a younger man who began practice soon after his graduation from Indianapolis Medical School in 1902, was also active in civic affairs, taking the lead in the establishment of the Colored YMCA and Lincoln Hospital, a private institution for blacks, and in Witherspoon Presbyterian Church.[55]

Although they had no voice in shaping educational policies, black citizens believed firmly in the importance of education. African American teachers were looked upon as leaders, and black schools were important centers of community life. Evansville's most highly respected spokesman for blacks was probably William E. Best, principal of Clark High School. A native of the West Indies, he came to Indiana from New York, graduated from Indiana State Teachers College at Terre Haute, and received a master's degree from Indiana University. He was respected by whites, but was no "Uncle Tom," serving as president of a short-lived branch of the NAACP. Similarly, the most important black woman leader in Evansville was educator Sallie Stewart, whose community activities are described below. For many years dean of students at Clark High School, she was an important role model for black students, particularly for girls.[56]

In Indianapolis, where there was no black high school, teachers and principals of the colored elementary schools were leaders in community and church affairs. One of the most influential was Mary Cable, a Kansas teacher's college graduate who enriched her own education by doing post-graduate work at Columbia and Chicago Universities and by European travel. As a teacher and principal she emphasized training for citizenship and developed innovative strategies to compensate for the cultural limitations of her pupils. She was active in women's clubs, advocated women's suffrage, and took the lead in establishing the Indianapolis branch of the NAACP.[57]

Regardless of their training and abilities, black physicians were barred from hospitals for whites and almost never had white patients. Black lawyers served only black clients, and black teachers taught only black pupils. Physicians in Indianapolis organized the Aesculapian Society, which affiliated with the Indiana Association of Negro Physicians, Dentists, and Pharmacists in 1908 and which in turn affiliated with the National Medical Association. The Indiana association held annual conventions at which colleagues read papers about developments in their respective fields. Black lawyers were members of the National Bar Association. The Indiana affiliate of the National Association of Teachers in Colored Schools met annually at the same time as the Indiana State Teachers Association but held a different program at a different place.[58]

While all members of the professions enjoyed great prestige, blacks traditionally looked to their ministers for leadership and guidance, in secular as well as religious affairs. Churches were of central importance in their lives, and members, who usually had little in the way of material resources, were willing to sacrifice to support the minister and to pay for constructing and maintaining the church edifice. A substantial part of the wealth of the black community was invested in church buildings, and congregations often struggled for years to repay debts incurred in building newer and larger structures. Even more than for most whites, the church was the center of social and cultural life and of benevolent and welfare activities in black communities. In their churches, blacks had the dignity and status denied them in the white world; they also had opportunities for self-development and leadership. As one writer put it, the church provided a sense of "somebodiness," as well as being a "carrier of the black folk culture."[59]

Some of the pioneer churches, founded as soon as the first blacks arrived, survived in rural communities into the twentieth century. As the black population increased and became urbanized, the number of churches grew. Churches were of special importance in the lives of new migrants from the South, who sometimes founded their congregations in storerooms and private homes.

While Indiana's African American churches and their ministers are too diverse and numerous to be treated individually in this study, some general characteristics and a few examples follow. In Indianapolis and Evansville and in the other older communities in the southern counties the first congregations were affiliated with the African Methodist Episcopal (AME) Church. An AME church was founded in Evansville in 1843. The oldest church in Indianapolis was Bethel AME, also founded before the Civil War; the second oldest was Allen Chapel AME, founded in 1866 by settlers who came northward during the war. In Gary, the first AME church was opened in 1909 in a portable school building after a group of blacks appealed to the bishop in Chicago for an elder to organize their congregation. As the number of black Methodist churches grew, most remained affiliated with the AME Church, but a few AME Zion congregations were also founded, as well as some that affiliated with the Colored Methodist Episcopal (CME) Church. Like their white counterparts, the black Methodist Episcopal churches were governed by a hierarchy of clergy under bishops. Ministers were assigned to churches by annual conferences, had a maximum tenure of five years, and seldom had previous connections with local persons; consequently, their ties to the community were not as close as those of ministers of other denominations. Boards of lay members governed the secular affairs of the churches, supervising finances and church maintenance.[60]

Black Baptists soon outnumbered Methodists after the Civil War, and their numbers continued to grow as more settlers arrived from the South. Baptist churches, unlike those of Methodists, were autonomous and self-governing. Individual preachers sometimes founded their own churches and often served the congregation for their entire lives. For example, Nathaniel Seymour served as pastor of New Bethel Baptist Church in Indianapolis from 1879 to 1927, and Charles Hawkins was pastor of First Baptist Church in Gary from 1913 to 1944. The character and success of Baptist churches depended to a large degree upon the personality and success of the pastor.

In larger communities with several churches, Colored Ministerial Alliances served to unify and support Baptist ministers. Most congregations were affiliated with the Indiana Association of Negro Baptist Churches and the Indiana Missionary Baptist Association. By 1916, thirty churches in Indianapolis were represented in the latter organization. The 1920 meeting of the National Baptist Convention in Indianapolis was an event of major importance to the local black community. Under headlines that claimed "HOOSIERDOM ALL AGLOW WITH RELIGIOUS SPIRIT," the *Freeman* announced that more than six thousand delegates and many other visitors were pouring into the city from all parts of the country to attend the convention. At the headquarters in Tomlinson Hall, church choirs from St. Louis and Chicago as well as from Indianapolis were to sing, and there was to be a pageant that portrayed "the leading attainments of our race." In addition to hearing lectures by preachers, educators, and white politicians, convention visitors could enjoy refreshments and buy souvenirs in tents on the courthouse lawn.[61]

While only a few of Indiana's African American citizens became members of the Christian Church (Disciples of Christ), a denomination with a large white membership in the state, Second Christian Church was one of the most influential black churches in Indianapolis. Founded during the Civil War as a mission church for freedmen through the efforts of Ovid Butler, the founder of Butler University and a strong opponent of slavery, it continued to receive some support from the Board of Christian Missions of the Christian Church. But its growth and influence for many years were largely due to Reverend Henry L. Herod, who came from Kentucky to take charge of a struggling congregation in 1898 and remained its pastor until his death in 1935. Membership grew as more migrants arrived from the South, but at Herod's church they found dignity and formality in church services and an emphasis upon the importance of educational and cultural activities new to them. One of Herod's principal interests was the preservation and performance of Negro spirituals, which he considered the only true American music.[62] Herod's influence extended beyond his church to many community projects, including Flanner House, a black settlement house, for which he served as board member and president.

While most blacks were Baptists or Methodists, a few were Presbyterians, Episcopalians, Christians, and Roman Catholics. In the early years of the twentieth century, some began to leave the established denominations and join Pentecostal congregations. This movement, little noticed at first, developed by the closing years of this century into the most rapidly growing religious group in the United States. Starting in Los Angeles but growing most rapidly in the Middle West, Pentecostal congregations sought a return to primitive Christianity and individual communication with God, which sometimes manifested itself when a convert began "speaking in voices." One of the most important figures in the history of the Pentecostal movement was a black Indianan, Garfield Thomas Haywood of Indianapolis.

Born in Greencastle, he attended elementary school and Shortridge High School in Indianapolis, where his parents had moved in order to obtain better educational opportunities for their children. As a young man he attended meetings conducted by a pastor from Los Angeles and was converted in 1905, along with a few other blacks, most of them from Bethel AME Church. He began preaching in 1909 and soon gained a following as a dynamic speaker, "preaching always under the anointing of the Holy Spirit." Although his formal education was limited, he read widely and acquired an extensive library, including books on history and current affairs as well as theology. Beginning with a congregation of thirteen, which met in a tin shop, his following grew rapidly and moved to a larger storeroom. For several years meetings were held in a tent. By the 1920s, after the congregation had increased to more than a thousand members, they built Christ Temple on Fall Creek Boulevard, which was then on the outer fringe of the black community. When Haywood began preaching, some of his followers were whites, and his congregation continued to be racially mixed after the move to Christ Temple. But the national organization with which his church was affiliated, the Pentecostal Assemblies of the World, split at a 1925 meeting in Chicago when white members withdrew and adopted a new name. Thereafter, the Pentecostal Assemblies of the World moved its headquarters to Indianapolis, with Haywood serving as Presiding Bishop.[63]

In spite of differences in doctrine and church government, functions and activities of Baptist and Methodist churches were much the same. Singing in the choir and participating in music were an important part of religion in all black churches. Missionary societies, welfare societies to help the needy, literary clubs, and cultural activities, as well as an almost continuous succession of fairs and other fund-raising projects, were characteristic of major denominations. Women members played an important part in all of these activities. Money for much of the churches' work, including paying the pastor's salary, was acquired in large part as a result of efforts made by women's groups. A typical example was the Ladies Alliance of Corinthian Baptist Church in Indianapolis, which had as its motto, "Not what we give, but what we share, for the gift without the giver is bare." Members helped raise money to build and furnish a new church and eventually contributed eight hundred dollars toward an organ. Other women's groups helped to make churches centers of aid for the needy and of welcome to newcomers. Through a variety of activities they also taught women how to care for their children and improve their lives.[64]

Serving their churches and the community gave women experience in leadership and helped them to develop positive self-images. Church groups, says Darlene Clark Hine, "nurtured and created a black female community and cultural network."[65]

Next to churches, fraternal organizations were probably the strongest cohesive force and source of leadership for men in black communities. Such organizations furnished aid to sick and needy members and helped to pay for funeral expenses. Much of black social life centered on events sponsored by the various orders and the women's auxiliaries. Lodges of the Prince Hall Masonic order had been founded in Indiana before the Civil War, and as new settlers from the South arrived after the war, many other fraternal orders were established. It was not uncommon for a person to belong to more than one order. Darrel Bigham found that there were twenty fraternal groups in Evansville by 1909, and almost twice that number by the 1920s. Most numerous were twelve lodges of the United Brothers of Friendship (UBF), eight Odd Fellow lodges, six Masons, six Knights of Pythias, and smaller numbers of Elks, Knights of Tabor, and Templars. No similar compilation has been made for Indianapolis, but the same fraternal orders existed there, with even more individual lodges. In Gary, St. Luke's Lodge of Colored Masons was recruiting members by 1908. Soon there were more Masonic lodges, as well as Colored Odd Fellows, Knights of Pythias, and other orders. A club was organized in 1919 to buy land for a hall that all lodges could share.[66] By 1901 there were four Masonic lodges in Terre Haute and one Odd Fellows; by 1910 there were also two Knights of Pythias lodges.[67]

These same fraternal orders were found all over the state in towns where the black population was increasing, but as blacks left older communities in the Ohio River counties, some lodges disbanded.[68]

Community leaders and politicians were nearly always identified with membership in one or more fraternal order. Membership in Masonic lodges continued to be regarded as more prestigious than that of other orders, although some Masons were common laborers. But the Knights of Pythias, an order founded in 1864, experienced spectacular growth in size and influence. The career of Ernest Tidrington, the most powerful black politician in Indiana in the twenties, was due in part to his position as Grand Chancellor of the Knights of Pythias of Indiana.[69]

Most fraternal orders were founded as mutual aid societies—to care for sick and needy members and to provide decent burials. These functions continued to be important, but the rituals and drama of their ceremonies also attracted members. Funerals for members were impressive affairs. Members and nonmembers packed churches to hear the music, the reading of scripture, and the eulogies, and to see the uniforms and the rites performed by fellow members. The various orders held annual state or regional meetings that included parades and other ceremonies. Installations of new officers were also important events, usually followed by banquets.[70]

Women's auxiliaries of these fraternal orders provided opportunities for social life and leadership for some women, but they were, of course, merely "auxiliaries" to male-dominated organizations. Church organizations offered a broader scope for women's activities, but they were limited in membership and programs. The women's clubs that were beginning to develop in the early years of the century were even more significant in making contributions to the community and prompting the personal development of black women.

There were similarities between the white women's and black women's club movements, but there were also significant differences. Educated, upper-middle-class women, often with servants, were the prime movers in the clubs of white women. Members seldom had careers outside the home and found in club activities opportunities for self-fulfillment. Black clubwomen usually worked outside the home, sometimes as teachers or in business, more often as domestic servants, with the responsibility of caring for their own homes and children as well. Grace Julian Clarke, a white leader of the Indiana Federation of Women's Clubs, observed that black women, because they were often breadwinners, were less economically dependent than white women and tended to show more initiative than their white sisters. "If you have ever visited one of them [black women's clubs]," she wrote, "you have noted an earnestness and alertness and a genuine eagerness for enlightenment that by no means characterize our own [white] societies. It is my opinion that the great mass of colored people must be reached through their women."[71]

By 1920 there was a large network of black women's clubs all over Indiana, not only in the cities but in many small towns as well. Their varied purposes and programs are suggested by the names of some Indianapolis clubs: the Florence Nightingale Club, Regina Embroidery Club, Sisters of Charity, Alpha Home Trustees, Dressmakers Relief Club, Auxiliary of the Lincoln Hospital, and Rosebud Needle Club. While some groups were obviously philanthropic from the outset, other clubs that began as social or cultural organizations often expanded their programs to include community service.[72] The Women's Improvement Club (WIC) was founded as a literary club in Indianapolis in 1903 by two black professional women —Lillian Thomas Fox, the first black woman to be employed as a journalist by the Indianapolis *News,* and Beulah Wright Porter, the first black female physician in the city—, but it moved away from its initial goal of self-improvement to undertake a program to fight tuberculosis. In 1905 the club opened a summer camp for black children, who were considered particularly susceptible to the disease. WIC also began a program for training black nurses, who were barred from training in hospitals. With meager financial resources, the camp was operated largely by club members and by black physicians who donated their services.[73]

Fox also took the lead in organizing the Indiana State Federation of Colored Women's Clubs, which held its first meeting in Indianapolis in 1904. All clubs working on "religious, moral, educational or charitable lines" were invited to send delegates. Nineteen clubs, with a total membership of about five hundred, were represented at the first convention, which met at Bethel AME Church. At this first meeting, delegates passed resolutions deploring the spread of lynchings and the increase in prejudice and disfranchisement and pledged themselves to work for racial fair play. During the next few years as more and more clubs were organized, local federations were

Oak Hill Camp for tuberculosis patients was run by the Woman's Improvement Club of Indianapolis, 1905–1916. Indiana Historical Society Library.

formed in towns with two or more clubs. These federations, in turn, sent delegates to the state conventions, which met in different cities each year to discuss issues of interest and concern to members. They also appointed state chairpersons for committees on "mothers' department," juvenile court work, domestic science, education, and folklore and storytelling.[74]

Indiana women also participated in the National Association of Colored Women, with which the Indiana Federation was affiliated. Teacher Sallie Wyatt Stewart of Evansville was the most prominent. She succeeded Fox as organizer, traveling all over the state to encourage formation of new clubs and membership in the state federation. Stewart also took the lead in a number of efforts to improve the condition of blacks in Evansville; for example, she organized the Colored Association of Charities

to cooperate with the township trustee in providing aid to indigent blacks. This project later led to the founding of the Evansville Federation of Colored Women's Clubs. Stewart became president of the Indiana Federation in 1921 and president of the National Association of Colored Women in 1928, succeeding Mary McLeod Bethune in that office.[75]

The Indiana Federation of Colored Women's Clubs and the National Association of Colored Women were not affiliated with their white counterparts, the Indiana State Federation of Women's Clubs and the General Federation of Women's Clubs. A few white women's clubs protested against their exclusion, and in Indiana some prominent white clubwomen and feminists made efforts to cooperate with and assist the black organizations. Among them was May Wright Sewall of Indianapolis, the president of the International Council of Women, who spoke at the first convention of the Indiana Federation of Colored Women's Clubs.[76]

There was some cooperation between white and African American women on two issues important in the Progressive era—temperance and suffrage. A standing committee of the Women's Christian Temperance Union (WCTU) worked with black women in the union's colored branches, and white women lecturers from WCTU frequently spoke at black churches and before other black groups. Black women, as well as white, braved ridicule to work at the polls on election day for candidates who supported Prohibition.[77]

Black and white women and a few men also cooperated to a limited degree in efforts to educate members of both races and sexes on the importance of voting rights for women. A colored branch of the Equal Suffrage League, organized in Indianapolis in 1912, which included men, met every month with the six white branches of the league. The president of the black women's group reported that meetings were well attended because "We all feel that colored women have the need for the ballot that white women have, and a great many more needs that they have not."[78]

Besides church groups, women's clubs, and fraternal orders, there were also institutions created specifically to deal with social problems. In some cases these were sustained entirely through resources and efforts of blacks; in others they were aided by white philanthropy. In the early years of the century, the most important example was Flanner House in Indianapolis. It began as an offshoot of a white settlement house, Indiana Neighborhood House, established by the Charity Organization Society in 1897, which was at first expected to serve members of both races; but very soon officers decided that it was "inexpedient to have colored and white children attending the same institution" because of the "special needs" of Negroes. The next year Frank Flanner, a white businessman, donated a cottage for the use of black children. It opened in 1900 as the Flanner Guild (later Flanner House), with furnishings donated by blacks.

From its beginning the settlement was governed by a biracial board. The first head was Dr. Benjamin Morgan, a black physician and an employee of the settlement. In the early years, several others held the position, among them attorney Brokenburr and his wife Alice, a schoolteacher. Members of the black middle class gave enthusiastic support to the institution as a means of uplifting the lower classes and instilling middle-class values in them. Board member Dr. Sumner Furniss said in an address that members of his class should "urge those around us to more personal cleanliness, insist on a pure home life, and less dissipation and intemperance; to have fewer picnics and save more money for a rainy day."[79] The program of Flanner House was built on the principles of Booker T. Washington's Tuskegee Institute, and its stated goals reflected his philosophy. The educational program was intended to train blacks for domestic service and other jobs that were customarily open to them. Unlike programs in settlement houses for white immigrants, the Flanner House program for women was not intended as preparation for their roles as wives and mothers, but as preparation for service in the homes of whites. The settlement's most important function appears to have been training domestic workers and providing an employment service for them and a day nursery for their children. Although Flanner House offered some classes in sewing and millinery, its financial resources were too limited to permit a real vocational education program.

Flanner House survived its early years through the unpaid services of social workers, doctors, and other volunteers. Later its financial problems were eased somewhat by funds from the Indianapolis Community Fund, but its program continued to be hampered by a lack of money. Despite its limitations, the settlement was nevertheless at the heart of many community activities. A women's auxiliary carried on a number of fund-raising activities—carnivals, fairs, and other events. One of the most ambitious was the "Children's House," held annually at Tomlinson Hall during the Christmas season. Children's choirs and other musical groups from all over the city participated. Proceeds in 1914 were used to buy land for a small playground next to Flanner House.[80]

Flanner House remained the only social service center of its kind in Indiana until the Great Migration during World War I brought large numbers of blacks into the state. Other settlement houses served European immigrants only. One of them, Christamore House in Indianapolis, moved to another part of the city rather than extend services to blacks in a neighborhood where by 1910 half the residents were black. The manager of Christamore House regarded any "mixing" of whites and blacks as "degenerate."[81]

The Indianapolis Colored YMCA, founded about the same time as Flanner House, served a broader and more varied segment of the community. Although some of the same black men served on the boards of both and some of the programs were similar, the paternalistic atmosphere of Flanner House was absent from the "Y." Blacks organized the separate YMCA in 1900, after the Central YMCA repeatedly rejected applications for memberships from blacks, although it had no written rule barring them. Dr. Henry L. Hummons, a young doctor recently arrived from Tennessee, took the lead; he and other young doctors formed the "Colored Young Men's Prayer Band," which met at first at Flanner Guild. In 1902 the group was admitted to membership in the state YMCA.[82] Membership and programs for the new organization grew rapidly. The Colored YMCA was soon offering Bible classes and basic education for adults at night and sponsoring lectures called "Monster Meetings" at churches, featuring speakers like the president of the National Colored Anti-Saloon League. A Ladies Auxiliary was active as early as 1904. A grant from white philanthropist Julius Rosenwald, who offered $25,000 toward the cost of a Negro YMCA in any city where $75,000 was raised by popular subscription, made a permanent building possible. The Indianapolis branch accepted Rosenwald's challenge and by 1912 it had succeeded; with contributions from blacks and even larger contributions from white organizations and individuals, they broke ground for a building expected to cost $100,000 on Senate Avenue. After its completion, the Colored YMCA was popularly known as the Senate Avenue YMCA.[83]

The construction of the new building and the arrival of a new staff member signaled the beginning of a new era for the "Y." Faburn DeFrantz came as director of physical education in 1912 and was made executive director in 1915, a post he continued to hold until 1951. A native of Kansas, DeFrantz attended segregated schools in Topeka and the University of Kansas at Washburn and later studied at the Indiana University School of Social Work and Kent Law School. He was an impressive figure—more than six feet tall, aggressive, and articulate. Under him the Senate Avenue "Y" continued to attract the physicians, lawyers, and teachers who furnished leadership for its many activities, but most of its adult members were unskilled laborers in personal or domestic service. There was also a large youth membership, usually sons of working-class parents. By 1917 the Indianapolis branch had the largest membership of any colored YMCA in the United States.

Activities at the Senate Avenue "Y" emphasized physical fitness—gymnasium classes for young and older boys, ball games, and other athletic contests. A variety of adult teams competed on its basketball court. An adult education program offered classes ranging from high school English and algebra to vocational skills. Under DeFrantz

Members of Indiana's black elite and Booker T. Washington at the dedication of the Senate Avenue YMCA in Indianapolis, 1913; *left to right:* George Knox, Madam C. J. Walker, Freeman B. Ransom, Booker T. Washington, Alexander Manning, Dr. Joseph Ward, R. W. Bullock, Thomas A. Taylor. Madam C. J. Walker Collection, Indiana Historical Society Library.

the "Monster Meetings" attracted national attention. Begun as primarily evangelical religious lectures, they soon came to explore social and political subjects, some of them controversial.[84]

In Evansville, as in Indianapolis, the Colored YMCA was the center for many activities in the black community. Indianapolis publisher George Knox, a strong supporter of the Indianapolis "Y," helped to spur interest in an Evansville branch in 1907 when he spoke at several Evansville churches, asking for support and contributions. With the aid of black businessmen and the clergy and some help from the white YMCA, a branch was established. A white philanthropist contributed money to buy and renovate a vacant storeroom, which furnished meeting rooms and space for a gymnasium.[85]

In 1914 a move to organize a colored branch of the Young Women's Christian Association (YWCA) in Indianapolis began with the support of Madam Walker and other prominent women. The group was granted provisional status from the national YWCA and began a drive for members and funds that met with early success. However, a permanent branch, the Phyllis Wheatley YWCA, did not receive official recognition until 1923.[86]

Women's clubs, fraternal organizations, and church groups contributed to several other welfare and self-help organizations. One of the oldest was the Alpha Home for Aged Colored Women in Indianapolis, which opened in 1886 as the first institution of its kind in the United States. Established with a gift of a small house from a white woman, it was maintained by contributions from black organizations, which carried on fund-raising affairs to support it.[87]

Black women also opened day nurseries for children of working mothers in Evansville, Terre Haute, and other communities and supported them out of the meager resources of blacks, sometimes supplemented by contributions from whites. The matron of the Terre Haute nursery, who took in washing to support herself, served without pay. Although mothers paid only ten cents a day for each child, the nursery was able to provide meals for the children.[88]

More ambitious were efforts by blacks to care for health needs by establishing their own hospitals served by black physicians, who were barred from practice even in the "colored" wing of the tax-supported Indianapolis City Hospital. In 1909 Lincoln Hospital opened in Indianapolis with a staff of nineteen physicians and five dentists. It was founded to fill the "need for a colored institution open freely to all cases of curable and non-contagious cases, where any reputable physician could bring his cases and treat them . . . and colored nurses could be trained." Housed in a frame residence of twelve rooms, Lincoln Hospital could accommodate seventeen patients. There were two medical wards, two surgical wards, and one for obstetrics. In the first year, eleven students were enrolled in a two-year training program for nurses. A ladies' auxiliary, open to any woman interested in civic welfare, sponsored fairs, "tag days," and other fund-raising events.[89]

In 1911 another hospital was opened in a two-story frame house in Indianapolis by the Sisters of Charity, an organization founded in 1874 by women of Bethel AME Church to provide health care for needy blacks. The hospital, which later became interdenominational, was entirely a charity institution, supported by fund-raising activities and contributions, some from white organizations. Like Lincoln Hospital, it offered a training program for nurses.[90]

Although both Lincoln and the Sisters of Charity hospitals began with laudable intentions of filling some of the most serious needs of the African American community, they lacked the financial resources to buy equipment and to provide services required for national accreditation, and both institutions closed after a few years.

In contrast to the enthusiastic support they gave to churches and other community organizations, blacks appeared to be apathetic about politics, and their participation was largely perfunctory. The fact that African Americans accepted, with little protest, denial of equal treatment in tax-supported institutions like Indianapolis City Hospital was evidence of their political powerlessness in the early years of the twentieth century. Before 1900, Republicans had assiduously sought black votes, particularly in Indianapolis, where they might furnish the margin of victory in contests in which the two major political parties seemed evenly matched. A few black members from Indianapolis and other cities had been elected to the state legislature and to city offices. But as the "lily-white" movement gained strength after 1900, black candidates were ignored by state and local Republican organizations. Not a single African American member was elected to the state legislature from 1896 to 1932. A state law passed in 1909 virtually ensured that no black would be elected to the Indianapolis City Council, by providing that members were to be elected from the city at large rather than from wards.[91]

The black vote remained solidly Republican, but black "leaders" were usually selected by whites. During the early years of the century Knox, publisher of the *Freeman,* developed ties with Republican leaders through his work as a barber and established his leadership among blacks by his success as a businessman and through his work in church, fraternal, and civic organizations; he was generally recognized as the most powerful black political leader in the state. Although he never held public office, he was a member of the Republican state central committee.[92]

During political campaigns, white politicians came into black districts to give stereotyped speeches in which they reminded their audiences of their obligation to the GOP, the party of Lincoln, which had emancipated the slaves and given political rights to members of their race. They assailed all Democrats as allies of southerners, who were responsible for disfranchisement and lynching.

In the weeks before elections, numerous political advertisements, with pictures and promises of Republican candidates, appeared in black newspapers, and, not surprisingly, the papers publicized their speeches and usually endorsed their candidacies. White candidates also sought support by dispensing money, although evidence of these subsidies is elusive. Black ministers, who had great influence over their congregations and often delivered political speeches from the pulpit, were undoubtedly sometimes influenced by contributions to their churches.[93]

For black party workers the rewards for election victories were meager. In Evansville, Ernest Tidrington, the "czar" of black politics, dispensed party funds to African Americans during campaigns and awarded patronage afterwards, but the only civil service positions under his control were those that were open to "colored"—street cleaners and janitors of public buildings. Rewards were similar in Indianapolis. After a Republican victory in a city election, the *Recorder,* in a front-page article under large headlines, announced the names of blacks appointed to jobs at City Hall: two custodians, one night watchman, and nine janitors.[94]

The only black elected to public office in Indiana between 1900 and 1920 was Dr. Sumner Furniss, who was elected to the Indianapolis City Council in 1917. Furniss was an elitist who carefully cultivated the support of whites, and he was endorsed by the Republican organization, the members of which regarded him as "safe," a man not likely to embarrass white party members. After the direct primary replaced party caucuses and conventions as means of nominating candidates for state and local offices, a few blacks sought nomination. But the white-dominated party organization controlled the new system as effectively as it had controlled the old one. Lawyers Bailey, Brokenburr, and Ransom all unsuccessfully sought nomination for the state legislature, probably as much to publicize their names in the black community as in hope of winning.[95]

White politicians never referred to discrimination against black citizens or denial of black rights guaranteed by law in their campaign speeches, and although blacks might resent indignities and injustices, most of them appeared to accept the white denial of black civil rights as inevitable. As an editorial in the Indianapolis *Ledger* said,

> There are a great many civil rights in Indianapolis that are denied to Afro-Americans, just as there are in all large cities . . . and the people feel them keenly and resent them openly, but it does not amount to much because those who make the denial insist that they [the rights] are of a social character—such as theaters, churches, schools, hotels and restaurants. [However] . . . we have our own theaters, churches, schools, hotels and restaurants, and the like, and shall have to keep them and improve them, so that after a while they will be just as good in every way as those the whites reserve for themselves.[96]

But to a small minority of blacks this philosophy of acquiescence and accommodation was unacceptable. The most significant evidence of this was the organization of the Indianapolis branch of the NAACP, which was granted a charter in 1913, just three years after the founding of the national organization. School principal Mary Cable, president of the Colored Women's Civic Club, and a group of women associated with her headed the drive for the Indianapolis branch. Mary White Ovington of the national office came from New York to describe the work of the NAACP, and meetings were held in churches and private homes to attract members. Cable was the president of the new branch, and all the other officers and members of the board were women; but men, including ministers and able lawyers, gave them support. Robert L. Brokenburr succeeded Cable as president in 1914, and his associates Bailey and Ransom along with W. S. Henderson contributed legal services to the new organization.[97]

During the first year the Indianapolis branch enlisted more than two hundred members, but activities and growth were the result of grueling efforts by a few. In a private letter Mary Cable said that while she would "never cease struggling," she found the burden of leadership "too much" in addition to her school responsibilities. In her final annual report she said: "We have done much to convince the indifferent that a membership fee would aid much in helping the downtrodden brother who has fewer privileges." But she was discouraged by the apathy of most middle-class blacks: "It will take a torrent that will almost sweep us from our feet before we will band as one power, forgetful of everything other than [that] we are part of the government and must be dealt with as men [sic] receiving all the rights and privileges of citizenship."

After succeeding Cable as president, attorney Brokenburr was soon complaining that membership had declined. In 1918 he wrote to the national office, "Our local branch is very inactive indeed. The fact is we have only the shadow of an organization."[98] But in spite of a repeated pattern of growth, decline, and revival, the Indianapolis branch became the most significant force for civil rights in the state in following years.

In Indianapolis a few prominent whites, including the rabbi of Indianapolis Hebrew Temple and the minister of the Unitarian Church, gave support to the NAACP, but blacks furnished the leadership and carried on the work of the branch. In Gary, by contrast, a white man, Judge William E. Dunn, took the initiative for a branch. A Yale graduate, he served as president of the Gary NAACP, which was chartered in 1916. By 1917 the Gary group was involved in such issues as housing, voter registration, and protesting the segregationist policies initiated by Superintendent Wirt in the schools. Like other NAACP branches throughout the United States, the Gary branch won publicity by its opposition to the showing of *Birth of a Nation,* the notoriously racist motion picture about the Reconstruction era in the South.[99] In Evansville opposition to *Birth of a Nation* was the immediate reason for the founding of an NAACP branch, with William Best as president and Sallie Stewart as secretary. However, the branch showed little vitality and went out of existence soon after World War I.[100] Branches were also chartered in Terre Haute, Muncie, and Marion before 1920. Some collapsed after a few years and were later revived.[101]

While opposition to *Birth of a Nation* was a stimulus to NAACP membership, a much more pervasive and persistent grievance against which branches of the organization protested was whites' denial to blacks of equal access to theaters and other places of entertainment that catered to white patrons. As already noted, most establishments either refused admission to blacks or seated them in "jim crow" galleries. In smaller communities blacks had few options: they could either accept humiliating treatment and sit in the segregated section or take legal action, which was usually futile. In larger communities, notably Indianapolis, denying blacks admission to "white" places of entertainment acted as a stimulus to black enterprise and talent. Out of necessity, African Americans developed their own distinctive forms of music and entertainment, which whites subsequently enjoyed and tried to imitate.

In support of one enterprise that it commended as worthy of support by "every lover of Race pride" the *Recorder* said,

> On account of the vast discrimination existing in virtually all of the places of public entertainment in this city, and in order that the colored people may have a place of amuse-

ment of their own and where their pride will be free from embarrassing situations and other unpleasantness, the Union Amusement Co. composed of reputable colored citizens of this city have organized a stock company to present to the general public the best shows and amusement that can be secured.[102]

As an important railroad center with the largest black population in the state, Indianapolis attracted traveling shows. Several vaudeville houses featuring black entertainers from other cities as well as some local talent were opened during the first two decades of the century. By 1920 motion pictures were drawing audiences away from vaudeville, but many theaters continued to present vaudeville and musical acts along with silent movies. The Indianapolis *Freeman* gave extensive coverage to shows in Indianapolis as well as those in other cities throughout the country. A typical bill at the Washington Theater in 1917 included Ora Criswell, a monologist noted for her beautiful costumes; "Jules and Maggie," an act composed of a popular male drummer and a songstress known for her rendition of "Don't Leave Me, Daddy"; and a group of male singers who were applauded for their performance of "Don't Lay It All on Broadway."

The Walker Theater, managed by Earl Walker, featured traveling vaudeville performers and also a public ballroom. The white-owned Astor Theater opened in 1917 across the street from the new Senate Avenue YMCA and announced that it was "a theater for all . . . and the colored people of this city are welcome and a special invitation is extended to them."[103] In this pre-jazz era of ragtime and the beginning of the "blues," local musicians learned of current trends from the bands and individuals who performed in these theaters. Local players in turn formed their own bands, which often played at dances at white clubs and ballrooms as well as for blacks. In addition to music popular with blacks, which whites were beginning to enjoy, black bands also played the music to which whites were accustomed to dance—waltzes, two-steps, and foxtrots.[104]

Indiana Avenue, the center of black business in Indianapolis, was even better known as the center of entertainment and recreation. Along with theaters and motion picture houses there were dance halls, taverns, and "clubs" where blacks mingled after working hours. Some were patronized by "respectable" men and women, but others, sometimes owned by whites, were regarded as centers of gambling and vice, sometimes including prostitution. Some legitimate businesses like shoe-shining parlors were fronts for illegal gambling. Proprietors of saloons and liquor stores tried to persuade the public through advertisements in the black press that they were "respectable family" institutions that catered only to "gentlemen and ladies," but African American clergymen, church groups, and the black press constantly inveighed against Indiana Avenue as a center of vice. The poolrooms on "the Avenue," said a typical editorial in the *Recorder,* were "infected with young men whose only aim in life is to live easy, without the least semblance of honest toil." In every municipal election campaign, candidates for mayor pledged themselves to "clean up" Indiana Avenue. They promised law-abiding citizens they would drive out the "toughs," suppress gambling, and close saloons and theaters on Sunday. But efforts to stamp out these practices were sporadic, without lasting results. Meanwhile, working-class blacks continued to patronize the establishments along "the Avenue," while clergy-men and reformers continued to denounce them.[105]

While clergymen and some church groups looked askance at dancing and vaude-ville shows, nearly all black Americans showed enthusiasm for organized sports, both as spectators and participants. Before 1900 there were professional black baseball teams in Indianapolis and Evansville and numerous amateur teams in smaller communi-ties. There were also amateur basketball teams throughout the state. The Senate Av-enue YMCA in Indianapolis boasted teams that won victories against colored "Y"s in Louisville, Chicago, and Cincinnati, as well as defeating other Indiana teams. In 1919 the Senate Avenue team, having won the Midwest championship among black teams, was invited to play the team of the white Central YMCA and a white team from Fort Benjamin Harrison. Teams from other clubs and organizations also used the basketball court of the Senate Avenue building. There were also amateur football squads in black communities all over the state. By 1914 there were enough black stu-dents at Indiana University to form a team that defeated the Indianapolis Royal Ath-letes and the Muncie Athletic Club.[106] And in addition to the athletes and the spec-tators were the sports fans who followed their teams' fortunes in the newspapers; the black press, particularly the Indianapolis *Freeman,* gave extensive coverage to sports events all over the United States.

In most fields of recreation and entertainment, blacks followed white models while adapting them to their own tastes and talents. But Emancipation Day was unique to blacks—their most important secular holiday, comparable to the Fourth of July among whites. Celebrations to commemorate Lincoln's Proclamation and the end of slavery began soon after the Civil War and continued in the twentieth century. Most often they were held in September or late summer but sometimes in January. Pro-grams varied, but there were always speeches on the progress of the race since Eman-cipation, stressing the importance of education, and there was always music. In 1909 in Indianapolis, Emancipation was celebrated in January with a series of events at Bethel AME Church in which most churches and fraternal organizations joined. The highlight was a speech by Booker T. Washington.

Emancipation Day celebrations in late summer were held outdoors and usually featured marching bands, processions, and picnics as well as speeches. In 1900 two or three thousand people, white as well as black, gathered at Marion to watch a pa-rade and hear two brass bands as well as speeches. Sometimes several communities joined together in celebration. In 1909 blacks from North Madison, Columbus, and Seymour gathered at North Vernon for a day of oratory and a parade by members of the Knights of Pythias, Odd Fellows, and other fraternal orders and school children, to the music of the Knights of Pythias band. Observances in 1913, the fiftieth an-niversary of Lincoln's Proclamation, were of special importance nationwide as well as in Indiana. Ceremonies all over the state were held to give thanks to God for free-dom, to review the record of progress since Emancipation, and to predict a future when every vestige of slavery and discrimination would disappear.[107]

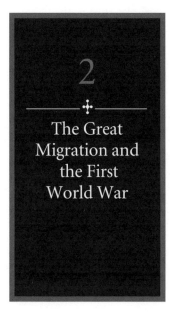

2

The Great
Migration and
the First
World War

To most Americans and certainly to southern blacks, the assassination of Archduke Ferdinand, heir to the Austro-Hungarian throne, in Sarajevo during the summer of 1914 seemed remote from their lives, but the general European war that followed was an important factor in bringing about the most profound change in black society since Emancipation—the Great Migration from the rural South to the urban North.

In 1910, 89 percent of African Americans in the United States lived in the South, and 72.6 percent of them were classified in the United States census as rural.[1] The Great Migration that occurred in the following decade was not really so "great" in numbers as the movement northward during the Second World War and after, but it set in motion demographic, economic, and social changes of tremendous significance. By 1970 the total number of blacks in the South was approximately equal to the number in the North and West, and blacks were the most highly urbanized element in the entire population.

Much has been written on the Great Migration but little of it about Indiana, and research materials such as letters from Indiana migrants are few; but it is safe to assume the motives and experiences of those who came northward to Indiana were similar to those in neighboring states. While scholars debate some aspects of the Great Migration, they agree that both "push" and "pull" factors were involved.

Economic conditions in the South certainly constituted a strong "push." The early years of the twentieth century marked the decline of cotton growing and the one-crop system in much of the South. A number of factors contributed to the decline—soil exhaustion, droughts, and floods. Added to these was the invasion of the boll weevil, which moved eastward through the cotton belt, ruining crops and worsening the condition of tenant farmers and sharecroppers. In cities and towns, the rise of large-scale industries that did not employ African Americans made some traditional occupations of black workers obsolete and impelled them to leave.[2] Economic changes resulting from the outbreak of the European war created a powerful "pull," drawing southern blacks to northern cities. Iron and steel producers and related manufacturing plants in Chicago, Cleveland, Pittsburgh, and the Calumet area faced labor shortages as the war stopped the flow of immigrants and, in some cases, reversed it at the very time when the war generated an increasing demand for American products. Later, the entry of the United States into the war created still greater labor shortages. These developments led to employment opportunities in manufacturing for blacks, who had generally been excluded from such jobs before the war.

While hopes of better jobs, higher wages, and an improved standard of living were powerful motives for migration, less tangible factors were also important. Letters from migrants indicate that they wanted to escape the oppressive racial system of the South—that they envisioned a North where there was no racial segregation, where they could enjoy full citizenship, and where their children could have educational opportunities equal to those of whites. Although there was no single spokesman for the migrants, their actions and their letters rejected Booker T. Washington's dictum that the South was the "natural home" for blacks and that blacks would make better progress by remaining there and accommodating to the prejudices and mores of the "better class" of whites. Washington's followers at Tuskegee and Hampton continued to preach his philosophy after his death in 1915, warning against the dangers of the urban North, but the migrants showed by their actions that they rejected these admonitions.[3]

Southern blacks learned of opportunities in the North through a variety of channels. Letters from relatives and friends who had already migrated prompted some to follow them. Robert Abbott kept up a steady stream of articles and editorials extolling opportunities in Chicago in his Chicago *Defender,* which Pullman porters distributed throughout the South. Labor agents were sent out by some northern industries to recruit workers. In some cases individual men went north, leaving their families behind with the expectation that they would earn money to send for them. But frequently entire families sold their furniture and other possessions and came as a group. Sometimes the entire congregation of a church came with their pastor.

In the Middle West by far the largest number of migrants headed for Chicago, where the number of African American residents grew from 44,103 in 1910 to 109,458 in 1920—an increase of 148 percent in ten years. In Detroit and Cleveland, where the black communities were smaller, increases in the years of the great migration were even more spectacular. In Detroit, where the census showed only 5,741 blacks in 1910, the number grew to 40,838 in 1920, an increase of 611 percent. The number in Cleveland increased from 8,448 to 34,451, or 307 percent.[4]

In Indiana, where the total black population had shown only a modest increase during the first decade of the century, the number grew from 60,000 to 80,000. Few of the new arrivals settled in the southern half of the state, from which, as we have already seen, earlier black residents had already begun to leave in favor of towns and cities in the north and central parts of the state. In Evansville, where the number of blacks had actually declined slightly between 1900 and 1910, it increased a mere 2 percent between 1910 and 1920.[5]

The number of African Americans in Indianapolis grew from 21,816 in 1910 to 34,678 in 1920, an increase of 29 percent. The black population continued to increase during the 1920s, but at a slower rate, bringing the total in 1930 to 43,967, or more than 12 percent of the whole. In absolute numbers, the increase in the black population of Indianapolis was the largest in the state during the Great Migration, but the percentage of increase was far greater in the northern part of the state, particularly in the Calumet area along Lake Michigan, the center of the steel industry. The most dramatic growth was in Gary, where from 383 blacks in 1910 the number rose to 5,299 in 1920—a rise of 1,283 percent. By 1930 Gary's black population numbered 17,922 or almost 18 percent of a total population of 100,426. In nearby East Chicago, where the 1910 census showed a mere 28 Negroes, the number had grown to 1,424 by 1920 and to 5,088 by 1930, about 9 percent of a total population of 54,784.[6]

South Bend and Fort Wayne, where there had been few blacks, also attracted migrants during the war years and in the 1920s. In South Bend by 1930 blacks numbered 3,431 in a total of 104,193. In Fort Wayne they numbered 2,360 of a total of 114,946. In Muncie, Anderson, Richmond, and other smaller cities where industries were developing, there were sharp increases in the black population, while the black population continued to decline in southern towns like Jeffersonville, New Albany, and Madison. Somewhat surprisingly, Terre Haute, a railroad center and site of several industries, also showed a decrease in black residents.[7]

During the years of the Great Migration, for the first time sizable numbers of African Americans from the lower South came to Indiana. Before 1910 most settlers had come from the border states and the upper South. The census of 1930 showed that, of a total of 110,837 black residents in the state, 32.2 percent were natives of Indiana, while 67.8 percent had been born in other states. Kentucky and Tennessee, with 22.8 percent and 12.4 percent respectively, still contributed the largest numbers, but by 1930 more than 7,000 black residents of Indiana claimed Mississippi as their birthplace, while more than 6,000 were natives of Alabama and more than 4,000 were born in Georgia.

Most newcomers from the lower South were headed for the Chicago industrial area. They bypassed Indianapolis and the smaller cities in the central part of the state and went instead to Gary and the neighboring industrial centers. The 1930 census showed that the black population of Gary came from forty-four states and the District of Columbia. In 1920, 93 percent of the black residents had been born outside of Indiana. Ten years later the percentage had dropped to 86, but at that date the number of native Indiana blacks in Gary was smaller than the number from each of six southern states—Alabama, Tennessee, Arkansas, Georgia, Mississippi, and Kentucky.[8]

The experience of new arrivals in Indianapolis was different from that of those in the frontier-like towns of the Calumet area. In the state capital, where there was already a well-established black community, older residents had mixed feelings about the prospect of a sharp increase in their numbers. While they sympathized with the problems of their southern brethren, some were apprehensive over the effects of their arrival. In editorial after editorial, the Indianapolis *Freeman* expressed disapproval of the mass exodus from the South. George L. Knox, a longtime friend and disciple of Booker T. Washington, continued to express the Tuskegeean point of view that blacks should remain in the South. In response to an editorial in *The Crisis,* a publication of the NAACP that encouraged the exodus, the *Freeman* argued that the advantages for blacks in the North were few. Although there was greater political freedom in the North, economic opportunities were limited. The North was no Utopia, Knox asserted, adding, "There is such a thing as making it in any section of the country. This is the lesson to be taught instead of that of unrest." Other editorials frankly stated another reason for deploring the arrival of large numbers of newcomers—the fear that it would arouse prejudice and have an adverse effect upon older black residents. In contrast to the *Freeman* editorials, the Indianapolis *Recorder* declared that the influx of migrants was not causing problems and that "our organized institutions should see to it that they are not only made welcome but that their freedom should begin under the most favorable influences."[9]

The "organized institutions" to which the *Recorder* referred—churches, YMCA, fraternal organizations, and Flanner House—all tried to come to the aid of the new arrivals to help them adjust to their new environment, but they had insufficient resources to deal with the continuing influx. In other northern cities, notably Chicago, affiliates of the National Urban League took care of the migrants' immediate needs for shelter and other necessities. However, in Indianapolis there was no Urban League, although some local organizations, particularly black women's clubs, showed an interest in organizing one. After a meeting held in April 1916, at the Senate Avenue YMCA to announce the formation of an Indianapolis Urban League, the effort collapsed.[10]

Flanner House, black churches, YMCA, and women's clubs made valiant efforts to help the newcomers, but they lacked funds and the services of trained social workers. Consequently, most migrants were forced to seek housing and jobs through their own efforts.

Unlike the burgeoning steel-dominated towns in the Calumet, Indianapolis was home to a variety of small and medium-sized manufacturing establishments. These included Kingan Meat Packing Company and smaller meatpacking plants, lumber mills, iron and steel foundries, and factories that produced a variety of finished products. The numerous railroads converging in the city also created jobs for many residents. But few black migrants or older black residents were employed in these establishments. Most newcomers, if they found jobs, were consigned to traditional low-paying, unskilled, service occupations. A social worker, commenting on conditions of black workers, said that the fact that 90 percent of them were in unskilled jobs was in part because they had recently arrived from the rural South, but it was also because racial discrimination barred them from most kinds of employment.[11]

The entry of the United States into the World War in 1917 and the resulting manpower shortages created new employment opportunities for some black men, at least for the duration of the conflict. The few available statistics do not reveal whether the new employees were recent migrants, but they show an increase in the number of black workers in some of the largest establishments. For example, at Kingan Meat Packing Company the number of blacks increased from 225 in 1916 to 450 in 1918. At National Malleable and Casting Company the number increased from 300 to 450 in that same period; at Citizens Gas Company, from 225 to 450. The Link Belt Chain Company, one of the largest manufacturing plants in the city, began to hire black men for semiskilled jobs, and after the end of the war the company continued to advertise in the Indianapolis *Freeman* for men who wanted to learn the molder's trade.[12]

Black women traditionally worked outside the home in large numbers, usually in domestic service or as "day workers," and the Great Migration brought more black women into the workforce. They were compelled to work when husbands and fathers failed to find jobs or were paid too little to support their families. Besides wives and mothers seeking employment, young unmarried women from the rural South also looked for work in the city and were particularly vulnerable to exploitation by unscrupulous men.

The general assumption of employers and social workers was that black women would enter domestic service or similar fields. One of the most important functions of Flanner House was training and finding jobs for women who did domestic work by the day. The settlement attempted to establish a standard for daily wages and for the length of the working day. A circular publicizing the services of Flanner House stated that its purpose was to provide homes that needed servants by the day or week "with the best colored help that can be procured." Workers were divided into categories. In class A were experienced workers with good records. In 1922 they were paid $2.35 for eight hours of work. Class B workers were less experienced, "average" ones, who received $2.00 for eight hours. All workers were expected to pay their own streetcar fares, but employers were expected to furnish "a good hot lunch" at noon.[13]

Not all women workers had the protection that Flanner House afforded. The *Freeman* reported in 1924 that some women domestics were working for four or five dollars a week. Others were being "lured into lives of immorality" by men who persuaded them that "good morals have no place in a northern big city if they are to survive."[14]

The entry of the United States into the war and the shortage of male workers opened opportunities, temporarily at least, for a few black women in jobs previously held only by men. The Link Belt Chain Company, which had already employed black men as molders, was possibly the first factory in the United States to hire women molders in its foundries. When the company advertised for more molders, six sturdy black women appeared to the surprise of the superintendent, who nevertheless hired them and provided training. After six months the man assigned to give them the necessary training reported that they were "proving satisfactory to all concerned." Other factories and businesses also hired women to replace men. The *Freeman* reported, "An overall clad Negress [*sic*] polishing automobile bodies is not an uncommon sight around garages." The usual daily wage for such workers was three dollars, which, the *Freeman* said, "beats the hitherto six dollars a week which, it is strange to say, was regarded as logical and just remuneration for the average working woman."

But opportunities for black women, like those for black men, were usually limited to the heaviest, least attractive kinds of work. When local canning factories advertised for white women workers, a group of black women protested. But the always-accommodationist editor of the Indianapolis *World* chided them, pointing out that there were plenty of opportunities "for colored girls" in "high class domestic work," which, while not so spectacular, was just as patriotic as any other kind of work.[15]

However, opportunities for work other than domestic service were short-lived. When the war and war contracts ended and the servicemen returned, women workers were dismissed. Many black men who had been hired during the war also lost their jobs. As a result more women than ever were forced to turn to "day work" to support husbands and children. A report for 1920–1921 said that of the 610 women who applied for work through Flanner House, about a third were married women with husbands. They were seeking work for the first time in years because their husbands were unemployed. It was easier for wives to get domestic employment than for men to get jobs to support a family.

For most of the new arrivals in Indianapolis, finding housing was even more urgent than finding a job. Some moved in with relatives, while others were given temporary shelter by churches and church organizations. But when they tried to find permanent homes, African American migrants were confronted with exorbitant rents for shabby, substandard housing. The housing shortage was made more acute by an influx of whites who also hoped to find jobs in war industries. Many blacks could not pay the rents demanded by landlords, even when several families crowded into a single-family dwelling, as they often did. "Wherever the housing problem is bad for white people, it is worse for colored people," a white social worker observed. Unable to pay the excessive rents, many crowded into makeshift shelters in alleys and back streets, which became breeding centers for vice and disease, particularly tuberculosis. In the years after the war, as migration from the South continued into a city where employment opportunities were declining and housing problems were becoming more acute, some social workers advised migrants to go back to the South.[16]

For black families who moved northward in hope of finding better schools, Indianapolis offered new opportunities. Many adults and older children who were forced to work during the day to supplement family income eagerly enrolled in night classes. But many children did not attend school regularly or did not attend school at all. Truancy rates were high in the most congested school districts in black neighborhoods, and juvenile crime was increasing. Truancy officers, who were the only kind of social workers in the Indianapolis school system, reported a variety of reasons for lack of school attendance. Some families were so poor that children had to go without shoes and decent clothing. Some parents thought schooling pointless. Persons who came North expecting that increased schooling would open new economic opportunities became disillusioned when they saw boys with high school diplomas forced to work at the same kinds of menial jobs as their illiterate fathers, while the only jobs for girl graduates were in domestic service.[17]

At the same time, the increase in enrollments resulting from the influx from the South crowded the school buildings and placed new burdens on the public school system. When the colored schools were unable to accommodate more students, some black children were sent to previously all-white schools. Another source of tension was the increased congestion in black neighborhoods that were forced to make room for the newcomers, which prompted older black residents to seek homes in formerly all-white neighborhoods. Consequently, some members of the white community made demands for complete racial segregation in the schools and some tried to bar blacks from moving into "white" residential areas.

While the arrival of large numbers of blacks in Indianapolis was changing the black community and arousing fears among whites, the communities in the Calumet area were also absorbing a larger percentage of newcomers. In Gary, East Chicago, and Indiana Harbor—where there were no equivalents of Flanner House to serve new arrivals—schools were just being established, and there were few established black institutions of any kind. In his early study of the Great Migration, Emmet Scott described the alienation felt by migrants from rural Alabama and Georgia to East Chicago and Indiana Harbor, towns populated almost entirely by Hungarians, Poles, and Italians. The blacks complained about the "wickedness" of East Chicago, where there were no churches for them to attend. They wanted to found their own church where they "could sing without appearing strange" and pray as they were accustomed to pray, but their first effort to organize a church met with such hostility among their white neighbors that it was abandoned. Nevertheless they stayed on, and by 1920 about

Many black homes were without running water in Indianapolis before World War II.
Indianapolis *Recorder* Collection, Indiana Historical Society.

two hundred black men were working in brickyards, while others were employed in foundries and chemical companies.[18]

A much larger number of blacks arrived in Gary from the South, hoping to find jobs in the steel mills. In 1910 there were only about one hundred blacks in the mills, but hiring of blacks began in earnest after the war stopped the flow of European immigrants and caused some of them to return to their native lands. Earlier blacks had been hired only for janitorial jobs, but by 1919 more than 1,300 were working in the mills in a variety of jobs and at higher pay. By 1920, after the onset of the Great Steel Strike, the number had increased to more than two thousand. Management hoped to break the strike by hiring blacks, a move which met with some success, although African Americans were seldom trained to perform the more skilled kinds of work. Many of the blacks were brought into the mills surreptitiously and were kept within the buildings, where they were fed, furnished with cots for sleeping, entertained with movies, and paid higher wages than they had ever received.

Replacing white strikers with African Americans threatened to create serious racial tensions. The Gary branch of the NAACP worked to prevent incidents of racial violence such as those that swept other cities where blacks had been hired as strikebreakers. Louis Caldwell, the local leader, warned black workers that management was trying to break the strike by pitting one race against the other, but his admonition did not deter some men from taking jobs that offered higher pay than they had ever received before. Whites tried to retaliate against the "scabs" in a number of incidents, but there were no serious racial disorders in Gary as the result of the strikebreaking strategy.[19]

As new federal laws reduced immigration from Europe in the postwar years, the steel industry continued to recruit black workers from the South, partly because they were regarded as more amenable and less likely to strike than native whites. By 1928, before the onslaught of the Great Depression, 2,683 blacks were working in the mills, almost 17 percent of the total number of workers.

The steel mills did not employ black women in any capacity, but the fact that many of the men who worked in the mills, both black and white, did not have families created the need for services that women could furnish. Some black women ran boardinghouses for steelworkers; others took in laundry. As in Indianapolis and other cities, a much larger percentage of black women worked outside the home than did native-born and foreign white women. Most black women, including mothers of small children, worked for wages, usually as domestic "day workers."

As previously noted, most early black residents in Gary settled in the marshy area known as the "Patch," a district that lacked both paved streets and sanitary facilities. Some families lived in shacks they built themselves, and others lived in row houses built by the steel companies, where nine or ten families shared a single pump and a single outdoor toilet. A survey on the condition of preschool children done by the Children's Bureau of the United States Department of Labor found that housing conditions for black families in Gary were far inferior to those for foreign-born whites.[20]

Housing for blacks was not included in plans for the development of residential areas in the new city, which included streets and schools for white workers. But the flood of blacks during the war years led steel mill officials and civic leaders, as well as real estate developers, to plan to keep blacks in separate areas from whites. In 1918 the Gary Land Company, a creation of United States Steel, announced it would build low-cost housing for blacks in an area south of the tracks of the Michigan Central Railroad. Some black leaders denounced the plan for being designed primarily to perpetuate segregation, but the Calumet Church Federation, composed of white churches,

The "Patch" in Gary, Broadway at 19th Street. Courtesy of Calumet Regional Archives, Indiana University Northwest.

praised the Gary Land Company and urged them to continue to develop subdivisions "which they have set aside for these people." The Gary *Evening Post* also applauded, saying, "Colored people everywhere prefer to live together and this new subdivision . . . is going to permit them to live in the same neighborhood decently and well."[21] With no alternative, African Americans had to move into the new development if they sought better housing, and segregated housing patterns continued as the black population of the city increased.

Other Indiana cities saw no increase in black population comparable to that in Gary and Indianapolis, but in most of the cities in the north and central parts of the state, where there had been only a few black families before the war, blacks arrived from nearby rural communities as well as from the South, hoping for jobs in factories. In South Bend, where it was estimated there were three thousand blacks by 1923, they found jobs at Studebaker Corporation, the Oliver Chilled Plow Works, Westinghouse Company, and in construction. During the war Studebaker employed as many as seven hundred blacks, including some women. After the war, employment shrank. Many men were unemployed, and women could find work only as domestics.

There had been no recognizable black neighborhood in South Bend before the war, and blacks had been accepted in the same restaurants and other places of public accommodation patronized by whites. But as the number of blacks increased, whites tried to distance themselves from them. Most of all they wanted to confine blacks to certain areas and prevent them from moving into white neighborhoods. Consequently, even blacks who were earning good wages were forced to live in crowded quarters. Some families were crammed into single rooms without heat. Congested, unsanitary living conditions and a lack of social services and recreational facilities were conducive to the spread of disease and vice, but at the same time, the growth of the black community created opportunities for black-owned businesses and the establishment of black churches and other institutions.[22]

Before the war, conditions in Fort Wayne were similar to those in South Bend. The few black residents were employed in jobs traditional for members of their race—domestic service and unskilled labor. Their numbers were so small that there was little concern about race relations. A strike in the railroad shops in the city in 1907 brought the first large group of black laborers. Increasing job opportunities during the war brought more blacks and led to problems in housing and race relations. As in other cities, population growth created opportunities for black businesses and led to the establishment of churches and other black institutions. Among them was the Wheatley Community Center, organized in 1920 primarily as a recreation center. In 1930 it was affiliated with the National Urban League and began to develop the programs for housing, vocational guidance, and training typical of other branches of the Urban League.

Meanwhile in Evansville, a city comparable in size to Fort Wayne and South Bend, the black population actually had declined by 1940, a fact which probably reduced the likelihood of racial conflicts. Although there was some industrial growth in the city, blacks did not share in new employment opportunities. The only factory jobs open to them were janitorial. After the war, traffic on the Ohio River declined, depriving some black men of jobs traditionally open to them.[23]

For thousands of African Americans in Indiana, both native-born and newcomers from the South, the World War raised hopes of better jobs and better lives. But for others the war also meant a stint of military service.

The outbreak of war in Europe in 1914 received little attention in the black press in Indianapolis, but once the United States became a participant, the newspapers loudly and continuously proclaimed support for the war and the loyalty of black citizens. As in earlier wars, blacks hoped that proving their devotion to the United States, even when they were denied full rights of citizenship, would help the race in attaining the same rights enjoyed by whites.

When a separate training camp for black officers was announced by military authorities, the *Freeman* said that, in general, segregation should be deplored but not in this particular case. As a group of Indianapolis men, mostly members of the professions, set off for training in Des Moines, Iowa, the paper said that the camp for training black officers was "of vast importance to the country, to the race and to individuals. More respect will attach to the race because of these men. . . . Our men are measuring up to the tests, waging a war in the interests of the world's higher citizenship, despite the fact that our own [citizenship] lacks completeness." When black men in Indianapolis lined up to register after the adoption of the Selective Service Act in May 1917, the *Freeman* said that young men were anxious to do what was expected of them, and because they responded to the call of duty, it predicted that future demands for consideration of rights would not be met with indifference.[24]

As the war progressed, the black press kept up a litany of editorials supporting the war and criticizing those who did not show the same enthusiasm. A succession of speakers at the Senate Avenue YMCA and at churches and rallies throughout the state repeated the same message—that after the war blacks would be granted the rights of full citizenship as rewards for loyalty and military service. Rarely did a speaker strike a different note.[25]

Young men who volunteered for service during the first months of the war were likely to be rejected because there were as yet no facilities for training black recruits. But once the Selective Service Act was implemented and draft boards were operating, black men from all over the state began to register.

In Indianapolis, where registration began in June 1917, the Senate Avenue YMCA served as headquarters for registration for all men in the Fourth Municipal District, white as well as black. The "Y" furnished some of the clerks and also physicians for physical examinations. Actual induction of draftees did not get under way on a large scale until 1918. In late April the first group from Indianapolis, about three hundred, were given a sendoff by the "Y." Hundreds of family members of the drafted men were entertained at lunch in the gymnasium. Then the draftees marched to the Union Station along streets lined with cheering spectators. Mayor Charles Jewett made a farewell speech to them in which he spoke of the honor of standing for the flag of the United States.[26] A much larger contingent, more than 1,200 in number, who left Indianapolis in August were given a similar parade and farewell. Gary's black community gave the first drafted men a huge farewell party; James Weldon Johnson of the national office of the NAACP was the featured speaker and the mayor of the city an honored guest, and the recruits were escorted to the railroad station by a jazz band. There were similar festivities for later groups of inductees. The first large group of draftees in Evansville was honored by a parade of members of fraternal orders and Boy Scouts and an oration by Ernest Tidrington. In smaller cities like Muncie, the black community demonstrated its pride in the soldiers in similar ways, by church services, parades, and ceremonies at the railroad station.[27]

The largest numbers of blacks from Indiana were sent to Camp Dodge in Iowa. Others were sent to Camp Zachary Taylor in Louisville and Camp Custer in Michigan. The most publicized black soldiers from Indiana were the group of officers from Indianapolis trained at Des Moines, Iowa, where a camp had been established through the efforts of the Colored Department of the International YMCA. Among the 639 officers commissioned in October 1917 were ten men from Indianapolis. They included lawyers, doctors, and Elder Diggs, principal of an elementary school. After receiving their commissions, some of the men served in France in the 365th and 368th Infantry Regiments. Others served in medical and dental corps. Best known among them was Major Joseph Ward, who later headed the Veterans Hospital at Tuskegee, Alabama.[28]

Only a small fraction of black enlisted men saw combat overseas. There was a widespread suspicion among blacks, and some evidence to support it, that military authorities were reluctant to send black troops into combat. Instead, a disproportionate number were assigned to various kinds of service in labor units. Even the Indianapolis *Freeman* complained that there was evidence of a policy to keep blacks from fighting units. "The cry has gone forth," it said, "that the Negroes will do the laboring part, while white men carry the guns."[29]

The first stevedore battalion of American blacks arrived in France in June 1917. Thereafter other service battalions continued to arrive to unload ships and perform other kinds of manual labor. Early in 1918 the first black combat troops arrived, and they moved to the front in April. Among them were soldiers from Indiana. As in all infantry troops in all wars, individual infantrymen seldom received recognition. But one Indiana black, Second Lieutenant Aaron Fisher, was singled out for acts of heroism. As a member of the 366th Infantry Regiment of the all-black 92nd Infantry Division in France, Fisher received the Distinguished Service Cross for heroism in defending his men and leading a counterattack against German troops. For wounds he received in this encounter he received the Purple Heart, while the French awarded him the Croix de Guerre.[30]

Some Indiana men died while in military service, but a Gold Star Honor Roll, which carefully identifies men who were "colored," shows that few Indiana blacks died on the battlefield. Of the thirteen black servicemen from Marion County on the list, only one died in action. Six died of influenza or pneumonia in training camps before leaving the United States. One died at sea en route to France; five died of pneumonia in France.[31]

On the home front, black churches, civic, social and fraternal organizations, and individuals gave enthusiastic support to the war effort. In Indianapolis, according to Elder Diggs, the Senate Avenue YMCA "represented the rallying point for those [men] who because of age, economic, or social condition would not be accepted for active service in the army." As noted, "Monster Meetings" were used as forums for instilling patriotism and support for the war, and the "Y" played a prominent part in patriotic demonstrations and ceremonies for departing troops. Members of the staff also led other activities to aid the war effort, such as speaking as "Four Minute Men" to promote the sale of Liberty Bonds.

Women whose husbands, sons, and other relatives were in service gave support in many ways. The most active women's organization was the Circle for War Relief, which included about twenty branch groups sponsored by churches and social organizations, such as the War Workers Club, the Patriotic Knitting Club, the Cosmo Embroidery Club, a Red Cross unit, and similar groups. The Red Cross unit, with headquarters at Flanner House, had more than forty members who worked two days a week making various articles of clothing, including pajamas and underwear for soldiers but also dresses for women and children refugees. The Red Cross also organized classes in nursing at Flanner House, and during the influenza epidemic of 1918 students from the classes performed valuable services. Children in the public schools also made contributions. Under the direction of Principal Mary Cable, pupils at the McCoy Colored School collected magazines, sold Thrift Stamps, and raised war gardens.

Despite its limited resources, the black community gave strong support to the sale of liberty bonds. Churches, social organizations, and lodges helped to sell bonds; and blacks employed in factories and mills bought bonds through the places where they worked.[32] The government in Washington, using the slogan "Food Will Win the War," called upon civilians to raise victory gardens and to can and preserve the products of the gardens. Freeman Ransom, state director of Colored Food Clubs, toured the state to encourage the organization of local food clubs. In Marion County, blacks organized twenty-eight clubs that held classes in canning and preserving food. During the summer of 1918, black men were recruited along with whites to help harvest wheat in Marion and surrounding counties.[33]

In Gary, Evansville, and smaller cities black citizens supported the war effort through organizations similar to those in Indianapolis. Officials of the steel companies in Gary assumed the responsibility of making sure that all employees contributed to the Red Cross and bought war bonds by deductions from paychecks. Members of black churches throughout the state, particularly women's groups, supported Red Cross activities and promoted the sale of war bonds. In addition to efforts to help soldiers and support military needs, black organizations also worked to help wives and children of soldiers. Representatives of the National Soldiers' Comfort Committee were active in towns with sizable black communities, raising money and providing food and other necessities for soldiers' families. In Evansville, the committee raised money for a day nursery for children of servicemen whose wives were working.[34]

Most of these civilian efforts were scarcely under way and large numbers of enlisted men were still in training camps when the armistice ending the war was signed in November 1918. Blacks greeted the news with high hopes. An effusive editorial in the *Freeman*, entitled "Necessary Justice," expressed the aspirations of many. Now that the "world's fight for democracy" had been won, it said,

> our people are naturally anxious that something be done for correcting once and for all time, the many vexatious and long-standing grievances with which they have had to contend for so many years. . . . It is to be expected that in recognition of the splendid patriotism of our people and the now historic and gallant service of soldiers on the battlefields . . . it will not be long before we are given our just share of that human justice for which the Colored American has so long yearned.[35]

As black troops began to return home early in 1919, they were greeted with parades and ceremonies similar to those that had celebrated their departure for training camp. But it was symbolic that in parades in which both black and white soldiers marched, black troops were at the end of the procession.

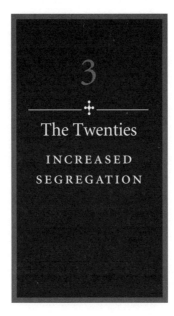

3

The Twenties

INCREASED
SEGREGATION

The optimism of black Americans was short-lived. It soon became clear that for them the war's promise "to make the world safe for democracy" was a mockery. During the war and postwar years, racial violence increased in all parts of the United States. A riot between black soldiers and white civilians in Houston, Texas, resulted in a military trial in which thirteen soldiers were sentenced to death by hanging and forty-one others to life imprisonment. A riot in East St. Louis in which at least forty blacks died was followed by riots in Chicago and Washington and other northern cities. At least thirty-eight blacks were lynched in 1917 and fifty-eight the following year.[1]

There were no large-scale disorders in Indiana in the immediate postwar years, but throughout the state, in small communities as well as larger cities, there was evidence of increasing prejudice and discrimination and white demands to tighten racial restrictions.

In Indianapolis housing shortages resulting from the rapid increase in black population caused older middle-class black residents to seek homes in previously all-white neighborhoods, and whites responded by forming a White Supremacy League in 1922. The constitution of the organization, which was also sometimes called the White Protective Association, demanded separate schools, separate churches, separate hotels, separate theaters, separate recreational facilities, and, most of all, separate residential zones. In virulently racist publications, the organization played upon white fears of "racial amalgamation and social equality" and denounced "impudent Negroes" and whites who sought "unnatural and unwholesome associations . . . contrary to the civilized laws of decency."[2]

No organization as blatantly racist as the White Supremacy League appears to have operated in other cities in the state, but everywhere there were signs of increasing prejudice. In Gary, where foreign-born whites had formerly associated with black neighbors on friendly terms, foreigners as well as native whites sought to distance themselves from African Americans. But some whites spoke out against increasing racism. A white Protestant minister in South Bend deplored the attitudes of whites who were interested in "Americanizing" foreign immigrants but were indifferent to the needs of blacks who had recently moved into the community.[3]

The increase in evidence of racial fears and hatred and demands for tightening racial restrictions in the 1920s coincided with the period of ascendancy of the Ku Klux Klan in Indiana politics and society. Much has been written about the Klan in Indiana, the state where the organization achieved its greatest political power in the twenties, and an extended treatment is beyond the scope of this book. Because of its political power and its creed of white supremacy, both writers and the general public have assumed that the Klan fomented racial hatred and was responsible for measures to intimidate and segregate blacks. However, recent research casts doubt on the implication that the Klan was an extremist fringe group. Analysis of Klan membership lists for several Indiana cities shows that members were representative of the mainstream of native white Indianans. Klan members came from every stratum of society—farmers, factory workers, businessmen, professionals, and ministers—and the organization was strong in both urban and rural areas in all parts of the state. It is estimated that at least 25 percent of all native-born white males in the state were Klan members.[4]

White Protestant ministers and their congregations were drawn to the Klan by its strong support of Prohibition and its opposition to Catholicism. In most parts of the state the Klan emphasized anti-Catholicism and hostility to foreigners more than opposition to blacks. A Klan klavern was organized in Gary in 1921 with the announced purpose of fighting anarchists and creating an extra-legal police force to assist in breaking up "red" meetings. A Klan organizer in Evansville declared that the Klan of the 1920s was "not an outgrowth of the old, pillaging, night-riding lawless bands . . . [but] a clean organization, standing for the uplift and protection of untainted Americanism." In that city, where there had been no marked increase in the black population, opposition to blacks played little part in the Klan's appeal. The Klan's main targets in Evansville were Catholics of German ancestry, who were powerful in the Democratic Party; the Klan had close ties with the Republican Party and concentrated its attacks on "bootlegging Catholic Democrats."

Klansmen admitted that they believed in white supremacy and separation of the races, but they insisted that this was in the interests of blacks as well as whites. Editorials in the *Fiery Cross,* the Klan newspaper, declared that the organization was not the enemy of Negroes, but editorials and Klan orators played upon fears of "racial mixing."[5]

Despite their rhetoric, Klan members had no clear agenda for putting their racist doctrines into effect. It was not the Klan itself but the White Supremacy League and other groups, all of which undoubtedly included many Klansmen in their membership, who were more directly responsible for measures to segregate the races.

Nevertheless, to many blacks the Klan and its white-hooded members epitomized race hatred. The Klan, probably more than any other movement, prompted educated, middle-class northern blacks to resist threats to their rights by organizing. This was evident in the increased membership of the National Association for the Advancement of Colored People in Indiana. As early as 1921 the Indianapolis branch was sounding an alarm over the Klan and recruiting members on the grounds that the NAACP was the most potent organization fighting segregation, lynching, the Klan, and "all other wrongs to which colored citizens are subjected." Under the leadership of lawyers Brokenburr, Bailey, W. S. Henry, and Freeman Ransom (now a member of the national NAACP board), and with support from other black professionals, teachers, and businessmen, the branch grew in membership during the 1920s and took the lead in Indiana in resisting the growing threat of segregation.[6]

NAACP branches were also organized or revived in other cities and towns. By 1926 the NAACP was active in Fort Wayne, Gary, South Bend, Terre Haute, East Chicago, Michigan City, and several smaller communities, including French Lick, Brazil, and Rushville. Not all of the branches survived, but correspondence in NAACP Records in the Library of Congress shows that in Terre Haute, Gary, and South Bend members were engaged in litigation to challenge white businessmen's refusal to admit blacks to places of public accommodation and to protect the rights of persons accused of crime.[7]

The political power of the Indiana Klan reached its zenith in 1924 as it gained control of the Republican Party and dictated the nomination of candidates for state offices.

Apprehension over possible consequences for members of their race caused many stalwart black Republicans to desert the party and vote the Democratic ticket for the first time. For many years the most powerful black Republican in the state was George L. Knox, owner of the Indianapolis *Freeman,* but after the primary elections showed the strength of the Klan, the *Freeman* declared, "The Republican Party as now constituted is the Ku Klux Klan of Indiana. The nominees for Governor, House, Senate and County offices are all Klansmen." Saying, in fact, that there was no Republican Party, the paper called upon Negroes to support the Democrats to show they were worthy of the right to vote. "The ballot," it said, "is the only weapon of a civilized people and it is up to the Negro to use that weapon as do other civilized groups."[8] The Indianapolis *Recorder* and the Indianapolis *World* also rejected the Klan-dominated Republican Party and urged support for the Democrats.

NAACP leaders in Indianapolis responded to the Klan threat by organizing the Independent Voters League to enlist black voters to support Democrats. At an organizational meeting, Robert L. Bailey presented a proposed constitution, while Freeman Ransom said that even if the Klan were not against the Negro he would oppose it because it was un-American. While the national office of the NAACP reminded the president of the Indianapolis branch that it must maintain its nonpolitical character and not accept financial contributions from the Democrats, it nevertheless supported a huge rally sponsored by the newly organized league and the Indianapolis branch. A rally at Tomlinson Hall was planned in conjunction with the first annual meeting of the NAACP's state conference and was attended by several thousand blacks from all over Indiana, who proceeded to endorse the entire Democratic state ticket.[9] The regular Democratic organization supported efforts to recruit black voters, sending anti-Klan speakers into black districts and funding black political meetings. The local Republican organization continued to use its customary methods to hold the African American vote. It sent black patronage workers into black districts to rally support for the Klan-endorsed candidates and sought the customary support of black ministers. But these efforts evoked little enthusiasm. An unusually large turnout of black voters was reported on election day, and for the first time in the history of Indianapolis, large numbers of black voters deserted the Republican Party. Democratic candidates won a majority of the votes in all the black wards in the city.[10]

However, the Klan issue failed to arouse an equally strong response of black voters in communities outside of Indianapolis. Ernest Tidrington, who had succeeded George L. Knox as the most powerful black Republican in the state, scoffed at efforts to portray the Klan as a menace and urged support of Republicans through the customary tactic of linking northern Democrats with southern demagogues. Republicans carried all the black precincts in Evansville. Thus African American voters contributed, probably unwittingly, to giving control of the state government to the Klan. Gary's black leaders rejected overtures from Klan leaders and supported the Lake County Good Government Club, which opposed the Klan and announced that it welcomed support from all citizens—Jews, Catholics, Protestants, and Negroes. Nevertheless, Klan-backed candidates were swept into office in Lake County, as they were throughout the state.[11]

Ed Jackson, who did not deny that he was a member of the Klan, was elected governor; other Klan members or Klan-supported candidates were elected to other state offices; and Klan-endorsed candidates dominated the new General Assembly. However, at its 1925 session the legislature failed to enact any measures that reflected the racist and religious views of the Klan. No proposal for segregation was introduced, and none of the bills intended to limit Catholic influence in the public schools was adopted.[12]

The prestige and power of the Indiana Klan were shattered by November 1925, when municipal elections were held in most of the larger cities in the state. The Klan's rapid decline was due in part to internal rivalries and feuds, but the most publicized reason was the disgrace of D. C. Stephenson, the once powerful Grand Dragon, who was on trial during the political campaign on charges of murder in a particularly sordid sex crime. Protestant ministers, church members, and others who had supported the Klan as a reform movement hastened to dissociate themselves from it.[13]

Despite internal feuding, the Klan in Indianapolis continued to dominate the Republican organization and was able to nominate the candidates for mayor, city council, and the board of school commissioners in 1925. Since the Klan issue was not publicized during the campaign, black voters were not aroused as they had been in 1924. The Indianapolis *News* reported that, except for party workers, blacks showed little enthusiasm for John Duvall, the Republican candidate for mayor, and on election day fewer black voters went to the polls than the year before. Hence, black wards that had been carried by the Democrats in 1924 returned to the Republican fold in 1925. But a few months later the black community was aroused as never before when the Klan-dominated city council adopted a residential zoning law.[14]

The most conspicuous and lasting evidence of the rising tide of racial prejudice was the effort to segregate housing, by preventing blacks from moving into neighborhoods that white homeowners declared belonged exclusively to them, and to segregate all white and black pupils in separate schools. Aside from what they described as "natural repugnance" at the prospect of black neighbors, white homeowners were obsessively afraid that the movement of African Americans into their neighborhoods would mean a drastic decline in the value of their property. For these whites, usually members of the lower middle class living in fringe areas where blacks were most likely to move, their houses represented by far their most important financial investment.

Soon after the beginning of the Great Migration, both Baltimore and St. Louis passed ordinances proscribing blacks from living in city blocks where most residents were white. White real estate agents in many other cities agreed not to sell property to blacks in white neighborhoods. News of the ordinances led the usually accommodationist Indianapolis *Freeman* to declare that, while blacks had learned to forego some rights that were legally theirs, they could not give up the right to live where they chose. But in the years after the war, as whites increasingly resisted the push of blacks seeking to escape from the crowded slums in the center of the city by moving further north, the *Freeman* admitted, "That segregation . . . is slowly but surely becoming an established fact in Indianapolis cannot be denied."[15]

The Indianapolis Real Estate Board followed a policy of discouraging the sale of property in "white" neighborhoods on the grounds that such sales would depress property values, and they defended the practice by saying, "We feel that the leading members of the colored race feel that the best interests of both races are served by segregation in real estate areas." Neighborhood civic associations, which were less vocal than the White Citizens Protective League but probably more effective, gladly cooperated with the Real Estate Board. In a report of civic leagues' activities in 1923, the Mapleton Civic League, located in the northwest part of the city, said its principal purpose was to protect property owners within its borders, explaining that, since it was a strictly residential district without factories or railroads, one of its chief concerns was "to prevent members of the colored race from moving into our midst, thereby depreciating the property values fifty percent or more." To achieve this goal each member of the association pledged not to sell or lease property to nonwhites. As a result of the league's efforts, some colored families had moved away, and none had moved into the district since the founding of the league in 1920.[16]

Other groups adopted more aggressive tactics. When Dr. Lucian B. Meriwether, a young black dentist, bought a house on North Capitol Avenue, neighbors who were members of the Capitol Avenue Protective Association built high fences, more than six feet tall, on both sides of his property. With Robert L. Bailey as his legal counsel, Meriwether sued the neighbors for damages on the grounds that the fences were built with malicious intent. The Marion County Superior Court ordered the neighbors to pay cash damages to Meriwether, a decision upheld by the Indiana Appellate Court.[17]

The *Freeman* responded to the white groups with an editorial, "Living Next to Negroes":

> If they want Negroes to stay in strictly Negro neighborhoods, why don't they get busy and see to it that the Negro gets good streets, lights and police protection in such neighborhoods? There is no problem or mystery about it. The Negro is just a man like any other man. He moves for the same reason that any white man moves. The question of social equality no more enters into the matter with the Negro than it does with the white man.

As efforts by private groups proved inadequate and blacks continued to move north of the boundaries that whites tried to impose, civic groups demanded government action, a development made possible by the election of the Klan-dominated city government in 1925. In March 1926, the Indianapolis City Council responded with a bill backed by the White Peoples Protective League.

Several hundred clapping, cheering, stamping whites crowded into the council chambers to witness the adoption of the measure, for which all members except a lone Democratic dissenter voted "yea."[18] The ordinance made it unlawful for whites to establish residence in a city block inhabited principally by Negroes or for Negroes to establish residence in a block inhabited principally by whites without the written consent of the dominant race. Although both the legal counsel for the city and the state attorney general had given opinions that the ordinance was unconstitutional, Mayor Duvall signed it.[19]

Members of the White Peoples Protective League and their allies cheered the adoption of the ordinance, and even the respected Indianapolis *News* said that, although of doubtful constitutionality, it was "an effort to solve a vexed problem" and represented "sincere convictions."

The Indianapolis *Recorder,* under headlines "JIM CROW BILL BEFORE COUNCIL," said that the Negro had "sat idly by" while discrimination had increased; but now Rome was burning, and Negro citizens must prepare themselves for a legal battle.[20]

The Indianapolis NAACP had already planned to challenge the ordinance and had received word that the national office was ready to give financial support. An aroused local community responded with pledges of support from churches, fraternal organizations, social clubs, and other groups. A prestigious firm of local white lawyers was employed to develop a test case with assistance from black lawyers W. S. Henry and Robert L. Brokenburr.[21] Brought in Marion County Circuit Court, the case arose from the refusal of Dr. Guy L. Grant, a black physician, to fulfill a contract for the purchase of real estate in a predominately white neighborhood on the grounds that the zoning ordinance would prevent him from occupying the property. In November 1926, Judge Harry O. Chamberlin ruled that the zoning ordinance was a violation of the Fourteenth Amendment and that there was no legal impediment to prevent Grant from fulfilling the contract.[22]

After this rebuff the White Peoples Protective League announced that they intended to appeal the decision. But segregationists' hopes of successful appeal were dashed when the United States Supreme Court declared a New Orleans ordinance similar to the one adopted in Indianapolis unconstitutional.[23]

The NAACP and the African American citizens of Indianapolis had won a signal legal victory, but it did not result in access to housing for them in white neighborhoods. The same restrictions that existed before the adoption of the ordinance continued to be used—agreements among white realtors, opposition by white civic clubs, restrictive covenants, and, occasionally, use of intimidation and violence.

Efforts to confine blacks to certain sections and prevent them from moving into areas whites claimed as their domain were not limited to Indianapolis, although no other city appears to have attempted to adopt a residential zoning ordinance. The fact that Indianapolis had both a larger black population and a larger black middle class that could afford to buy decent housing, as well as an aggressive NAACP branch and black newspapers, meant that efforts to segregate blacks received more attention in the capital than in other communities. But similar restrictions were used in other cities.

In Gary residential segregation increased and the burgeoning black population became more concentrated. Families who tried to move into outlying areas received threats of bombings and other forms of intimidation. White real estate agents cooperated in efforts to prevent blacks from buying property, and some landlords refused to rent to them. In 1923, when the Gary Health Department ordered black families to be evicted from shacks in the area south of the Wabash Railroad, many resisted because no other housing was available to them. A survey by the Gary Interracial Commission showed that African Americans sometimes paid twice as much rent as whites for substandard housing on Gary's southside.[24]

Blacks not only paid exorbitant rents for inferior housing, but they also lacked the services and amenities that city governments provided for white residents. After the court decision nullified the residential zoning ordinance, the Indianapolis *News,* in an editorial not unlike the *Freeman* editorial quoted above, said that one thing that could be done to prevent blacks from moving into white neighborhoods was to pave streets in black districts. Their surroundings should be made as good as those in white sections so that they would not want to move. The advice was sound, although it showed that the *News* did not understand the magnitude of the housing problem, but city authorities continued to ignore it. Black civic groups continued in vain to protest against the lack of public services in black areas. Even in small communities the "colored section" was always identifiable not only by the shabbiness of the houses but by unpaved streets and absence of sidewalks, sewers, and streetlights.

The movement for separate schools went along with the movement for residential segregation. The same civic groups that fought to keep blacks from moving into their neighborhoods also supported segregated schools. But separate schools had even wider support; well-to-do whites who deplored the tactics of the extremists and who were not threatened by the possibility of black neighbors also urged separate schools.

Because most African American children were already concentrated in certain areas, the movement for separate elementary schools did not encounter much opposition among blacks. Parents usually wanted to send their children to the nearest school. They asked only that old buildings be replaced or renovated. But efforts to establish separate high schools aroused intense opposition in Indianapolis and Gary, the two cities with the largest black populations. The Board of School Commissioners that was elected in Indianapolis in 1921, the first school board election after the war, made the crucial decision for a completely segregated school system, including a separate high school.

Under state law the Indianapolis public schools were incorporated separately from the City of Indianapolis and were governed by a board elected every four years on the same date as elections for mayor and members of the city council. However, the law provided that the elections be nonpartisan. Although members were nominated individually by petition, they usually ran as members of a slate endorsed by a committee of interested citizens.[25] The school board nominees in 1921 were backed by the Citizens Committee, a group which included prestigious civic leaders, members of the Chamber of Commerce, and persons powerful in financial and legal circles. During the campaign, candidates emphasized economy and businesslike methods while at the same time promising modern school buildings with capacity for every pupil. Once in office, however, they found it difficult to fulfill those promises, since they confronted increased enrollments of both white and black pupils along with demands from white groups for complete segregation.

So crowded were the colored schools by 1919 that more than five hundred pupils were compelled to attend half-day sessions. To alleviate the crowding, other black pupils from the seventh and eighth grades were sent all over the city to white schools where there was room for them, their parents paying the costs of transportation. This led to protests from parents who complained about sending their children to distant neighborhoods where they sometimes met a hostile reception. To remedy the situation, parents asked for new and larger colored schools to replace the crowded substandard buildings—requests that the school board said they lacked funds to fulfill.[26]

Motivated by complaints from white groups, during the early 1920s the school board moved with little publicity toward complete segregation of elementary schools. In 1923 the board set up new boundaries, removing black children from schools that previously were racially mixed and removing white children from schools in areas that were becoming predominantly black. When black parents protested their children's transfers to schools more distant than the ones they had previously attended, the attorney for the school board upheld the transfers.

By the beginning of 1924, the Mapleton Civic League was able to report with satisfaction, "Through our efforts the School Board has promised to provide separate schools for the colored pupils of the city, especially a high school of their own." Although the Mapleton group exaggerated its own influence, the Indianapolis school board had responded to pressure from civic clubs, the Chamber of Commerce, and other respected "establishment" groups by authorizing the building of a separate high school for blacks, a decision that aroused intense opposition among the most respected and influential leaders of the African American community, the same group that led the fight against the residential zoning ordinance.

As previously discussed, black students had attended Indianapolis High School, later named Shortridge, since the 1870s and also Manual Training and Technical, which had been built more recently. Though few blacks graduated from the high schools, larger numbers attended them. By 1922 it was estimated that almost eight hundred were enrolled, most of them at Shortridge, which was located near the central city, not far from areas populated mostly by blacks.[27] While Shortridge was one of the most academically prestigious public high schools in the United States, its students were crowded into classrooms in old buildings that were in a state of deterioration. Along with demands that blacks be removed from Shortridge, patrons were also demanding that the school be moved to new buildings in a new location.

On May 27, 1922, under the headline "SEGREGATION OF NEGROES IS ADVOCATED," the Indianapolis *Times* reported a meeting of the Indianapolis Federation of Civic Clubs, held at the Chamber of Commerce, which recommended a separate high school for African Americans. Resolutions presented and adopted at the meeting said that, although the school board was unable to meet all demands for new buildings because of limited funds, the black high school should have priority over other building plans. The most urgent reason for segregating blacks, according to the newspaper account, was their susceptibility to tuberculosis. "Whereas the public schools have a large number of colored children in the incipient stages of tuberculosis" as a result of crowded and unsanitary housing, the resolutions declared, "Be it resolved that the honorable members of the board of school commissioners make plans for separate schools for colored children as soon as is practical and that they secure colored teachers for these schools in all branches."

In discussion following the presentation of the resolutions, when some members suggested that there was danger of arousing racial hatred that might embroil the fed-

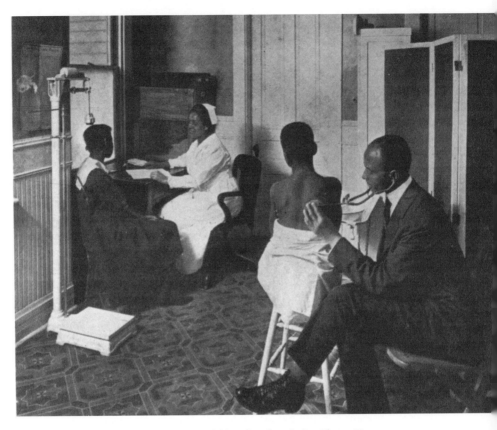

Dr. Henry Hummons screening children for tuberculosis at Flanner House.
Flanner House Collection, Indiana Historical Society.

eration in disputes, the chairman of the committee replied: "There is no use going behind the bush on this proposition. We've all been afraid to get up and say what our sentiments are on this question for business and political reasons"; but pupils with measles and chicken pox were quarantined, he pointed out, and tuberculosis was much deadlier than these. Hence, crowded classrooms with mixed enrollments were a menace to whites.

When they presented their resolutions to the school board, representatives of the federation reiterated that the prevalence of tuberculosis among Negro children was a menace to white pupils and a reason for separate schools. Ironically, members of the civic clubs did not seem to recognize that their efforts to enforce residential segregation contributed to the crowded and unsanitary conditions that made black neighborhoods breeding grounds for tuberculosis.

At a later meeting a representative from the Chamber of Commerce presented a petition that stressed the "necessity" for "a separate modern, completely equipped and adequate high school for colored students." Representatives of women's clubs and civic groups and the principal of Shortridge High School and other well-known whites also appeared before the board to ask for a separate high school.[28]

Meanwhile, leading black citizens who were also members of the NAACP campaigned against the proposed high school, and the national NAACP headquarters also expressed concern over the situation. Both the Indianapolis *Freeman* and the Indianapolis *Recorder* expressed opposition to a "jim crow" high school. A petition from the Better Indianapolis Civic League presented to the school board by Robert Lee Brokenburr eloquently defended public education and equality of opportunity and protested against segregation. The proposal for separate schools, it said, sprang from "class feeling, the desire to separate the children of the schools not only on the basis of color and ancestry, but to separate as far as possible the richer and more fortunate from the poorer for whom they are responsible." Another delegation of black ministers and NAACP leaders told the board that segregation inevitably meant inequality of opportunity, and that the Chamber of Commerce, which advocated separate schools, was pervaded by "a malicious spirit which would produce a serf class."[29]

But members of the school board had already made their decision—that a separate high school for blacks would be built at once, while a new building for Shortridge High School would come later. In making his recommendation, the chairman of the committee said that, while the large numbers of Negroes enrolled in high school "showed a laudable desire on their part and on the part of their parents for a high school education[,] . . . the maximum educational opportunity for these pupils will be best provided for by a new, modern, well-equipped high school." Such a school would provide "the fullest opportunity for the development of the initiative and self reliance and other qualities needed for good citizenship." Moreover, the new school would be staffed by Negro teachers.

Leaders of the black community opposed the proposal for a segregated school and rejected the board's patronizing view that such a school was needed to develop in Negro students the qualities necessary for good citizenship. The local NAACP, with the support of the national office, began to prepare for legal action to stop construction.

Robert L. Bailey immediately offered his services. In Marion County Superior Court he and two other black lawyers asked for an injunction. They argued that the proposed high school could not meet the requirement of equality under the "separate but equal" doctrine: it could not equal the three city high schools already in operation because a single school could not offer the range of academic, technical, and vocational courses offered in the existing schools. When the local judge refused to grant the injunction, the Indianapolis school board voted to go ahead with construction, even though the case was being appealed.[30]

School board minutes and other contemporary materials do not record any petitions by blacks who favored a black high school. But after the building was under construction and the board promised that it would have a staff of African American teachers, some support for it developed, since it would mean jobs for black teachers who were barred from positions in the white high schools. It was rumored that some blacks had met secretly with school board members to endorse the separate school, a movement that the *Freeman* and NAACP leaders regarded as a betrayal.

Crispus Attucks High School, completed in 1927. Bass Photo Company Collection, Indiana Historical Society.

In 1926, only a little more than a year before the school was expected to open, the Indiana Supreme Court finally handed down a decision upholding the Marion County court that had refused an injunction against construction. If, after the school was in operation, the high court said, a case should arise in which a Negro pupil was denied some advantages open to pupils in the other high schools, then proceedings could be taken. Meanwhile, the court would not issue an injunction "merely to allay fears and apprehensions of individuals."[31]

Named after Crispus Attucks, the black patriot of the American Revolution, the new high school opened in September 1927, but from the foregoing account it is clear that the decisions to build the black high school and to continue construction while the appeal to the state supreme court was pending were made by the school board elected in 1921. The so-called "Klan board" was not elected until November 1925. These facts refute the popular tradition that the "Klan board" was responsible for authorizing a segregated high school.

Running under the name United Protestant, the "Klan board" was elected at the same time as Mayor John Duvall and the Klan-dominated city council. Although the state law said that the school board election should be nonpartisan, school board candidates sometimes appeared at Republican rallies. At the end of the campaign the Exalted Cyclops of Marion County Klan No. 3 presided at a high victory rally, at which the newly elected United Protestant school board members were present and recognized by name. However, in newspaper accounts of the campaign there was no evidence that the issue of segregation was mentioned by school board candidates.[32]

Once in office the Klan-backed board continued segregation policies begun by the previous board. Construction of the black high school proceeded, and in 1926 the new board authorized the building of three new colored elementary schools. In 1929 more black pupils were moved from racially mixed schools to colored schools. By that date, out of a total of ninety-one elementary schools in Indianapolis, thirteen were all-black. Although a few new elementary schools were built for black students, in most cases blacks were transferred to older schools in neighborhoods where the racial mix was changing, and whites were moved to new buildings.

By 1929, when members of the "Klan board" again faced Indianapolis voters, the city had gone through a traumatic political experience. Stephenson was in prison, convicted of second-degree murder; Governor Jackson, tried on a charge of bribery, had escaped conviction on a technicality; Mayor Duvall and some members of the city council had been jailed for violation of the Corrupt Practices Act.[33] These developments led to a sweeping Democratic victory in the city election and inevitably brought the school board identified with the Klan into disrepute. In 1929 a slate chosen by a revitalized Citizens Committee overwhelmingly defeated all members of the school board who sought reelection. In a reform campaign, civic leaders from both political parties denounced the incumbent school board, and all three Indianapolis newspapers gave enthusiastic support to the Citizens' ticket. But it is significant for the purposes of this study that, while the "Klan board" was accused of loose financial practices, politicizing the school system, and nepotism, they were neither charged with racism nor criticized for segregating the schools. Not until many years later, after the state law that abolished school segregation was adopted in 1949 and "establishment" whites wanted to remove the stigma of racism represented by segregated schools, did the tradition develop that the Klan was responsible for Crispus Attucks High School.[34]

There is no evidence that students at Shortridge High School protested the presence of blacks or played a part in the movement for a separate black high school, but protests over the presence of a handful of blacks at the recently constructed Emerson High School in Gary gave the final impetus to the decision for an all-black high school. Gary schools were not officially segregated; but William Wirt, the powerful school superintendent, firmly believed in separate education for blacks and established a curious system of internal segregation.

In Gary, more than in Indianapolis, the school system was confronted with an almost overwhelming increase in school enrollments after the war, as black and white migrants from the South arrived in hopes of jobs in the steel mills. From 1920 to 1930 the total number of pupils and teachers more than doubled. Black enrollments increased from 634 to 2,759. Most black students were assigned to the Froebel School, but other schools operated in portable buildings in predominantly black districts. In 1918 the Virginia Street School was opened in the area where the Gary Land Company was building a housing development for African Americans. In another district, the same white principal was in charge of two segregated buildings: Roosevelt School for whites and Roosevelt annex for blacks.

At the opening of the school year in September 1927, six black students were already assigned to the recently opened Emerson School. After the term began, Superintendent Wirt transferred eighteen more blacks to the school to relieve overcrowding at the Virginia Street School. The following Monday hundreds of white students marched out of the school, chanting, "Let's get out of here until they get rid of the niggers." They then paraded down Broadway with placards that said, "We won't go back until Emerson's white." Wirt threatened to expel the student strikers, but the number of participants increased. After four more days, the strike was settled by an agreement that the strikers would not be penalized and the black students would remain at Emerson temporarily, until a black high school was built. Meanwhile, blacks would not be permitted to participate in athletics or social events.[35]

Members of the African American community united in opposition to the strike and to an attempt by the city council to appropriate money for a portable building to serve as a temporary school for the black students. When the NAACP sought an injunction against the appropriation, the council rescinded its action.

School authorities made some renovations at the Virginia Street School after the strike, and at the end of the Christmas vacation in January 1928, they transferred all blacks except three graduating seniors from Emerson to either Froebel or Virginia Street. At the latter school there were classes for ninth and tenth grade pupils as well as elementary grades, but it was not an accredited high school. There were no science laboratories, no library, no gymnasium, and the building was considered a fire and health hazard. Parents of three of the girls who were transferred filed a suit, asking that their daughters be sent back to Emerson; they claimed that the Virginia Street School did not meet the requirements of the Indiana school law of 1877, which said that facilities in colored schools should be equal to those in schools for whites. They pointed out that some courses taught at Emerson were not available at the Virginia Street School. Lawyers Edward Bacoyn of Gary and Robert Lee Bailey of Indianapolis represented the black girls in the suit, which was tried under a change in venue to Valparaiso in LaPorte County. After the trial judge refused to order the pupils transferred back to Emerson, Bacoyn and Bailey, with assistance from the national NAACP, appealed the ruling to the state supreme court.[36] The Indiana court finally rejected the appeal in January 1932, saying that the fact that the Virginia Street School did not offer all the courses for ninth and tenth grade pupils that were given at Froebel and Emerson was not a violation of the 1877 law.

Before the Indiana Supreme Court handed down its decision, the new black high school, promised in 1927, was dedicated in April 1931. The Roosevelt School, which included all the grades from kindergarten through four years of high school, met all requirements of equality in its physical facilities. Even the Gary *American,* a black newspaper that opposed separate schools, praised the new school's equipment and the quality of its teachers. The white press also praised the building and the appointment of F. C. McFarlane, a controversial figure among blacks, as principal.

Even after the opening of Roosevelt, large numbers of blacks still attended Froebel, where internal segregation policies continued. Black students were denied access to extracurricular and social events and were permitted to use the swimming pool only on the day before it was cleaned.[37] In 1938, as black enrollments continued to increase, the school board changed the districts for Froebel and Roosevelt, moving the boundary for Roosevelt further north, thus reducing the number of blacks at Froebel. But some blacks continued to be assigned to Froebel and continued to be denied privileges enjoyed by whites.

Although there was evidence of increased race prejudice in other cities in the north and central parts of the state, only Indianapolis and Gary built segregated high schools.

In most cities the small number of blacks who attended high school went to pre-dominantly white schools. Black students mixed with whites in the classrooms and in some cases participated in athletics, but black teachers were never employed in these schools. In Muncie, where there was no segregation in the schools, some African Americans campaigned for a separate elementary school as a means of employing black teachers, but opposition from other blacks defeated the move. Segregation was unofficial in some communities: the schools in areas where the black population was concentrated were sometimes designated as "colored" and were taught by black teach-ers. But in Elkhart, where black children had previously attended a racially mixed school, segregation became the official policy in 1929. White pupils were transferred to a newly built school, and three black teachers were hired for the ninety-five black pupils who remained in the old building.

In the south and south central counties in the state, small towns and rural areas continued to operate separate schools in spite of dwindling numbers of black stu-dents. In 1924 the Indianapolis *Freeman* described a school in Rockville in Parke County as one "which would do credit to the most wretched tale of a Mississippi plan-tation." One teacher taught everything from the first grade through four years of high school. For high school students there were no laboratories and no courses in science or foreign languages. This, said the *Freeman,* was one of many schools in the state "where the blight of segregation feeds on the hearts and vitals of thousands of inno-cent children."[38]

By contrast, Evansville, which had the largest black population in the southern part of the state, improved its educational facilities for blacks significantly. In 1924 a new school board announced plans to purchase land for an elementary and high school and playground in an area more attractive than the site of the old Clark High School, arguing that "colored boys and girls should be encouraged by surroundings in which they can take more pride." A group of whites appeared before the board to protest, claiming that the plan would encourage more blacks to move into the neighborhood of the school and reduce the value of white-owned real estate, but the school board went ahead with construction of the new school. The Lincoln School opened in 1928 with classrooms for both elementary and high school pupils, a large gymnasium, and manual training facilities. Although blacks were not involved in planning the school, it soon became an object of pride and center for community activities for them.[39]

Lincoln of Evansville, Roosevelt of Gary, and Attucks of Indianapolis, the three academically accredited black high schools in the state, were barred from member-ship in the Indiana High School Athletic Association (IHSAA). This meant that they were not allowed to participate in athletic events with other accredited high schools in Indiana and could only compete with each other or with teams of black high schools in other states. However, in a few high schools with racially mixed enrollments, black athletes participated in athletics along with white teammates.[40]

Efforts of whites to enforce residential segregation and establish separate schools were part of a larger pattern of increasing separation between blacks and whites. A grow-ing black population, confined to limited areas, offered new opportunities for black businessmen and other entrepreneurs. The Great Migration brought more members to older churches and often enabled congregations to build new churches in new locations. Newcomers from the South also organized their own congregations, most often Baptist, with their own ministers and styles of worship. Membership in older fraternal orders grew, along with a variety of social clubs and musical and literary societies. The Indiana Federation of Colored Women's Clubs acquired new members; African American veterans formed their separate American Legion Posts; and Greek letter fraternities and sororities became important in community life as more blacks attended college.

While isolation from whites strengthened their sense of community, most black leaders and members of the middle class opposed legalized segregation and remained committed to the ideal of an integrated society. NAACP branches, and especially NAACP lawyers, constantly protested against segregation measures. Largely through the efforts of Robert Lee Bailey, an Indiana conference of NAACP branches was organized. The subject of the 1929 meeting, "The Increasing Prejudice and Injustice against Negroes in Indiana and What Shall We Do about It?" was indicative of the deteriorating state of integrationist ideals.[41]

In sharp contrast to the NAACP's ideology was that of the Universal Negro Improvement Association (UNIA), founded by Jamaican-born Marcus Garvey. Garvey admired Booker T. Washington and preached Washingtonian doctrines of self-help and economic independence; he also advocated separation of the races, even legalized segregation in some cases. Historians have only recently begun to recognize the importance of his message in arousing race pride and feelings of self-worth among blacks. Even supporters of the NAACP sometimes admired Garvey.[42]

Several chapters of UNIA were reported in Indianapolis, but no prominent leader was identified with the movement. Garvey had a large following in Gary, however, including black ministers and professional men. The Gary *Sun,* the city's only black newspaper until 1927, was a strong Garvey supporter. UNIA groups held meetings in all the black churches and at the YMCA and Roosevelt School. The most influential and outspoken Garveyite in the city was Frederick C. McFarlane, principal of Roosevelt School. Members of UNIA had openly advocated a separate school, in contrast to the followers of the NAACP, arguing that race consciousness and pride would be destroyed by integration. The choice of McFarlane to head the new school was, of course, welcomed by the Garveyites, although his white admirers were probably responsible for the appointment.[43]

While integrationists and separatists carried on an ideological debate, the reality of life in black communities was a mixture of, and a compromise between, integration and separatism. Even integrationists sometimes made concessions when confronted with the choice between a segregated facility and no facility at all. An example of this was access to public parks. Despite earlier statements of city authorities that Indianapolis parks were open to all citizens, Douglass Park opened in 1921 in a largely black residential area with the general understanding that it was to be the park for blacks. The swimming pool and playground were labeled "Negroes only." Thereafter, black organizations were denied permission to hold functions in other parks, and individual African Americans who ventured into them were likely to be ordered to leave by park authorities.[44]

The head of Gary's park board made it clear that the park system was segregated and that only one park was open for such functions as Emancipation Day celebrations. Blacks seldom ventured into other parks and even more rarely onto public beaches. Members of the NAACP urged citizens to ignore the regulations, which were clearly a violation of the Civil Rights Law; but segregation continued.[45]

The "jim crow" wing at Indianapolis City Hospital, a tax-supported institution, and in particular the segregated facilities for training interns and nurses posed a more serious problem for integrationists and aroused more intense feeling than the question of access to public parks. Facilities at City Hospital, the only public hospital in the state that accepted blacks, were woefully inadequate. In 1926, in a city with a black population of almost 40,000, there were only about 70 hospital beds available, and black males were assigned to a ward in the basement. Only white physicians and surgeons were allowed to practice in the hospital. Black doctors could not care for their own patients, and blacks, even those who had graduated from the Indiana University School of Medicine, were denied internships. Although the hospital maintained a school of nursing, young black women were forced to seek nurses' training outside the state.[46]

At the time Attucks High School was nearing completion in 1927, an interracial committee of the Indianapolis Council of Social Agencies proposed construction of a separate wing at City Hospital where black interns and nurses could receive training. Rev. H. L. Herod, then director of Flanner House and a member of the committee, supported the proposal, as did DeFrantz of the YMCA. Other black leaders were strenuously opposed, and members of the NAACP were divided.

Plans for the "jim crow" wing were temporarily set aside, but the issue of inadequate facilities and the need for training of interns and nurses was kept alive by editorials in the *Recorder,* letters to the editor, and delegations which appeared before city authorities asking for improved facilities on a nonsegregated basis.[47]

Faced with the denial of hospital facilities to black medical professionals, a group of black physicians, most prominent of whom was Dr. Mark D. Batties, tried to raise funds for a private hospital, despite the failure of earlier efforts, such as Lincoln Hospital. The new institution, Community Hospital, began with hopes of expanding to a capacity of one hundred beds and struggled on for a time; but its founders' inability to raise funds, made more difficult by the Great Depression, led to its closing.[48]

Outside of Indianapolis there were no public hospitals in Indiana that admitted African Americans; in the rest of the state, blacks were entirely dependent on private medical institutions. During the 1920s, black doctors made several attempts to establish private hospitals in Gary. The most successful was Hedrich Hospital (later called St. John), which operated for several years with a staff of black surgeons and nurses. Gary's Methodist and Mercy hospitals, white-operated private institutions, refused to admit black patients until the 1930s, and then they were put in separate wards.[49]

Statistics provided by the United States census furnish abundant evidence of the effects of poverty, substandard housing, and inadequate health care in the black communities. Infant mortality rates for black babies were double those for whites, and black deaths from tuberculosis were more than double those of whites. In general, the life expectancy for African Americans was lower than it was for whites.[50]

With only limited success, social service centers and social workers tried to alleviate some of the problems of health and poverty that were enlarged by the rapid increase in black population. Social workers supplemented hospital facilities by opening clinics and teaching personal hygiene; they also provided job training and employment services. Although with few exceptions blacks were served in separate institutions from whites, those institutions depended largely on white philanthropy. In Indianapolis, Flanner House moved into larger quarters in 1918 and expanded its services. In addition to training women for domestic service and acting as an employment agency, the settlement enlarged its other training programs, expanded the day nursery, and campaigned against tuberculosis in cooperation with the Women's Improvement Club.[51]

In 1923, after a successful campaign to raise money for a building and acquire a membership of more than one thousand, the Phyllis Wheatley YWCA received official recognition from the national headquarters. Its first important activity was a study of community problems, with emphasis on the special needs of young black women in such areas as health care, working conditions, and recreation, as well as religious education.[52]

The Senate Avenue YMCA expanded its programs of education and recreation for men and boys. It continued to be the meeting place for numerous organizations and, through its "Monster Meetings," to stimulate and enlighten the entire black community. The Senate Avenue "Y," the Phyllis Wheatley "Y," and Flanner House were all dependent on financial support from whites. However, in Indianapolis there was no single white institution with all-pervasive power such as the United States Steel Corporation exercised in Gary.

In its zeal to suppress radicalism among employees, United States Steel supported and controlled several institutions for blacks. The most notable example was Stewart House, a settlement house opened in 1921 with Rev. Frank S. Delaney as superintendent. Delaney, an admirer of Marcus Garvey and his separatist doctrines, was also minister of Trinity Methodist Church, which was supported by subsidiaries of United States Steel.

Stewart House served blacks exclusively, and as the number of blacks in Gary increased, other settlement houses that had been founded to care for the needs of European immigrants also began to admit blacks. Neighborhood House, founded and financed by Presbyterians to serve foreigners, began serving blacks soon after the war. By 1925 half of the children in its kindergarten were black. Campbell House, founded in 1914 by Methodists to serve Europeans, at first excluded blacks, but in 1929 it opened its program to them and hired a black social worker.[53]

Black high schools, like "Y"s and settlement houses, were also centers of community life, and high school teachers were influential in civic and cultural affairs. Most black leaders were opposed to a separate high school in Indianapolis, although a few favored it because it offered an opportunity for employment for black teachers. In an editorial published on the eve of the opening of Attucks High School, the Indianapolis

Recorder again rejected the opportunity for jobs as justification for the school, asserting that "the claims for a Negro high school are overbalanced by the disadvantages" to the black population as a whole. But after the school opened, the tone of *Recorder* editorials soon changed, and the school became an object of pride to the entire black community. Partly because opportunities for educated blacks in other fields were so limited, Attucks was able to recruit teachers who were probably academically superior to most of those in the white high schools.[54]

In Gary even NAACP members who opposed segregation took pride in black schools and their teachers. Although Principal McFarlane of Roosevelt School continued to arouse controversy, no one denied his ability to instill pride and self-respect in students. Explaining his educational philosophy, he told an audience that the Negro was done with apology: "A race must have pride in itself in order to win the respect of other races." He explained, "The Negro has done itself [*sic*] a terrible harm. In some subtle way it has learned to despise itself. At Roosevelt we will try to teach the Negro youth to value his own background with its African backgrounds."[55]

Evansville's Lincoln High School, which opened in 1927, was named without consulting blacks, some of whom had petitioned that it be called the Frederick Douglass School. Nevertheless, the building of a modern facility was a significant step in making Lincoln equal to the white schools of the city. Teachers at Lincoln were respected leaders in the black community. They were the "backbone of the black middle class and upper class and the role models for hundreds of black Evansvillians," according to Darrel Bigham.[56]

Blacks from all parts of the state gave enthusiastic support to the athletic teams of the three black high schools—Attucks, Roosevelt, and Lincoln. Their teams played each other and also teams of black high schools in other states. African Americans also showed enthusiasm for baseball, and several professional teams were organized in Indianapolis. For a few years in the twenties, blacks also organized their own automobile races, which were held at the State Fairground.[57]

In the years after the World War, for African Americans as well as for whites, motion pictures became an increasingly important form of entertainment. "Downtown" theaters that were built for white patrons either barred blacks entirely or seated them in "jim crow" sections, but in the black sections of Gary and Indianapolis, businessmen, often white, opened movie houses catering to African Americans. Black audiences flocked to them, although the motion pictures portrayed white society and ignored blacks, except for an occasional stereotyped comic character.

In Indianapolis, Indiana Avenue continued to be the center for movie houses and all other forms of entertainment. Although there had been a few black-owned and operated theaters earlier, the opening of the Walker Theater on Indiana Avenue in 1927 was a major event in business and community life. The Walker Building was financed with funds from the Walker Manufacturing Company, partly as a memorial to Madam Walker, who had died in 1919. It was a lavish structure in African-Egyptian style, a fine example of the Art Deco period. Managed by Freeman Ransom, the building included a ballroom, beauty shop, numerous offices, and a restaurant as well as the theater.[58]

While the Walker Theater and other black theaters showed motion pictures produced and acted by whites, they also always featured a stage show with black entertainers in addition to the movie. Vaudeville houses and burlesque theaters also featured traveling black companies, often with local black musicians in the orchestra pit. Both local and nationally known dance bands played at the Walker Ballroom, the Cotton Club, the Sunset Ballroom, and other nightspots.[59]

When a craze for the Charleston, a dance that originated among blacks, swept the country in the 1920s, some whites—even in Indianapolis, center of the Ku Klux Klan—enjoyed black jazz and were fascinated by performances of the Charleston. They frequented "black and tan" nightspots along Indiana Avenue and its environs, coming to listen to black singers and to dance to the music of black bands. Some whites also came to drink the "bootleg liquor" available along "the Avenue" during the Prohibition era and to gamble in spots called "recreational halls" and "billiard halls."[60] Although police occasionally raided the nightspots and some club owners were indicted by grand juries, police were not very vigilant in enforcing Prohibition and laws against vice on Indiana Avenue. And even in an era of increasing segregation and restrictions on black citizens, some whites were willing to cross the "color line" to enjoy performances of black singers and musicians and to applaud the prowess of black athletes.

A decade of increasing racial tensions, discrimination, and segregation climaxed in the most heinous of race crimes—a lynching—in Marion, northeast of Indianapolis. The county seat of Grant County, Marion had a total population of about 20,000. Although the black community numbered only about one thousand, much of the white community, as well as residents of neighboring communities, gave signs of racial hostility. Nevertheless, in spite of their small numbers and the unfriendly atmosphere, the black citizens organized a small but vigorous branch of the NAACP. The most influential members were Katherine Bailey, who was also president of the recently organized state conference of the NAACP, and her husband Walter, a physician.[61]

The essential facts about the lynching appear to be the following: A young white man, Claude Deeter, sitting with his fiancée in a parked car on a lonely road near Marion on August 7, 1930, was shot by two young black men, Tom Shipp and Abram Smith, in an attempted holdup. Deeter later died from the injury. The blacks were also accused of attempting to rape Deeter's companion, but apparently this was not true. Shipp and Smith were arrested immediately and taken to the Marion jail. A third black, sixteen-year-old Herbert Cameron, who had been riding with Shipp and Smith but ran away before the shooting, was also arrested and jailed.[62]

As news of the shooting and alleged rape circulated, a mob began to assemble outside the jail. It grew rapidly to an estimated 5,000 persons and continued to grow until it numbered between 10,000 and 20,000—perhaps the majority of the inhabitants of Grant County. It included white men and boys and also women, some with babies and small children. As the leaders of the mob advanced toward the jail, the county sheriff, standing on the steps, pleaded with them to disperse. He later said that he did not shoot because he was afraid that he might hit women and babies. Members of the mob, some of whom came equipped with crowbars, apparently found entrance to the jail easier than they had expected because some of the doors were unlocked. They seized Shipp and Smith and beat them to death with crowbars and then hanged their bodies from trees on the courthouse lawn. Another black inmate, accused of an unrelated crime, was beaten so severely that he later died, but young Cameron succeeded in hiding in the jail and escaped death.

For several days after the lynching Marion's black community feared further violence, but the city remained outwardly calm although public opinion clearly supported the mob action. The local newspaper, the Marion *Chronicle,* attributed the lynching to "a state of mind" in which respect for law had declined because of delays and obstructions in punishment of crime. The lynching, it said, was not carried out by men of "lawless disposition," but by men, ordinarily good citizens, who lacked confidence in the courts. The tone of the Indianapolis press was not very different. The Indianapolis *Star,* while deploring the lynching, nevertheless said it was understandable since maneuvers by defense attorneys had become so time-consuming and delays in punishment had become so long that the public had lost confidence in the courts.[63]

Meanwhile, units of the National Guard were sent to Marion, in part, it was reported, to quell possible acts of reprisal by blacks, but also at the urging of local members of the NAACP and Walter White of the national NAACP office, who sent a letter to Governor Harry G. Leslie asking for protection of the black community. The Marion branch of the NAACP, the state organization, and the national NAACP office all agreed upon two goals: removing Sheriff Jacob C. Campbell from office and prosecuting the leaders of the mob. They called for action under a state law adopted in 1901, which provided that a sheriff who surrendered a prisoner to a mob could be removed from office either through indictment by a grand jury or through the office of the state attorney general. The law also provided penalties for persons who participated in a lynching. The Baileys, at considerable personal risk, led these efforts, gathering the names of the leaders from witnesses of the lynching. When local authorities showed little disposition to act, a group of black leaders principally from the Indianapolis branch of the NAACP sought a meeting with the governor at which they called for state action to prosecute the lynchers and to protect the citizens who testified against them. However, the representatives of the attorney general's office who were sent to Marion seemed reluctant to act. The sheriff surrendered to them, but charges against him were dropped.[64]

From the NAACP national office Walter White sent the names of twenty-seven persons who were alleged to have participated in the lynching to both the attorney general and Governor Leslie, along with evidence to support the accusations. Ultimately seven people were arrested, but only two were brought to trial, and both were acquitted. The first man to be tried was acquitted by the jury after only thirty minutes of deliberation by the jury. At the trial of the second man, which lasted several days, the antagonism against the blacks who attended it was described by a representative of the national NAACP as "appalling." Most of the whites who packed the courtroom were jubilant when the accused man was acquitted. All night long they celebrated by driving through the streets of the black section of Marion, blowing their horns and shouting.[65]

White hostility was still strong in July 1931, when Herbert Cameron was brought to trial. The sixteen-year-old youth, who had been arrested with Shipp and Smith, was indicted by a grand jury on charges of murder while committing a robbery and faced a prosecutor who sought to send him to the electric chair. But young Cameron had the good fortune to have as his lawyers Robert Lee Bailey and Robert Lee Brokenburr, who represented him without charge. Their first legal victory was to secure a change of venue from the hostile atmosphere of Grant County to the circuit court of neighboring Madison County before an impartial judge. At the trial, which lasted eight days, the two lawyers were under threats of reprisals from hostile whites and were under constant protection of sheriff's deputies. A complete record of the trial is not available and newspaper reports are sketchy, but it is obvious that the black lawyers won an impressive victory. They produced evidence that Cameron had not been present at the shooting of Deeter and, of course, had not participated in the alleged rape. Instead of finding Cameron an accessory to murder in the first degree, the jury found him guilty of being an accessory to voluntary manslaughter, a crime that carried a possible sentence of imprisonment for two to twenty years. However, because of Cameron's youth the judge sentenced him to only one year at the state reformatory.[66]

The Marion lynching started a movement led by NAACP lawyers to strengthen the anti-lynching law passed in 1901. The General Assembly that met in 1931 passed a law giving the governor authority to suspend any sheriff or deputy if a prisoner was taken from his custody and lynched. It also provided for monetary damages to be paid by local governments to heirs and dependents of victims of lynchings and for damages to be paid to persons who survived assaults by lynch mobs. However, at the next legislative session, the lawmakers, in spite of the efforts of the NAACP and black clergymen, repealed the parts of the law which made local governments liable for payment of damages.[67]

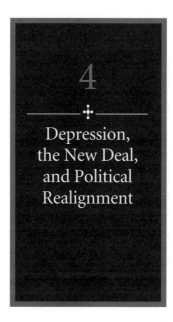

4

✛

Depression,
the New Deal,
and Political
Realignment

After a decade of increasing discrimination and segregation in the 1920s, Indiana's African Americans endured the added burden of mass unemployment and increased poverty during the 1930s. For most, life became a struggle for survival. As conditions worsened, growing numbers of both whites and blacks were jobless or working at drastically reduced wages. All estimates of the numbers of the unemployed are mere guesses, since neither the U.S. Department of Labor nor any other government agency had begun to keep such statistics. However, there is no question that a disproportionately large percentage of blacks were unemployed. As marginal, unskilled workers, African Americans were always less secure in their jobs than whites, and as more and more whites lost their jobs, they frequently replaced black workers, although in better times whites would have shunned the menial jobs for which blacks were normally hired.

According to one estimate, by the end of 1929 more than 2,000 black laborers in Indianapolis (foundry men, porters, janitors, elevator operators, and domestic servants) had been dismissed. As whites replaced more black domestics, the *Recorder* charged that there was a concerted effort to find jobs for unemployed whites by firing blacks. By 1932, when it was estimated that as many as three-fourths of the working-age population in industrial centers were unemployed, the *Recorder* commented that

Members of the Jones Tabernacle AME Zion Church and friends photographed at a church picnic in 1937. While they were fortunate to be employed during the Depression, their occupations reflected the limited job opportunities for black men in Indianapolis: janitor, waiter, vegetable huckster; the man second from the end on the left, Frank Chowning, was a dentist.
Photograph courtesy of Frances Linthecome.

it was undeniable that blacks as a group were more severely affected than whites, adding, "We know of no cases where white citizens have been turned away by employment agencies with the advice 'to let your own people find work for you.' But this happens to us every day."[1]

In Gary, where blacks made up about 10 percent of the population, it was estimated that by 1930 they made up half of the unemployed. As conditions in that city grew worse, black men were more willing to take hazardous jobs in the steel mills, which had been hard to fill in more prosperous times. In 1934 a foreman told two economists who were studying labor conditions in the mills, "Things got so bad, the colored are anxious to do that dangerous work when he [*sic*] can't get anything better. . . . Because this work is so hard on men, I think that is why you find the death rate among colored so high." Some men worked under heat so intense that their clothes caught on fire and they were seriously burned. Workers said that when men hesitated the boss ordered them to "get the hell out of there as they have men . . . who are ready to take their jobs."[2]

As men lost their jobs, more African American women were forced to seek work outside the home, although jobs for domestic workers were dwindling and more white women were applying for them. This competition led to the increasing exploitation of black women, some of whom worked long hours for a mere pittance or for only enough food to keep their families from starving.[3]

Unemployment, lack of money for rent and food, crowded, unsanitary living conditions, homelessness—these were already chronic problems in the black community; but they were made more acute by the Depression and led to increasingly desperate behavior. Black men and women without jobs increasingly turned to gambling, prostitution, and violence. Crime, particularly assault and battery, increased in all large communities. More and more blacks were arrested for major crimes, but many were also booked for vagrancy. In a single year (1933), the overall rate of crimes by blacks in Indianapolis rose by 20 percent, and there was an increase of 100 percent in petty thefts of food and clothing. Twenty-five percent of all persons brought before municipal courts were Negroes. Violent crime also increased—nineteen murders in one year, most of them blacks killing blacks. A front page editorial in the *Recorder* said that blacks killed blacks "with savage impunity at the slightest provocation," a fact which it attributed in part to "official negligence," a system which meted out punishment only when a Negro killed a white.[4]

Juvenile delinquency also increased at the same time that funds for programs for young people were cut. Some programs, such as the Negro YMCA in Gary, were closed altogether. A study of juvenile delinquency in Indianapolis showed an increase in deviant behavior among blacks and whites of both sexes, but there was a greater increase among blacks. Some delinquency among blacks appeared to be the result of families breaking up due to overcrowded, unwholesome housing conditions. Black delinquents were more likely than whites to be children who did not live in a two-parent household.[5]

As the Depression dragged on and the numbers of the unemployed grew, government revenues declined, and some of the increase in crime and juvenile delinquency may have been due to reductions in public services generally, especially in funds for schools. Although migration from the South almost stopped during the Depression and the total African American population of Indiana cities showed little growth, black school attendance increased, particularly among teenage students who remained in school because there were no opportunities for jobs. Unemployed adults also showed more interest in enrolling in night school at a time when school systems were being forced to cut budgets and services.

Completion of Gary's Roosevelt School improved the physical facilities available to black students there, but a drastic decline in revenues meant that summer school programs and night classes were reduced or eliminated. The school year itself was cut from ten to nine months. Substantial numbers of teachers were dismissed, while those who remained suffered salary cuts of 25 percent and were paid in scrip.[6]

In Indianapolis as in Gary, students and teachers, both black and white, suffered as the result of decline in public revenues, but in Gary there were no charges that school officials discriminated against African Americans. Salary scales for teachers of both races were the same; salary cuts of both groups were equal; and physical facilities and equipment for all schools were about the same.[7] But in Indianapolis African Americans were convinced that the school board and school officials discriminated against the black community.

As in Gary, the growth rate of the black school population in Indianapolis was greater than that of the black population as a whole. By 1934 total enrollment in the colored schools was almost 8,000, and there was a black teaching staff of 260. Enrollment at Attucks High School was more than 1,600, and by 1936 about two thousand students were crowded into a building designed for one thousand.

In 1932 the school board announced that as an economy measure night school programs, which had benefited large numbers of African American adults, were to be closed. When protests from a wide spectrum of black civic and fraternal organizations failed to persuade school authorities to reconsider the decision, the Senate Avenue YMCA attempted to remedy the loss by offering a broad range of night classes taught by members of the Attucks faculty and others free of charge to all persons who enrolled.

As the Depression worsened and revenues declined, salaries for all Indianapolis teachers and school administrators were drastically reduced. There were continuing charges from the black community that salary cuts for African American teachers were greater than for whites and that black teachers with higher academic qualifications were paid less than less-qualified whites, charges that the school board continued to deny.[8]

As public services declined, private charitable organizations and social agencies increased their efforts to deal with growing numbers of indigents of both races. In towns and cities all over the state, community chests and other private groups expanded efforts to raise money, concentrating on relief of the needy. By February 1930, the Family Welfare Society of Indianapolis reported that the "employment situation" was the worst it had been in the history of the organization—that demands for help in January had been twice as great as in the previous year. In the capital city, a new organization, the City Employment Relief Organization, also tried to raise funds from those who were still employed to buy coal and food for those who had lost their jobs. American Legion Posts acted as relief organizations in several cities. It was reported that more than 4,000 Indianapolis residents had received clothing from the Legion during the winter of 1930 but that supplies had not been adequate to meet the needs of a thousand more. Most churches and other organizations and newly organized volunteer groups also carried on relief activities. In some Indianapolis schools, Parent-Teacher Associations began furnishing lunches for pupils. Few figures are available to show how much of the relief from private sources went to African Americans, but the *Recorder* reported that, of 3,837 families receiving aid from the Family Welfare Association in 1931, about 30 percent were Negroes, although Negroes were only about 11 percent of the total population of the city.[9]

In addition to efforts by private organizations, local governments furnished relief to some of the needy. However, existing relief systems had been designed to care for persons deemed unemployable —the aged and the disabled—and the Depression imposed demands upon these systems which they could not meet. As their funds were exhausted, more and more able-bodied jobless workers turned to government in order to survive. Under Indiana law, elected township trustees administered relief from taxes levied by the county. Even in rural counties public funds were not equal to meeting the demands imposed by the Depression, and in urban counties, such as Marion and Lake, the burden of relief was far too great. By 1932 funds were exhausted in Lake County, and officials were forced to issue scrip to people who qualified for relief to enable them to purchase groceries and coal. Two townships in the county had overdrawn their relief funds by more than 2.4 million dollars and were using tax warrants from funds anticipated for 1933 and 1934 to pay current bills.[10]

Although it was evident that the burden of providing relief for persons impoverished by unemployment was too great a task for private charity and local governments, state and federal governments were reluctant to assume responsibility. Officials at both levels hoped that problems could be solved by voluntary efforts. Some professed to believe that "odd jobs" and "self help" and added contributions to community funds would solve joblessness. Throughout his administration, President Herbert Hoover remained convinced that unemployment was a local responsibility, that, in his words, the nation's "sense of voluntary organization and community service would take care of the jobless." In October 1930, the president asked industry and private enterprise to cooperate in solving the problem of unemployment. He urged industrialists to avoid layoffs by "spreading" existing jobs among current employees, shortening the number of hours each worked. He also urged employers not to cut wages, a plea that proved to be quite futile.[11]

In response to the president's plea, Governor Harry G. Leslie called a conference of leaders of industry, chambers of commerce, banks, and a sprinkling of leaders of the American Federation of Labor (AFL) unions to urge them to cooperate with a national group to be named by Hoover. At the meeting Leslie cautioned against any plans that would have the effect of "pauperizing people" and urged that the proposed county committees be "job-finding units and not charity dispensing groups." He also suggested that married women whose husbands were employed be dismissed from their jobs so that unemployed men could replace them.

In his message to the General Assembly in January 1931, the governor made no mention of unemployment or relief, nor did the legislature take any action on these problems. A commission on unemployment appointed later by the governor continued to look to voluntary action as the solution. Their proposal was the so-called "friendly five" system, under which five families would cooperate in caring for the needs of jobless workers and their families. A relief committee was appointed in every county to seek support for the plan, and in each of the fifty-two counties where there were Negroes, a separate Negro committee was appointed.[12]

Meanwhile, Indianapolis's African American community was trying to deal with the worsening situation through its own voluntary efforts. An editorial in the *Recorder* declared, "The poor of this city, through no fault of their own, are in dire circumstances. A large number of them are crying for a few lumps of coal, a suit of warm clothing, a pair of shoes. And by all means they must be given shelter." All citizens must sacrifice to help those in need; "What are you doing about it, Mr. Fortunate Citizen?" the editor asked.

Churches redoubled their efforts to collect, preserve, and distribute food and to clothe the needy, particularly children who could not attend school because they lacked shoes and warm clothing. Numerous neighborhood groups were also organized to arouse awareness and combat problems arising from the Depression. In several places citizens organized to prevent the eviction of families who were unable to pay rent.[13]

In Gary, Indianapolis, and other cities, blacks organized to persuade or compel white-owned businesses in black neighborhoods to hire African Americans. Gary's Negro YMCA, NAACP, churches, and schools united to form the Civic Affairs Committee, whose slogan was "Don't spend your money where you can't work." The campaign seems to have had little success, but efforts of the Youth Council of the Gary NAACP were more productive.[14]

In Indianapolis the local NAACP launched a concerted drive for jobs for African Americans at a mass meeting called in early 1930. Leaders initially tried to use persuasion rather than boycotts. A survey done by the Monday Luncheon Club, a group that included lawyers, doctors, educators, and businessmen, showed that more than 100 grocery stores and 40 drugstores in predominantly black neighborhoods had no black employees, while in a variety of other businesses in those neighborhoods, blacks had never been employed except in menial, janitorial-type jobs. A committee headed by Freeman Ransom began to urge these businesses to employ African Americans. Continuing intermittently for several years, the campaign was supported by a variety of organizations, particularly women's clubs and churches. At first, leaders expected to rely on persuasion and negotiation, but after a few months some of them began to urge direct action—to announce to store managers that if they did not hire black employees, blacks would take their business elsewhere. Sometimes pickets tried to dissuade customers from entering stores that did not cooperate. After a few months, the "Don't buy where you can't work" campaign concentrated on two food chains—Kroger and Standard stores—that had acquired a major part of the patron-age of black neighborhoods as small individually owned meat markets and groceries disappeared. When one of these chain stores hired a black salesperson, the *Recorder* hailed it as a victory; but the campaign produced only meager results. However, by 1934, several Kroger stores, threatened by loss of black patronage, had hired a few African American salespersons. The campaign was also credited with the hiring of several black attendants at gasoline service stations.[15]

The NAACP's "Don't buy where you can't work" drive depended upon winning concessions from whites, and its largely symbolic victories had little effect upon the magnitude of black unemployment. The combination of declining black incomes and the failure of the jobs campaign resulted in the NAACP's losing members locally and nationally. The large-scale replacement of blacks by white workers also contributed to skepticism about the NAACP vision of a racially integrated society and convinced many African Americans that economic independence from whites was the solution to race problems, which was the doctrine of the UNIA.

Although Marcus Garvey was living in exile after being convicted in federal court for mail fraud, the Garvey movement was not dead and seemed to gain renewed strength as a result of the Depression. In both Gary and Indianapolis, parades and celebrations were held in July 1931, in observance of the founding of the UNIA. Al-though the organization's claim of 2,000 members in Gary was doubtful, the move-ment was sufficiently strong that the Gary *American,* usually a strong opponent of black separatism, conceded, "If the Universal Negro Improvement Association has done nothing but inspire race pride and hopefulness among a few Negroes, Garvey's labors have not been in vain." The Indianapolis *Recorder,* while continuing to praise the NAACP, said the race was "as righteously proud of the U.N.I.A. as the N.A.A.C.P."

Early in the Depression, the Gary UNIA began a program of feeding the destitute and later participated in protesting evictions of tenants for failure to pay rent. Crowds gathered in Indianapolis to listen to Garveyite speakers, who urged economic inde-pendence as the way to stave off economic disaster. Delegates from both Indianapo-lis and Gary attended the national UNIA convention in 1935.[16]

Although there is no clear evidence that UNIA organizations were directly involved in the efforts of the National Negro Cooperative League to establish cooperatives to free African Americans from economic dependence on whites, the strategy reflected Garveyite ideology. Few Negro cooperatives ever got beyond the planning stage, and most of those survived only a short time. One of the most successful was the Gary Consumer Trading Company, incorporated in 1932 with the slogan "The Negro in Gary needs more cooperation than charity." Its leaders planned to buy goods from wholesalers, sell them at cooperative stores, and use the proceeds for welfare work in the black community. Begun with contributions from a small club, the cooperative store was grossing $200 a week by 1933. The company opened a second store and a gasoline station in 1936 and also organized a credit union. The success of the Gary cooperative was due largely to its founder, Jacob Lorenzo Reddix, a teacher at Roo-sevelt High School who, like the Roosevelt principal McFarlane, believed in black schools as a means of fostering race pride and self-respect. The Consumer Trading

Company continued to operate successfully so long as Reddix remained to advise the operations, but it declined after he left Gary in 1940.[17]

In comparison with the modest scope of the Gary Consumers Trading Company, Dr. Benjamin Osborne's cooperative venture in Indianapolis was ambitious. Osborne was a chiropractor who had moved to Indianapolis from British Guiana in 1920; he became an American citizen and a respected civic leader, active in the Monday Luncheon Club. An admirer of Garvey, Osborne was convinced that the remedy for the economic deprivations suffered by African Americans was for them to become economically independent.

In 1933 he conceived the idea of a cooperative organization, not to provide immediate relief for the jobless but to enable the "Indianapolis Negro . . . [to] lift himself out of the mire of economic serfdom to a point of economic stability by producing and marketing some of the necessities of life instead of remaining a dependent consumer factor." Consumer Unit, the organization he started, soon claimed a membership of more than a thousand, opened an office in the Walker Building, and held meetings in churches to explain their plans. They planned to grow, can, and sell fruits and vegetables on a cooperative basis, i.e., the land and the canning factory would be cooperatively owned and sales would be managed by the cooperative. The program was to be financed by membership fees ranging from one to ten dollars, with no one allowed to contribute more than ten dollars. Members of the experimental station at Purdue University were reported to have promised their cooperation.[18]

The Consumers Unit group was unable to collect enough money to buy the land on which its plan depended. However, undeterred, Osborne and his associates turned to plans for a Homestead Project, where city workers would be able to buy homes and supplement their wages by growing some of their food. They hoped for support from the Rural Resettlement Administration, which was created in the early days of the New Deal. A committee headed by Ransom and including other civic leaders and ministers submitted the plan to federal authorities requesting funds to buy 325 acres of land in Wayne Township, southwest of the city limits, to build homes for low-income workers. The development was not planned exclusively for black homeowners, but it was expected that most residents would be African Americans. To qualify, workers had to be regularly employed with incomes of $700 a year. The houses were to range in price from $2,400 to $3,500 and would be paid for over a period of thirty years. The proposal was not presented as a relief measure, but as a way to improve homeowners' standard of living by permitting them to raise part of their food. Authorities in the Rural Resettlement Administration were reported to have given tentative approval and indicated that $425,000 might be available.[19]

However, backers of the project had not taken into account opposition from white residents in Wayne Township. Individual owners who protested were joined by such groups as the Kiwanis Club, the Home Builders Association, and a newly formed group, the Wayne Township Taxpayers League. The powerful Indianapolis Real Estate Board also voiced opposition, which blacks attributed to "unwillingness to see colored tenants escape the exploitation of the 'rent hogs' who charge them 100 to 300 percent more than white tenants pay for similar houses and apartments."

Organizations in the African American community tried to counter the flow of rumors and misinformation about the project, writing to members of Congress and other state and federal authorities. But their hopes were finally dashed when spokesmen for the Rural Resettlement Administration announced in August that there would be no Homestead Project on the proposed site in Wayne Township and that there was little likelihood of any such project in the Indianapolis area.[20]

While African Americans gave some support to cooperatives and other self-help programs and, as the Depression grew worse, looked increasingly to aid from government, few of them saw Communism as the answer to their problems. Because the vast majority of blacks belonged to the working class and were obviously often victims of discrimination and oppression, Communists hoped to win their support. In the Gary area, the Steel and Metal Workers Industrial Union, a Communist-dominated group, made strenuous efforts to enlist unemployed blacks, but with little success. In Indianapolis, where the Communist Party was so insignificant as to attract little attention from the white press, the *Recorder* reported an occasional rally at which white Communists harangued blacks, but few listeners were converted. As conditions grew worse and more black workers lost their jobs to whites, the *Recorder* admitted, "We do know that Communism is today far less unpopular among our people than as heretofore [*sic*]." But, it added, the rank and file of the black community would not be influenced by the Communist ploy of nominating blacks for political office. They would recognize this as an effort by Communists "to draw their chestnuts from the hot fire by using the paws of Negroes."[21]

While they were not attracted to the Communist Party, a few Indiana African Americans were attracted to the National Negro Congress, which Communists hoped to make a front for their efforts. The idea for the Congress came from more militant black intellectuals who rejected the NAACP, with its legalistic approach to race problems and its middle-class membership, as inadequate to meet the crisis of the Depression. They hoped for a truly mass organization, embracing all kinds of black organizations and all segments of the population. The first meeting in Chicago, in February 1936, attracted delegates from 28 states representing a wide spectrum of organizations. Besides leaders from older organizations there were many young people, some of them members of recently organized CIO unions. A. Philip Randolph, president of the Brotherhood of Sleeping Car Porters, was elected president of the new organization.

The call for the Chicago meeting was greeted with interest in Indianapolis, where the *Recorder* said the proposed Congress showed the indispensable prerequisite for a successful race organization—"a deep seated and burning determination to work out its own salvation." Several representatives from the city, most of them ministers or people active in the NAACP, went to Chicago and reported to a meeting at the Senate Avenue YMCA upon their return, expressing hopes that a branch of the National Negro Congress would be established in Indianapolis.

Although an Indianapolis branch does not appear to have materialized, one was organized in Gary by a group that included some Garveyites associated with the UNIA. However, after the first flurry of enthusiasm, interest in the National Negro Congress declined in Indiana and elsewhere. Ralph Bunche, who had been a leader at the Chicago meeting, admitted later that it was fallacious to think that "the assumption of the common denominator of race would weld together all kinds of Negroes." Branches in a few communities showed some vitality, but a second meeting of the Congress in 1940 was marred by efforts of Communists to dominate it. After that the movement disappeared.[22]

The economic crisis of the Depression and the failure of government to take effective steps to relieve distress caused voters to desert the Republican Party in 1932 and turn to a Democratic presidential candidate who promised a "New Deal." They also elected a Democratic Congress, and Democrats were swept into power in most state governments.

Democrats won control of the state legislature in Indiana and voters elected a Democratic governor, Paul V. McNutt. To African Americans, who had abandoned their traditional allegiance to the Republican Party in droves and voted for Democrats, the new governor's inaugural address was heartening. Said McNutt, "A hungry man is never rational toward the life of the community or toward his own life. Therefore it is the business of government to make those adjustments which guarantee the right to live as a normal human being." The *Recorder* declared that the governor's message caused colored citizens to feel "a new hope, a new ideal, a new determination to live."[23]

The inauguration of President Franklin D. Roosevelt a few weeks later, the beginning of the New Deal, and measures taken in Indiana to supplement New Deal measures ushered in a new era in which functions of both state and federal governments greatly expanded. In the early years of the New Deal, programs were begun in such rapid succession and variety that the general public could not distinguish among them. But they all had the same objectives—to furnish jobs and relief and to stimulate economic recovery. During the first months of the Roosevelt administration, Congress authorized the Federal Emergency Relief Administration (FERA), the Public Works Administration (PWA), the Civil Works Administration (CWA), and the Civilian Conservation Corps (CCC). From 1933 to 1935, FERA, which was funded by federal grants to the states and administered by the Governor's Commission on Unemployment Relief, provided the largest share of relief in Indiana. This commission also administered the CWA program of "made work," which provided more than 100,000 needy persons in the state with jobs such as street maintenance and work on highways. By December 1933, it was estimated that nearly three thousand black men in Indianapolis were employed on such projects as painting the interior of Attucks High School and working in public parks. The PWA, administered through the U.S. Department of the Interior, furnished federal funds for permanent large-scale construction projects such as highways and public housing. The CCC provided work for unemployed young men in camps where they carried on various conservation activities. Blacks as well as whites were recruited for the CCC, and black leaders were watchful to see that young African Americans received their share of assignments. Blacks and whites in most camps seem to have lived together amicably. Black youths from Indianapolis reported enthusiastically that there was no "jim crowism" in their camp

A letter from W. E. Mayo, a black Civilian Conservations Corps worker, to his friend
Ruth Greathouse of Indianapolis, August 1934. Ruth Greathouse Collection,
Indiana Historical Society.

in California or in nearby towns. But whites in rural Indiana sometimes showed resentment when blacks from neighboring camps came into town seeking recreation. A segregated camp for blacks was maintained in Wadeville, west of Evansville.[24]

By 1935, as it became evident that extensive unemployment would probably continue for a long time, Congress created the Works Progress Administration (WPA) to provide work for able-bodied unemployed persons, while people too old or disabled to work and needy children would be cared for by state agencies with assistance from federal funds. The WPA, the longest lasting of the relief agencies, initiated programs that provided employment for persons ranging from unskilled laborers to artists and writers. For blacks in cities, where their rates of unemployment were higher than those of whites, WPA jobs were literally a means of survival. The percentage of African Americans receiving relief was always disproportionately high, in part, as an officer of the National Urban League pointed out, "because of a tendency to uproot Negroes from their traditional employment and replace them with white workers" and because when a few job opportunities appeared in the private sector, they went to whites.[25]

In the counties with the largest numbers of African Americans—Marion, Lake, Vanderburgh, Allen, St. Joseph, and Vigo—thousands of black men and a smaller number of black women worked on WPA projects. Unskilled male workers were put to work constructing and maintaining roads, streets, and other public facilities. Many worked on projects that improved the black sections of cities. They cleaned and repaired school buildings and built or improved playgrounds, parks, and community centers.

Under FERA programs, a few black women were employed as seamstresses and cooks. Adult education classes offered by FERA in cooking, laundry work, and child care were clearly intended to keep women in domestic service, while classes for men in plumbing and repairing electrical appliances prepared them for skilled or semiskilled jobs. Under WPA programs opportunities for women, while limited, were somewhat enlarged. Both black and white unemployed teachers were trained to teach general education classes, including literacy as well as vocational courses. Women participated in directing a wide range of recreational programs for both adults and young people. Both blacks and whites participated in the WPA-sponsored Federal Theater Project, which included classes in drama and dancing and mounted theatrical productions and performances. One of the most successful, "Basin Street Blues," a black musical directed by David Mitcham of Indianapolis, toured the state, attracting large audiences.[26]

Through the National Youth Administration (NYA), a part of the WPA, high school students and other young people under the age of twenty-five could earn small amounts of money and take part in activities that benefited their community as well as themselves. About three hundred young Indianapolis blacks took part in various kinds of work and training. Job training for boys included wood and metal work, used in renovating the Colored Orphans Home and converting it to a center for children who needed institutional care. For girls, in addition to the usual classes in sewing, cooking, and laundry work, there were classes in typing and clerical work. Some girls worked in the day nursery and recreational programs at Flanner House, the Senate Avenue YMCA, and the recently completed Lockefield Gardens. In other cities throughout the state, there were similar NYA programs, both for young people who had completed high school and for those who had dropped out. The NYA also furnished funds for students enrolled in high school; from the money they earned, students were able to pay for lunches, carfare, and clothes.[27]

While African Americans looked upon the New Deal jobs programs as a godsend and showed their gratitude through their votes for Franklin D. Roosevelt and other Democrats, they frequently complained of discrimination in the administration of New Deal programs, and there is evidence to support these complaints. Early in the New Deal, the Indianapolis *Recorder* reported that black workers were paid less than whites for the same kinds of work—a disparity for which it blamed the labor unions, which excluded blacks. "We refuse to believe," it said, "that it was the intention of the government to inject discriminatory practices into CWA activities here," but if reports were true, government administrators should act to stop discrimination.

Complaints of discriminatory practices continued, and the discrimination was attributed to the fact that blacks had little voice in the administration of New Deal programs. Black doctors and dentists complained they were not employed in programs to provide medical services for persons on relief. Black social workers complained that although the largest numbers of recipients of aid from public and private welfare agencies were blacks, few African American professionals were hired to deal with them. A group of black social workers in Indianapolis formed a Social Workers Fellowship, claiming that, "because of the enforced isolation of colored citizens," members of their race could best deal with their problems.[28]

Housing projects probably showed more discriminatory practices than other New Deal programs and also demonstrated how the economic interests of whites were sometimes more influential than the needs of blacks. From the outset it was taken for granted that public housing projects would be racially segregated. Though blacks might disagree with this policy in principle, there were few protests because of the desperate need for decent housing in the black community.

The most important housing project in Indiana, Lockefield Gardens in Indianapolis, demonstrated the conflicting interests of white labor unions and unemployed black laborers. Before the Depression, black civic groups had complained without success to city authorities about conditions in certain slums, in particular the city's failure to enforce an ordinance requiring the removal of outdoor toilets. After federal money became available during the early months of the New Deal, the Indianapolis Chamber of Commerce took the initiative in seeking a loan to finance a slum-clearance program and the building of privately owned, low-cost housing for Negroes. The proposal was endorsed by white labor unions and most black civic organizations, but the Indianapolis Real Estate Board lobbied successfully to block the original proposal.[29]

Although the Real Estate Board continued its opposition, by the summer of 1934 a plan was approved for a housing project in an area near the City Hospital and Attucks High School, to be constructed by the PWA—under the jurisdiction of the Interior Department—and owned by the federal government. The PWA purchased the land for the project at prices determined by local real estate experts, and the land was condemned if owners were unwilling to sell. After clearance began, some persons living in houses scheduled for demolition resisted moving because no other quarters were available to them.[30]

As news of the project became known, hundreds of unemployed blacks, most of them unskilled laborers, swamped employment offices, and most jobs in demolishing and clearing the building sites went to black workers. But opportunities for skilled African American laborers were another matter. Nearly all unions in the building trades, all affiliated with the AFL, had long excluded black members. The only exceptions were the Hod Carriers Union, which was largely black, and the Cement Finishers Union.[31]

Because of the New Deal requirement that contractors employ only union labor for construction and the unwillingness of unions to admit blacks to membership, prospects for skilled black workers to work in construction of housing planned for members of their race seemed bleak. To deal with the problem, a committee of local

Lockefield Gardens, Indianapolis, public housing for African Americans built during the New Deal. Indiana State Library.

leaders, including Ransom, Benjamin Osborne, DeFrantz, Clarence Scott (managing editor of the *Recorder*), and headed by Rev. Marshall Talley, announced the formation of the Negro Welfare Committee, which was intended to enlist skilled African American workers in a union of their own and thus prevent the white unions from being recognized as the only agents for dealing with contractors. Although the committee made persistent efforts and invited representatives from cities in other states to join in the movement to organize black workers, it met with little success.

In spite of a ruling by Secretary of the Interior Harold Ickes that 12 percent of the jobs in the project should go to black workers, the unions persisted in exclusionary policies. The contract for construction that was finally signed provided that 3 percent of skilled jobs should go to African Americans, but even that minimal requirement apparently was not fulfilled.[32]

Once construction was under way, the project was delayed by a series of jurisdictional disputes among the various unions. When the building was supposedly finished, government inspectors refused to approve it for occupancy until defects that caused damp walls were corrected. The first tenants did not move in until February 1938, nearly four years after the plan had been approved.[33]

Lockefield Gardens (named for one of the streets that formed the boundary of the project) consisted of twenty-four well-designed fire-resistant buildings, which included 748 apartments, twelve stores, several offices, and forty garages. The apartments, which varied in size, all had cross-ventilation, electric stoves and refrigerators, and steam heat. Each had its own backyard. In addition, there were central laundry facilities and a playground for children. Tenants were selected by a Housing Advisory Committee from "self-sustaining families of limited income," and government regulations specified the amount of income that determined eligibility.

Lionel Artis, longtime member of the staff of the Senate Avenue YMCA and an active civic leader, was named resident manager of the complex. Under his leadership and an elected tenant council, residents developed a variety of community activities, including publication of a mimeographed news sheet. Mothers of small children started a nursery school. Two Girl Scout troops were organized. Adult classes in sewing, music, and shorthand were offered in cooperation with Flanner House, and the Indianapolis Power and Light Company sponsored classes in meal planning and electric cooking. A branch of the Indianapolis Public Library was opened after a few months and enjoyed a large circulation.[34]

In spite of prejudice and race friction during construction, Lockefield Gardens became an example of successful cooperative black enterprise and an institution in which the African American community took pride. It was architecturally innovative and attractive and offered tenants comforts they had never enjoyed before. Nevertheless, private real estate interests, anti–New Deal Republicans, and the influential Indianapolis *News* opposed it from the beginning. The *News* and political groups opposed to government subsidies attacked the project as financially unsound. Consequently, in Indianapolis, unlike other cities in the state, the city council refused to authorize a Federal Housing Authority, and virtually no more public housing was built in the city for many years.[35]

In Gary in 1938 the Federal Housing Authority approved a housing project of three hundred units for blacks on a site near Roosevelt High School. Almost immediately dissension developed between black civic leaders and white authorities, because African Americans had been given no voice in planning the project, even though they petitioned for an advisory committee to help plan and manage it and to study methods for selecting tenants. As construction for Delany Community (named after the black Methodist minister) got under way, blacks were denied an opportunity to see plans or specifications for the buildings. As the buildings neared completion, the Gary Ministerial Association took the lead in organizing meetings to protest the way the project was proceeding. They complained about negligence on the part of the local housing authority that resulted in conflicts of interest among some of the companies and individuals involved in construction. They also called attention to defects in construction and architectural details. Protesters demanded that an African American be appointed as manager of the project and sent two delegations to Washington to present their grievances to federal authorities. After some delay the Gary Housing Authority announced that William Lane, a coach and teacher in the Gary schools, would manage Delany Community, with another black as his assistant. The Gary *American* had warm praise for the protesters: "This event marks the first time in the history of Gary that there has been a united effort on the part of Negroes to right a wrong. Had the same militant spirit existed twenty years ago . . . there would have been no need for [Negro] slum clearance as such. Neither would [there] have been all the segregation, discrimination, police brutality, and other attendant evils that the Negro is facing daily."[36]

In Evansville a 1930 proposal to demolish houses in the Baptisttown slums and develop a public park in the area had been abandoned because it made no provision for housing the black residents whose homes would be demolished. When federal funding became available in 1934, an application was made for PWA funds to demolish houses in the same area and replace them with two hundred modern units of four and five rooms. Plans for recreational and parking areas were also included. As in Indianapolis, problems arose when families whose houses would be demolished could not find places to move, but contracts were signed in spite of obstacles and construction began in 1936. The kinds of problems that arose in Gary were avoided by including two prominent black Democrats on a planning committee and by appointing one of them, Dr. Robert King, as manager of the project. Opened in 1938, a few weeks after Lockefield Gardens, the units in Lincoln Gardens were soon occupied, and the project was regarded with pride by black citizens.[37]

African Americans settled for "half a loaf" in accepting the New Deal's segregated housing policies and were the first beneficiaries of public housing in Indiana. Because the need for housing was so acute and protests over segregation would have been futile, black leaders acquiesced in racially separate projects, asking only that they have a voice in planning and administration.

In another area of acute need, black access to Indianapolis City Hospital, African Americans won only a partial victory when PWA funds were used to construct a new wing for the hospital. It was generally understood that the new wing would be used for black patients, but city and hospital authorities continued to equivocate on the question of admitting black doctors and training black interns and nurses. A bill introduced into the state legislature in 1939 requiring the hospital to use Negro interns and nurses passed the house of representatives without dissent but, according to the *Recorder,* was killed in the senate because of opposition by city authorities.[38]

In September 1939, perhaps at the urging of city council member Ransom, who was the most influential black Democrat in the state, Mayor Reginald Sullivan (a Democrat) received a letter from PWA authorities containing a "sharp inquiry" asking why blacks were not to receive training in the new wing and reminding the mayor that the application for funding made by his predecessor in 1936 had included an agreement that Negroes would be trained in the new facility. The Indianapolis *Star,* always critical of New Deal measures, called the letter another example of a "Federal government bureau attempting to dictate to a city government." At a meeting with black leaders, including Ransom and DeFrantz and a number of black physicians, the mayor insisted that the plans for admitting black interns and nurses were "evolutionary," not "revolutionary." The appointments for 1939 had already been made, he said, but blacks would be appointed in future years.[39]

In November 1939, it was announced that Dr. Clarence A. Lucas, son of a prominent African American physician and a graduate of Dartmouth and Indiana University School of Medicine, had been appointed as an intern at City Hospital, the first such appointment in twenty-two years. However, Lucas was summarily dismissed a few weeks after beginning his internship for violating the rules under which he had been admitted—"specifically for eating in the white dining room," although most of the white interns, many of whom had been fellow students with him in medical school, indicated they were willing to accept him. The dismissal caused a furor among black physicians and other influential members of the black community and led one of them, Dr. Theodore Cable, to threaten to withdraw as a candidate for the state senate. Apparently Lucas was readmitted, but thereafter only a few black interns were admitted for several years.[40]

Two young African American women were admitted to the nursing school of City Hospital in 1940. By 1942, there were five black students, and in 1943 two were graduated, the first members of their race to do so in the sixty-three-year history of the Indianapolis City Hospital School of Nursing. By 1943, black nurses were also being hired as members of the hospital staff.[41]

In 1943 Dr. Paul A. Batties was the first African American to be appointed to the surgery staff at City Hospital. The first black cardiologist, Dr. Harvey Middleton, joined the staff at about the same time.[42]

One lasting legacy of the Great Depression and the New Deal era among African Americans has been in the political realm. In Indiana, as in the rest of the nation, black voters abandoned their traditional loyalty to the Republican Party and turned to the party of Franklin D. Roosevelt and the New Deal, and for the most part they have remained loyal Democrats.

Except for the flurry over the Ku Klux Klan in 1924, which caused numbers of blacks, principally in Indianapolis, to vote for Democrats, the black vote had remained solidly Republican throughout the 1920s. The most powerful African American politician in the state during those years was Ernest Tidrington of Evansville, a lawyer who kept black voters in line in 1924 by minimizing the Klan issue. His popularity and prestige among black voters was partly due to his position as Grand Chancellor of the Knights of Pythias of Indiana. Among white politicians his influence reflected the fact that he was regarded as a protégé of Jim Watson, longtime United States Senator. In 1920 the Republicans had named Tidrington county chairman for Colored People of Vanderburgh County. After this appointment he was regarded as the "czar" of black politics in Evansville, able to control two or three thousand votes. So successful was he in his home community that he was appointed head of the Colored Bureau of the Indiana Republican Party and a member of the National Colored Republican League. President Coolidge named him to a committee to study "Negro conditions" in the United States.[43]

While three black Republicans were elected to Gary's city council in the 1920s, blacks in Indianapolis who sought nomination to local office were ignored by the Republican organization. Nevertheless, most of the black leaders who had deserted the party in 1924 returned to the GOP in 1926. Both Robert Lee Bailey and Robert Lee Brokenburr, who had bolted the Republican Party in 1924, supported the Republican ticket in 1926. In 1928 Bailey stumped the state on behalf of the Republican State Committee, assailing Al Smith, the Democratic presidential candidate, as a Tammany man who would not give a colored man a job sweeping the street in New York and praising his opponent, Herbert Hoover, as a man who had always taken a firm stand for "equality for all, irrespective of race or color." On election day in 1928, as usual, black voters cast their votes for Hoover and for Republican Harry G. Leslie as governor.[44]

Bailey and Brokenburr remained Republicans for the rest of their lives, but by 1930 other black leaders were identifying themselves as Democrats. Ransom was campaigning for Democratic candidates, as were Osborne and Cable. Young attorney Henry J. Richardson failed in his attempt to win nomination for state representative, but he became a familiar figure in white Democratic circles as he campaigned for other Democratic candidates. The Indianapolis Recorder continued to support Republicans in its editorial columns, but just before the 1930 election it published a large advertisement signed by a group of black converts to the Democrats. Declaring "the Republican Party has rebuked, humiliated, insulted and debauched unbelievably its Negro voters who were once loyal to it," the group cited among reasons for leaving the party its ties with the Ku Klux Klan and the recent lynching in Marion, where Republican city officials had failed to remove a Republican sheriff who had "permitted" the lynching. A Democratic victory, the advertisement promised, would mean the "beginning of a new day politically and economically, ending an era of bigotry and economic stagnation."[45]

In November 1930, Democrats swept the state, winning control of state and local offices. As the Depression deepened, many more voters, white and black, who had supported Republican candidates two years earlier voted for Democrats for the first time. Over 200,000 more citizens voted in 1930 than in 1928. Although the surge of African American voters to the Democrats was not as large as it would become in 1932 and in 1936, they contributed to the victory. In Evansville for the first time Democrats made inroads into traditionally black precincts. The Democrats won two normally Republican wards in Indianapolis, and the Democratic county chairman expressed thanks to black voters for their "enthusiastic and militant support."[46]

By 1932 both political parties were actively campaigning for African American votes. In Marion and Lake Counties, the white-dominated organizations of both parties adopted a tactic that guaranteed the election of one black from each county to the state house of representatives, and this became customary. In Lake County, which sent five members to the house, Republicans nominated Milo Murray, a Gary lawyer; Democrats nominated Dr. Robert Stanton of East Chicago, a dentist. Other black aspirants were defeated in the primary. The same pattern prevailed in Indianapolis as Republicans nominated Brokenburr, and Democrats nominated Richardson. In 1932 the largest number of black delegates in years were chosen to the Republican state convention, and, for the first time, there were black delegates at the Democratic convention. Each party sent a single black to its national convention as an alternate.[47]

At political rallies white speakers from both parties assured black audiences of a new concern for their rights, and African Americans everywhere were showing an increased interest in politics. A *Recorder* columnist said that the Depression had brought home to all blacks the awareness that government, local and national, concerned them. The state conference of the NAACP reaffirmed the organization's traditional nonpartisan position, but in a speech to the group White, the national secretary, predicted "the greatest political revolt" among black voters "ever known in a national election."[48]

The prediction appeared to be fulfilled when voters all over the country flocked to the polls to elect President Franklin D. Roosevelt and a Democratic Congress as well as Democratic governors and legislatures in most states. McNutt was elected Indiana's governor along with other Democratic state officers and a General Assembly with a Democratic majority. Two black members, Stanton of East Chicago and Richardson of Indianapolis, were elected to the lower house, the first Democrats of their race to serve in that body. Dr. Stanton was a native of Arkansas who had moved to East Chicago to open a practice after graduating from Meharry Medical College with a degree in dentistry. At a time when African American Democrats were almost nonexistent in Lake County, Stanton had pioneered in establishing a local party organization. Richardson, born in Huntsville, Alabama, had moved to Indianapolis while in his teens and worked as a waiter to earn money to attend Shortridge High School. After attending the law school of the University of Illinois on a scholarship for two years, he transferred to the Indianapolis Law School, where he received his LL.B. degree in 1928. By 1932 he had established himself as a lawyer ready to fight for civil rights.[49]

The political tide toward the Democrats continued in 1934, and more blacks joined the party. In Gary for the first time in many years Democrats were victorious in local elections, partly because many blacks, heretofore staunch Republicans, were converted by A. B. Whitlock, editor of the Gary *American,* a strongly Democratic publi-

State representative Henry J. Richardson of Indianapolis in the 1930s,
when he introduced civil rights legislation in the General Assembly.
Henry J. Richardson, Jr., Collection, Indiana Historical Society.

cation. William Anderson, a black Democrat, defeated Wilbur Hathaway, a longtime Republican member of the city council. Bailey failed to win nomination as a candidate for city council in Indianapolis, but Cable, a dentist, was nominated in the Democratic primary and elected in November, becoming the first black Democrat to serve on the council. Brokenburr, the only African American Republican nominated in Indianapolis, was again defeated by Richardson, who along with Stanton was elected to the house of representatives for a second term.[50]

Dr. Stanton appears to have been a conscientious though unobtrusive lawmaker; but it was evident from the time the house of representatives convened in 1933 that Richardson was to be an aggressive advocate for members of his race—a kind of African American politician previously unknown in Indiana. During his first term he received a considerable amount of publicity as one of the sponsors of a law that required contracts for public buildings to contain agreements not to discriminate because of race or color in the employment of workers. Richardson also introduced a bill in 1933 to strengthen the 1885 Civil Rights Law, but, although it received a committee recommendation that it pass, it was not heard of again.[51]

After his reelection in 1934, Richardson and six other Democrats cosponsored a bill to "put teeth" into the 1885 Civil Rights Law. In a speech at a public hearing, Richardson declared that denial of the rights that the law purported to protect was "unconstitutional, un-Christian and anti-social." Although few members of the house of representatives openly opposed the measure, it appears that they were under pressure to kill it from lobbyists for hotels, theaters, and restaurants. White Democrats from Marion and Lake Counties continued to support the bill, but other Democrats joined Republican representatives to defeat it by delaying tactics.[52]

In 1936, when the New Deal was at its zenith, the coalition of voters that was to constitute the Democratic Party for the next generation consolidated. Increasing numbers of African Americans contributed to the sweeping victory of Franklin Roosevelt in Indiana and in the nation as a whole. However, despite the fact that they increased Democratic majorities, black voters received little recognition in Indiana when white-dominated party organizations selected and endorsed candidates for office. In Indianapolis, where Richardson sought renomination, Ransom and Osborne formed a Democratic Workers Council to demand that the Democratic organization give more attention to their interests and evaluate candidates in terms of their position on questions affecting race. The state executive board of the NAACP went on record as opposing renomination of any candidate for the state legislature who voted against strengthening the 1885 Civil Rights Law. On the eve of the primary in a fiery speech in which he urged a black audience to demand their legal rights, Richardson declared, "Whether you realize it or not the self respect of your race is on the spot. . . ." But he failed to win renomination when the party organization threw its support to Rev. Marshall Talley, a Baptist minister who apparently was persuaded by white party officials to oppose Richardson. In Lake County, Dr. Stanton was also defeated in his bid for renomination.[53]

These rebuffs did little to diminish the black enthusiasm for Democratic candidates. For most African Americans, President Roosevelt was the symbol of his party, and speakers, white and black, dwelt on him and the benefits conferred by the New Deal. Ransom, designated to head the drive for black votes for FDR by the National Democratic Committee, campaigned vigorously throughout the state, saying, "I don't see how the Negro will go back on our great President who has done much to restore stability.... Through the New Deal every Negro in the state has benefited [in] some way." A speaker at a rally in Gary said that colored people and poor whites would be "ungrateful for all he has done for us if we did not give President Roosevelt another term."[54]

African Americans voted in unprecedented numbers in November 1936 and contributed to another huge victory for Roosevelt and the Democratic state ticket. In Indianapolis, Lake County, and Evansville it was estimated that as many as 75 percent of African Americans gave their support to the party of the New Deal. However, few blacks were elected to office, and only one, Talley, to the state legislature.[55]

In 1938, in the normally Republican state of Indiana, enough white voters returned to the GOP to enable Republicans to win most state and local offices, but blacks continued to give overwhelming support to Democrats. Although Republicans won control of the state house of representatives, two black Democrats were elected to that body—Cable of Indianapolis and Chester A. Allen of South Bend. At the same time, Ransom was elected to the Indianapolis City Council, and in East Chicago voters elected the first African American member of the city council, James Dent.[56]

In the legislature, Allen and Cable cosponsored a number of measures intended to remedy some discriminatory practices and improve the status of African Americans, although Allen was the more aggressive of the two men. One bill amended the 1885 Civil Rights Law to outlaw discrimination in hospitals and colleges and universities. Another, aimed at the Indiana High School Athletic Association, banned discrimination against black athletes or teams of public schools. A third required jury commissioners to swear that they would not discriminate against a prospective juror because of race or sex. All of these bills were assigned to committees, reported favorably, and not heard of again—the fate of nearly all civil rights bills for many years. Two less-controversial measures sponsored by Allen were adopted. One amended the law on first-degree murder to permit life imprisonment as an alternative to the death penalty. The second mandated appointment of a Negro member to the State Board of Public Instruction.[57]

The election of 1940 ended a decade of Democratic Party dominance in Indiana politics and government. Indiana cast its electoral votes for Republican Wendell Willkie, a native son, and elected a slate of Republican state officers and a Republican-dominated General Assembly. The single important Democratic victory was the election of Governor Henry F. Schricker, who although a Democrat was regarded as nonpartisan on most issues. In Marion County (Indianapolis), both Republican and Democratic parties endorsed and nominated black candidates for the state senate—Democrat George Cable and Republican Brokenburr. The Republican victory made Brokenburr the first member of his race to sit in the upper house. Mercer Mance, a Democrat nominated for the state house of representatives in Indianapolis, was defeated in November. But South Bend voters elected Allen for a second term in the house. He was joined by another black representative, James S. Hunter of East Chicago, who for the next twenty-five years was to be one of the most influential Democrats in the state legislature. In 1942 Hunter was joined by Jesse Dickinson of South Bend, another Democrat, who became an effective spokesman for civil rights. After serving six terms in the lower house he was elected to the state senate in 1958. Republicans in Indianapolis were again victorious in 1942; Wilbur Grant, a lawyer who had been active in Republican politics for twenty years, was elected a state representative, and Dr. Lucian Meriwether, another African American Republican, was elected to the city council. Two years later Dickinson, Hunter, and Grant were reelected to the house of representatives, and Brokenburr was reelected to the state senate.[58]

In 1944, at the height of the Second World War, when African American units were fighting in all quarters of the globe and growth of wartime industries was brightening economic prospects of black civilians, the Indianapolis *Recorder* took the unprecedented and politically significant step of endorsing Roosevelt for reelection. In a front-page editorial, the paper said that although it had supported Republican candidates and principles for forty-seven years, it found that Republican "promises" were "unfortunately empty." Under Roosevelt, it continued, "the nation can know it will continue forward, out of the darkness of racial hatred [and] intolerance toward the shining goal of peace and prosperity based on the principles of the Atlantic Charter." "For Negroes," the editorial continued, "who have the intelligence to weigh the empty promises of the Republicans since Emancipation against solid performance there can be but one avenue of hope—Roosevelt and the liberal elements among the people, regardless of party."[59]

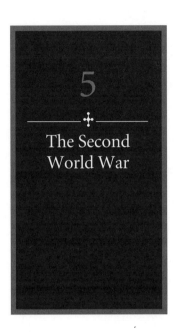

5

✝

The Second
World War

As Hitler rose to power and Germany began to build a war machine, most African Americans in Indiana appear to have been indifferent to signs of a possible European war. But Mussolini's invasion of Ethiopia, a black African nation, aroused interest and sympathy, particularly among persons with Garveyite leanings. However, once the Second World War began in September 1939, black newspapers focused attention on the conflict. The Gary *American* predicted at the war's outset that the United States would be drawn into the conflict, and almost immediately blacks, recalling the First World War, began to raise questions about discrimination in the armed forces. After Congress authorized the first peacetime draft in history, the Indianapolis *Recorder* warned of likely discrimination by draft boards. The *Recorder* scoffed at the claim that this was a war for democracy, asking what democracy there was in the British empire, where "millions of dark people [are] unable to run their lives." An editorial entitled "Billions for Europe but Nothing for U.S." said that if the sums of money being requested for Europe had been spent to eradicate depression, hunger, and disease at home "our democracy would be much safer" and that economic democracy and "full guarantees of civil rights" were better armaments than aid to foreign nations.[1]

After the attack on Pearl Harbor, the black press and black organizations pledged unqualified support for their country. Under headlines declaring "THE AMERICAN NEGRO PLEDGES HIS ALLEGIANCE TO HIS FLAG AND TO HIS COUNTRY," a front-page editorial in the Gary *American* reflected the attitude of most African Americans. But another editorial in the same paper, "Negroes Fight on Two Fronts," emphasized a theme expressed by other black newspapers and race leaders. The editorial said that the United States was at war with a dastardly foreign foe and that Negroes would shed their blood until victory was won in that war, but it also predicted they would fight on the home front the evils of "race hatred, intolerance, segregation, discrimination and mob violence." A short-lived black newspaper in Evansville, the *Argos,* while giving support to the war, also declared a wartime platform for blacks—abolition of discrimination in the armed forces and in training defense workers and also government provision of better housing. The commander of the local black American Legion Post said blacks must wage two wars—one against the Axis powers, the other for full citizenship at home. Throughout the war newspaper editorials, letters to the editor, and speeches by black leaders, while continuing to assert the loyalty of African Americans and their support for the war, pointed out the discrepancy between the war aims proclaimed by the United States and the realities of the black experience at home. Editorials also emphasized the inequities in conscription and segregation in the armed forces. After Pearl Harbor, blacks answered calls for volunteers, only to be rejected because Negro units were already filled, while white volunteers continued to be accepted. The *Recorder* pointed out that naturalized citizens could enter any branch of service without being subjected to discrimination, while young African Americans "whose parents and grandparents helped to build this great nation, will be segregated, put into a program of militarization not anxious to have them nor even ready for their coming."[2]

In spite of a clause in the Selective Service Act that prohibited discrimination in selection and training, the practices of some draft boards were undoubtedly discriminatory, and blacks who were inducted often encountered prejudiced white officers. Those who were sent to training camps in the South encountered the same kind of degrading treatment by white civilians to which all blacks were subjected, and white civilians in the North were often equally prejudiced. Nevertheless, on the whole, treatment of black servicemen was more impartial than it had been in the First World War.

Few blacks were drafted at first, and throughout the war the rate of rejection among African Americans was higher than for whites. But by 1944 there were more than 700,000 African Americans in the army, about 165,000 in the navy, and smaller numbers in the marines and coast guard. Black ground troops served in every theater of the war in Europe and the Pacific and were used for a greater variety of activities, including combat, than in earlier wars. When preparation for combat began, blacks in the United States Navy (about 4,000) were nearly all messmen, barred from opportunities to become combat seamen or to enter the training programs open to whites. At first, in spite of protests, officials said there would be no change in these policies, but in April 1942, the secretary of the navy announced that Negroes would be accepted for general service and as noncommissioned officers. At the same time, it was announced that Negroes would be accepted in the marines. After this, thousands of blacks were trained to perform a variety of technical and combat jobs. Black women were also admitted to the WACs (Women's Auxiliary Corps) in the army and to the WAVES, the navy counterpart.[3]

Late in 1940 the war department announced that Negroes would be trained as aviation pilots in a special school at Tuskegee, Alabama. Although some blacks objected to segregated training, more welcomed the opportunity to serve in the air force for the first time. Before the end of the war, about six hundred African Americans had become pilots.[4]

Names and exploits of African American men and women in the armed forces were recorded in detail in the Indianapolis *Recorder* and the Gary *American* and occasionally in the white press. The black papers urged parents and friends to send in names and service records of black servicemen, and they printed the names of all who served, calling attention to families in which several children were in service and to black officers who were commissioned in the various branches of service. Press and public appeared to take special pride in the young men who were commissioned as pilots in the air force. Particularly noteworthy was Charles Hall of Brazil, a graduate of Brazil High School and Eastern Illinois Normal College, who became the first African American to be awarded the Distinguished Flying Cross after he shot down German planes in the battles over Italy.[5]

Most Indiana men and women received their training in camps outside the state before being assigned to service overseas, but a few were assigned to camps in Indiana. Fort Benjamin Harrison, on the outskirts of Indianapolis, which had been opened before the First World War, was important as a reception center. Camp Atterbury, south of Indianapolis, which opened in 1942 as a training camp for combat troops, included more than forty thousand acres in Johnson, Bartholomew, and Brown Coun-

BUREAU OF PUBLIC RELATIONS, WAR DEPARTMENT
WASHINGTON 25, D.C.

FOR IMMEDIATE RELEASE

    U.S. FORWARD AIR BASE---Lieutenant Clinton B. Mills, of Durham, North
Carolina, talks over his exploits in the air with Lieutenant Wilson V. Eagelson,
of Bloomington, Indiana. The two bagged three Focke-Wulf 190s, with Eagleson
taking the lead. They are assigned to the Ninety-ninth Fighter Squadron. (Army
Air Forces photo.) 23 March 44.

Serving in a segregated unit in the Army Air Forces, Bloomington pilot Wilson Eagleson shot down
German fighter planes in World War II. Indianapolis *Recorder* Collection, Indiana Historical Society.

ties and was the largest military camp in the state. Other military camps in the state
were Baer Field, near Fort Wayne; Bunker Hill, a United States Air Station near Peru;
and Freeman Field, south of Seymour. Military personnel were also stationed at the
Jefferson Proving Ground, which included parts of Jefferson, Ripley, and Jennings
Counties, and at the Crane Naval Depot in Martin County. Only white troops were
assigned to some camps, but members of both races were assigned to others. As early
as January 1941, a group of black enlisted men arrived at Fort Benjamin Harrison.
The 64th Aviation Squadron, made up of 250 black troops, was stationed at Baer Field
for several months of training. Freeman Field was base for 500 aviation cadets and
their officers and more than 2,000 enlisted men of the air force who performed a variety of duties. Among the enlisted men was a squadron of blacks assigned such work
as preparing food for the mess hall, even though the squadron included men who
were skilled industrial workers. Black troops were also stationed at Atterbury at various times. Among them were two bombardment squadrons of African American avi-

ators who arrived in 1944. As the war was nearing an end in 1945, two more bombardment squadrons moved into Atterbury but were later transferred to Freeman Field. African American WACs were also stationed at Atterbury, where they took over work formerly performed by men as medical technicians, ward attendants, and ambulance drivers. Others were dietitians.[6]

The presence of large numbers of servicemen, white and black, stationed at camps throughout the state, at Camp Breckenridge in Kentucky across the Ohio River from Evansville, and at George Field across the Wabash from Vincennes, meant large numbers of soldiers with weekend passes flocking into Indiana cities and towns in search of lodging and recreation. In all the large cities, white citizens were eager to help establish USO centers for servicemen, but they took for granted that they would be for whites only, in spite of an official USO statement against discrimination. This meant that members of black communities were forced to assume responsibility for furnishing facilities for African American servicemen and women. NAACP members in Indianapolis criticized the establishment of a separate center as a step toward increased discrimination that would create ill feeling at a time when national unity was being emphasized, but since there was no alternative, leaders who were opposed to segregation nevertheless gave their support to separate facilities. As soon as black soldiers began to arrive in the city, the Indianapolis Park Board designated the Northwest Community Center as recreation center for black servicemen, but this was soon inadequate. A "Colored Citizens Selective Steering Committee," including most African American civic leaders, expanded and coordinated efforts to provide facilities, with the aid of some government funds. Churches, Flanner House, and Lockefield Gardens opened their doors and developed recreational programs, but the Senate Avenue YMCA became the planning center for most activities. In 1942 a second building on Senate Avenue near the "Y" was rented to expand services, and more committees were appointed to direct activities. Nettie Ransom headed a committee of Volunteer City Wide Activities for Service Men, which coordinated activities of young women cadets and older women who acted as chaperons for social events and also operated a library and reading room. The Senate Avenue annex, a three-story building, included a floor where food (much of it contributed by churches) was prepared and served, a ballroom where weekly dances were held, and sleeping rooms. But since no hotel would accept blacks, the number of rooms was inadequate, and many private families offered hospitality to servicemen and women.[7]

Churches and fraternal orders in Gary organized a Service Men's Cheer Group to serve the large numbers of African Americans stationed at naval bases in the vicinity. The first center proved inadequate, and a second was opened at Stewart House.[8]

In Evansville, only thirty miles from Camp Breckenridge where there were 2,000 black soldiers, visiting servicemen found facilities as segregated as in any city in the South. Women from Lincoln Gardens started the Lincoln USO club for black servicemen and women in 1943. With Sallie Stewart heading the committee of hostesses, it operated under the Negro YMCA and received some public funds. The regular program included weekly Saturday night dances and Sunday breakfast. It also offered sleeping accommodations and facilities for billiards and tennis.[9]

In Indianapolis, Gary, and Evansville, where there were large black populations, and in some places, including Terre Haute and Fort Wayne, where the numbers were smaller, local citizens contributed enthusiastically to hospitality and entertainment; but in smaller communities near camps where there were large numbers of black troops and few black residents, the situation was different. This was particularly true of towns near Atterbury, especially Columbus, in a county with no restaurants or other facilities that served blacks. When a new contingent of black troops arrived at Atterbury in 1944, twenty-five African American soldiers, apparently unaware of local customs, went to the white USO club, expecting to be served supper. Some of the startled white girls who were serving walked out rather than serve the unexpected patrons, and the manager of the club, fearing trouble, closed the club. Irate whites protested to the commanding officer at Atterbury, and he responded with an apology to the townspeople, promising that in the future black soldiers would go elsewhere. After the incident, blacks at Atterbury were transported to Franklin, a town farther away from camp than Columbus, where there was a somewhat larger African American community and a USO club for black servicemen.[10]

Some of the most glaring examples of discrimination were in the military camps themselves, in spite of orders from President Roosevelt against the practice. In 1944 the Indianapolis *Recorder* asked the war department to investigate treatment of black soldiers at Camp Atterbury, citing reports that they were served inferior food and housed in inferior barracks, and called "niggers" by white officers. A few months later one of the most notorious incidents of the war occurred at Freeman Field in southern Indiana. The camp, which had been temporarily closed, reopened in January 1945, and members of the 477th Bombardment Group, some of whose members had been recognized for distinguished service overseas, were transferred there from Atterbury. When three African American officers began a boycott of a separate officers' club for Negroes and attempted to enter the club for white officers, they were arrested and charged with jostling a provost marshal. Later, other black officers who tried to enter the club were also arrested. Altogether about one hundred Negro officers were arrested when they refused orders from the commanding officers to promise that they would not try to use the facilities at the white officers' club. The three who had begun the protest were later transferred to Godman Field in Kentucky and brought before a court martial on charges of violating Articles of War. Although the officers were subsequently acquitted, the war department failed to make a statement against the policies that had led to their arrest.[11]

So long as black servicemen confined themselves to the segregated USO centers there was no trouble, but those who ventured into restaurants, taverns, or motion picture houses that catered only to whites were likely to be refused service, even though they wore the uniforms and insignia of the United States. Numerous instances of refusal of service were reported in the black press. In one incident, two African American lieutenants from Atterbury were refused service at the downtown bus station in Indianapolis. When one of them protested, he was arrested by police, who charged him with disorderly conduct and resisting arrest. In a few cases white soldiers protested against discrimination directed at their black comrades. When black soldiers were refused service at an Evansville restaurant and told that they could not be served in the restaurant but could go outside to eat, twenty white soldiers who were seated inside the restaurant walked out. Black waitresses in a downtown Indianapolis chili parlor quit their jobs when the manager refused service to black soldiers.[12]

Protests of this sort against discriminatory treatment of servicemen were a sign that more widespread opposition to racial discrimination was brewing among civilians. For example, when a black draft inductee in East Chicago was beaten by police for alleged disorderly conduct, a mass protest meeting of African Americans set off a drive against discrimination in law enforcement and other areas, including refusal of service in restaurants and segregated seating in theaters.[13]

As thousands of young men—white and black—left the state for military service, thousands of new residents—white and black—flocked into Indiana cities, seeking jobs created by the war. Some of the migrants were from smaller communities in Indiana and neighboring states. Many whites came from Kentucky and Appalachia; many of the blacks came from farther south. The northward movement of southern blacks, which had almost stopped during the Depression, revived and continued unabated until the 1970s. Nearly all of them crowded into cities, continuing the urbanization that had begun during the Great Migration of the First World War period.

Accurate estimates of the number of newcomers who came into the state during the Second World War years are impossible, since the most reliable statistics are furnished by the decennial United State Census reports. The 1950 census showed that the total population of the state increased by almost four million, or 14.8 percent, between 1940 and 1950. By 1950 there were 30,796 African Americans in Indianapolis out of a total population of 551,777. The proportion in Gary was higher—19,413 out of a total of 133,911. In Evansville the number was 4,404 out of a total of 160,422. In cities in the northern part of the state where there had been few blacks before the war, their numbers increased substantially: in South Bend to 4,312 out of a total of 205,058; in Fort Wayne to 2,513 out of 183,722. In smaller industrial cities there were also increases; in Muncie, for example, to 2,174 out of 90,252.[14]

The migrants came in anticipation of jobs, but their immediate problem was finding a place to live, and, although many found employment with higher wages than they had ever enjoyed before, they were unable to find decent housing and were forced to pay exorbitant rents to live in crowded hovels. Older black residents who also found better-paying jobs resented the newcomers because landlords used the housing shortage created by their arrival as an excuse for raising rents.[15]

Indianapolis was the destination of the largest number of new arrivals, but housing there for African Americans was grossly inadequate and substandard before the war, and the problem grew more acute during the war years. A report by a Citizens Housing Committee made in 1940, describing slum areas where most of the black population lived, said that "unregulated building of low cost frame structures without sanitary facilities, was for many years, allowed to take place. Such areas were bad to start with, and grew worse as they grew older."[16]

Blacks with sufficient funds to make a down payment to buy a home found that virtually no houses were available to them, and banks were reluctant to make loans. A report of a Governor's Housing Commission appointed in 1941 said there was "no housing whatever available to Negroes regardless of the price range or quality of housing sought." Consequently, several families were often crowded into single-family dwellings. The Board of Health said that at least six hundred of these buildings should be condemned and torn down, but there was no place for the occupants to move. An editorial in the Indianapolis *Recorder* said that under the "vicious system of housing" in the city, there were few areas open to blacks that were not in slums—that "the average person wishing adequate housing finds himself ringed by prejudice, slums, and outlandish market prices," and the influx of newcomers made the situation worse. As a result, blacks were in a "housing vise not of their own making and from which there appears little escape."[17]

The situation became more desperate as war industries expanded and more new settlers arrived. A Better Housing Committee seeking federal aid to construct temporary housing estimated in 1944 that 27,000 war workers had moved into the city since 1942. Families of black workers were living in coal sheds, garages, and attics. Often six members of a family were crowded into one room.[18]

The one bright spot in the dismal housing picture was Lockefield Gardens, but tenants who had taken jobs in war industries and whose income exceeded the limits set up by the U.S. Housing Authority were told they would have to move. Later, however, the same authority granted indefinite tenure to tenants whose income was greater than the established maximum and gave wives whose husbands were in military service permission to continue to live in Lockefield Gardens, adjusting rents to the wages of the wife if she was employed or to the military allotment she received if she was not employed.[19]

The need for housing spurred demands for more public housing. Petitions from church, civic, and labor groups were presented to mayors John Kern and Reginald Sullivan (both Democrats), but the city authorities and the city council failed to act. *Recorder* editorials insisted that building the kinds of needed housing could not be left entirely to private enterprise and asked for exposure of efforts of "the people or influences . . . devoted to the eminent prerogative of private enterprise" who were responsible for repeated rebuffs to advocates of public housing.[20]

As the writer of the editorials was fully aware, the most influential opponents of public housing in the city were the Indianapolis Real Estate Board and the Indianapolis Chamber of Commerce, which for years adamantly continued to insist that any form of government interference or competition with private enterprise was dangerous. In other industrial cities in the state where opposition to federal authority was not so intense, local federal housing authorities were more cooperative. But once the war began they could do little that was effective in providing housing for workers who flocked to their communities because of the shortage of building materials caused by the war and because of internal disputes that delayed construction.[21]

Fewer African Americans migrated to Gary than to Indianapolis during the war, but they made up a larger percentage of the whole in the smaller city. As already noted, Delaney Project built during the New Deal had only black tenants. In two other public housing projects there were white as well as black tenants. But the three projects were already inadequate to provide decent housing for black residents before the war and became much more inadequate with the influx of newcomers. In the areas of the city where African Americans were concentrated, 50 percent of the rental units were substandard, and more than half of the houses occupied by black owners were classified as substandard. Many of them lacked indoor plumbing, and as late as 1943 the city building department continued to issue permits for construction of buildings that did not meet standards. As in Indianapolis, blacks with money enough to buy a decent home found that realtors refused to show them houses in "white" neighborhoods, and bank loans were difficult or impossible to obtain.[22]

The story was much the same in South Bend, where hundreds of African Americans migrated, seeking jobs with the Studebaker Corporation and other industries with war contracts. Black families were crowded into one or two rooms in substandard buildings. A total of 750 units were constructed for white workers, but a 1942 petition from black leaders and labor leaders for additional housing brought no results. Whites owning real estate in an area under consideration for a housing project for blacks protested "the building of additional houses for colored people in this section." A few temporary units were built expressly for Negroes, but there was nothing else before the end of the war.[23]

In Fort Wayne the 1940 census showed that 21 percent of buildings occupied by nonwhites were in need of major repairs. A petition by a group calling themselves the Negro Home Owners Taxpayers Association charged that Negroes were paying exorbitant rents for shacks that were "unfit for human habitation" and a menace to health and morals and urged the local housing authority and the city council to build apartments. As more workers moved into the city to take war jobs, little was done to relieve the housing situation, and a growing number of families crowded into existing buildings. In 1945, as the war was drawing to an end, it was reported that the City Planning Commission and the Fort Wayne Housing Authority would make a study of the "housing needs of Negroes."[24]

The city of Evansville became an important center for war contracts, and it was estimated that the city's total population increased by about one-third during the war years and that by 1943 about two thousand black families had arrived. Before the war, a majority of African Americans lived in housing described as "poor or bad," and, as in other cities, conditions deteriorated with the arrival of new settlers. Some of them were housed in fifty trailers that the city bought from the federal government, and by the end of the war, about 150 permanent units were opened in a segregated area in the city. In Evansville, as in the other cities in the state, it was taken for granted that such housing as *was* built, whether temporary or permanent, would be racially segregated.[25]

But in spite of physical discomfort and potential dangers to health and safety caused by the lack of decent housing, for most blacks in Indiana, both older residents and newcomers, the war years were a period of hope and rising expectations. At last, after years of unemployment and WPA, there were prospects of jobs. Few African Americans had gained employment during the limited economic recovery under the New Deal. A disproportionate number remained on WPA jobs or on relief rolls. Of Indiana's entire population, 5.5 percent were on WPA rolls in 1940, according to the U.S. Census, but 16 percent of black males and 11.3 percent of black women were on WPA.[26] Of course in cities, where the black population was concentrated, the percentage of blacks on WPA was much higher. On the eve of the war, more than half of Gary's black population was receiving some form of government relief. But, as one writer has said, "Pearl Harbor cleared the decks for social reform and opened up possibilities for the Negro, who had known only a combination of bread lines, relief, and WPA" during the 1930s. However, blacks' access to jobs in war industries was limited by three factors: their lack of training in necessary skills and lack of opportunities to acquire training after the war began; reluctance of white employers to hire blacks; and prejudice of white workers, who sometimes went on strike rather than work with blacks.[27]

The dearth of blacks among skilled workers was due in part to the exclusionary policies of labor unions, which prevented them from serving needed apprenticeships, and also to the inadequacies of the "manual training" and "vocational" courses taught in segregated high schools, which did not prepare students for work in modern industry. Once the defense buildup began, government programs offered training in needed skills, but few blacks were able to enroll in them. In Evansville, where welders were needed for work in the shipyards, a Mechanical Arts School at first refused to accept black applicants. The school officially began to admit them in 1942, but classes were held from one to six o'clock in the afternoon, which prevented men with jobs from attending. The classes were later offered at night, but facilities for black students continued to be limited, and there were long waiting lists of those who wanted to enroll. In Gary, at the only high school where blacks could receive mechanical training, the only classes for them were held at hours that prevented many from enrolling. The school board and war industries in Indianapolis announced a plan to offer needed courses at Attucks High School for men at least eighteen years old, but throughout the war blacks complained that training facilities were inadequate.[28]

During the early months of the defense buildup, as the state WPA began to comb rolls to find persons with needed skills for jobs in factories with war contracts, the Indianapolis *Recorder* claimed that both the WPA administrators and the state employment agency were reluctant to refer African American workers to defense jobs or training programs.[29]

When the state legislature convened in 1941, Chester Allen introduced House Bill 445, which was intended to prevent racial discrimination in employment and promotion in factories with war contracts. Later explaining the need for the bill, Allen said that industries in South Bend and Mishawaka had received war contracts for more than twenty million dollars and this had resulted in substantial reductions in the numbers of whites on WPA rolls; but the percentage of blacks on WPA rolls did not change. When he brought this fact to the attention of the local chamber of commerce, its members were indifferent. Allen said he introduced H.B. 445 as a means of giving employers a larger pool of workers, reducing relief rolls, and giving African Americans more faith in American democracy.[30]

The bill met no opposition in the lower chamber, where it was passed unanimously,

Frances Jenkins Linthecome recalled that when she was photographed
by a roving sidewalk photographer in the early 1940s, she had one
of the best jobs for which black women were eligible in Indianapolis:
she was an elevator operator at L. S. Ayres & Co. Several of her
co-workers had bachelor's degrees in education but could not
find teaching jobs because of segregation in the schools.
Photograph courtesy of Frances Linthecome.

but in the senate it encountered the delaying tactics that usually killed antidiscrimination measures. Representatives of the AFL spoke against the bill on the grounds that it would weaken collective bargaining, but the most effective resistance came from the Indiana Chamber of Commerce, which freely admitted to taking the lead "in making public the vicious character of the proposed law" and denounced the "dangerous and undemocratic principle involved in legislation which compels the employment of any class, creed or color of people." A Citizens Defense Council appointed by Governor Schricker supported the bill, saying they were less concerned about "regimentation of business" than in getting people off of relief and back into "contributing channels in the American scheme of industry." The bill remained in the hands of the senate judiciary committee until the closing days of the session, when it was recommended for passage with amendments. But it was killed on the last day of the session when two Democratic members moved that it be sent to the committee on military affairs, a motion passed with only three dissenting votes, one of them cast by Senator Brokenburr, the only black in the chamber.[31]

Having succeeded in killing H.B. 445, the Indiana Chamber of Commerce attempted to prevent federal intervention to remove racial barriers to employment, which Washington considered essential to filling war contracts, by announcing the creation of the Indiana Plan of Bi-Racial Cooperation. This involved cooperation between a Chamber of Commerce committee and the State Defense Council appointed by Governor Schricker and Chester Allen, whom Schricker appointed Coordinator of Negro Affairs.[32]

Meanwhile, President Roosevelt faced increasing pressure to take action to prevent racial discrimination in employment by industries with war contracts. In January 1941 A. Philip Randolph announced plans for a massive march on Washington by perhaps as many as 100,000 blacks to demand employment of blacks in war industries. The plan met with enthusiastic support in Indianapolis and other Indiana cities. Indianapolis's Federation of Associated Clubs sponsored a mass meeting at the Senate Avenue YMCA to forge a group from civic, church, and other organizations to join the march. A local committee was appointed that included well-known civic and political figures. Officials in Washington were alarmed at the prospect of thousands of African Americans descending upon the nation's capital, but Randolph was not dissuaded until the President promised to issue an executive order "with teeth." Finally on June 25, 1941, Roosevelt issued Executive Order 8802, which declared, "There shall be no discrimination in the employment of workers in defense industries or government because of race, creed, color, or national origins" and that it was the duty of employers and labor unions "to provide for the full and equitable participation of all workers in defense industries without discrimination because of race." Thereafter, clauses prohibiting discrimination were included in all defense contracts, and a Committee on Fair Employment Practices was appointed to investigate complaints of violations.[33]

Executive Order 8802 was issued shortly after the creation of the Indiana Committee on Bi-Racial Cooperation and the appointment of Allen as Coordinator of Negro Affairs, but the Indiana Chamber of Commerce continued to insist that only voluntary action should be used to fill manpower needs and prevent discrimination. Nevertheless, Allen sometimes invoked Order 8802 and threats of federal investigation to persuade management to employ and upgrade black workers. While the Bi-Racial Committee did recognize that discrimination in employment existed and published pamphlets and carried on other forms of publicity urging employers to employ blacks, at the same time the committee advised Negroes not to seek "unwarranted advancement."[34]

Besides appointing Allen as statewide Coordinator of Negro Affairs, the governor also appointed a committee of sixteen black leaders drawn from all parts of the state and an equal number of industrialists chosen by the Chamber of Commerce to monitor black employment in war industries. The committee asked the Indiana Employment Security Division to appoint black interviewers in cities with large African American populations. Local committees were also organized to cooperate with the state group. They also cooperated in cities where there were affiliates of the National Urban League. Allen traveled tirelessly over the state, speaking principally to employers but also to representatives of labor unions and other groups, including white ministerial organizations. After a meeting at night, he often had to travel many miles to find accommodations that would accept African Americans.[35]

After the Committee for Bi-Racial Cooperation and the rest of the plans to open employment to blacks began to operate, unemployment among African Americans was sharply reduced, but how much this was due to the work of the committee and Allen and how much to the growing labor shortage created by the draft and the demands of industry cannot be calculated accurately. The first opportunities for black workers came when white workers left employment in nondefense businesses to work for higher wages in factories with war contracts and employers, for the first time, hired blacks to replace them. In factories without war contracts, increasing numbers of African Americans were hired as unskilled or semiskilled workers. In some businesses black women were hired for clerical jobs for the first time, but in many businesses and factories janitorial jobs remained the only work available for blacks.[36]

Efforts to promote employment of African Americans in factories with war contracts met with varying responses from management. Some plants sent their representatives to Kentucky and Tennessee to recruit white workers in order to avoid employing blacks. In other cases, management itself took the initiative in hiring and training blacks. At Allison General Motors in Indianapolis, management appointed a committee on industrial placement of colored workers with instructions to study ways of placing them in skilled brackets and also to study ways of employing black women. Indianapolis's Lukas Herald Factory, where large numbers of blacks worked in janitorial jobs, began to train them for skilled or semiskilled jobs with the cooperation of the U.S. Employment Service.[37]

Increasing numbers of black workers were hired in Gary's steel mills. The Steel Workers Organizing Committee (SWOC) of the CIO, the union's bargaining agent, claimed to have six thousand African American members in the mills. A few of them were upgraded to skilled positions but most remained in unskilled or semiskilled positions, and there were no black foremen. Evansville's Chrysler and Sunbeam Corporations hired and trained black workers as machine operators, but on the whole FDR's Executive Order 8802 had little effect, and few black workers were employed in better jobs than before the war. The Bendix Corporation in South Bend hired black workers for the first time, but blacks complained that they were not given opportunities for upgrading. At the Studebaker Corporation, which had some of the largest war contracts in the state, there was evidence that management and union membership worked together to restrict blacks to the least desirable jobs.[38]

Opportunities for African Americans in smaller industrial communities varied. An influx of southern whites limited opportunities for blacks in Muncie, but as the war continued, some industries reluctantly began to hire blacks for positions other than janitorial ones. In nearby Anderson, where there were several industries that were subsidiaries of General Motors, the CIO of Madison County voted to end "jim crowism" in employment, but few jobs above the janitorial level opened for blacks.[39]

The manpower shortage created by the war led to new employment opportunities for women, both white and black. However, there was evidence that whites opposed employing African American women even more than they did African American men. This was partly due to general resistance to women's doing what was traditionally "men's work," but there was also evidence that white women objected more strenuously than white men to working with blacks. Therefore, probably the greatest gains for African American women were opportunities in jobs vacated by white women who left for more lucrative work in war industries. The Indianapolis *Recorder* charged that the U.S. Employment Service and the Indianapolis Public Schools avoided enrolling black women in training programs for work in industry. Nevertheless, as the labor shortage became more acute, African American women were hired for assembly line work in war industries in most Indiana cities. Black women also did heavy manual labor previously regarded as exclusively "men's work," such as that of "Pan Men" in Gary steel mills and loading coal, washing engines, and cleaning passenger cars for the Chicago and Eastern Railroad in Evansville. Even the women who remained available for domestic "day work" enjoyed higher wages because of the shortage of labor.[40]

Employers frequently cited opposition by white workers as their reason for not hiring blacks, and there were numerous instances of strikes, work stoppages, and occasional acts of sabotage to protest the employment of blacks. The most publicized incident occurred at Indianapolis's Allison General Motors plant, the largest defense plant in the city, where several hundred white workers went on strike when black men began working on the assembly line. However, management remained firm, insisting that African Americans would remain on the machines, and after a few hours the men returned to their jobs. When the Curtis Wright Corporation, where blacks had previously been employed only in the service department, announced plans to put a few of them on machines, twenty-five white workers quit their jobs rather than work beside blacks. White workers at the Chrysler Corporation in Evansville went on strike when blacks were employed in the salvage department. The strike began in the salvage department but spread to other departments, tying up production for several hours. In some plants where blacks were hired, white workers insisted that they be segregated. They were put on separate assembly lines in some instances. At Evansville's Chrysler Corporation there was an agreement that blacks would work only in certain departments in order to avoid trouble with Kentucky-born white workers. In some factories, blacks were barred from the cafeterias and required to use separate toilets.[41]

African American workers found support against discrimination in unions affiliated with the CIO, which had won the position of bargaining agent in some factories. The United Automobile Workers (UAW) and the SWOC had won elections in many plants with war contracts. Some local unions balked at carrying out policies approved by CIO governing bodies, but the rise of the CIO and the labor shortages during the war for the first time opened the way for significant participation by blacks in labor unions.[42]

Before the New Deal most blacks had been hostile to labor unions because of the exclusionary policies of the American Federation of Labor. They viewed with skepticism the New Deal measures designed to guarantee collective bargaining. A 1935 editorial in the *Recorder* described legislation protecting the closed shop as "nothing but a contraption of the labor unions intended to legalize what is now a fixed determination on the part of those organizations to deny the Negro of his right to earn a living" and urged black voters to oppose it. The Gary *American* pointed out the long history of discrimination against African Americans in the labor movement, and most blacks in the steel mills remained dubious about measures to encourage unionization, even though the state's NAACP branches and the affiliates of the National Urban League endorsed them. Most Indiana blacks were skeptical when in 1936 the CIO was created to encourage formation of industrial unions that would include all levels of workers in mass industries instead of the craft unions, which included only those with special skills.[43]

The SWOC began a drive in the Gary mills in 1936. Although black ministers, lawyers, and most civic leaders remained hostile, the group that attended the meeting of the National Negro Congress in Chicago was converted when the Congress passed a resolution in support of the SWOC. Local black organizers began an intensive campaign to win support for the union. United States Steel signed a contract with the SWOC in 1937, and black employees, most of them unskilled workers, began to find in the union a new weapon against discrimination.[44]

CIO unions in other parts of the state made little progress before the war. Indiana had the reputation of being a nonunion state, and in Indianapolis in particular employers and the city government had a long record of hostility to organized labor and the closed shop. Nevertheless, as the CIO won victories in neighboring states, the UAW won recognition in some of the subsidiaries of General Motors and in the Bendix plant in South Bend.[45] Although the only black employees in these factories were janitors, they were admitted to membership in the UAW.

At its annual convention in 1942, the Indiana CIO adopted a strong statement on discrimination that declared, "the ugliest obstacle to the all-out war effort and complete national unity is discrimination because of race, color or creed." Indiana, it said, had discrimination of many kinds but "the worst and most prevalent is discrimination against the Negro people, Jim Crowism." The policy of the national CIO and the Indiana CIO, it continued, was "complete, irreconcilable opposition to any and all forms of discrimination."[46]

As more African Americans were hired by industries with war contracts, the position of the national and state CIO organizations on racial discrimination was clear, but the willingness of all members to comply with these policies varied from place to place. In some communities, local CIO unions took the initiative in encouraging employment of black workers. The Elkhart County CIO adopted resolutions in 1942 calling on aircraft and defense plants in the area to hire blacks. Local unions in Gary urged the promotion of blacks to supervisory positions. Black workers themselves, particularly those who were recent arrivals, were frequently diffident about active participation in unions, but a few were elected officers. Hurley Goodall, a future member of the state legislature, was president of the UAW at the Muncie Malleable Foundry.[47]

White union members often appeared to regard African American coworkers as "second-class members." At a coke plant in Gary where blacks went on strike to protest discriminatory treatment by white foremen after white workers promised to support them, only one white joined in the strike. In some cases, white union members cooperated with management in perpetuating discriminatory practices. One of the most notorious examples of this was at the Delco Remy plant, a General Motors subsidiary in Anderson. Local 662 of the UAW, in collusion with management, was able to prevent the upgrading of black members in many job classifications and also to deny them privileges in the union hall, where there were signs "For whites only." Black members were given an ultimatum not to attend a dance at the union hall, although they paid the same dues as white members. The UAW's international executive board stepped in when alerted to the situation and insisted that discriminatory practices cease and that Executive Order 8802 be obeyed. A hearing of the Fair Employment Practices Committee led to an order to remove restrictive job classifications, and the union voted to open the union hall to all members. That the question of African American participation in union-sponsored social events was a troubling one is not surprising in an age when white society looked askance at any sign of "racial mixing" and when police sometimes broke up interracial gatherings.[48]

Although the most significant gains in union membership and participation by African Americans were in CIO affiliates, there was some relaxation of racial barriers in AFL unions during the war. The national AFL convention in 1941, while voting to support the war against Hitler in the name of democracy, refused to endorse a resolution offered by A. Philip Randolph for appointment of a committee to survey racial discrimination. But meeting earlier in Evansville, the Indiana AFL, after listening to a speech by Allen, adopted resolutions urging employers in factories with war contracts to abide by FDR's Executive Order 8802 and also asking the state federation to cooperate with the Indiana Defense Council to solve problems "of discrimination in job opportunities for skilled Negro people." As he traveled over the state, Allen found local AFL unions less cooperative than the ones affiliated with the CIO, but many unions gave him assurances of support.[49]

In Indianapolis and most other industrial cities in the state, the participation of blacks in labor unions appears to have had little effect on race relations, but in Gary, where the steel mills were strongly unionized, the CIO had a much greater influence. A 1944 study made by the National Urban League for the Gary Council of Social Agencies said, "The unions play an important role in the life of Gary Negroes. Their influence has also been extended in beneficial ways to help improve some of the social problems faced by the community."[50]

As the war began to draw to a close and war production began to taper off, African American organizations began efforts to extend fair employment practices adopted as war measures to the postwar era. In September 1943, the Federation of Associated Clubs in Indianapolis began a "Hold Your Job Program" to expand job opportunities after the war. They sponsored meetings at which personnel directors in industry and business spoke to African American groups. They also sponsored mass meetings of black men and women at which speakers emphasized the need for interracial cooperation and "correct" behavior on the job. Some meetings were held exclusively for women workers.[51]

At the 1945 session of the General Assembly during the closing months of the war, Senator Brokenburr and Charles Fleming, a white senator from Hammond, introduced a bill to create a Fair Employment Practices Commission (FEPC) with enforcement powers—a measure similar to one sponsored by Governor Thomas Dewey that was before the New York state legislature and was being studied as a model by legislatures in several states. The Indiana bill had strong support by the Democratic minority in both chambers and was reported to have support, with some reservations, from powerful Republicans, including Governor Ralph Gates and other Republican state officers as well as the floor leaders in both houses of the legislature. At the urging of the NAACP, black leaders organized a coalition headed by Mrs. Jessie Jacobs, a Republican, to coordinate lobbying for the bill. Walter Frisbee, secretary-treasurer of the Indiana CIO, was a strong supporter of the measure; numerous African American organizations joined the coalition; and Mrs. Jacobs appealed to all minority groups—Jews, Catholics, and foreign-born—to join forces to support the bill.

A Fair Employment Practices Law was finally adopted, but in a drastically modified form. The Indianapolis Chamber of Commerce, the Retail Merchants Association, and other employer groups demanded that the power of the commission be reduced and that the penalties be eliminated. The law as finally enacted said it was the policy of the state to oppose discrimination in access to employment. The FEPC was given authority to "request" (not subpoena) testimony of witnesses and to receive written complaints of discrimination based on race, color, creed, and national origin and to investigate such complaints "as it deems meritorious." In a final speech supporting the amended version, Brokenburr said the law was "not all we wanted" but that it was "the most we can get at this time and a grand stride in the right direction." However, *Federation News,* the publication of the Indianapolis Federation of Associated Clubs, labeled the law "a shameful fraud upon the minority groups of Indiana," and the Gary *American* called it a "four flushing, emasculated bill, stripped of everything except its undies, for the purpose of fooling the small following of Negroes left in the Republican fold." Indiana boasted that it had the distinction of passing the first state FEPC law in the United States, but for more than a decade after 1945, at every session of the General Assembly there were efforts to strengthen the law, and William J. Hardaway, a black Republican from Gary who was appointed to administer the law, resigned in 1949 out of frustration over its weaknesses.[52]

Jobs and good wages increased the self-confidence of African American men and women and made them determined to keep the gains they had won during the war. The presence of black workers on assembly lines and other jobs formerly closed to them and their demands for fair treatment made them more visible to whites. Other factors also contributed to increased awareness by whites of blacks and racial problems. Growing numbers of whites, particularly in church groups, perceived the inconsistency between the American creed and war aims proclaimed by the United States, on the one hand, and the second-class status accorded black citizens, on the other. Other whites were motivated primarily by fear of racial troubles, as wartime race riots erupted in several American cities. In Evansville, where white workers from the South probably added to racial tensions, rumors began in one factory that a riot would occur; this led city officials to call in military police to patrol the streets, causing some black workers to be afraid to report for work. Terre Haute's local NAACP sponsored a meeting at which Henry J. Richardson pleaded with blacks to put a stop to rumors.[53]

The state CIO condemned the spread of rumors and racial violence. It urged Governor Schricker to take steps to prevent racial clashes and urged the mayors of Indiana cities to appoint biracial committees representative of all elements of the community to work to prevent racial incidents and improve race relations. Other groups were also organizing or urging the formation of interracial committees. As a result, in every large city in the state and in many smaller communities, from Evansville in the south to Gary in the north, such committees were organized. Mayors took the initiative in some cases; in others, private organizations were responsible.[54]

Racial incidents in Evansville in 1943 led to the reactivation of an Inter-Racial Commission that had been created in the 1930s. In February 1944 the Evansville commission, along with the local YMCA and YWCA, sponsored the first regional conference on race relations in the area. About three hundred delegates from Evansville and neighboring states attended. Blacks took part and spoke freely about problems they faced. When launching a drive for members later, the Evansville commission issued a policy statement: their aim was to improve race relations and dispel misconceptions through discussion of problems, but in seeking better health and recreation facilities for the black community, they reassured whites, their approach would be "gradual." The Catholic diocese took more immediate action. The bishop announced that qualified black students would be admitted the next term to Reitz Memorial High School, which had formerly been for whites only.[55]

In the summer of 1943, the Indianapolis Church Federation announced the formation of the Indianapolis Citizens Council "to work for the peaceful and constructive solution of community problems involving race or religion." The Church Federation, the Catholic Diocese, the Jewish Federation, the Seventh District of Women's Clubs, the League of Women Voters, the Central Labor Union, the CIO, the Indianapolis Council of Social Agencies, the Federation of Associated Clubs, and other organizations joined the council. In June 1945, the group sponsored a two-day meeting to analyze race problems and recommend remedies. Dr. Howard J. Baumgartel, executive secretary of the Church Federation, later recalled that the proposal for the "clinic," as it was called, "presented difficulties." He said, "We found immediately that the decision makers of the city had considerable misgivings about the clinic being held," warning that it might lead to racial tensions. Nevertheless, the conference was held, and out of it came the Community Relations Council, a permanent organization with a full-time executive secretary. Most, but not all, of the organizations that had been represented in the earlier Citizens Council became members, and they were joined by the Indianapolis branch of the NAACP, which played an important part in the new group.[56]

Of all Indiana cities, the one that appeared to have the greatest potential for racial violence was Gary, with its concentration of African Americans, many of them recent arrivals to the city. After riots in other cities, the Office of Community War Services of the Federal Security Agency in Chicago compiled a confidential "Report on Racial Situation in Gary, Indiana." The report listed areas of racial tension that had been important in riots in other cities—recreation, schools, transportation, and housing. The report on Gary emphasized the very limited recreational facilities available to blacks compared to those available for whites. A conspicuous example was the lack of beaches for African Americans on Lake Michigan, as well as the lack of adequate gymnasiums and other recreational facilities in the public parks. In education, the report pointed out the absence of opportunities for vocational training and the fact that black students were not allowed to use the swimming pool at Froebel High School or take part in some extracurricular activities. There was no public transportation in some heavily black areas, and on Broadway, where a large percentage of riders were black, the railway company operated two sets of streetcars, one stopping for black passengers, the other passing them by. Housing for blacks was more concentrated and crowded and generally inferior to housing in white neighborhoods, and the report pointed out, "Poor housing conditions are usually in that section of the city which includes the more lawless and vicious elements." The report also noted that, although the Gary Chamber of Commerce had appointed a committee to work on racial problems, the committee did not represent the views of all segments of the white community and did not include any African Americans. It recommended that a more representative committee, including both black and white members, be appointed to study problems and make recommendations on racial problems.[57]

A few months after the report, although not necessarily because of it, the Gary Chamber of Commerce announced the appointment of an enlarged committee and declared, "We believe that there are no superior or inferior races but that all mankind is one" and that interracial problems were "solvable but they will not solve themselves." There was a need, the Chamber's statement went on, for a "positive program arrived at in an atmosphere of understanding, cooperation and mutual respect by men of good will." Chairman of the committee was H. B. Snyder, editor of the Gary *Post Tribune,* the only daily newspaper in the city. Snyder was a man who had long shown

concern for Gary's blacks and had recently hired the paper's first full-time black reporter. Black members of the committee, who were nominated by African Americans, included two attorneys, two clergymen, a steel mill employee active in the SWOC,
and the editor of the Gary *American*.[58]

During the following year, in the closing months of the war, the Gary Council of
Social Agencies adopted a series of recommendations from a group named by the
National Urban League to promote harmony and prevent racial clashes. The recommendations reflected the same problems that had been identified in the 1944 report
on the racial situation in Gary but they addressed the issues in greater detail. Among
other things, the group recommended the organization of a Gary affiliate of the National Urban League, which was accomplished later in 1945.[59]

Soon after the report of the Council of Social Agencies, the mayor of Gary recommended that a nonsegregated beach playground be provided on Lake Michigan;
but, he said, the section of the beach at Marquette Park should remain for whites only.
Gary, he explained, was not yet ready for "immediate co-mingling of the races at Marquette Park."[60]

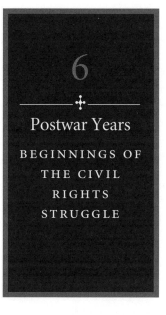

6

Postwar Years

BEGINNINGS OF
THE CIVIL
RIGHTS
STRUGGLE

The migration of African Americans from the South to the cities of the North continued and accelerated in the decades after World War II. Most of those coming to Indiana do not appear to have come directly from rural areas but instead came from the rural South via southern towns and cities. In Indiana they headed directly to larger cities, where the black population grew more rapidly than the white. Between 1950 and 1960 the state's African American population increased by almost 55 percent, but in 46 counties the number of blacks declined, as more and more moved from small towns and rural areas to find jobs in the cities.[1]

In Indianapolis, where blacks made up about 15 percent of the population in 1950, the percentage grew to 20 percent in 1960 and was estimated to be 24 percent of the whole in 1965. In Gary, where blacks made up approximately 38 percent of the population in 1950, they had become a majority by 1965. In nearby East Chicago, African Americans made up 24 percent of the whole in 1960. In other industrial cities in the northern part of the state, where there had been few blacks before the war, percentages remained small, but the numbers increased; South Bend's black population was almost 10 percent of the total in 1960, while Fort Wayne's grew to 7.4 percent. Blacks remained about 6 percent of Evansville's population.[2]

By 1960, 79 percent of the nonwhite population in the state was concentrated in Indianapolis, Gary, Fort Wayne, South Bend, Evansville, and East Chicago. There were some areas of the state where there were very few African Americans. In 1960 there was only one black, a woman, in Beech Grove, an incorporated city of more than 20,000 in Marion County southeast of Indianapolis; in Speedway City, on the western fringe of the city, there were three blacks out of a total population of more than nine thousand. There were two African Americans out of a total of 9,309 residents in East Gary. In some towns in the state there were no blacks at all. The total absence of African Americans in some communities was attributed to vestiges of the so-called "Sundown Laws."[3]

While blacks came to comprise a larger part of the population in Indiana cities, they continued to be concentrated in small areas within those cities. African Americans made up a majority of Gary's population by 1966, but they occupied less than 13 percent of the total residential area of the city. They were concentrated mainly in Midtown West, a community where blacks made up 95 percent of the whole.[4]

In Marion County (Indianapolis) the black population increased by 54 percent between 1950 and 1960; the white population grew by only 23 percent. Nearly all blacks were concentrated in Center Township, where the percentage of black residents increased by 51 percent between 1950 and 1960. Although in the following decade (1960–1970) the total population of the township declined by nearly 18 percent, the percentage of blacks rose again as many whites moved away from the area.[5]

As whites moved northward to parts of the city outside the township, a growing number of African Americans moved into formerly all-white neighborhoods within the township. Many whites also moved beyond city limits to the suburbs. Between 1950 and 1960, population within the city grew by only 10 percent, but population in the suburban areas of Marion County increased 76 percent, and there was also rapid growth in the counties surrounding Marion.[6]

With the assistance of Lafayette builder Floyd B. Lux, Collins Ferguson migrated from Alabama to Indiana in 1947 after graduating from Tuskegee Institute with advanced skills in construction work. Photograph courtesy of Collins Ferguson.

Willard Ransom, son of Freeman Ransom, graduate of Harvard Law School and veteran of World War II, was a longtime president of the state NAACP; he took a lead in challenging segregation in Indiana after the war. He is shown here in 1948 with fellow Progressive Party activist Senator Glen Hearst Taylor of Idaho. Indianapolis *Recorder* Collection, Indiana Historical Society.

As their numbers increased, African Americans became more active in politics, but they remained a fringe group with little influence on government policies. Since 1940, Republicans had been dominant in state politics, and in the years following the war, they asserted "states' rights," rejecting Washington and all policies associated with the New Deal era. A joint resolution adopted by the General Assembly in 1947 epitomized the political philosophy of the dominant party:

> Be it resolved Indiana needs no guardian and intends to have none. We Hoosiers—like the people of our sister states—were fooled for quite a spell with the magician's tricks that a dollar taxed out of our pockets and sent to Washington will be bigger when it comes back to us. We have taken a good look at said dollar. We find that it lost its weight in its journey to Washington and back. . . .
>
> So we propose henceforward to tax ourselves. We are fed up with subsidies, doles and paternalism. We are no one's stepchild. We have grown up. We serve notice that we will resist Washington, D.C. adopting us. . . .
>
> We respectfully petition and urge Indiana's Congressmen and Senators to fetch our county court houses and city halls back from Pennsylvania Avenue. We want government to come home. . . .[7]

In the elections of 1946, which marked the high tide of Republican power after the war, African American Democrat Jesse Dickinson of South Bend, although renominated, was defeated in November by Zilford Carter, a black Republican. Two other black Republicans, Wilbur Grant of Indianapolis and Charles Decker of Evansville, were also elected to the Indiana house of representatives.[8]

Although in 1948 Indiana cast its electoral votes for Republican Thomas Dewey for president, the state's voters elected Henry Schricker governor a second time, and Democrats gained control of the lower house of the General Assembly. In Marion County, where blacks gave strong support to the election of President Truman, their votes were crucial in electing a Democratic delegation to the state house of representatives. Democrat Forrest Littlejohn was the only black elected in the county. Republican Brokenburr, who had been nominated for the state senate, and Rufus Kuykendall, who ran for the lower house, were defeated.[9] James Hunter, who was also elected, became chairman of the Democratic caucus in the house of representatives in 1949.

The 1948 campaign was enlivened for African Americans by the candidacy of Henry Wallace, presidential candidate of the Progressive Party, who as Vice President during FDR's third term had taken a strong stand for civil rights; he also opposed Truman's cold war position against the Soviet Union and was often accused of being pro-Communist. Willard Ransom, eldest son of Freeman Ransom and president of the Indiana state conference of the NAACP, was Wallace's most noted supporter in the state. A Harvard Law School graduate who served in the Adjutant General's Office during the war, Ransom had returned from the war determined to fight for civil rights and full citizenship for African Americans. He headed the Indiana delegation at the 1948 national convention of the Progressive Party and addressed the convention. He himself was nominated as the party's candidate for Congress, becoming the first black candidate for that office in Indiana history. The Gary *Ameri-*

can announced its support of Wallace because of his strong commitment to civil rights, saying, "Wallace aligned himself with the future." Wallace also had some support among members of CIO, but the Gary branch of the NAACP strongly opposed him and Ransom's support of him, as did other prominent members of the NAACP.[10]

While Republicans were dominant in state politics in the 1950s and most blacks voted Democratic, a handful of blacks from both parties continued to serve in the state legislature during the decade. In the 1950 Indianapolis primary several blacks from both major parties sought nomination to the state house of representatives, but there appears to have been an agreement between the Republican and Democratic organizations that each would endorse only one black candidate. The Republicans named William D. Mackey, an insurance executive, and the Democrats supported Forrest Littlejohn. Republicans again swept the state in November, but South Bend's Jesse Dickinson and Democrat Hunter of East Chicago were elected (again) along with Mackey.[11]

In the presidential campaign of 1952, the state Republican organization made vigorous efforts to win the support of African Americans by playing upon the theme of the power of southern racists in the Democratic Party. A full-page advertisement in the Indianapolis *Recorder* warned against the Democratic vice presidential candidate under headlines saying "Jim Crow Sparkman One Heart Beat From the White House." A front-page editorial entitled "Help Emancipate the White Folks!" called upon blacks to vote Republican to diminish the influence of southern whites. On election day it was estimated that 30 percent of Indianapolis blacks voted the Republican ticket, while 70 percent remained loyal to the Democrats. Nevertheless, Republicans carried Marion County, and Brokenburr and Mackey were reelected to the General Assembly; but Democrats Dickinson and Hunter were also elected, Hunter winning a seventh term in the house of representatives.[12]

Republicans again won throughout the state in 1954, and Mercer Mance, a black lawyer nominated by the Democrats in Indianapolis, was defeated in his race for state representative. In the northern part of the state, where the CIO had considerable power in the Democratic Party, Hunter and Dickinson were reelected. Republicans were also victorious statewide in 1956, and Brokenburr was returned to the senate, although black districts in Indianapolis remained heavily Democratic. South Bend voters elected Democrat Dickinson to the senate, where he became the second African American member of the upper house, and Hunter was returned again to the house of representatives.[13]

In the General Assembly most white Democrats as well as the dominant Republicans appeared to resist efforts to change the status quo. Although the state constitution required reapportionment of state legislative districts every six years, no apportionment had taken place since 1927. This obviously had the effect of reducing the influence of cities and the power of the thousands of African Americans who had migrated to Indiana. Even the Indianapolis *Recorder,* usually Republican in politics, criticized the record of the 1955 General Assembly for "unceremoniously" ignoring civil rights bills and giving the "bum's rush" to other measures, including the reapportionment mandated by the state constitution.[14]

Even in the cities where African Americans were concentrated, their influence was not proportionate to their numbers. No black was nominated to run for the city council in Indianapolis between 1944, when Dr. Lucian B. Meriwether was nominated and elected, and the early 1960s. More militant African Americans complained of the indifference of black voters and their passive acceptance of "leaders" chosen by whites. White politicians sometimes appeared to be reluctant to support black candidates because they feared white backlash. There seemed to be a tacit understanding among white leaders of both parties that white prejudice would be neutralized if each party nominated a black candidate for the same office. For example, in 1958 both parties endorsed African American candidates for a particular municipal judgeship in Indianapolis. Both candidates were able lawyers, but the extent of white prejudice was shown by the circulation of racist leaflets by Republicans, which pointed out that most cases judges would hear involved whites and asked, "Are we really ready to have members of the colored race judge us?"[15]

Richardson castigated both political parties for exploiting black voters and claimed the political situation had reached a "dangerous state," which threatened gains the race had made under the New Deal. In his weekly column in the *Recorder*, Andrew Ramsey, one of the NAACP's most ardent members, also criticized local African Americans for their political apathy and failure to retaliate against exploitation by white party bosses.[16]

At every session of the General Assembly, bills were introduced to strengthen the Fair Employment Practices Commission and to "put teeth" into the 1885 Civil Rights Law, but, with the notable exception of the 1949 law abolishing segregation in public education, no civil rights legislation was adopted between the end of the war and 1961. Nevertheless, in spite of obstructionist tactics in the state legislature, there was evidence that the times were ripe for change and a meaningful struggle for civil rights, and there were beginnings of progress toward attaining some long-sought goals. Some changes in attitudes of both African Americans and whites had occurred during the war years, and after the war many veterans demanded that the democratic principles the United States had proclaimed as its war goals for the rest of the world be made a reality for all citizens here at home.

At the national level, President Harry Truman responded in 1946 by appointing a distinguished committee to study and make recommendations on civil rights. In its report "To Secure These Rights," the committee called for a program that would lead to "elimination of segregation based on race, color, creed, or national origin from American life." Truman later issued executive orders toward this goal, requiring fair employment practices in government service and integrating the armed forces.[17]

The initiative in the struggle for civil rights in Indiana was taken by members of the NAACP, notably by Willard Ransom, president of the state conference that was revived in 1947, and by a revitalized Indianapolis branch, which played a leading part because of its location in the state capital. Indianapolis leaders included both Democrats and Republicans. President of the branch was William T. Ray, a realtor and son-in-law of state senator Brokenburr. Jessie Jacobs, another Republican and the

Andrew Ramsey, Indianapolis *Recorder* columnist and civil rights activist.
Indianapolis *Recorder* Collection, Indiana Historical Society.

first black woman to seek a seat in the state legislature, was a tireless worker, as was Ramsey, a Democrat who taught at Attucks High School and later became president of the Indianapolis branch and also of the state conference. Richardson continued to help frame legislation and to give legal advice.[18]

In other cities and towns in the state, NAACP branches were revived and new ones founded. Whites as well as African Americans served on NAACP boards, and in Fort Wayne, where a new branch was chartered in 1946, the first president was the Unitarian minister, a white man.[19]

The National Association for the Advancement of Colored People was never a mass movement, and although membership increased during and after the war, its membership included only a small fraction of the total black population; and the number of African Americans in the state legislature was minuscule. This meant that the principal contribution of the NAACP was arousing public opinion and lobbying, but effective lobbying required a coalition of allies, whites as well as blacks.

Among middle-class African Americans throughout the state there was a network of organizations and institutions with a strong sense of community whose members could be called upon to rally to support efforts against discrimination and prejudice. In Gary there was the United Council of Negro Organizations, which included a revitalized NAACP branch, the Urban League, the interdenominational ministerial association of black churches, and other fraternal groups, which both protested against local examples of discrimination and lobbied in the state legislature.[20]

Indianapolis's Federation of Associated Clubs (FAC) was a particularly effective instrument for arousing middle-class African Americans. Its affiliates included a wide variety of clubs, ranging from cultural and musical groups and bridge clubs to labor unions and an American Legion post. Starling James, the president, was a strong supporter of the NAACP and its goals. The monthly publication of the FAC included editorials written by Richardson urging members to join in "fighting for the economic, civil, and social liberties of our People," as well as reports of social events. FAC's total membership numbered in the thousands, while the NAACP included only a small fraction of that number.[21]

In all communities black fraternal organizations, Greek letter fraternities and sororities, ministerial associations, and other civic groups could be called upon to protest or support racial policies. But more important in obtaining civil rights goals, particularly in the state legislature, was support from members of the white majority. In the General Assembly and in lobbying at the state level, the CIO and its affiliates often cooperated with the NAACP and provided much-needed support. At a 1945 meeting in Gary, the state CIO Anti-Discrimination Committee made plans for a drive against racial discrimination in every community and asked every local to form an antidiscrimination committee. There was a considerable amount of overlapping of membership in the NAACP and the CIO. The two most influential black Democrats in the General Assembly in the postwar years, Hunter and Dickinson, were CIO members, and in Muncie the president of the local NAACP also served as chairman of the antidiscrimination committee of the United Automobile Workers.[22]

In legislative lobbying and local campaigns against discrimination, a variety of predominantly white organizations and groups participated. Among the most active were religious groups, particularly those affiliated with the Indianapolis Federation of Churches and church federations from other cities. The Indianapolis Jewish Community Relations Council and other Jewish organizations gave active support to civil rights measures in Indianapolis. The Indiana Congress of Parents and Teachers and local PTAs lobbied for the end of segregated schools, and the Indiana League of Women Voters and local leagues actively supported antidiscrimination measures.

In most of the larger cities in the state, interracial committees, usually organized by the local church federations, had existed before the war, and these groups expanded their voluntary efforts during the war. In the postwar years, human relations commissions with some public funding were organized in several cities. One example was Evansville, where the Mayor's Commission on Human Rights was established by city ordinance in 1948. A year later the commission reported some progress against "jim crowism," including abolishing segregated washrooms in public buildings and in one city park; desegregating city playgrounds; and establishing a training school on race relations for the police department.[23]

A mayor's committee on race relations had existed in Indianapolis since 1945, and in 1952 Mayor Alex Clark, a Republican, asked that it be placed on a permanent basis "to promote amicable relations among racial and cultural groups within the community." In 1953 the city council responded by passing an ordinance creating the Indianapolis Commission on Human Rights, which was authorized to "take appropriate steps by conference and education to deal with conditions which strain relationships," to collect factual information, and to work with private organizations. Apparently, the council also provided the commission with some funding for 1953, but by 1955 funding was withdrawn. The Indianapolis *News* reported that Indianapolis was the only major northern city with a Human Rights Commission that had no budget or staff and made no reports. Thereafter, for several years the commission was largely symbolic. In 1958 the city council appropriated $12,000 for the commission, including the salary of an executive director.[24]

The authority of local committees and commissions, whether voluntary or created by municipal law, was limited. Stronger laws and commissions with enforcement powers were needed, and this required action by the state. The NAACP branches that met to establish the state conference in 1947 resolved that "Negroes in the state of Indiana are, in many areas, denied rights and privileges guaranteed by the Constitution and laws of the United States and this state" and listed demands that became the basic program of the civil rights movement in Indiana.

First on the list was equal access to public accommodations. Noting that the state already had a law (the 1885 Civil Rights Law) prohibiting discrimination, the resolutions declared that the law was almost "universally violated" and asked that the NAACP conference publicize the existence of the law, that members exercise their rights under the law, and that law enforcement authorities investigate and vigorously prosecute violations of the law.

The second item on the list of demands dealt with housing. The NAACP pointed out that the housing shortage was particularly acute among Negroes, that no long-range government program provided for adequate housing, and that the problem was made more difficult by restrictive covenants and the refusal of many private and public housing developments to admit Negroes solely because of their race. The conference demanded that the state institute a long-range program of public housing, us-

ing public funds when available, and that the program be carried out without discrimination on account of race.

The list also included a stronger FEPC law. Noting that since the end of the war
there had been an "alarming rise in discrimination in employment" and that the present law was ineffectual, the resolutions called for amended legislation providing criminal penalties for violations.

The NAACP also demanded an end to segregated schools. Although the state did
not require segregation, in most communities Negro children were "unlawfully discriminated against by being segregated . . . solely because of their race . . . and qualified
Negroes . . . are denied . . . the opportunity to teach or are restricted to teaching in
segregated schools."[25]

The resolutions of the state conference in 1947 did not ask for a new or stronger
public accommodations measure than the 1885 law but simply for publicizing the
rights already guaranteed by existing law and vigorously enforcing it.

The 1885 Civil Rights Law was largely a dead letter, partly because prosecutors ignored it and refused to enforce it. When cases were brought to court, judges gave the
law the narrowest possible interpretation. In one case the state appellate court had
ruled that the statute did not include ice cream parlors, and in 1953 a South Bend
judge ruled that the law did not apply to taverns.[26]

There had been some relaxation of barriers in Indianapolis during the war years
as black soldiers came into the city, seeking recreation. After a long campaign in which
the Federation of Associated Clubs played an important part, the management of the
Circle and Indiana Theaters, the principal downtown motion picture houses, agreed
in 1943 to admit blacks. The manager of the Circle Theater was reported to have said,
"Yes, we are admitting colored people to our theater. As long as they are presentable,
we don't turn them away." But, he added, some whites were objecting to the change
in policy, and he hoped blacks would come gradually and not in large numbers.[27]

Hotels and restaurants in the state capital regularly refused service to African
Americans—a fact that was particularly burdensome to travelers. Dickinson, a longtime member of the General Assembly, said that when he came to the state capital to
attend legislative sessions, he was forced to stay at the Senate Avenue YMCA or in
private homes and to eat at the snack bar in the basement of the state house. When
athletic teams traveled to Indianapolis from Muncie Central High School, a nonsegregated school, white team members stayed at downtown hotels, while black members were sent to room "with nice colored families in the colored section." White athletes ate in good restaurants, but their black teammates were forced to eat sandwiches
on the bus. When the National Bar Association met in Indianapolis, black members
stayed in private homes because they were not accepted in hotels. The United Council of Church Women decided to meet in another city because Indianapolis hotels
barred blacks. The state CIO protested publicly in 1942 when the Claypool Hotel refused to accept black delegates to their convention, and later the CIO played a leading part in efforts to compel hotels to abide by the 1885 law.[28]

After the war a coalition of African Americans and white groups undertook a serious nonviolent direct-action campaign to gain admission to and end discrimina-

tion in hotels, restaurants, recreation facilities, and other public places. Unlike the "sit-in" movements in the South, which protested state and local laws that authorized segregation, the Indianapolis groups were merely demanding the recognition and enforcement of existing law. Leaders met with managers of establishments that refused service to blacks and with government officials. These meetings were followed by nonviolent attempts, usually by racially mixed groups, to secure service. If service was refused, they sometimes appealed to law enforcement officials.[29]

Most of the action was centered in Indianapolis, home to the largest African American population in the state, including a large black middle class with enough money to pay for service in first-class establishments, but there were similar efforts in smaller cities all over the state.

In 1946 the CIO laid plans for an attack on "jim crow" at its state convention in Indianapolis. After informing city officials of their plans, members targeted six of the best downtown restaurants, which, having been warned in advance, served the racially mixed groups without protest. "In the biggest demonstration against jim crow in the history of Indianapolis," CIO leaders exulted, "we proved to everyone's satisfaction that jim crow can be beaten."[30]

However, the CIO effort was a one-day affair and did not produce lasting results. Early in the following year, a group in Indianapolis under NAACP leadership began an "eating crusade" intended to be more effective. A Civil Rights Committee made up of members of the NAACP, black clubs and fraternal organizations, and white church groups and white members of labor unions was formed with Wilson Head, a member of the staff of Flanner House, as its leader.[31]

The Civil Rights Committee's meeting with the secretary of the Indiana Restaurant Association brought no promise of cooperation except for the secretary's grudging agreement to send copies of the 1885 law to restaurants. Nevertheless, members of the "eating crusade" began to invade all sorts of eating establishments, from lunch counters at drugstores to the most expensive restaurants, carrying copies of the law to present to proprietors if they encountered refusals. In some places, the crusaders were served without question, but more frequently they met with obstacles. When racially mixed groups appeared in some restaurants, they were served but were seated behind screens or in distant corners. Other restaurants and lunch counters suddenly closed rather than serve the unwanted patrons, and some places simply turned them away.[32]

The committee made some efforts to file suits against businesses that refused to comply with the law, but officials were reluctant to prosecute, partly because they sympathized with proprietors who feared that serving blacks would drive away white customers. A Marion County prosecutor was quoted as saying to a reporter, "I'm for the enforcement of all laws, but this is a delicate question." Finally in 1950 a restaurant employee who refused to serve a black high school teacher was found guilty of discrimination and fined ten dollars, but the presiding judge then criticized the teacher for having waved a copy of the civil rights law in the face of the defendant, saying, "the problem could not be worked out by such methods."[33]

There were efforts to invoke the law in other cities. Suits in South Bend and Fort Wayne were won against restaurants that refused to serve blacks or racially mixed groups. In Bloomington, where Indiana University students had organized a branch of the NAACP, student protests ended discrimination against blacks in most restaurants near the campus, but in other places in the same city there were still signs reading, "We do not cater to the colored trade." African Americans in some areas seemed apathetic and accepted continued discrimination without protest. In Terre Haute, one of the most segregated communities in the state, hotels refused rooms to blacks; only a few lunch counters and snack bars would serve them; and only one motion picture theater allowed them unrestricted seating. The secretary of the NAACP branch complained that blacks in the community wanted relief from discrimination but were unwilling to protest openly. Most communities in the southern half of the state accepted segregation without protest. At a regional meeting of NAACP branches in 1949, an attorney from the national office complained that in most places little was being done to break down segregation, with the result that the civil rights legislation was not enforced, and African Americans were still barred from hotels and restaurants and were refused first-class seats in theaters.[34]

In several areas in the state there were efforts to end discrimination in parks and recreational centers as well as restaurants and hotels. In some cities YWCA and YMCA facilities that had formerly been open to only whites were made available to African Americans. For example, in Gary, where the YWCA had been closed to blacks, all facilities opened to them in 1943; black women began to serve on committees, and a teacher at Roosevelt High School was appointed to the board. However, Boy Scout troops continued to be segregated, and black troops were assigned to the Boy Scout camp only for the final week of the summer.[35]

The question of the black citizen's use of public parks and beaches was a focal issue in the right to public accommodations. In Indianapolis's black community it was generally conceded that certain public parks and playgrounds and golf courses were "for colored" and others were for whites only. However, the Civil Rights Committee of the NAACP began a campaign to persuade members of black clubs and churches to assert their right to use all parks and playgrounds. A particularly bitter and prolonged issue in the city was whether blacks would have access to Riverside Park, a privately owned amusement park that displayed signs "For whites only." It became customary for the management of the park, in response to requests from black organizations, to set aside one day a year as "Negro Day." For several years black patrons flocked to the park on their special day, which black charitable organizations used as a time for fundraising. But as African Americans became more sensitive to discrimination, black leaders, particularly black veterans, denounced "Negro Day" and all it symbolized. Starling James and the Federated Association of Clubs urged a boycott by the "thoughtless Negroes" who went to the park. "The first step to becoming first class citizens in this country," said James, "is to avoid insults whenever and wherever they may come." Consequently, only a few blacks, mostly children, attended Negro Day, and the Indianapolis *Recorder* exulted that "Riverside Park 'jim crow' season suffered what may be a mortal blow." However, Riverside Park continued to display signs saying, "White Patronage Only Solicited," and the Marion County prosecutor failed to take action to enforce the 1885 law.[36]

Riverside Park in Indianapolis long refused admission to blacks; these NAACP members in the early 1960s protested the policy. Indianapolis *Recorder* Collection, Indiana Historical Society.

In cities such as South Bend and Fort Wayne, public parks and playgrounds had never been segregated. Parks and playgrounds in Evansville were opened to blacks by the Mayor's Commission on Human Rights. In most places desegregating parks did not cause friction, perhaps because few blacks went to those formerly reserved for whites. However, in Gary, although the city council had declared parks open to all residents, blacks who ventured into formerly white parks and beaches risked attacks by rowdies, and police rarely interfered to protect them. A serious racial incident occurred at Marquette Park in 1949 at an interracial rally to commemorate the fifth anniversary of the landing at Salerno in the recent war. When a mob attacked participants in the rally, police offered no protection to the marchers but simply closed the beach. Some state parks were also off-limits to blacks. In 1945 a guard refused use of park facilities at the Lincoln Trail Park near Rockport to a Sunday school picnic group, and another guard drove away blacks who tried to swim in a lake in the park. The CIO was refused permission to hold interracial camp schools in state parks. Governor Gates insisted that the refusal was not racially motivated but that state policy was to limit use of the parks to groups interested in nature study and conservation.[37]

Access to swimming pools on a nonsegregated basis was more difficult for whites to accept than admitting African Americans to parks and playgrounds. But as they gained access to parks, blacks also began to demand use of public swimming pools. When confronted with delegations from the NAACP, mayors sometimes offered the use of pools at certain times on certain days of the week; but these offers were usually rejected, and blacks countered with threats of lawsuits. Perhaps the most significant case arose in Marion, where lawyer Willard Ransom responded to the city's refusal to permit blacks access to a public pool by threatening to file suit in federal court, charging that denying use of the pool was a violation of the Fourteenth Amendment rather than merely a violation of the state law. City officials responded by opening the pool to African Americans but expressed fear that it would lead to racial disturbances, and some white groups formed private swimming clubs rather than share the public pool with blacks.[38]

Meanwhile, in the postwar years, blacks were gaining increased access to public and private hospitals, and more African American physicians and surgeons were winning the right to practice in hospitals in all parts of the state, although many hospitals continued to operate on a "closed staff" basis and the number of beds allotted to blacks was limited. In 1949 the "jim crow" ward was abolished in the Indianapolis General Hospital, and in 1953, when all hospitals in the city were beginning a fund drive, the Indianapolis Development Association gave assurances that in the future there would be no discrimination or segregation in the private hospitals participating in the drive. In 1954 five hospitals in the state (in Indianapolis, Muncie, Hammond, Fort Wayne, and South Bend) had granted staff membership to black doctors, and in 1947, after a long fight, two Gary hospitals agreed to admit black doctors to their staffs.[39]

Although some gains had been made by 1950 in access to both public and private places of public accommodation, it was evident that voluntary efforts by members of the NAACP and other organizations to secure enforcement of the weak civil rights law of 1885 were not adequate to win the struggle against entrenched custom and prejudice. An enforceable law, "with teeth," was necessary, and beginning with the legislative session of 1949, bills to achieve this goal were introduced at every session of the General Assembly. All were defeated by the obstructionist tactics of lawmakers who wanted to preserve the existing system.

Exclusion from hotels, restaurants, places of entertainment, and parks in obvious violation of the law were indignities that a growing black middle class resented and resisted, but an issue of more fundamental importance to African Americans was discrimination in employment. During the war years, as we have seen, manpower shortages and government policies opened a variety of jobs formerly open only to white workers. After the war, African Americans lost some of the gains they had made during the war, and many who had worked on factory assembly lines were forced to return to menial, unskilled jobs. In industries with war contracts, dismissals were due in part to cancellation of contracts, and some other blacks were downgraded because of lack of seniority. These changes were not always due to discrimination, but the final report of the federal Fair Employment Practices Commission showed that job losses among blacks in Indianapolis were relatively more widespread than in other large northern cities, although some industries tried to maintain standards set during the war.[40]

Part of the problem in Indianapolis and other cities in the state continued to be the discriminatory practices of labor unions. Work in Indianapolis's building trades remained closed to blacks because of policies of AFL unions, even when there was evidence that contractors were quite ready to accept removal of the restrictions. Although the state CIO played a conspicuous part in the fight against all forms of discrimination, some affiliates did not cooperate. The constitution of the United Automobile Workers mandated that every local establish a Fair Employment Practices Committee, but in 1949 fewer than half the locals in Indiana had such committees.[41]

In the eyes of black leaders and their white supporters, the way to eliminate discrimination in employment was to strengthen the weak state FEPC law adopted in 1945 and give the commission authority to impose penalties. In its 1946 platform, the Democratic Party pledged to "expunge the phony FEPC act adopted by the Republican Assembly as a political gesture to minorities," but the sweeping Republican victory that year eliminated any possibility of adopting stronger law in the next legislative session.[42]

In 1949 a bill almost identical to the one rejected in 1947 received support from the NAACP, other black groups, the Indianapolis Jewish Community Relations Council, and other Jewish organizations, as well as the CIO. It provided for a Fair Employment Board with authority to receive complaints, hold hearings, and issue cease-and-desist orders enforceable through the courts. Among the discriminatory practices it would have outlawed were employment advertisements that specified race. The principal opposition to the measure came from the Indiana Chamber of Commerce and the Indianapolis *Star,* as well as from Republican members of the legislature. A spokesman for the Chamber of Commerce pleaded for "cooperation" instead of the "club" that the bill would provide and said that his organization preferred "love" to an approach that depended on "fear." A columnist for the *Star* said the bill violated "civil rights" and "might endanger national security."[43]

A similar but stronger bill was introduced in 1951 that prohibited discrimination by labor unions as well as employers and prohibited employers from asking questions about race in job applications as well as outlawing mentioning race in newspaper advertisements. As at previous legislative sessions, both black and white supporters from all the industrial cities in the state journeyed to the state capital to testify in favor of the measure, and, as in previous sessions, the Chamber of Commerce voiced strong opposition. The bill passed the house of representatives in amended form after some of the "teeth" had been extracted. It then went to the senate, where it was referred to a committee and died. Democrats in the upper house tried to "blast" the bill from the committee, but Republicans prevented a vote on it.[44]

The fate of the 1951 FEPC bill was typical of all FEPC bills and most civil rights measures introduced in the 1950s. Few lawmakers were as outspoken in their opposition as the spokesmen for the Chamber of Commerce, and most preferred to kill bills by delay and obstructionist tactics. A member of the NAACP described this process as a "shell game," saying,

> There will be plenty of credit to pass around, but no civil rights laws. The bill is referred to committee and the committee sits on it for three weeks. Finally the committee decides to report it out. That makes them "champions of civil rights."
>
> But it's too late to get the bill passed—which has been the idea of committee members all along. Or maybe the House makes a superhuman effort and passes the bill. All . . . who vote for it are thus recorded as champions of civil rights.
>
> The Senate of course has no time to act on the measure. The Senators claim that they too are champions of civil rights but [the bill] never had a chance.[45]

Members of some city councils, frustrated by the weakness of the 1945 law and the legislature's tactics, introduced bills for local FEPC ordinances. In Indianapolis in 1946 Dr. Lucas Meriweather, a Republican council member, introduced a bill patterned after a Chicago ordinance. It had the support of the Indianapolis NAACP and labor groups, and at a public hearing, a variety of speakers representing both white and black organizations spoke in favor of it: no one spoke in opposition. James, speaking for the FAC, told the council, "We're not the same group of colored people that used to come to you before the war. We want and demand the same things as all other members of society. . . .We are watching everything that you do. Do not be deceived into thinking that all is well. All is not well."[46]

Meriweather's bill prohibited the city from making contracts with any business that discriminated in its employment policies because of race. After Mayor Robert Tyndall vetoed the bill, on the grounds that it was probably illegal because a state law dealt with the same subject, Meriweather introduced an amended bill somewhat narrower in scope. It passed the council by a vote of eight to one, but Tyndall also vetoed the second version.[47]

In contrast to Indianapolis, Gary created a city Fair Employment Practices Commission in 1950. The bill was framed by NAACP lawyers and backed by CIO unions and civic groups. Ministers, members of the American Legion, a representative from the Urban League, and others spoke in favor of the bill at a public hearing. The only opposition came from AFL building-trade unions. The bill, which was passed in amended form, created a five-member commission authorized to hear complaints of discrimination by employees. East Chicago, which passed a measure similar to the one in Gary, and Gary were the only Indiana cities to adopt FEPC ordinances. Elkhart's city council failed to adopt a proposal for an FEPC in spite of two public hearings at which blacks complained of lack of employment opportunities due to discrimination. However, after rejecting the ordinance, the council passed a resolution calling upon both employers and labor unions to help increase employment opportunities for Negroes.[48]

Despite the lack of a state agency authorized to enforce fair employment practices and although unemployment increased in the immediate postwar years, more jobs became available to African Americans in the 1950s as the United States entered a long period of unprecedented prosperity and economic growth. Some new jobs were in industries formerly closed to blacks. One example was the Eli Lilly Pharmaceutical Company, one of the largest employers in Indianapolis. During the 1940s it had begun to hire and upgrade blacks, partly because of labor shortages caused by the war. After the war, Lilly adopted the goal of employing blacks in proportion to their share of the population of Marion County. As the plant expanded, African Americans with the necessary skills were employed as carpenters and electricians and in other construction jobs. Although blacks had been employed before the war in janitorial and custodial jobs only, some were now given opportunities in the laboratories, a few of them in research. The company announced in 1951 that in the future all cafeterias, restrooms, and recreational rooms would be open to all employees without regard to race.[49]

In both Gary and Indianapolis, black operators were hired for streetcars and buses. Black men and a few women were hired in growing numbers for work on assembly lines in various factories. Banks began to hire both African American men and women, and increasing numbers of black women were hired as secretaries and bookkeepers, particularly in smaller companies and offices. Department stores, where blacks had worked behind the scenes in stockrooms or as waitresses and busboys in tearooms, began to hire a few women as salespersons. Black men were also hired as salesmen in certain departments, and a few men were hired as salesmen in other types of stores and businesses. Some large food chains began to employ more blacks in sales and in clerical jobs. Similar changes took place in cities with smaller black populations. Black physicians, dentists, and lawyers, whose patients and clients continued to be drawn almost entirely from the black community, also prospered, as did some types of black-owned businesses as the overall economy expanded.[50]

In Indianapolis, some employment of African Americans in kinds of work formerly closed to them was the result of efforts of the Association for Merit Employment, a private organization founded by the American Friends Service Committee. Its interfaith governing board was racially mixed. During its most successful years (1956–1961), its director was Harold Hatcher, a white Quaker who became the first director of the Indiana Civil Rights Commission.

The purpose of the association was to "work with management, labor and other groups and agencies in spreading the policy and practice of employing and upgrading the best qualified applicants for vacancies regardless of the applicant's race, religion, or national origin." It was not an "employment agency for Negroes." Instead of trying to place large numbers in jobs traditionally open to them, its purpose was to change community employment patterns and open opportunities for blacks in new fields and places. Its work included establishing contacts with employers, interviewing, testing, counseling applicants, and disseminating occupational information to high school and college students and to other groups.[51]

Although the Merit Employment Association increased awareness that many African Americans were capable of successful performance in various fields, its successes were limited. The number of positions it was able to fill represented a small fraction of the number of applicants in its files. A report of the State Advisory Com-

Despite the state's Fair Employment Practices Commission, most African Americans in Indiana were confined to jobs such as janitor, domestic servant, or laborer. George Jenkins, pictured here in 1954, was head waiter at the Indianapolis Athletic Club. Photograph courtesy of Frances Linthecome.

mittee to the U.S. Commission on Civil Rights for 1959 showed that most blacks were still confined to the jobs traditionally open to members of their race. The report showed that most employers did not discriminate in hiring unskilled workers, and nearly half of those surveyed did not discriminate in hiring semiskilled workers on the basis of merit. But, the report said, "approximately nine tenths raise barriers to the employment of particular groups [blacks] in office, engineering, and sales occupations." The commission thought that the discrimination was usually "unpremeditated or inadvertent" and that "tradition" and "company policy" were most often cited as the principal reasons for failure to employ African Americans.[52]

A lack of decent housing had always been a problem for African American citizens, a problem made more acute during the war years by the influx of thousands of migrants seeking work in factories with war contracts. Opposing discrimination in access to housing became one of the main objectives of the civil rights struggle.

The report of the Race Relations Clinic sponsored by the Indianapolis Church Federation in 1945 helped set the agenda for the civil rights efforts of the postwar years; this report pointed out some of the obstacles faced by blacks who sought to buy homes. The underlying cause, according to the report, was white prejudice. In most of the desirable residential neighborhoods, homeowners had signed restrictive covenants that included penalties for owners who sold their property to nonwhites. In most new developments, similar covenants were attached to property titles. These covenants were one reason that banks refused to loan money to blacks. In other cases, particularly in "changing neighborhoods," white owners asked exorbitant prices from blacks. Banks and lending agencies were reluctant to make loans to African Americans and required higher down payments from them than from whites. Blacks had no representatives in the banks; real estate boards barred them from membership; and white members of the boards refused to show houses to blacks. The report concluded that the usual defense of these discriminatory practices was that "the government has built Lockefield Gardens for Negroes, and Negroes should fix up their homes in the Negro neighborhoods where the Negro schools are located."[53]

When, in spite of these obstacles, a few blacks began to move into "white" neighborhoods, older residents sometimes tried to intimidate them and force them to leave. In 1944 when two black families moved into houses on Indianapolis's Twenty-ninth Street, a few blocks north of neighborhoods recognized as "colored," they were confronted by a mob of whites who said it was a "restricted" area. A group of black leaders who protested were told by representatives of the North Indianapolis Civic League that they had established "an arbitrary restricted residential area in which Negroes will not be permitted to live or buy homes" between Twenty-eighth and Thirty-eighth streets. At a meeting with members of the Indianapolis Chamber of Commerce, Freeman Ransom deplored the policy, saying that America had no greater asset than the "hard working, home owning, church going Negroes." Those who moved into white neighborhoods were "seeking the same thing a white man seeks who moves into a better neighborhood, better streets, adequate police protection, garbage removal, and so forth."[54]

Few black families had money to buy homes outside the "colored" neighborhoods, and most of the houses in those neighborhoods were classified as substandard. However, in Indianapolis and Gary African Americans were not crowded into multi-storied tenements of the kinds found in New York and Chicago. Except for Lockefield Gardens and other public housing projects there were few apartments designated "for colored." Most of the black population lived in single-family or two-family units. Most of these dwellings had no bathtubs, and some had no inside plumbing. Landlords charged the many families who rented their homes rents at least 20 percent higher than those paid by whites for similar accommodations.[55]

Black leaders attributed the high crime rate among members of their race to inferior, crowded housing and slum conditions. Statistics gathered by a reporter for the Indianapolis *News* supported this view. The ratio of arrests of African Americans for crimes of all kinds was higher than their ratio to the entire population of the city. In an area of Indianapolis that included some of the worst housing, police reports for 1946–1947 showed one arrest for every 3.54 residents. In Lockefield Gardens, in contrast, there was only one arrest for every 17.56 persons.[56]

These figures suggest that the crime rate was much lower where blacks lived in decent housing and wholesome surroundings, but white political and civic leaders were ardent defenders of private enterprise and adamantly opposed housing financed by government funds, with standards imposed by "Washington bureaucrats."

The Indianapolis Chamber of Commerce and other white leaders had other plans for African Americans in postwar Indianapolis. They envisaged a program under which the city would buy an area including the worst slum areas in the city, divide it into lots, install public utilities, and then sell the lots to individual blacks to build houses. It would, said a spokesman, be a "social experiment in Negro housing." A carefully selected group of Negroes would build their own homes in a "self-help" plan. "We look for this plan," he said, "in the course of years, to contribute greatly to the stability and improvement of the citizenship of the Negro population of Indianapolis." The plan would be carried out "without having to resort to public housing with all its attendant evils." He admitted that Indianapolis had much bad housing, but, he said, more government housing was not the answer. Private enterprise could build houses more economically.[57]

In 1945 the Indiana General Assembly passed a bill which authorized Class I cities (i.e., Indianapolis) to condemn and buy slum property; the bill also provided for a Redevelopment Commission, to which the older Ransom was later appointed as the sole black member. Flanner House Homes, Inc., which was modeled after a somewhat similar program developed by the American Friends Service Committee in rural Pennsylvania, was authorized to raise money to buy land in the designated slum area. Under the dynamic leadership of Cleo Blackburn, the director of Flanner House, Flanner House Homes attracted national attention as a model self-help program. Through a revolving loan fund Flanner House paid for the land and most of the materials used in construction of the houses. The houses were built by a select group of veterans.[58]

The Indianapolis school board, which agreed to pay qualified instructors for the veterans, was later reimbursed by the Veterans Administration. The project furnished on-the-job training in skills in the building trades. Construction did not actually begin until 1950, and no houses were completed until 1953. By 1959 a total of 205 houses had been finished.

Flanner House had a trained caseworker to decide the eligibility and suitability of applicants who wanted to buy the houses. Although Flanner House publicized the buyers as coming from the worst slums, the families selected did not in fact represent the most poverty-stricken and least-educated blacks. Of the original families selected, all the men had steady employment and were not considered to be financial risks.[59]

The Flanner House Homes program provided modern, well-equipped houses in a landscaped area for a tiny fraction of the African Americans in Indianapolis who desperately needed better housing. But the men who wielded the political and finan-

cial power in the city continued to oppose seeking government money for larger public housing projects. Barrington Heights, a housing project for blacks in a southeast-
ern section of the city, was opened in 1950. It consisted of ranch-style one-story units.
It helped fill the need for housing for 338 families, but thereafter no public housing
was built for more than a decade. At the 1949 session of the General Assembly, when
Democrats had a majority in the house of representatives, a bill was introduced to
amend the slum clearance act of 1945 to provide authority to make contracts with
the United States agencies for federal loans and other assistance. The bill passed the
lower house but was tabled in the senate and did not come to a vote.[60]

Opposition to public housing and use of government funds in other Indiana cities
was less intense. All cities with sizable numbers of African Americans had housing
authorities, but public housing continued to be inadequate to meet the needs of the
growing number of blacks, and a disproportionate number continued to live in
slums. Gary seems to have been the only city where there were housing projects in
which both black and white tenants lived. In other cities all projects were racially
segregated, and those for blacks were sometimes inferior to those for whites. In 1945
federal authorities approved an application by the South Bend Housing Authority
for two projects—one for Negroes, one for whites. The one for Negroes (100 units)
was to cost $440,000; the larger one for whites (200 units) was to cost $1,200,000. In
Evansville, where blacks had always been assigned to housing units built especially
for members of their race, an attorney for the housing authority said that the policy
was "to provide equal facilities but not identical." However, when a new low-rent project for whites was opened in 1953, a group of black women applied for admission
and won a suit against the Evansville Housing Authority in the federal district court.
Judge William E. Steckler ruled that the housing authority must accept the women's
applications, holding that the right to rent was a civil right protected by the "equal
protection" clause of the Fourteenth Amendment.[61]

Ironically, this decision, which appeared to end legalized segregation in public
housing, was used in Indianapolis to kill prospects for any kind of public housing,
segregated or non-segregated.

In 1950 the Indianapolis City Council had revived the Indianapolis Housing Authority in spite of intense opposition from the Indianapolis Real Estate Board, which
assailed possible interference from "Washington experts." The housing authority later
announced plans for seven projects. Only one of those was to be for Negroes, on the
grounds that there were already two projects for Negroes and none for whites.[62]

Protests immediately arose from civic groups in the neighborhoods where the new
projects would be built. The Highland Park Citizens Committee claimed that the
"cheap housing project" planned in its area would destroy the value of all homes in
the area. The committee hired two lawyers from one of the most prestigious and expensive law firms in the city to find a way to halt the proposed construction. The
lawyers, apparently relying on the Evansville decision as precedent, argued that, since
public funds would be used for construction for the Indianapolis housing projects,
the plan to bar Negroes from the units reserved for whites would violate the Fourteenth Amendment. They threatened to seek an injunction in federal court.[63]

In view of the possibility that blacks would now be able to live in all public housing, the city council sought a way out. At a meeting in the council chamber, packed by five hundred angry citizens, the council voted by a margin of six to three to repeal all the measures enacted to give the housing authority power to build the seven proposed projects. While this action did not abolish the housing authority, it meant that no new projects could be undertaken without authorization from the council. The vote was along party lines, six Republicans in favor, three Democrats against. Most of the audience applauded, but representatives of labor unions and civil rights advocates assailed the Indianapolis newspapers and the Chamber of Commerce and banks for killing prospects for better housing for people with low incomes. A former director of the Indianapolis Housing Authority said the council's action had a "flimsy veneer" of attacking "socialism" and "decreased property values" but was really racially motivated.[64]

No more public housing was built in Indianapolis, but neither the Indianapolis Real Estate Board nor neighborhood civic groups were able to stem the northward movement of African Americans in the city. The members of the real estate board continued to refuse to show a house to Negroes unless two black families already lived in the city block where the house was located. But well-to-do blacks sometimes evaded this restriction by the subterfuge of having a friendly white buy the property they wanted and then buying it from the white purchaser.

The largest movement of African Americans was to an area north and slightly west of the central city; but at the same time black neighborhoods in the eastern part of the city also expanded northward. During the war, the North Indianapolis Civic League had decreed that no blacks should reside between Twenty-eighth and Thirty-eighth streets, but by 1957 in the area between Twenty-eighth and Thirty-fourth streets west of Boulevard Place the proportion of blacks grew from 3 percent to an estimated 87 percent. To the north of this area, between Thirty-fourth and Thirty-eighth streets, black residents had increased to an estimated 75 percent of the whole, and substantial numbers were moving into the area north of Thirty-eighth Street.[65]

In some cases when a house became vacant in a neighborhood threatened by racial change, white homeowners banded together to buy the house to prevent it from being sold to an unwelcome black neighbor. In one area a group calling itself the Fairmap Realty Company attempted to forestall black home-buying by purchasing houses in their neighborhood, but the attempt was abandoned when it became evident that money could not be raised quickly enough to buy all of the houses put up for sale by whites fleeing to the suburbs. Moreover, in this particular area not all the whites wanted to flee. The neighborhood in which the Fairmap Company attempted to operate was an upper-middle-class area of attractive homes near the campus of Butler University. Instead of succumbing to panic selling, some householders decided to stay and welcome African American neighbors and work toward maintaining a racially integrated neighborhood where householders took pride in maintaining their houses. The Butler Tarkington Neighborhood Association became the first and probably the most successful of several neighborhood organizations in which blacks participated along with whites in maintaining racial balance.[66]

The most substantial gains in improved housing were made by middle-class blacks who bought well-built homes in older neighborhoods. By the late 1950s a few well-to-do African American families began to build homes in fashionable Washington Township, beyond the Indianapolis boundaries. That African Americans could own homes in the suburbs and in the Butler Tarkington area was evidence that some black families had incomes comparable to middle-class whites.[67]

7

School
Desegregation

The 1949 law abolishing segregation in public education from the kindergarten level to state universities was the first important civil rights measure passed by the Indiana state legislature and the only significant one adopted before 1960. However, although it was adopted earlier and with less opposition than other civil rights laws, implementation of the school law proved more difficult and controversial than any of the other laws, particularly after the question of busing as a remedy for segregation became the focal issue. Because debates over school desegregation were more prolonged and the legal questions more complex than in other civil rights areas a separate chapter is devoted to it.

The school law of 1877, under which public schools operated until 1949, gave local school authorities freedom to provide schools for Negroes but said that, where there were no separate schools, "colored children shall be allowed to attend the public schools with white children."[1]

In the years between 1877 and 1949, school systems had carried out the law in a variety of ways. In the southern half of the state, schools were usually segregated. With the largest black population in the area, Evansville's elementary schools were segregated, and some of the rooms in Clark elementary school served as the high school until the construction of Lincoln High School, the only colored school in the area with physical facilities equal to those in the high schools for whites. Segregation was the rule in other towns and in rural areas in southern Indiana as well. Elementary schools for black children were sometimes brick, sometimes frame buildings of one or two rooms, often with outside toilets and only stoves for heating. "High schools," not usually accredited, were ordinarily one or two rooms in elementary school buildings. In a few cities, such as Bloomington and Terre Haute, while there were separate elementary schools, the few blacks who attended high school went to the same school as whites.

In Indianapolis, where about half of the state's African American students lived, elementary schools were segregated with few exceptions, and segregation had tightened as the black population increased during and after World War I. After the opening of Crispus Attucks High School in 1927, there was a separate high school for African Americans.

School systems in the cities and towns north of Indianapolis were seldom officially segregated, but in communities where the black population was concentrated in a particular residential area, there was often a "colored" elementary school, usually taught by an African American teacher. Gary, which did not exist until after 1900, developed its own peculiar system of segregation, with black and white children sometimes in the same building but taught in separate classes. Both whites and African Americans were enrolled in Froebel High School, but the black students were barred from some classes and activities. In 1931 Roosevelt High School, a modern building with facilities equal to or better than those in the schools for whites, was opened as an all-Negro school.

African Americans taught in most of the segregated elementary schools in the state, but in nonsegregated school systems with racially mixed student bodies, there were only white teachers. This practice greatly reduced job opportunities for educated blacks, who sometimes had better academic qualifications than white teachers; consequently, it was sometimes argued that separate schools should be maintained to offer jobs to educated blacks. There were African American teachers and administrators at Attucks High School in Indianapolis, Roosevelt in Gary, and Lincoln in Evansville, but except for these three high schools and the inferior "high schools" in the towns in the south, there were no opportunities for black high school teachers, even for those with advanced degrees.

Before the Second World War, except for the protests in Indianapolis and Gary against separate high schools, blacks generally accepted segregation as inevitable and normal, although some complained about inferior buildings in many colored schools and the lack of equal facilities and equipment. During the war, black complaints increased as a lack of equipment and opportunities for vocational training prevented African Americans from acquiring the skills needed for new opportunities in industry.

Somewhat surprisingly, the first attempt to force a school corporation to equalize opportunities for vocational training through an appeal to the courts began in Jeffersonville, a small town on the Ohio River. In 1941 George Martin, a black student, filed a suit in the federal district court for admission to the all-white Jefferson High School to enroll in courses for physical education and commerce, which were not offered at the Negro school. After the school board refused to admit him, he filed a suit for damages and an injunction. The suit was the culmination of a long campaign by African Americans in Jeffersonville and the local branch of the NAACP to improve or rebuild the Negro high school, which had been constructed in 1891, was still heated by a stove, and lacked both plumbing and a gymnasium. When the school board announced plans for a new vocational training school open only to whites, resentment in the black community came to a head. The NAACP hired a Louisville lawyer and began legal action. The lawyer, Prentice Thomas, in turn sought advice from Thurgood Marshall in the NAACP's national office. Details of the litigation are not clear, but Judge Robert Baltzell dismissed the suit, perhaps because Thomas had not been admitted to the Indiana bar.[2]

The desegregation effort in Jeffersonville had little impact in the southern counties of the state. But during the war years, racial tensions and fear of racial disturbances in the northern part of the state, particularly in Gary, led to efforts by the Gary Chamber of Commerce and members of the white establishment to take steps to eliminate discriminatory policies. As part of these efforts, the Gary school board announced a policy statement in August 1946 that students should not be discriminated against because of race, color, or religion in the district where they lived or in the schools they attended.[3]

The school board took this action after a prolonged strike at Froebel High School. In September 1945, white students walked out of Froebel, demanding the removal of all black students and the replacement of the Froebel principal. Receiving national publicity, the strike revealed the deep divisions in Gary between the black community and the white immigrant working-class parents, who encouraged their children to strike and offered them support. The students finally returned to classes after the school board promised an investigation of the Froebel principal, but racial tensions did not subside. Nevertheless, community leaders and organizations, including the Urban League, the League of Women Voters, the YWCA, and the Gary Council of Churches, sponsored human relations workshops and worked behind the scenes to persuade the school board to move toward integration of all public schools. The board finally issued the statement in August 1946, but implementation did not begin until September 1947.[4]

To carry out the announced policy, the board redrew school districts and assigned all students to the school district in which they lived. The principle of integration was established, but because of residential patterns, enrollments in most schools remained predominantly white or black. Only a total of 116 African Americans enrolled in previously all-white schools. Among them were thirty-eight who were assigned to Emerson High School. In response, about 80 percent of the whites at Emerson boycotted classes for ten days. White students and other demonstrators gathered every day to jeer and threaten black students. However, the school board refused to negotiate with the truants, and when their leaders were ordered to appear in juvenile court the boycott ended.[5]

Abolition of segregation in Gary schools was followed by ending discriminatory policies in nearby East Chicago. There were no separate schools for African Americans in that city, but for twenty-five years school authorities had followed a policy of excluding them from extracurricular activities and social events. In 1947 a coalition of citizens from a variety of organizations began to push for ending these practices. James Hunter, a longtime member of the state legislature, joined the president of the Chamber of Commerce and the president of the League of Women Voters to form a committee to carry out this objective. At their urging, the city council, which had the authority to appoint the school board, passed a resolution demanding that the school board end discriminatory policies.[6]

In Elkhart, where all African American elementary pupils were schooled in an antiquated, substandard building, the local CIO and a revitalized NAACP branch supported black parents in a campaign to enroll their children in the nearest neighborhood schools. With support from the ministerial alliance, PTAs, and other organizations, they persuaded the school board to close the colored elementary school and redraw school districts.[7]

The actions in Gary and the other cities in the northern part of the state in 1946 and 1947 left Indianapolis and Evansville the only large American cities outside the South with segregated school systems.

After 1927, when the NAACP and other African American groups had lost their fight against building a segregated high school in Indianapolis, the black community had become reconciled to its existence; they took pride in Attucks High School's teachers and in the achievements of its students, particularly in athletics.[8] But after Attucks opened, some of Indianapolis's black leaders, especially those who were members of the Monday Luncheon Club, mounted an ongoing campaign to press the school board either to increase course offerings at Attucks, especially in vocational and technical subjects, or to admit black students to white high schools where these

White students at Gary Emerson High School went on strike to protest the desegregation of the school in 1947. Calumet Regional Archives, Indiana University Northwest.

courses were taught. In 1933, with the slogan "Make Attucks the equal of other city high schools or close it up," the club appointed a committee to investigate whether it was the purpose of the school board "to treat the Negro as a separate and distinct unit in educational affairs" and whether white children had priority over colored children in securing a technical education. When the committee appeared before the school board, they met with an icy reception, the first of many such confrontations between African American citizens and the all-white school board.[9]

In 1934 the Monday Luncheon Club began the first serious effort to elect a black member to the school board by seeking the all-powerful Citizens Committee's endorsement of black candidates. The Citizens Committee had led the campaign to oust the "Klan" school board in 1929 and continued to dominate the Indianapolis Board of School Commissioners for almost a half century thereafter. Two able African Americans, M. D. Batties, a physician, and Guy L. Grant, a dentist, expressed their willingness to be candidates, but the Citizens Committee, using an argument that was to be repeated many times in future years, refused to endorse either man on the grounds that "the racial issue should not be injected into the campaign."[10]

The school board's requirement that all black high school students attend Attucks led to another continuing complaint among black citizens of Indianapolis, particularly those who were parents, since many Attucks students were forced to travel long distances to the school and to pay for their own transportation. To remedy this problem some demanded a second black high school on the city's east side.[11]

By the 1935–1936 school year, about 2,000 Attucks students were crowded into a building intended for half that number. Parent-Teacher Associations, civic clubs, and fraternal organizations launched a campaign to publicize the need for another high school and presented petitions to the school board. But the board rejected the proposal for a new high school and instead announced plans to build an annex to Attucks by renovating a nearby elementary school to house first-year Attucks students. A few months later, in another rebuff to the African American community, the board announced plans for an eastside high school for whites in Irvington.[12]

During the Second World War, blacks increasingly complained about the inadequate facilities available to them for vocational and technical training, and after the war, groups of black veterans appeared before the Indianapolis school board to demand more opportunities for job training. Meanwhile, growing numbers of white delegations representing church groups, labor unions, PTAs, the League of Women Voters, and others were urging the end of segregation in the city schools.

A fire that gutted a Negro elementary school in January 1946 appeared to offer an opportunity to begin desegregation by admitting the black pupils to nearby white schools where there were empty seats and where the principals expressed willingness to accept them. A delegation from the NAACP, the CIO, the Senate Avenue YMCA, and other groups appeared before the school board to ask that pupils displaced by the fire be allowed to attend neighborhood schools, but the board replied that they had already appropriated funds to bus the children across the city to a previously abandoned building. At the same meeting, the board announced plans to build a ten-room addition to School 26, a Negro school that was already the largest elementary school in the city.[13]

A few weeks later, another delegation representing a broad spectrum of organizations appeared before the board to ask that Indianapolis follow the example of Gary and announce a date for ending segregation in the schools. This delegation also addressed the issue of whether Negro teachers would be hired in desegregated schools, which some people regarded as an obstacle to ending segregation; the delegation argued that in an integrated system there should be Negro teachers and administrators as well as whites.[14]

During the following months, more groups asking for an end to segregation continued to appear before the board and continued to be rebuffed, but during the first part of 1947, organizations urging desegregation concentrated their efforts on the Republican-dominated General Assembly. Early in the session, two Republicans from Marion County—William Fortune, a white representative, and Wilbur Grant, a black—introduced a bill to abolish segregation in all public schools, including state colleges and universities. Under the measure, which was in large part the work of the Race Relations Committee of the Indianapolis Church Federation, desegregation would have taken place gradually over a period of years. At a public hearing, representatives from groups supporting the bill pointed out that Indianapolis was the only large city in the North with a segregated school system and called the segregated system "expensive, unfair, undemocratic, unreasonable, and immoral." Spokesmen from opposing groups predicted that adoption of the measure would lead to racial troubles and would endanger the jobs of Negro teachers. Most damaging to prospects for adoption of the proposed law was the opposition of the Indianapolis school board, which predicted dire results if the bill was passed. The board repeated the arguments of the bill's opponents that in a city where separation of the races was the norm in employment and in social relations, desegregation would lead to racial problems.[15]

Opposition by the Indianapolis school board killed the possibility that the bill would be adopted. Representative Hunter tried in vain to pry it from the education committee, but the house voted by a margin of 46 to 25 to table his motion to bring it to a vote.[16]

Following the defeat of this bill, antisegregation forces in Indianapolis increased their efforts, sending more and more delegations to appear before the school board. They also tried to gain a voice in the selection of school board members, but their efforts to induce the Citizens Committee, which dominated school board selection, to name a black candidate failed.[17]

In 1947, Henry J. Richardson and his intrepid wife Roselyn tried to enroll their son in the neighborhood school near their home, but the boy was refused admission and was sent back to the colored school, which was several miles distant. A similar effort by Clarence Nelson, a black Methodist minister, also failed.[18]

After these rebuffs, the Indianapolis Branch of the NAACP began to consider court action to force the school board to change its policy. In September 1948, Richardson presented a plan to the school board for ending segregation in the Indianapolis schools within three years, and he threatened to appeal to the courts if the board rejected his proposal.[19] This was no idle threat; members of the Indianapolis NAACP were already appealing to the national office for financial support, and Indianapolis lawyers Richardson and Willard Ransom were consulting with Thurgood Marshall, chief counsel for the NAACP Legal Defense Fund, about legal strategies to end school segregation. However, Richardson and Ransom decided not to institute a suit until after a survey had been made that would prove that Negro schools did not have equal facilities and did not receive equal funding with the schools for whites.[20]

State and local NAACP officers decided to concentrate their efforts on obtaining a law abolishing segregation at the 1949 session of the General Assembly. Prospects for such a law were improved when Democrats won control of the house of representatives and Democrat Henry J. Schricker was elected governor on a state platform that included a strong civil rights plank. Meanwhile, the Indianapolis school board showed no sign of retreating from its policy of segregation and announced plans to spend half a million dollars on Negro schools to accommodate growing numbers of black students.[21]

In 1949, Ransom, Richardson, and other lawyers wrote a new bill, more carefully

Roselyn and Henry J. Richardson, Jr., and sons Henry III and Rodney are shown here in 1947, when the Richardsons challenged Indianapolis school segregation by seeking admission to the public school near their home. Roselyn Richardson Papers, Indiana Historical Society.

drawn than the one defeated in 1947. It abolished segregation in public education, provided a schedule for implementation, and also included protection for African American teachers. The bill was introduced by Hunter and a white Democratic member from Indianapolis. After being reported favorably by the committee on education with only minor changes, it passed the house of representatives by a vote of 58 to 21.[22]

After the bill went to the Republican-dominated senate, there were rumors that the education committee intended to kill the bill by failing to act on it. At this point, Governor Schricker, who had not previously committed himself, met with Democratic senators and urged them to support the bill. The measure had impressive support in Indianapolis from whites as well as from the African American community. Endorsement by the white press was also important in influencing public opinion.[23]

Under prodding, the senate education committee brought the bill to the floor with a recommendation that it pass. Republicans attempted to emasculate it by offering restrictive amendments, but finally, despite delaying tactics, the senate passed the bill.[24]

The law as finally enacted declared that it was the public policy of the state to pro-hibit segregation and discrimination "in the public kindergartens, common schools, colleges, and universities of the state," and it provided for gradual implementation over a period of years. No new segregated schools were to be built or established, and beginning in September 1949 pupils entering kindergarten and the first year of ele-mentary school were to attend the kindergarten or school in the district where they lived. Abolition of segregation in elementary and high schools was to be completed by 1954. In addition to providing for desegregation of students, the law also guaran-teed that no public school, college, or university should "discriminate in hiring, up-grading tenure or placement of any teacher on the basis of race, creed or color."[25]

African Americans and their white supporters were jubilant. A "Monster Meet-ing" at the Senate Avenue YMCA celebrated the victory. Willard Ransom reported to the NAACP's national office that the school law "marked, for the first time, a real death blow at segregation in Indiana, together with the unification of all groups in-terested in civil rights working for the passage of this legislation." He singled out William Ray and Jessie Jacobs, both Republicans, as the "real spearhead in the suc-cessful fight for the law."[26]

Indianapolis, where school authorities had resisted efforts to abolish the segrega-tion of the largest African American school population in the state, became the focal point of implementation of the 1949 law. In April 1949 the school board ended its formal opposition to desegregation and announced a plan for compliance. Under the plan, children entering kindergarten or the first grade of elementary school would enroll in the school nearest to their residence. This meant that desegregation would be carried out one year at a time. The plan for high school students was more com-plex. Before the adoption of the new law there had been no high school districts in the city. Negroes were assigned to Attucks regardless of where they lived, while white students might attend any of the other high schools. Under the new plan, two factors were to be considered in assigning first-year high school students: the high school to which a pupil graduating from elementary schools had previously been assigned (a provision which would obviously preserve segregation) and the distance of that high school from the pupil's place of residence. Students dissatisfied with their assignment would be given "special consideration for change" if they lived more than two miles from the high school to which they were assigned. After their parents requested a change, eighteen black students from School 18, less than two miles from Shortridge High School, were reassigned to Shortridge, while the remaining forty-two members of their class went to Attucks.[27]

As a result of the new districts for elementary schools, a few black first-graders at-tended previously all-white schools, but even fewer white children went to former Negro schools. By the opening of the school year in 1953, about two-thirds of ele-mentary pupils attended schools with racially mixed enrollments. Of the fifty-three elementary schools reported as "integrated," blacks were in a minority in forty-nine, whites were a minority in only four. In two of these "integrated" schools there was only one white pupil, in two others a single Negro. About 175 African Americans were still being bused outside the district where they lived. School authorities said that this

Jessie Jacobs in 1981; along with realtor and NAACP president William T. Ray,
Jacobs led the movement to pass the 1949 state school desegregation law.
Indianapolis *Recorder* Collection, Indiana Historical Society.

was because space for them was not available in the neighborhood schools, but they insisted that selection of the children to be bused was "not based simply on race."[28]

Integration of teachers did not begin until 1951. By 1953, there were seven African American teachers in formerly white elementary schools, and a black principal was assigned to an elementary school with a mixed enrollment. It was announced that the program of desegregation in Indianapolis was completed ahead of the schedule permitted by Indiana law. As protests and plans for resistance developed in the South after the Supreme Court decision in *Brown* v. *Board of Education* in 1954, the white press in Indianapolis contrasted these developments with the "peaceful" and "gradual" process of racial integration in the Indianapolis schools. The Indianapolis *Times* said that it had gone "so smoothly you'd hardly have known that it was going on. And if any one has been injured in the process we have yet to hear about it."[29]

The complacent, self-congratulatory perception of the process of desegregation as seen by the white press contrasted sharply with the views of the black community as reflected in the Indianapolis *Recorder*. From the outset, the *Recorder* and spokesmen for the NAACP were skeptical about the intentions of the school board, and by 1952 more and more African American parents were questioning the good faith of the board and school authorities. The loudest complaints were over evidence that the school board was gerrymandering school districts so as to perpetuate segregation. The most obvious example was the continuing all-black student body at Attucks.

In the 1960s the school board's choice of sites for building new high schools furnished further evidence of the their intention to evade the 1949 law. As the school population grew, reflecting the "baby boom" following the war, and as African Americans continued to move into formerly white neighborhoods, the school board authorized the building of three new high schools on the edges of the city, where nearly all the residents were white. Arlington in the northeast opened in 1961, Northwest on the west in 1963, and John Marshall at the eastern edge of the city in 1967.[30]

By the 1960s the emergence of what was called "de facto," as opposed to "de jure," segregation created new obstacles to genuine school desegregation. In Indianapolis and other northern cities, the schools were being "resegregated" as the result of changing residential patterns. Numerous elementary schools that had been predominantly white a few years earlier were becoming nearly all black as whites moved to the outer edges of the city or to the suburbs and black families replaced them in their old neighborhoods. In some areas where large houses formerly occupied by whites were converted to multiple-family units for blacks, elementary schools were not only becoming predominantly black but also seriously overcrowded. The school board responded to these changes by using portable buildings, rather than dedistricting the schools as the NAACP and supporters of school integration urged.[31]

While the school board and school authorities followed policies of delay and obstruction in the 1950s, impatient integrationists in Indianapolis tried to break the monopoly exercised by the Citizens Committee over the selection of school board members. In the years when it was at the height of its power, the committee was chaired by Judge John Niblack, a Republican. Candidates were not always Republicans, but they always represented the interests of the "white establishment" and usually came from the upper-class neighborhoods on the far north side of the city. Before 1955 no person was selected from the central areas where the African American population was concentrated, and spokesmen for the committee continued to reject recommendations that a black member could best represent the interest of the black community during a period of transition from a dual school system to a desegregated system.[32]

While Indianapolis took token steps to comply with the 1949 school law, in Evansville, the only other large Indiana city where schools were officially segregated, there were no signs at all of steps to desegregate. In May 1949 the Indianapolis *Recorder* reported that Vanderburgh County schools would postpone any steps toward school integration because of crowded conditions. At the beginning of the school year in 1950 conditions remained unchanged, and in 1951 the Indiana Parents Association, a white group, was organized to oppose any steps toward desegregation. In 1954 tentative compliance began when Harward Elementary School admitted thirty African American pupils whose parents demanded that their children attend the school in the district in which the parents paid taxes instead of being bused to colored schools. White parents responded by picketing the school, carrying signs that said "Go Back to Your Own School," and about 40 percent of the white pupils were absent. But after a few days, when protests had no effect, picketing ceased and white pupils returned.[33]

By 1957 about half the elementary schools in Evansville had racially mixed enrollments. All high schools had been officially desegregated. The NAACP continued to complain about the all-black enrollment at Lincoln School and the fact that other elementary schools remained entirely black in spite of claims that desegregation had been completed. A lawsuit to close Lincoln and to eliminate all the black elementary schools was begun in the federal district court presided over by Judge S. Hugh Dillin, who later was to hear the Indianapolis school desegregation suit.[34] In 1970 Judge Dillin accepted a plan that closed two black elementary schools and transferred their pupils to predominantly white schools. Meanwhile, in 1970 the school board had also adopted a plan for further desegregation of the high schools. The plans finally adopted for desegregating the city's elementary and high schools involved busing some 2,000 pupils "two ways"—i.e., black students would be bused to predominantly white schools and white students bused to predominantly black schools. This number represented a small fraction of the total number of pupils who regularly rode buses in the school district, which included the whole of Vanderburgh County as well as the city of Evansville. At first white parents, offended by the busing program, drove their children to school, but after a time they accepted the public transportation. The court rejected later complaints by dissatisfied African American groups, and except for some changes to adjust school districts to changes in population, the court-approved plan continued to operate.[35]

In other Ohio River towns, including Madison, New Albany, and Jeffersonville, dual school systems were also being abolished. As a growing number of African Americans had moved from these towns to larger industrial centers, the costs of maintaining dual systems had become burdensome, even though the black schools had received

Judge John Niblack, longtime head of the Indianapolis Citizens Committee that
dominated school board elections from the 1920s until the 1970s.
Indianapolis *Recorder* Collection, Indiana Historical Society.

only a fraction of the money spent on schools for whites. Closing the black schools
meant that more money was available for the schools that remained. However, while
black students attended formerly white schools, African American teachers faced
strong prejudice against their employment in the southern communities. Dual systems were also abolished in rural communities all over the state; primitive one- or

two-room colored schools were abandoned, and the few African American children who remained were bused to township schools.[36]

In a few communities, among them Terre Haute, school authorities initially evaded the intent of the 1949 law by drawing school districts to include both a white school and a colored school and allowing black parents a choice in deciding which school their children would attend. Black teachers, particularly those without tenure, were reported to be discouraging their pupils from transferring to the white schools because they were afraid of losing their jobs. However, the NAACP state board denounced all systems where parents were allowed to decide which school their children would attend, saying, "There is no provision giving a choice to officials, parents, or anyone else."[37]

In some cities and towns where schools had never been officially segregated, the 1949 law, which prohibited discrimination because of race in employment of teachers, opened the way for the first time for employing African American teachers in schools with racially mixed enrollments. For example, in Muncie, where African American graduates of Ball State Teachers College had previously never been hired to teach in the public schools, in 1952 Mrs. Gerald Finley became the first member of her race to be employed in an elementary school. Robert Foster became Muncie's first black administrator when he was appointed principal of an elementary school in 1956. A 1958 report on racial conditions in Elkhart claimed that the school city had "set the pace in merit employment by employing six Negro teachers" and that schools where blacks had once been barred from athletics and most extracurricular activities were "fully integrated."[38]

Desegregation in Gary had begun in 1946 by the process of drawing new school districts, and problems of resegregation and de facto segregation were more acute there than in Indianapolis. Although the total number of African Americans in Gary was smaller than in the capital city, they made up a much larger percentage of the whole. By 1961, 90 percent of the Gary public schools were either entirely black or almost all black. Ninety-seven percent of the 23,055 black students were in eighteen predominantly or entirely black schools where nearly all of the teachers and administrators were African Americans. By 1965, 90 percent of Gary's black teachers taught in black schools. During the 1950s, as the African American population grew, schools were so crowded that many children attended only half-day sessions. Construction of several new schools during the early 1960s eased the problem of overcrowding, but the new schools were as racially imbalanced as the old. The original school desegregation plan, based on the concept of neighborhood schools, did not take into consideration the problem of residential segregation, and the new schools were built in densely populated black neighborhoods. They were not located to ensure racially mixed enrollments.[39]

By 1962, of the forty-two public schools in Gary, enrollment in eighteen of them was almost entirely black, twenty were almost entirely white, and only four were racially mixed. In an effort to remedy the situation, which they regarded as discriminatory to African Americans, the Gary branch of the NAACP brought suit in the federal district court in Hammond, one of the first such suits in a northern city. In the trial, NAACP lawyers argued that the Gary school board and the superintendent had a "constitutional duty to provide and maintain a racially integrated school system" and that "school systems that are administered so that all or nearly all Negro children attend schools, separate and apart from all nearly all white students, are no less segregated than those systems where separate schools are mandated by state constitution and statute." Gary school authorities responded that they could not function as a resettlement commission or an open occupancy administration and that in selecting the sites for new schools they had no choice but to accept existing residential patterns.

The plaintiffs did not present either effective arguments or convincing evidence that school board decisions on school sites were racially motivated, and their case was weakened by testimony by the president of the school board, an African American, that race had never been a consideration in drawing school districts. District court Judge George N. Beamer ruled that the plaintiffs had failed to prove that the Gary school board had "deliberately or purposefully segregated the Gary schools"; the Seventh Circuit Court of Appeals upheld his decision, and the Supreme Court refused to review.[40]

Roosevelt High School, Gary, 1951. Calumet Regional Archives, Indiana University Northwest.

The white press in Indianapolis expressed satisfaction with the rulings of the courts, and in a statement published in the Indianapolis *Star,* Judge Niblack quoted the part of the opinion that said desegregation did not mean that there must be "intermingling of the races in all school districts," only that pupils must not be prevented from going to school together because of race. He added that the Civil Rights Act of 1964 recently passed by Congress made it clear that desegregation did not mean "assignment to public schools in order to overcome racial imbalance."[41]

As early as 1951, leaders of the Indianapolis NAACP had charged that the school board was "shuffling the cards" so that Indianapolis schools would "continue to have colored schools with colored teachers and white schools with white teachers," regardless of the letter and spirit of the 1949 law, and subsequent actions of the board did not cause them to change their view of the board's intentions.[42]

NAACP members, as well as school officials in Indianapolis, had followed the Gary trial with intense interest, and the former were disappointed with the outcome; but that did not deter them from efforts to bring representatives of the federal government to investigate school policies in Indianapolis. Most active in seeking intervention by federal authorities was Andrew Ramsey, president of the NAACP state conference. In 1967 he wrote to John Gardner, Secretary of Health, Education, and Welfare, requesting a federal investigation of discrimination in assignment of teachers. This led to a visit by the regional director of the U.S. Civil Rights Commission.[43]

A few weeks after this visit, the Assistant Attorney General for Civil Rights of the U.S. Justice Department charged the Indianapolis school system with "overt racial discrimination in the assignment of students and faculty members." This action was based on a section of the Civil Rights Act of 1964 that authorized the Attorney General to act if he received a complaint in writing by a parent or a group of parents that his or her children, as members of a class, were being deprived by school authorities of equal protection of the laws. If the complaint was found to have merit, and if school authorities did not correct the alleged conditions within a reasonable time, the Justice Department was authorized to institute a civil action in the district court in the name of the United States.[44]

When the Indianapolis schools failed to make a satisfactory response, the Justice Department filed an injunction at the end of May 1968 against Indianapolis Public Schools (IPS) in the federal district court. Defendants were the Board of School Commissioners of the city of Indianapolis and the Superintendent of Schools.[45]

By the time the Justice Department initiated the suit against the Indianapolis school board, experts in the field of education had become convinced that so long as more and more African Americans settled in northern cities and residential patterns remained unchanged, resegregation would continue, and the only realistic method of promoting desegregation would be to transport white pupils to predominantly black schools and black children to predominantly white schools. Earlier busing had been thought of as a means to improve the quality of rural and suburban education by transporting students to consolidated schools. But once the issue of busing as a method of promoting "racial mixing" of students was raised, prosegregation forces pounced upon it and denounced it, and politicians were afraid to endorse it. When the Indiana General Assembly was debating legislation in 1965 to strengthen the 1949 school law and promote desegregation, they were fearful of being accused of endorsing busing. While the law they passed gave school officials authority to take action to reduce segregation, it was clear that it did not provide for busing.[46]

The suit that began in 1968 was brought by the Justice Department at the instigation of the NAACP. Initiated when Lyndon Johnson was president, the case dragged on through the administrations of Richard Nixon and Gerald Ford and was not settled until 1981, when Jimmy Carter was president. During this prolonged legal battle, the positions of the Justice Department lawyers underwent significant changes that reflected the views of the successive presidents.

The IPS board responded to the Justice Department suit by claiming that there was "no hint of segregation" in assignment of pupils and teachers, that any one-race schools in Indianapolis were the result of "neighborhood characteristics," that the all-Negro enrollment at Attucks "reflected the composition of the neighborhood surrounding the school," and that there was "nothing in the system to desegregate."[47]

Nevertheless, despite these protestations, IPS began to take limited steps toward further desegregation; but even these limited measures aroused opposition from members of the white community who resented what they considered unwarranted federal interference with local schools. When twenty-nine white teachers were assigned to the Attucks facility, five of them resigned.[48]

While IPS tried to come up with a plan that would satisfy the various elements of the Indianapolis community and at the same time comply with the demands of the Justice Department, opponents to any changes became more shrill. Residents of the Northwest High School area organized Citizens for Quality Schools, announced plans to organize resistance to the Justice Department suit, and warned that they would take legal action to oppose involuntary assignment of teachers. A new school superintendent (Stanley Campbell) who hoped to be able to satisfy the Justice Department became an object of abuse and was dismissed. In an effort to show compliance with Justice Department demands, the school board at one point proposed to phase out both Attucks and Shortridge and to build a new Attucks in a different location. The Justice Department rejected the proposal because Attucks would have continued as a segregated school for at least three more years under the plan.[49]

The long-awaited trial did not take place until August 1971. The judge in the case was Dillin, who had been appointed to the bench by President Kennedy.[50]

At the trial, Justice Department lawyers presented an eighty-two-page report detailing the charges of de jure segregation by IPS and asked the court to order measures that would eliminate segregation "root and branch." On their side, lawyers for IPS denied the charges and insisted that racially identifiable schools were entirely the result of residential patterns and not due to policies of the school board.[51]

On August 18, Judge Dillin handed down a lengthy decision, finding IPS guilty of de jure segregation. In reaching the decision, he was following closely the guidelines written by Chief Justice Warren Burger in the case of *Swann* v. *Charlotte-Mecklenburg Board of Education,* which had been decided by a unanimous court the previous

April. In the decision, which upheld busing as an appropriate remedy to bring about the dismantling of a segregated school system, Burger pointed out a number of practices that might be used to maintain a dual system—including choosing locations for new schools and drawing school attendance boundaries, among others, to reinforce current patterns—and thus perpetuate unlawful segregation.[52]

In his opinion, Dillin cited IPS's drawing of school districts as a method of perpetuating segregation. Evidence presented by the Justice Department showed that of over 360 boundary changes since 1954, more than 90 percent had promoted segregation. "Feeder" elementary school districts had been drawn to prevent assignment of white pupils to Attucks. As the school population increased, the board had built additions to existing Negro schools instead of transferring black children to white schools with vacant classrooms. The board chose sites for new high schools on the edges of the city so as to minimize black enrollment. Having found IPS guilty, Dillin ordered the board to take the following steps: 1) immediately reassign personnel to ensure that no school was racially identifiable from the composition of faculty and staff; 2) immediately move to desegregate and relocate Attucks; 3) review transfer policies; 4) negotiate with suburban school corporations for possible transfer of minority students.[53]

In the first part of his opinion, Dillin stayed closely within the guidelines of *Swann v. Charlotte-Mecklenburg Board of Education.* However, he recognized that the steps he ordered would not lead to significant or lasting desegregation. In the second, more innovative part of his decision, he sought remedies that would lead to long-term desegregation. Although a plan that covered Indianapolis alone would furnish no lasting solution, the possibility of resegregation would be minimized if all schools in Marion County (the area included in the recently adopted UniGov law) and perhaps those in adjoining counties were included in the remedy.[54]

The UniGov law, adopted in 1969 *after* the Justice Department brought suit against IPS, consolidated some offices and powers of the city government of Indianapolis and Marion County, but it expressly provided that school corporations were not to be affected. In Marion County outside the boundaries of IPS, there were eight township school corporations and two more in the incorporated towns of Beech Grove and Speedway. Blacks made up only 2.62 percent of school enrollments in the outlying school systems, and out of more than three thousand teachers only fifteen were African Americans.[55]

Questions regarding the state's responsibility for perpetuating segregation by passage of the UniGov law and other actions led Dillin to order that the State of Indiana be made a defendant in the desegregation case and that school corporations outside the boundaries of IPS also be made defendants. Following Dillin's decision, the Indianapolis school board voted, by a margin of four to three, to appeal. A few days later, John Moss, a local black attorney, filed a motion to intervene in the case in behalf of added defendants Donney Buckley and Alycia Buckley as representing a class of Negro children of school age in Marion County. In his motion, Moss asked the federal court to require that defendants in the case submit a plan that conformed to the Equal Protection Clause of the Fourteenth Amendment, and he asked that parts

Federal Judge S. Hugh Dillin in 1971. Indianapolis *Star*.

of the UniGov law be declared unconstitutional. Thereafter, John Moss and his associate, John Preston Ward, played a more active and aggressive role in the litigation than the Justice Department lawyers.[56]

In February 1973, the Seventh Circuit Court of Appeals upheld Dillin's decision that IPS was guilty of de jure segregation, finding "a purposeful pattern of racial discrimination based on the aggregate of many decisions of the board and its agents." In June, the United States Supreme Court denied an appeal for review by the Indianapolis school board.[57]

While upholding Dillin's decision that IPS was guilty, the Seventh Circuit Court of Appeals sent back to the district court the question of determining the responsibility of the State of Indiana and the issue of whether the suburban school corporations should be included in the remedy for segregation in IPS.[58]

At the second trial before the district court in the summer of 1973, the Justice Department, now reflecting the Nixon administration's opposition to busing as a remedy for school segregation, sought a city-only plan. Moss, the attorney for local plaintiffs, rejected that approach and urged a unified school system for all of Marion County, arguing that UniGov was an act of legislative gerrymandering that denied minority students educational opportunities equal to those that students were offered in the township schools.

Much of the trial was consumed with the question of whether the state was responsible for perpetuating segregation. While lawyers for the state insisted that schools were entirely under local control in which the state had no part, Dillin cited voluminous evidence regarding the part that state agencies played in school systems. His decision found that the State Superintendent and State Board of Education had failed to fulfill their legal obligations to prevent continued school segregation.[59]

While holding that suburban school corporations had not been guilty of perpetuating de jure segregation, since there were virtually no black students in the suburbs, Dillin concluded that a lasting remedy to segregation in IPS was impossible without including the suburban schools. This would mean busing African American students from IPS to suburban schools, which the suburbs adamantly opposed on the grounds of opposition to "forced" busing, although most white children within their districts were bused to township schools. Dillin said that the General Assembly had the power to create a metropolitan school system for the whole of Marion County and urged that this be done; but he also said that if the legislature failed to act in a reasonable time, he would devise his own plan under his powers of equity.[60]

Although litigation dragged on for another eight years, for the most part Dillin's 1973 rulings were upheld and ultimately carried out. But the immediate reactions to his decision were principally cries of outrage by state officials and by whites, especially those who lived in the suburbs. Throughout the prolonged legal battle, suburban school corporations fought any desegregation plan that would involve busing students outside the boundaries of IPS, and they hired lawyers from the most prestigious and expensive law firms in Indianapolis to do so.

Judge Niblack and Dan Burton, a future member of Congress, began a movement to impeach Dillin, denouncing his decision as "unconstitutional, unlawful, and dictatorial."[61]

Nevertheless, although it refused to create a metropolitan school system for Marion County, the General Assembly complied with Dillin's instructions in creating legislation that would fulfill its obligations to desegregate the schools. In a lengthy measure dealing with court-ordered transfers of students from one school corporation to another, the law provided formulas for paying costs of transportation and tuition and distributing state funds.[62]

In August 1974, the Seventh Circuit Court of Appeals upheld Dillin's decision on the state's responsibility for perpetuating segregation but sent back to the district court the crucial question of whether the UniGov law was an attempt to perpetuate segregation and thus warranted an interdistrict remedy for segregation in IPS. In another opinion, Dillin found that, since evidence showed the UniGov law would not have been adopted without a provision explicitly excluding township schools, the law was intended to perpetuate segregation and, therefore, gave him authority to order busing to the township schools. At a trial resulting from an appeal on this decision, a majority of the justices of the Seventh Circuit Court of Appeals agreed that the UniGov provision for schools was racially motivated and justified an interdistrict remedy for segregation in IPS. This appeared to settle the issue of the state's responsibility for perpetuating de jure segregation.[63]

Meanwhile, though the question of an interdistrict remedy remained unsettled, important changes were taking place in IPS. The Citizens School Committee was in disarray, and its candidates lost elections to the school board. The seven members elected in 1976 were candidates of a group named CHOICE (Citizens Helping Our Indianapolis Children's Education). They favored measures to integrate the Indianapolis schools and IPS teachers, but they opposed Dillin's plan for one-way busing of African American students to the suburbs as discriminatory to those students on the grounds that it "cast the whole burden of desegregation on those whose rights were violated." Furthermore, they argued that one-way busing would lead to the dismissal of a substantial number of IPS teachers as IPS school population declined. Instead, the CHOICE board urged a unitary school system for all of Marion County, and if this was adopted, they favored busing from the township schools to IPS schools.[64]

Blacks and pro-integration white groups continued to protest against the injustice of one-way busing and its probable effect on IPS. Meanwhile, as litigation dragged on, the court of appeals ordered that an Indianapolis-only plan for desegregation be put into effect. This order presented new problems to the IPS board. Implementation meant drawing new school districts and making painful decisions to close some neighborhood schools. Compliance also required extensive busing within the IPS area. Some busing for desegregation had begun in 1973, but the numbers of students now involved were to be much larger. Over protests from neighborhood groups and threats of defiance, large scale two-way busing of blacks and whites within IPS boundaries began in September 1980.[65]

In a final opinion in the Indianapolis suit, the Seventh Circuit Court of Appeals affirmed one-way busing from Indianapolis to township schools as a remedy for segregation in IPS, noting that within the boundaries of pre-UniGov Indianapolis both black and white pupils would be bused. In October 1980 the Supreme Court again refused to grant a review of the Indianapolis case, as it had consistently done on previous appeals, and both IPS and state and township officials bowed to the inevitable.[66]

Buses to the suburban schools finally began to roll at the beginning of the 1981–82 school year. By that date the white press and civic leaders had changed from protesting court orders to urging peaceful compliance with them. A group of civic leaders organized an advisory council they called PRIDE (Peaceful Response to Indianapolis Desegregation Education). Mayor William Hudnut, who as a member of Congress had strongly opposed busing as a remedy for segregation, proclaimed the weekend before the opening of schools "School Desegregation With Pride" weekend. With rare exceptions suburban schools opened their doors to African Americans from IPS without disorder.[67]

The final orders for interdistrict busing did not include Speedway and Beech Grove (which retained a special status under UniGov), and two other townships in Marion County, Washington and Pike, were also excluded because their schools already had

sizable African American enrollments. This meant that six suburban townships—
Lawrence, Warren, Franklin, Perry, Decatur, and Wayne—were designated to receive
about 6,000 students from IPS.[68]

Several legal questions remained unanswered. When it became evident to opponents that interdistrict busing would be ordered, a number of bills intended to prevent the state's paying monetary costs were introduced to the General Assembly, but
none of them passed both houses. Dillin ruled that the state of Indiana, having been
found guilty of perpetuating unlawful segregation, should pay the costs of transporting
students to the township schools, and the governor grudgingly agreed.[69]

After the legal questions appeared to be settled, human relations problems arising
from desegregation both in IPS and in the township schools remained.[70]

The Justice Department suit against the Indianapolis Public Schools was more prolonged than any other litigation over school desegregation in Indiana, and the remedy was the only one that imposed one-way interdistrict busing as a remedy. But there
were numerous other desegregation suits settled by court rulings or consent decrees,
including the Evansville-Vanderburgh County case previously mentioned.

In 1967 United States District Judge Cale Holder ordered the closing of two predominantly black elementary schools in Kokomo as part of a settlement of a suit
brought by the local NAACP. In Terre Haute, where black students made up only
about 6 percent of the school population, the director of the Indiana Civil Rights
Commission brought a complaint in 1973 that led to a consent agreement for re-
districting to bring about racial balance in each school for both pupils and faculty
members.[71]

In Muncie, where schools had never been segregated officially, racial troubles at
Southside High School led to an investigation by the state advisory committee to the
U.S. Commission on Civil Rights and the Indiana Civil Rights Commission in 1968.
This led to an inconclusive suit against the Muncie school authorities, but in 1971
they began a voluntary program for further desegregation.[72]

In larger cities in the northern part of the state where there had been no official
segregation—Fort Wayne and South Bend—increasing black populations and their
limited access to housing led to predominantly black schools. In 1968 the office of
Civil Rights of the U.S. Department of Health and Welfare (the same agency that had
begun the investigation of Indianapolis schools) began to investigate possible violations of the Civil Rights Act of 1964 in Fort Wayne. They found some evidence of
gerrymandering of school districts, creating optional school districts, and possible
violation in selection of sites for new schools. More than 73 percent of minority pupils
(blacks and Hispanics) were enrolled in schools with predominantly minority enrollments. There was also evidence of discrimination in teacher assignments. After
this initial inquiry the Justice Department started a full investigation, and black parents produced evidence of discrimination. However, lawyers for the Justice Department decided that the evidence was insufficient to initiate a lawsuit.

The Indiana Civil Rights Commission later charged the school system with discrimination in hiring and promotion of teachers. As a result, school authorities un-

dertook a reorganization plan that included closing six elementary schools with predominantly black enrollments and negotiating an agreement about minority teacher assignments. African American parents complained that the plan, which involved busing black pupils to predominantly white schools, placed the entire burden of desegregation on the black community, and their complaints continued after the plan was implemented.[73]

In South Bend, where by the 1970s about one-fifth of public school pupils were African Americans, a civil suit was brought against the South Bend Community Schools in 1966. The case was settled the following year by a five-year reorganization plan involving new construction to replace some existing buildings, including Central High School, and new attendance zones to bring about racial balance. This plan led to busing about 1,900 pupils. However, complaints over racial imbalance continued, and more busing went into effect at the beginning of the 1981 school year.[74]

A full account of desegregation of colleges and universities in Indiana would require more research than the author has been able to carry out and require more space than this volume permits. What follows is a brief summary.

The 1949 law abolishing segregation in public institutions applied to state colleges and universities as well as to elementary and secondary schools. However, the press gave little attention to segregation at institutions of higher learning, partly because their policies were established by administrations and boards of trustees outside of local jurisdictions and because very few African Americans attended them in comparison with the number of white students. Press coverage of black college students was usually limited to athletes, who were often the most valuable players on college and university teams, to such matters as elections of African American beauty queens, and to sensational events, such as racial disorders; there was little attention to numbers of blacks enrolled and rates of retention.

Before the Second World War, black students at Indiana University were excluded from university dormitories, did not pay dues to the Student Union, and were not allowed to eat in the university cafeterias. They were also excluded from honorary and professional organizations. Privately owned eating-places near campus openly displayed signs that said, "We serve white patrons only."[75]

Things began to change during and following the war years. Returning veterans, white as well as black, gave an impetus to change, and the GI Bill of Rights brought more African Americans to Bloomington. In 1945 a student branch of NAACP was organized.

The university opened a dormitory for "colored girls" in 1944, and African American women were admitted to all university residence halls in 1947. The following year, male students were also admitted to university housing, and university cafeterias, barbershops, and recreational facilities were opened to all students. Access to privately owned restaurants presented greater barriers until the state legislature passed a stronger public accommodations law in 1963 and created a Civil Rights Commission with enforcement powers.[76]

Both Indiana and Purdue Universities, as well as Notre Dame, announced in 1956 that they would not compete with athletic teams of institutions that barred African American players.

At Purdue University, where before the Second World War most students were males enrolled in engineering or agriculture and where white students and faculty were less sensitive to racial issues than in Bloomington, enrollment of black students came slowly.[77]

After the war, the curriculum at Purdue was greatly broadened and new programs, many leading to the Ph.D. degree, were introduced in languages, literature, history, and psychology. The new programs made deep changes in the student body and brought in large numbers of new faculty members, many of whom were more interested in social and political issues than the older professors. Nevertheless, in spite of the changed atmosphere, the number of African American students grew slowly, partly because the location of the university offered few opportunities for students who needed to work.

In the years after the war, the two state teachers' colleges, Ball State in Muncie and Indiana State in Terre Haute, grew rapidly and expanded their curricula; they also hired many new faculty members and were granted the status of universities. During the sixties, the Indiana Civil Rights Commission worked actively with all the state universities as well as with some private institutions to eliminate discrimination and promote racial harmony.[78]

Adoption by Congress of the Civil Rights Act of 1964 gave a further impetus to eliminating discriminatory practices and to recruiting African American students. The law provided for withholding federal aid to schools that discriminated against racial minorities and caused many private as well as state institutions to increase their efforts to recruit African American students and faculty members.

8

The
Turbulent
Sixties

During the 1960s, race and race-related issues appeared to dominate the national scene. These were the years when Martin Luther King Jr. and nonviolent protest over-shadowed other events in the South and deeply influenced developments in the North—the years of the marches in Birmingham and Selma and student sit-ins. Partly as the result of these events, Congress passed the Civil Rights Act of 1964, the Voting Rights Act of 1965, and finally the Housing Act of 1968; and African Americans appeared to have won recognition of full citizenship rights at last.

But the 1960s were also a decade of increasing violence, particularly as the civil rights movement, previously centered in the South, moved into the cities of the North. It was also a decade of assassinations—President John F. Kennedy in 1963, Malcolm X in 1965, Martin Luther King Jr. in 1968, and a few months later, Robert F. Kennedy. There had been urban riots earlier, notably in Los Angeles and Detroit, but the assassination of King sparked riots nationwide.

Developments in Indiana reflected national trends, but there was little violence. After years of delaying tactics, the General Assembly finally enacted a series of civil rights measures that in some cases were adopted earlier and were stronger than the laws adopted by Congress.

Movements in the South influenced actions in Indiana. Sit-ins at southern lunch counters inspired sit-ins in Woolworth stores by youth groups in Indianapolis, Gary, and other cities. The 1959 appearance of Martin Luther King Jr. at a YMCA "Monster Meeting" in Cadle Tabernacle, the largest auditorium in Indianapolis, had widespread influence. There King proclaimed, "A new age of justice that is dawning for the Negro challenges him to love even his oppressors." King warned members of his race against attitudes of bitterness and recriminations against old injustices and cautioned, "We must learn to live together as brothers or we will die as fools." After King had made several other appearances in the city, Rev. Andrew Brown of St. John's Missionary Baptist Church took the lead in organizing an Indianapolis affiliate of the Southern Christian Leadership Conference (SCLC), and that group then formed a branch of Breadbasket, the SCLC offshoot concerned with efforts to improve the economic condition of poor blacks.[1]

The Indianapolis SCLC was but one of many African American protest groups that appeared in the state capital and other Indiana cities during the 1960s. A branch of CORE (Congress of Racial Equality), an organization that preceded SCLC and also emphasized nonviolence and peaceful protest, played a significant part in Indianapolis in registering black voters and worked, albeit unsuccessfully, for the desegregation of Attucks High School. John Torian, a twenty-six-year-old graduate of Tech High School, founded the CORE chapter in Indianapolis in 1964. Also a member of the NAACP, Torian expressed respect for the older organization with its "solid broad basis" but added, "We also need a smaller group like CORE that is more daring, more militant . . . a sort of shock troops in sensitive areas that other organizations are afraid to touch."[2]

While CORE and the NAACP shared the same goals, other groups preached "black power" and "black nationalism." The Black Muslims, disciples of Elijah Muhammed, who denounced white Christians as "white devils," made an appearance in Indi-

Members of CORE being arrested during a sit-in at the Indianapolis School Board building to protest school segregation and the segregation of teaching staffs in Indianapolis public schools, July 1964; CORE protesters, front to back, were John Torian, Alfonzo Black, and James Pond. Indianapolis *Star*.

anapolis in 1959, but their numbers were small and did not appear to grow. The president of the NAACP denounced them for preaching violence, but Dr. Joseph Taylor, director of Flanner House, blamed the community for permitting the social inequities that gave rise to such movements: "A social order which leaves a race largely frustrated also leaves them susceptible to those who promise to give them things they've been deprived of."[3]

Although the police viewed them with suspicion, the Muslims did not overtly advocate violence against whites, but the Black Panthers, who appeared in the late 1960s, were avowedly a revolutionary movement. The Indiana Panthers were headed by Fred Crawford, who had been associated with the organization in Oakland, California. The Panthers described themselves as a political party with the goal of helping black people gain control of their own communities, and they supported armed revolution if necessary to "free the black man." Crawford told a reporter from the Indianapolis *News*, "I don't feel we can gain our freedom without a revolution. This could only happen if the white man raised his feet off the black man's neck, but I don't think he'll ever do that."[4]

Compared with the Muslims and the Panthers, the NAACP, which remained the state's largest and most influential African American organization in the campaign for civil rights, was indeed moderate. Whereas it had once been denounced as "radical" and "militant," the Indianapolis *Times* now spoke of the NAACP as the "mature, organized bi-racial" movement for integration in contrast to the "noisy sit-ins and boycotts which mark the new-born Negro rights groups."[5]

However, NAACP leaders differed among themselves over matters of strategy. Virginia Davis, president of the Indianapolis branch in 1964, was less of an activist than Andrew Ramsey, president of the state conference. Ramsey frequently assailed Indianapolis blacks for their lethargy and failure to demand their rights and criticized Mrs. Davis for her cautious approach to problems, which he characterized as saying, "Let's not do this or that or we might get into trouble." Nevertheless, in spite of his militant statements, Ramsey and the NAACP had broad support from whites and white organizations.[6]

Apprehension over the growth of black radicalism was also a factor prompting leaders from both races to join together in 1965 to establish an affiliate of the National Urban League in Indianapolis. The Gary Urban League played an important role in race relations in that city, as did affiliates in Fort Wayne and South Bend in their communities. There were also leagues in Elkhart, Marion, and Anderson. However, several factors had prevented formation of a league in the state's largest city. Both African Americans and white leaders who wanted an Indianapolis Urban League cited the opposition of Flanner House and the influence of Cleo Blackburn, its powerful director, who had the support of ultraconservative white members on the Flanner House board. Willard Ransom, in an interview with the Indianapolis *News,* said Flanner House feared that an Urban League would take over some of its functions and lessen its financial support. Some white conservatives were undoubtedly also suspicious of any kind of a "national" organization.[7]

However, by 1964 there were powerful white leaders, including bankers and business executives, who recognized the growing influence and discontent of African Americans and supported the legitimacy of their demands, and they were meeting privately with black leaders and negotiating with officers of the National Urban League. Among the most influential of the founders were Thomas Binford, a white industrialist and banker, chairman of the health, education, welfare committee of the recently created Greater Indianapolis Progress Committee, and Richardson, the black attorney, who was also later to serve for several years as president of the Indianapolis league. Chartered in December 1965, the Indianapolis Urban League was soon firmly established with a biracial board of directors that included clergymen, bankers, and businessmen as well as social workers, members of the League of Women Voters, the Council of Jewish Women, and other public-spirited men and women. Sam Jones, a social worker who had been serving as executive director of the St. Paul–

Minneapolis Urban League, was brought to Indianapolis as director of the new affiliate and was later given the title of president.[8]

National Urban League policy prohibited its affiliates from engaging in political activity, in contrast to the NAACP. While NAACP branches were not supposed to engage in partisan politics, one of the organization's most important functions was lobbying for and against national, state, and local legislation. The NAACP had played an important part in writing the 1949 school law, rallying for its public support, and trying (unsuccessfully) to enact other civil rights laws during the 1950s. In the changing political atmosphere of the 1960s, the Indiana branches and their members spearheaded coalitions that lobbied successfully for effective civil rights laws.

The Federation of Associated Clubs of Indianapolis held a dinner in 1959 for lawmakers who supported civil rights legislation: *left to right,* Birch Bayh, James Hunter, unidentified, Robert L. Brokenburr, Henry J. Richardson, Jr., Jesse L. Dickinson, unidentified, unidentified, Mercer Mance, Matthew Welsh, unidentified, Starling James. Indianapolis *Recorder* Collection, Indiana Historical Society.

In 1960, both gubernatorial candidates, Democrat Matthew E. Welsh and Republican Crawford Parker, promised to support civil rights. At a rally in Indianapolis, Welsh gave the strongest commitment yet made by a candidate for governor. He called for an effective fair employment law, decent housing without discrimination, and improved educational opportunities for blacks; and he said that no person should be denied service in any hotel or restaurant because of race and promised to strengthen existing laws on public accommodations. He concluded by saying, "Your Indiana government must set the moral tone with bold, imaginative action—under the leadership of a Governor who is indignant enough about the present conditions to do something about them."[9]

At a pivotal meeting to form the Indiana Conference on Civil Rights Legislation, a coalition representing a broad spectrum of organizations and interests, Governor-elect Welsh promised to ask the General Assembly for a strong fair employment practices law as well as legislation to end discrimination in housing and in hotels and restaurants. The meeting also called for creation of a Commission on Human Rights to administer civil rights laws.[10]

In the General Assembly that convened in 1961, a public accommodations bill that also included provisions against discrimination in housing was introduced in the Democratic-controlled senate and was passed by a large margin. In the lower house, where Republicans were in the majority, the bill was drastically altered. Enforcement provisions were eliminated, and provisions against discrimination in housing were to apply only to housing owned by cities, towns, or the state.[11]

While the General Assembly deliberated, peaceful public rallies reinforced lobbying for the public accommodations bill. Supporters in the house of representatives made strenuous efforts to restore the language of the senate version. But the minority report, submitted by Hunter and Birch Bayh, was rejected. The weakened version passed the house by a vote of 89 to 9. Some senate Democrats argued that the bill should be scuttled, but Governor Welsh urged its adoption as the best possible bill under the circumstances. After his intervention, the senate voted to adopt the house version. The law as finally enacted strengthened the 1885 law by providing for criminal penalties and allowing individuals to initiate actions if the prosecutor failed to act.[12]

Meanwhile another, less controversial bill, dealing principally with discrimination in employment and creating a Civil Rights Commission, was introduced in the senate and passed both houses. The commission was not only authorized to hear complaints about employment practices, it was also empowered to receive written complaints of violations of the public accommodations law, to carry on investigations— even "in the absence of complaints when [the commission] deems it in the public interest"—and to transmit recommendations to the General Assembly.[13]

The laws that were finally adopted gave little protection against discrimination in housing, and groups that had worked so hard for a public accommodations law were disappointed that the Civil Rights Commission was given power only to investigate and make recommendations.

But the personality and performance of Harold Hatcher, whom Welsh appointed as the first director of the Civil Rights Commission, did much to convince both the public and the legislators that civil rights laws served a legitimate purpose; his leadership in investigating discriminatory practices and their effects and in collecting statistics paved the way for a stronger law adopted in 1963.[14]

In 1962, Governor Welsh promised to work for stronger civil rights legislation in the next General Assembly, but Democrats lost control of the senate in the 1962 elections, with the result that Republicans controlled both houses of the state legislature in 1963. Early in the session a stronger public accommodations bill, backed by the Civil Rights Commission, was introduced in the senate. The bill included stronger enforcement provisions, but to the disappointment of many African Americans, it did not include provisions about housing. It passed the senate with some amendments by a margin of 45 to 2. When the measure seemed to have bogged down in the house of representatives, the reactivated Conference on Civil Rights began intensive lobbying, and in the closing days of the session the lower house passed the senate bill with few amendments by a vote of 336 to 7.

Declaring that equal educational and employment opportunities and equal access to and use of public accommodations are civil rights, the law provided that the Civil Rights Commission was to induce compliance by persuasion and conciliation if possible. It was empowered upon receiving written complaints to make preliminary investigations, to hold public hearings, subpoena witnesses, take testimony under oath, and examine books and papers. Refusal to obey a subpoena constituted contempt, punishable by a circuit or superior court. The commission could issue cease-and-desist orders against persons found to have engaged in discriminatory practices and order them to take "affirmative action" to carry out the purposes of the law. Decisions of the commission were subject to court review, but in the absence of an appeal for judicial review, the commission could obtain a court decree for enforcement of its orders.[15]

Adoption of the 1963 law was a major step toward achieving the legislative goals of civil rights advocates. The fact that it did not include provisions against discrimination in housing was no doubt an important reason why lawmakers who had been unwilling to accept parts of the 1961 bill were now willing to give significant powers to the Civil Rights Commission.

The reluctance of a large part of the white public to accept government interference with their rights to buy, sell, and rent real estate was reinforced by powerful real estate interests, and adoption of a fair housing law proved more difficult than other legislative goals. Debate over local fair housing laws and actions by some city councils preceded adoption of state laws and paved the way for them.

Some of the obstacles faced by African Americans received fresh publicity in a hearing sponsored by the U.S. Civil Rights Commission in Indianapolis in 1963. William T. Ray, former president of the Indianapolis NAACP and one of the city's most successful black realtors, testified that Negroes were denied housing in 90 percent of Marion County by discriminatory policies of the Indianapolis Real Estate Board, which had an unwritten law not to show houses to prospective Negro buyers unless there were already two Negro families in the city block. The president of the board denied Ray's accusation, and while he admitted that the rules of the board barred Negroes from membership, he said he would personally be happy to see applications for membership decided "strictly on merit." The board presented a written statement to the commission that reflected the dominant thinking of white realtors: "It is our opinion that attitudes and feelings of relatively long standing cannot be made to disap-

Gary Mayor A. Martin Katz, pictured here with singer Mahalia Jackson, signed an Omnibus Civil
Rights Bill for Gary in 1965. Calumet Regional Archives, Indiana University Northwest.

pear overnight and that many ill-advised attempts to force integration and housing have done serious harm to the cause of good race relations."[16]

Meanwhile, an open housing ordinance introduced in Gary's city council in July 1963 was rejected by a vote of 6 to 3 along racial lines, and whites in suburban Glen Park formed an organization called the National Association for the Advancement of White People. In September 1963, following Martin Luther King Jr.'s March on Washington, organized protests against Gary's "ghettoized housing" were held. The following year, after his election as new mayor, A. Martin Katz urged creation of a Human Relations Council with power to combat discrimination in housing and other areas; but the ordinance, which was opposed by the Gary Board of Realtors and the Chamber of Commerce, was defeated by the city council by one vote. A few months later, after a council member resigned and was replaced by an appointee of Mayor Katz, the council passed an open housing ordinance by a margin of 5 to 3. The commission appointed to enforce the law had some success in opening the sale of private homes and in opening apartment rentals to blacks, but as a few African Americans appeared in hitherto all-white neighborhoods, many whites decided to move to the suburbs.[17]

Two African Americans were elected to Indianapolis's city council in 1963—Rufus Kuykendall, a Republican, and Rev. James Cummings, a Democrat—and they introduced an ordinance outlawing discrimination in the sale or renting of housing in 1964. The proposal was intended to increase the power of the Mayor's Human Rights Commission by giving it authority to subpoena and to turn evidence of discrimination over to the prosecutor. The Indianapolis Chamber of Commerce, which at first opposed the proposed ordinance, invited a select group of black leaders to a carefully planned dinner in a downtown hotel. At the beginning of the meeting, a member of the chamber read a statement denouncing the proposal and then asked the assembled African Americans their opinions. Second to speak was former state senator Robert Brokenburr, now seventy-seven years old. Brokenburr, a Republican who had long been considered among the most politically conservative members of his race and who was noted for his conciliatory attitude toward the white establishment, rose to his feet and, to the surprise of his audience, endorsed much of the tactics of activist groups in the civil rights movement, including sit-ins and picketing so long as they were lawful. "Anything that can be done legitimately to stir up the conscience of Indianapolis and America should be done," he said. "This is not only for the good of Negroes, but for the good of the whole country." He asked, "Can you move too fast in getting what is rightfully yours?" As for the proposed ordinance, he said, "There is no point in waiting any longer. We might as well face up to the issue. The time to act is now." Two days later the executive board of the Chamber of Commerce met and drafted a statement quite different from the one they had originally intended. It recognized that discrimination against Negroes in housing "clearly cannot be justified in any moral or economic consideration." This statement was subsequently presented to the meeting of the city council, which then passed the housing ordinance by a 5 to 4 vote.[18]

The Indianapolis ordinance was adopted as the presidential campaign was under way. In November, for the first time since 1936, Indiana cast its electoral votes for the Democratic presidential candidate. The election of President Lyndon Johnson was accompanied by the election of Democrat Roger Branigan as governor and by the election of Democrats to state offices. Branigan, a brilliant lawyer, was less dedicated to civil rights than Governor Welsh had been; he was quoted as saying that he favored "gradualism" in accomplishing the ideal of equal rights for all and that there were penalties in "pressing beyond the point of public acceptance."

The Indiana Conference on Civil Rights Legislation made a fair housing law its priority for the 1965 meeting of the General Assembly. John Preston Ward, vice chairman of the conference, pointed out that blacks had turned out in record numbers to vote for Democrats and expected the party to support civil rights legislation.[19]

When the legislature convened, Senator David Rogers of Bloomington sponsored a bill to amend the existing Civil Rights Law to ban discrimination in the sale or rental of real property and to extend the authority of the Civil Rights Commission to issue cease-and-desist orders to include sales of real estate and rentals. As expected, the Indiana Real Estate Association lobbied against the bill, and in the senate the cease-and-desist provisions in the original bill were amended to cover only public housing and federally financed housing. In this watered-down form, the bill passed the upper house and went to the house of representatives, where there were efforts to restore the bill to its original form. In its final form, as passed by both houses and signed by the governor, the law applied only to houses of more than four or more units. While the measure was being debated, the Indiana Conference on Civil Rights sponsored a march in which citizens from Gary, East Chicago, Fort Wayne, and Muncie came to Indianapolis to protest against the emasculation of the bill.[20]

After the measure had passed both houses, civil rights leaders continued to protest. Ward said it appeared that the Democratic Party owned the Negro vote and "did not fear reprisals even when it betrayed campaign promises." The bill as enacted, he said, applied only to a small fraction of houses and insulted the intelligence of blacks who had voted for Democrats.[21]

The amendments adopted at the next two sessions of the legislature strengthened the 1965 law and expanded the authority of the Civil Rights Commission. The new law covered all housing, including homes that were owner-occupied. The 1969 law also sought to eliminate "block busting" instigated by real estate brokers. It provided that licenses of real estate brokers and salesmen be revoked if they engaged in "unlawful discrimination" by appealing to race prejudice or fear to persuade owners to list their property for sale.[22]

In spite of the state's reputation for political conservatism, Indiana lawmakers moved earlier than Congress in enacting civil rights legislation. The laws of 1961 and 1963 that gave the Indiana Civil Rights Commission authority to act against discrimination in access to public accommodations and employment were adopted before the federal Civil Rights Law of 1964. The housing laws were in some respects stronger than the Federal Housing Law that Congress finally passed after the assassination of Martin Luther King Jr. Nevertheless, the existence of federal laws enhanced respect both for Indiana laws and for the Indiana Civil Rights Commission, and the existence of federal agencies such as the Equal Employment Opportunity Commission supplemented the work of the state commission.[23]

NAACP Freedom Rally, 1963, Indianapolis. Indianapolis
Recorder Collection, Indiana Historical Society.

Civil rights laws, in Indiana as elsewhere in the United States, were enacted by legislatures that were made up almost entirely of white members and in which African Americans formed a tiny minority; and although blacks spearheaded lobbying efforts, the laws would not have been adopted without the support of powerful white groups. For many whites, racial justice had become a compelling moral issue. After the adoption of the Civil Rights Law of 1963, Governor Welsh said that the "forthright role played by men and women of all faiths" was of major importance in the adoption of the law.[24]

Although the number of black elected officials remained very small, interest in political issues and political activity among African Americans increased in the 1960s. Developments in the South influenced attitudes of both blacks and whites. White organizations and lawmakers could not consistently denounce racism in the South while ignoring racial discrimination at home. Many previously indifferent African Americans were aroused to vote by television news reports of the reprisals that their brothers and sisters in the South encountered by merely attempting to vote.

In 1963, memorial services attended by black community leaders at St. John Missionary Baptist church in memory of Medgar Evers, the slain president of the Mississippi NAACP, led to formation of the Social Action Council, with Rev. Andrew Brown as president. NAACP member Herman Walker, the president of the AFL-CIO local meatpackers union, became executive director of the new group and explained that the new organization was intended to be an action arm of the NAACP, "not tied down by rules and regulations." Ransom was vice-president and Fay Williams, secretary. The first project of the Social Action Council was a highly successful voter registration drive, carried out with the support of the NAACP and CORE and in which CORE's Torian played an important part. Long lines of new voters, some of them old people who had never voted before, waited patiently to register. An African American veteran of the Korean War told a reporter, "Let's face it, civil rights is what's bringing them out. It's not the candidates or the issues here that's important, but what's going on in the South. Everyone's thinking 'If they are actually battling just to vote in Mississippi, at least I ought to go out and vote here.' We're really voting for the folks down there."[25]

Voter registration drive, 1963. Indianapolis *Recorder* Collection, Indiana Historical Society.

The drive resulted in unprecedented numbers of African Americans voting in the city elections in November 1963, and Rev. James Cummings was elected to the city council by the largest number of votes cast, exceeding the number for John Barton, the Democrat who was elected mayor.[26]

The record black vote and the increasing importance of racial issues in national and state politics brought about significant changes in Indianapolis after 1964. Mayor Barton was not regarded as a civil rights activist, but he recognized that current urban needs could not be met by outdated ideologies and policies. One of his most important actions was to appoint the Greater Indianapolis Progress Committee (GIPC), which included some of the city's most influential civic and financial leaders. The new willingness of those local leaders to accept federal aid was a significant change of policy that emerged in the 1960s. As one member of the committee said, "People realized the situation was getting worse year after year and nothing could be done about it. They were hearing the same old clichés about letting free enterprise do it. But many things can't be done by free enterprise because there is no profit in doing them." Another member said, "Now the highway problem comes along [the plan for a federal interstate highway to be routed directly through densely populated black neighborhoods], with 20,000 persons to be displaced. We've yakked and yakked about free enterprise, but when a family can pay only $40 dollars a month or less, I defy anyone to build them housing on a reasonable dividend basis."[27]

An August 1965 GIPC report endorsed federal aid for public housing that would "encourage a healthy racial mixture within the community" and said that families displaced by the planned new federal highway should be given "official encouragement to relocate in any available housing" in any location in the city. In accepting and endorsing the committee report, Mayor Barton said it was "most timely in light of the (racial) explosions in other parts of the country."[28]

African Americans made up more than half of Gary's population by the mid-1960s, and racial issues, race prejudice, and the increasing political power of blacks were far more conspicuous there than in Indianapolis. Although they made up more than half the population, blacks were confined to only about one-fourth of the city's housing units, and the dwindling white population of the city and the growing white population of the suburbs sought to prevent blacks from spreading into white areas, in spite of state and city fair housing laws. The fact that white supremacist Governor George Wallace of Alabama campaigned in the area and carried Lake County in the May 1964 Democratic presidential primary furnished clear evidence of the fear and prejudice of white voters. In Gary itself all white precincts gave Wallace a majority of their votes.[29]

However, in spite of white prejudice, an African American, Richard Hatcher, was elected mayor of Gary in November 1967, making him one of the few members of his race to become mayor of a city of more than 100,000 before 1970.

Hatcher was born the twelfth of thirteen children in 1933, during the Great Depression, and grew up in poverty in Michigan City. When his father lost his job with the Pullman Car Company, the family was forced to turn to welfare. Very early in his years in the Michigan City schools, Richard Hatcher decided he wanted to be a lawyer,

Gary attorney and city council member Richard Hatcher campaigning for mayor in 1967.
Calumet Regional Archives, Indiana University Northwest.

though his teachers tried to steer him into vocational courses. He entered Indiana University on an athletic scholarship in 1951 and received additional financial aid from his two older sisters. Hatcher soon learned that he needed more academic preparation and almost "flunked out." He gave up football and worked in a dormitory dining hall. While at the university, he became active in the NAACP and took part in demonstrations against segregated restaurants. He later earned a law degree at Valparaiso University while working full-time in a hospital. After passing the state bar examination in 1959, Hatcher entered legal practice in East Chicago. In 1962 he moved to Gary, where he immediately became involved in politics and civil rights, serving as one of the lawyers in the unsuccessful school desegregation case. (See chapter 7.) He entered the 1963 Democratic primary as a candidate for council member-at-large and was elected through the support of black voters. The city council members chose him to be council president, an unprecedented honor for a freshman member.[30]

While serving as council president in 1966, Hatcher announced he would be a candidate for mayor in 1967. After winning the Democratic nomination in a primary in which he faced two white opponents, he launched a campaign pledging to rid the city of "the shackles of graft, corruption, inefficiency, poverty, racism, and stagnation" of previous administrations. At the same time, he tried to prevent the campaign from degenerating into a "black-white" conflict.[31]

Since the days of the New Deal, Gary had been a solidly Democratic city, and in 1967 the Republican candidate, Joseph Radigan, would have had no hope of winning if Hatcher had not been an African American; but in spite of Hatcher's slogan, "Let's get ourselves together," and his assurances that the honest government he sought was not a racial issue, many white Democrats defected. The white Democratic Lake County chairman, while ostensibly supporting Hatcher, worked behind his back, suggesting that Hatcher was a dangerous radical and that he sympathized with Communism. Most white Democratic precinct chairmen also gave support to the Republican candidate. Partly because of the Democratic chairman's "smear" tactics, several nationally prominent Democrats, including Vice President Hubert Humphrey, Senator Robert Kennedy, and Senator Birch Bayh, became Hatcher's supporters. In November, Hatcher won a narrow victory of 1,865 votes out of a total of 77,759 votes. Ninety-six percent of Gary's African Americans voted for him and only 12 percent of white voters.[32]

During the campaign two political scientists observed that Hatcher "projected an image that black citizens had never before seen in their political leaders. He was young, intelligent, a reputable lawyer, and a capable city council member. Most important, he was down to earth." In his first inaugural address, Hatcher warned hoodlums to leave the city, and he called on business and industry to play a greater role in improving the city. "We cannot solve our problems, we cannot save our city if we are divided," he said. In hopes of placating whites, he named a white chief of police and ordered him to clean up the city.[33]

Hatcher's campaign and election attracted national attention, and his first term was notable for the amount of federal aid he was able to garner for Gary, described by some observers as an "urban laboratory" for President Johnson's "Great Society" experiments. More than $35 million in federal money was pledged by various agencies for housing, urban renewal, antipoverty programs, Head Start, public safety, and other programs. In addition to federal funds, Gary received large grants from private foundations, including the Ford Foundation, the Field Foundation, the Cummins Engine Foundation, and the Congress of Racial Equality.[34]

Two years later, however, after the Nixon administration came into office in 1969, much of the federal funding dried up, and Hatcher's goals of a crime-free city eluded him, despite his antivice campaign. In addition his efforts were marred by disputes with police, firemen, garbage collectors, and social workers.[35]

Hatcher's election gave a tremendous psychological lift to Gary's African American community, but as the political scientists noted, in spite of temporary federal aid, "In no area [of] substantive power to influence the distribution of resources . . . are blacks adequately represented." Black power in the central city was diluted by white control of the county and state government agencies.[36]

During Hatcher's 1967 campaign, Ramsey, in a prescient column in the Indianapolis *Recorder,* spoke of Negroes' gradual "inheritance" of cities as the result of the exodus of whites to the suburbs. He predicted that within fifteen years many cities would have Negro mayors, but that African Americans would remain a minority group in economic and "real power structure." The election of black mayors, he predicted, would come about not as the result of the erosion of racism but because of its increase. Blacks were inheriting dying cities.[37]

While Ramsey's predictions proved to be true for Gary and for many other cities large and small, they were not true for Indianapolis, which continued to have the largest African American population in Indiana. The power of the growing black minority there was diluted by incorporating the white suburbs into the city.

In the 1967 mayoral election in Indianapolis, Democrat John Barton was defeated by Republican Richard Lugar, a former member of the school board and future U.S. Senator. In 1969 a bill "Concerning reorganization of government of counties of the first class"—better known as the UniGov bill—was introduced in the General Assembly largely through the efforts of Mayor Lugar.

The idea of metropolitan government for Marion County was not new, and the possibility of a metropolitan school system had already been debated at length and rejected by the suburban schools. Several countywide agencies had been created by the state legislature and had resulted in a considerable amount of overlapping with city agencies. This situation suggested the desirability of a centralized authority for budget-making and taxation, which prompted Mayor Lugar to appoint a task force headed by the chairmen of the city and county councils to draw up a plan for consolidated government.

At the next session of the General Assembly, where Republicans controlled both houses, the UniGov law passed with little debate as the result of a carefully orchestrated public relations campaign by Lugar and Keith Bulen, Republican chairman of Marion County. The campaign was based on the "concept of metropolitan government, while avoiding arguments on the finer points of the bill," according to the authors of a scholarly analysis of the measure.[38]

The law as finally passed was the product of compromises and concessions to vested government and political interests. Numerous government agencies, including police and fire departments as well as township school corporations, were not included. UniGov provided for a mayor elected by voters from the entire county and a twenty-nine member city-county council, twenty-five from single member districts, four elected at large. Voters in three incorporated communities in the county—Beech Grove, Lawrence, and Speedway—continued to elect their own mayors and councils, while at the same time having the right to vote for the UniGov mayor.[39]

Indianapolis African Americans opposed the UniGov bill from the beginning. Richardson denounced it as "dangerous and maliciously motivated as to race and a political enslavement of minorities and an unfair power grab." The Indiana Conference on Civil and Human Rights opposed the legislation, both because it weakened the political power of black voters and because it excluded schools and metropolitan police and fire departments. Headlines in the Indianapolis *Recorder* cried, "NEGROES OPPOSE LUGAR UNIGOV PLAN," and the front-page article that followed suggested that the main purpose of UniGov was to eliminate the possibility of a black mayor like Hatcher in Indianapolis.[40]

By 1969 all the major legislative goals of civil rights advocates had been achieved through state and federal law. The Indiana Civil Rights Commission had authority to enforce the state laws, while agents of the federal government—EEOC, the U.S. Civil Rights Commission, and the U.S. Department of Justice—were available to hear complaints of violation of federal laws. In addition, all the larger cities in Indiana and many smaller ones had created their own agencies, usually with names like Human Relations Commissions, to hear complaints and enforce remedies.[41]

The adoption of laws and creation of commissions did not, of course, ensure compliance with the intentions of the lawmakers, and it is impossible to measure the results of the legislation with any degree of accuracy because of the effects of extraneous factors and unanticipated conditions. As indicated in the last chapter, implementing the 1949 school law that abolished segregation in public education was hampered by de facto segregation, caused by the concentration of blacks in inner cities and the movement of whites to the suburbs, and by opposition to busing as a remedy. Therefore, genuine racial integration in public schools became impossible.

In contrast to the obstacles associated with school integration, access to public accommodations, long denied to African American citizens in spite of the Civil Rights Act of 1885, came about in most places with relative ease and little friction. The proprietors of restaurants, hotels, theaters, and other places of recreation who had practiced discrimination because of fear of losing white patrons were ready to serve black patrons once strong state and federal laws were enacted.

After the adoption of the 1963 law giving enforcement powers to the Indiana Civil Rights Commission, Governor Welsh issued executive orders to all departments of state government involved in licensing or supervising organizations or persons offering places of "public accommodation" to take action to prevent at all times discrimination because of race, color, creed, or national origin. This meant that businesses like bars, restaurants, and hotels, which were licensed by the Alcoholic Beverage Commission or the Indiana State Board of Health, jeopardized renewal of their licenses if they did not comply. A survey by the Indiana Civil Rights Commission following the adoption of the 1963 law gave a summary of black access to accommodations in sixteen cities. It showed that African Americans expected to be served at nearly all lunch counters in drug and department stores in the state and that they could be served in 80 percent of the restaurants surveyed, the exceptions being small ones in all-white neighborhoods. Blacks could also expect to be turned away from about three out of five cocktail bars and taverns, except for bars in major hotels. Black travelers could expect to find lodging in about 80 percent of downtown hotels and about two-thirds of motels, particularly those that were part of national chains. Nearly all theaters, parks, public recreation centers, and bowling alleys admitted black patrons, but not all skating rinks did. The commission report concluded that "on the basis of present trends, all Indiana public accommodations should be available to citizens regardless of color at an early date."

Later developments appeared to justify this prediction. Complaints over denial of service steadily declined. In 1963 the Civil Rights Commission reported that 32 percent of the complaints filed with it were over access to public accommodations, but that by 1965 that figure had been reduced to 15 percent, and by 1967 there were only a few isolated complaints, which were settled by negotiation.[42] By the end of the 1960s, except in small towns in isolated rural communities, the sight of all-black or racially mixed groups being served in restaurants and bars or registering at motels no longer excited comment. Racial barriers at private clubs persisted, especially at country clubs and golf courses, and resulted in some complaints, but on the whole the battle over "public accommodations" had been won. The general acceptance of the public accommodations law allowed the Civil Rights Commission to devote more attention to discrimination in employment and housing.

Discrimination in employment, like denial of access to public accommodations, rested partly on custom and tradition. For example, testimony at a hearing before the U.S. Civil Rights Commission showed that nearly all African American employees at Allison Division of General Motors, one of the largest employers in Indianapolis, were still in maintenance and janitorial positions in 1963. One woman had only recently been promoted to the shipping department after seventeen years as a janitor, while another woman who attended college for two years had worked as a janitor for twenty years.[43]

A report of the Indiana Civil Rights Commission for the entire state in 1963 showed that blacks were employed in all major job categories, but 85 percent were still concentrated in blue-collar jobs that were most likely to be threatened by automation.[44]

Earlier, in 1961, the state-operated Indiana Employment Security Division had made an effort to weaken the custom of racial categories in employment by announcing that it would no longer deal with employers who listed race as a qualification in their job applications. At about the same time, the Indianapolis newspapers also agreed to end the practice of designating race in their advertisements for employment.[45]

Discrimination by labor unions continued to prevent the employment of African Americans. One black labor leader reported, for example, that blacks continued to be excluded from printing unions. All over the state in various kinds of industries it also appeared that union bargaining agents used antidiscrimination clauses in contracts as tools that could be surrendered at the bargaining table.[46]

The 1963 law gave the Indiana Civil Rights Commission authority to hold hearings, subpoena witnesses, and issue cease-and-desist orders in cases of discrimination because of race. Although the commission sometimes used these enforcement powers, its practice was usually to use conciliation and persuasion in cases of alleged discrimination in hiring and promotion. The state commission and its local representatives, together with human relations commissions and affiliates of the National Urban League all over the state, worked to educate the public as well as employers to open employment to African Americans in nontraditional jobs. Results were not spectacular, but reports of the Civil Rights Commission showed progress. One example was the employment of black women as telephone operators in several communities and as salespersons in department stores. Large food chains, such as Kroger, also increased the number of African American salespersons and clerical workers among their employees.[47]

Congress's adoption of the Civil Rights Act of 1964 and its creation of the Equal Employment Opportunity Commission (EEOC) with regional and state offices gave further impetus to opening new job opportunities. Increasing fears of urban unrest in the late 1960s also motivated some employers to hire African Americans for the first time.[48]

Help in increasing job opportunities for blacks in Indianapolis came from an unexpected source in late 1965, when the Indianapolis Chamber of Commerce announced that virtually every business in the city would be asked to join in a "vigorous program of employment opportunity especially benefiting members of minority groups." Businesses were expected to sign a formal pledge that said, "I reaffirm my company's commitment in recruiting and advancing the best qualified person without regard to race, color, religion or national origin." A steering committee made up of some of the city's most powerful figures in industry, banking, retailing, and public utilities was appointed to seek employer cooperation and to assist organizations with programs for employing minority groups. The group would also encourage on-the-job training programs and encourage blacks to complete high school.[49]

More trade unions also began to open membership to African American workers. In 1970 the city government in Indianapolis signed an agreement with the Marion County Building Trades Council providing that unions and contractors would give priority in hiring to residents of neighborhoods in which federally funded projects were being built.[50]

Meanwhile, more and more African Americans were finding employment outside the private sector, in government service. By 1962 a survey by the Indianapolis *Star* found that of 3,200 persons on the city payroll in the state capital, 751 were black. Of these, 334 were classified as skilled workers, 417 as common laborers.[51]

Governor Welsh issued an executive order in 1963 for departments of state government to end discrimination in hiring and urging them to employ more African Americans. As a result the number of clerical and professional staff increased substantially as well as the number of unskilled black workers, but some departments, among them the State Police, remained almost entirely white.[52]

The opening of the Army Finance Center at Fort Benjamin Harrison, described by the Indianapolis *Star* as the "Pentagon of the Prairies," also opened increased opportunities for African Americans. By 1959 of 4,500 civil service employees, 1,700 were black, and the percentage of black workers at the center continued to rise in later years.[53]

By 1970 the United States Census showed that, of 49,647 African American workers sixteen years of age or older in Indianapolis, 36,230 worked in private business, 1,513 were self-employed, and 11,851 were government employees. In Gary the total number employed was 30,223, of whom 24,405 were in the private sector, 593 were self-employed, and 5,171 were government employees. In neighboring East Chicago the total number employed was 36,501, of whom 29,754 were in the private sector, 694 were self-employed, and 5,994 government employees. However, an earlier study conducted by the Gary Human Relations Commission under a grant from EEOC showed that in that city, where blacks made up more than half the population, the largest corporations, among them United States Steel, did not employ African Americans in proportion to their percentage of the entire population in the city.[54]

Attempting to measure the effectiveness of laws against discrimination in the sale and rental of housing is even more elusive than measuring laws covering employment. Forces other than laws, including larger black incomes and the growth of a substantial African American middle class, were assisting the dispersal of blacks into new areas. But the fact that "it was the law," as J. Martin Crump, Director of the Indianapolis Human Relations Commission, pointed out, led formerly reluctant real estate agents to show houses to blacks and made some whites willing to accept them as neighbors.

In 1958, before the adoption of local and state open housing laws, the director of the Booker T. Washington Center in Elkhart wrote, "We do not need census tracts or block statistics to pinpoint occupancy since there is a definite Negro area in Elkhart. The number of Negroes residing outside the Negro area could be termed negligible. As the Negro area 'pushes out' or spreads 'For Sale' signs can be readily observed in the homes of white owners."[55]

What was true of Elkhart was also true of other Indiana cities with substantial black populations. In 1959 the United States Civil Rights Commission, after a study of conditions in South Bend, Fort Wayne, and Indianapolis, reported, "The area of discrimination in housing in Indiana is probably the greatest blight we are facing in the problems of discrimination affecting the Civil Rights Commission." The study showed that the percentage of substandard units occupied by nonwhites ranged from 50 to 95 percent and that minority groups had little share in new housing units. In South Bend less than 2 percent of new housing was available to blacks although they made up 9 percent of the population. Banks refused to extend credit to open-occupancy projects. In South Bend such public housing as had been built was occupied principally by blacks, but in Fort Wayne, where new public housing projects were being built, only one of three was to be open to blacks. In Indianapolis, Lockefield Gardens, which was operated by the federal government, was exclusively for Negroes.[56]

A 1959 Indianapolis *Times* report on the city's housing conditions found that a large percentage of the rental units available to blacks were substandard, in spite of the fact that some of the worst slum areas had been leveled by the Redevelopment Commission. The homes owned by African Americans were relatively much better than the housing they rented, and the rate of home ownership among blacks was almost as high as it was among whites. A typical black homeowner owned a thirty-year-old five-room dwelling with inside plumbing. But by 1959 a growing number of blacks with substantial buying power were tending to buy newer, better homes in what realtors called a pattern of "racial succession," when African Americans bought houses from whites who were moving into still better new houses, often in the suburbs. Most of the African American population in Indianapolis remained concentrated in Center Township, but some black families were moving north of Thirty-eighth Street, sometimes as the result of the Butler Tarkington Neighborhood Association and the more recently organized Meridian-Kessler Association. However, the policies of the Indianapolis Housing Authority, reactivated in 1964, contributed to keeping low-income blacks in Center Township. All of the public housing projects built in the 1960s were in that township, with the result that schools in the central city became more crowded and the problem of desegregation more difficult.[57]

After local housing ordinances and state laws were enacted, the Civil Rights Commission, local human rights commissions, and local urban leagues carried out programs to persuade white homeowners to accept black neighbors and to persuade managers of all-white apartments to accept black tenants. The issue on which these groups concentrated most intensely in the case of homeowners was to persuade them that the widely held perception that racially integrated housing led to a decline in real estate values was a myth. A survey conducted by the Indiana Civil Rights Commission showed that, contrary to popular belief, property values remained stable or actually increased in such neighborhoods if whites did not panic and flood the market in an effort to flee.[58]

However, in spite of a state law designed to penalize realtors guilty of "block busting," evasions of the intent of the law persisted. Black as well as white real estate brokers in Indianapolis were accused of sending letters to residents informing them of the sale of houses in a neighborhood and telling them who their new neighbors would be. Although realtors insisted that such information was not "block busting" (intending to induce panic selling), the practice in one neighborhood led to a suit and a public hearing against a real estate agency. However, the accused white real estate broker secured a temporary injunction from a sympathetic local judge, and the suit was later moved to Hancock County, where it languished.[59]

Although white real estate agents seldom simply refused to show a house to a potential black buyer, they sometimes continued the practice of claiming that the house had already been sold. This ruse was sometimes challenged when whites who were cooperating with the African Americans expressed an interest in the house and were told that it was available.

In 1972 two teams of employees of the Indianapolis *News* staged an experiment intended to test the availability of housing for blacks. The two teams—one a white couple, the other African Americans—made contacts with real estate companies. The white couple soon found out that none of the real estate agents was showing them houses in predominantly black neighborhoods. After inquiring about buying a house in Speedway (long a bastion of whites only), the white couple was immediately shown a house that the real estate agent priced at $17,000. When the black couple approached him, he reluctantly showed them the same house and said that the price was $23,000. The white couple also approached another realtor about buying a house in a suburb in southwestern Marion County, and he showed them a house in an upper-middle-class neighborhood. But upon visiting the same realtor, the black couple was shown houses in federally subsidized housing projects where most of the residents were black. When they asked about better houses in other neighborhoods, he told them that Indianapolis was "a lot like the South" and that they would not be happy in a white neighborhood. Only when the couple insisted upon looking at more expensive houses did the agent show them those houses and quote the same prices as he did to the white couple.[60]

Both "couples" were simply employees of the *News,* carrying out a project suggested by their editor. There is no evidence that they brought their findings to the attention of the Civil Rights Commission or the Indianapolis Human Relations Commission, and, in fact, few complaints regarding the sale of houses were brought, because discrimination was difficult to prove.

There were more complaints charging discrimination in apartment rentals. By the late 1960s many apartment buildings in predominantly white neighborhoods of Indianapolis were available to African Americans, although low incomes prevented many blacks from moving into them. But in spite of the city council's housing law and the state laws, agents and owners used a variety of ruses to prevent and discourage rental to blacks. It was a fairly common practice for managers to tell African Americans who inquired about rentals that there were no vacancies and that there was a long waiting list of applicants. When whites inquired about the same apartment, they were allowed to move in immediately, or if there was no current vacancy they were told that an apartment would be available in the near future.[61]

Although black homeowners gradually made their way outward from the central city in the process of "racial succession" described above and a few families found homes in racially integrated neighborhoods, African Americans were almost never found in white suburban areas. The only important exception in the state appears to have been the Grandview settlement in Washington Township, northwest of the city limits of Indianapolis in the most prestigious suburban area at the time. When the first houses in the settlement were built in the 1950s, there were some efforts to harass the black residents. As more houses were built and more African Americans moved into them, most whites moved away, leaving an almost entirely black community in what the white press sometimes referred to as the "golden ghetto." Residents organized the Grandview Civic Association and in 1969 built a recreational center and country club.[62]

A few of the families who moved to Grandview had earlier, along with other members of the black elite in Indianapolis and other cities, established an unusual summer resort for blacks on Fox Lake near Angola in northern Indiana. In 1927, after the Fox Lake Land Company had been incorporated, a builder from Fort Wayne built three cottages that were soon sold. These were followed by cottages constructed for African American families from Indianapolis, Chicago, Cleveland, Dayton, Cincinnati, and smaller Indiana cities. Later the Fox Lake Property Owners Association built roads and piers and employed a lifeguard. Eventually members built a lodge and social center where parties were held, and a Sunday School operated during the summer months. The resort reached its peak of popularity in the years following the Second World War, and it began to decline during the 1960s as children of original members grew up and civil rights laws and improved transportation made travel and admission to other resort areas more accessible to African Americans.[63]

In December 1968 an article in the Indianapolis *Sunday Star Magazine* entitled "The Indianapolis Formula For Racial Peace" attempted to analyze why the city had escaped race riots that had swept the country following the assassination of Martin Luther King Jr. the previous April. "There is something astonishing and marvelous about Indianapolis," said the writer. "It is the only city remotely near its size in the North . . . that hasn't had a single racial disturbance." He pointed out that about a quarter of the population of the city was African American and that much of the white population was of southern descent, and he acknowledged that the city had a long history of segregation and discrimination; but he emphasized that African Americans knew that progress toward solving racial problems was being made. He cited the growth of neighborhood associations like Butler Tarkington and Meridian-Kessler where whites had resisted the efforts of block busters. Most blacks lived in decent housing, he said, and were able to earn a decent living, thanks in part to the efforts of white businesses to make more and better jobs available to members of their race. But, in spite of the optimistic assessment, he acknowledged that relations between blacks and police were the most significant area of racial friction.[64]

Earlier in an interview with a reporter from the Indianapolis *News,* Rev. Brown of the local SCLC had a different explanation for the absence of racial disturbances. He attributed the quiescent attitudes, the "racial harmony," to the strength of the white power structure and said that blacks who had moved upward did not want to rock the boat. Of the typical African American who had succeeded in arriving in upper-income brackets Brown said, "When he [*sic*] arrives, so to speak, he sometimes forgets he's colored. If he has been sponsored by the white community certainly he has obligations to that community, more so than with the Negro community."[65]

Although the assassination of Martin Luther King Jr. did not lead to riots in Indianapolis, it had a profound effect upon the black community. That violence did not erupt was attributed in part to Senator Robert Kennedy, who was in the city seeking votes in his campaign for nomination as the Democratic candidate for President. Kennedy, who learned of the King assassination on his arrival in Indianapolis, insisted, against the advice of security agents, on speaking to a largely black audience of more than two thousand people who had been waiting for hours in a drizzling rain for his appearance, unaware of the death of their leader. When the shaken and white-faced Kennedy told them of King's death, the audience burst into shrieks and sobs, but Kennedy calmed them with a largely extemporaneous speech in which he pleaded with his audience to follow King's precepts of nonviolence and to "pray for our country which we all love . . . a prayer of understanding and compassion." A few days afterward, Mayor Richard Lugar made a similar plea in a radio address, and in a later speech the mayor said that he prayed that King's example "will make us all free at last" and that he would use the power of his office to prove that "human rights come first." He promised to curb police harassment and to work for better housing and better schools for minorities.[66]

Although the speeches of Kennedy and Lugar had a calming effect, groups and individuals within the black community probably were more important in preventing violence. Ministers, leaders of the Urban League and the NAACP, and especially youth groups urged peaceful protest rather than violence. Conspicuous among the young leaders was "Snooky" Hendricks, president of the recently organized Black Radical Action Project (BRAP).[67]

At a meeting called by CORE and the NAACP following King's assassination, representatives of many African American organizations and churches expressed not only grief but also frustration and bitterness at the failure of white society and government to deal with the many problems faced by members of their race. Earlier the Indianapolis NAACP had issued a statement that was, for that organization, militant in tone and also a warning. "With the violent death of Martin Luther King Jr.," it said, "America now stands at the crossroads. The black man will no longer continue to suffer the injustice heaped upon him by white America." The responsibility for the murder could not be attributed merely to a "madman," but the "American people are responsible for pulling that trigger, for such a dastardly thing could not have happened if America had not continuously denied black people the full equality they are so desperately seeking."[68]

Before King's assassination, NAACP leaders had urged steps to forestall possible racial disorders. At a meeting with Mayor Barton in July 1966, Ransom had said that while Indianapolis had been free from racial violence, the city was "far from being free from racial problems." In a written presentation the local NAACP called on city officials "to take every step possible to prevent these outbreaks of (racial) violence." They asked whether the police department had trained patrolmen in riot control and whether the police and the Human Relations Commission had established community contacts and programs "to identify potential trouble spots and whether the city had plans to mobilize community leaders and clergymen in case of trouble."[69]

The NAACP continued to urge a program of action in the event that violence threatened or occurred, but their urging had little effect in improving relations between the Indianapolis police and African Americans. From the beginning of the civil rights movement, the police had looked with suspicion on any sign of black militancy. In particular they targeted Black Muslims. The Muslims called all whites "white devils" and white political leaders, including President Kennedy, "frauds." The number of Muslims remained small, but the police followed their actions with suspicion and accumulated lengthy reports about their activities. When they first appeared in Indianapolis, members of the group, labeled "extremist" by the press and the police, tried to hold a meeting in a church. The first church they scheduled decided against holding the meeting, and plans to meet in Rev. Brown's Greater Zion Baptist Church were also withdrawn because of the large numbers of police and newspaper reporters who jammed the church. Before the meeting, a police inspector had read Indiana laws against racial hatred to Muslims. In protest against the indignities to which the police were subjecting them, the Muslims then canceled the meeting. Continuing police harassment of the Muslims led Rufus Kuykendall to threaten to ask for an investigation by the U.S. Department of Justice. Leaders in the black community asked Mayor Barton to appoint an "unbiased police study commission" to investigate police actions against black citizens. When Barton said he did not see the need for a special commission, Torian told the mayor if the Safety Board conducted the investigation, it would simply be "police investigating police." After Lugar took office, black activists met with the new mayor. When Lugar seemed to make no response to their request for action against two policemen they accused of brutality, the group said it looked as if "the city wanted a riot."[70]

The arrival of the Black Panthers, an avowedly revolutionary group, led to increased police surveillance in black neighborhoods. Two Panthers were arrested on charges that they were plotting to murder the Indianapolis chief of police and the head of the vice squad and were held for a long period without bail in the city jail; on the testimony of an undercover police officer they were finally brought to trial and convicted of conspiracy to murder. After the trial, Rev. Mozell Sanders, a prominent black Baptist minister, urged the Ministerial Alliance to alert the community to raise funds for lawyers' fees for an appeal.[71]

A few months later a genuine riot, thought by some to be in retaliation for the conviction of the two Panthers, erupted near Lockefield Gardens on Indiana Avenue, an area frequented by Panthers. The trouble began when two white officers sent to the area in response to a report of a fight were jumped by a group of about twenty young blacks, one of whom grabbed the officer's revolver and badge. A crowd of about three hundred, mostly boys and young men, quickly gathered. When more police arrived, they were met with a barrage of bricks and bottles, and a few shots were exchanged. Two policemen were injured, one wounded in the leg by a sniper and another beaten by members of the crowd. As the fray continued, windows of local businesses were smashed, and gasoline that had been tossed on the roof of the Lockefield Big Ten Market started a fire that consumed the entire building. Police quickly cordoned off the riot-torn area, and black leaders, including Rev. Sanders, "Snooky" Hendricks, and members of the Boys Club at Lockefield Gardens, called on the mob to leave peacefully. After peace had been restored, youths in the area were given an opportunity to air their grievances. These centered on police treatment of residents of the area. The group asked that most of the police patrols be removed and that only black officers be used in the area.[72]

Calm was restored, but the area continued to deteriorate. The white-operated businesses that had suffered during the riot, including the Lockefield Big Ten Market and a Hook's drugstore, announced that these enterprises would not be reopened.[73]

Following the riot in Indianapolis, racial disturbances broke out in other Indiana cities. In Kokomo, where the city government had long ignored the grievances of black citizens, two days of fire bombings and gunfire resulted in injuries to fourteen police officers, and the National Guard was called in to restore order. In Marion, which had a long record of police brutality and unprovoked attacks on blacks by white hoodlums, there was no riot during the summer of 1969, but at a statewide rally in the city addressed by Roy Wilkins of the national office of the NAACP, a crowd estimated at about three thousand marched in protest against police brutality and the denial of rights to African Americans arrested for petty crimes.[74]

Before 1969 there had been riots and racial disturbances in other cities in the state. In 1967 National Guardsmen and state troopers had been called to restore order after six people were injured in a riot in South Bend. A full-scale riot occurred in Evansville in August 1968, when police stopped two carloads of African Americans in cars that were alleged to have been stolen. Two nights of disorder and looting followed in which one policeman and one black woman were injured by gunfire. A fire in a lumber company in the black district and looting and destruction in other businesses caused heavy financial losses. Quiet was finally restored after the city council, meeting in emergency session in the absence of the mayor, ordered a curfew from 8 P.M. to 8 A.M. and prohibited the sale of ammunition and liquor.[75]

The presence in Gary of Mayor Hatcher, whom blacks trusted, probably prevented serious racial riots there. The disturbances that took place appeared to be intraracial rather than interracial. In 1966 when Hatcher was president of the city council, feuds between rival gangs of black youths threatened to erupt into violence. Hatcher brought the gang leaders together at a meeting with police where they were persuaded to cooperate in sponsoring various recreational programs rather than fighting with each other. Two years later, however, a "rumble" between two black motorcycle gangs led to a full-scale riot in which fires were started, store windows demolished, windows of passing cars shattered, and three persons injured by gunfire. City police, state police, and deputy sheriffs of Lake County restored order in the early morning. To prevent further disorders, Hatcher imposed a curfew in the black district and ordered the sale of liquor and gasoline in that area temporarily suspended. [76]

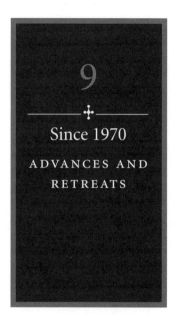

9

Since 1970

ADVANCES AND
RETREATS

The last two chapters of this book deal with the closing years of the twentieth century, after the peak of the civil rights movement—the period in which we are living—in which Indiana's African Americans faced new problems, and attitudes on race and race relations were changing. Because these events are so recent and so complex, any analysis runs the risk of being superficial and distorted by a close perspective. The judgment of history may be different from that of the present.

After 1970, migration of African Americans from the South to Indiana (and to the rest of the United States) slowed to a trickle, and consequently the black population growth in the state began to taper off. In Indiana the total increased from 356,379 in 1970 to 417,732 in 1980 and 432,092 in 1990, when blacks constituted about 7.8 percent of the entire population of the state. This relatively small segment of the population was concentrated in urban industrial centers, so that by 1980 two-thirds of the black population was in Marion and Lake Counties. In contrast, in 65 of the state's 92 counties, African Americans made up less than 1 percent of the population. In a few counties the U.S. census showed no black residents at all, and in many townships there was not a single black person.

In Lake County (Gary and East Chicago), African Americans made up 24.1 percent of the whole; in Marion, 20.3 percent. In Allen County (Fort Wayne) they made up 9 percent and in St Joseph (South Bend), 8.9 percent.[1]

In the largest urban counties, African Americans were usually concentrated in a single township. In Indianapolis in 1950 there were 59,530 blacks in Center Township, and the number grew to 89,903 by 1960, an increase of 51 percent in a single decade. During the 1960s the total population of the township declined by about 18 percent because whites left for other parts of the city or the suburbs. As a result, the percentage of blacks in the township increased.

There were similar trends in Gary and in other cities. Blacks made up more than half of Gary's total population by 1980, and 107,787 out of a total black population of 126,066 were concentrated in Calumet Township. In Allen County 22,021 of the 25,997 black residents were in Wayne Township. In St. Joseph County 20,260 out of 21,888 blacks were in Portage Township. In Vanderburgh County (Evansville) 9,499 of a total of 12,080 were in Pigeon Township.

More than half (86,342) of Marion County's total of 155,455 African Americans remained in Center Township in 1980, but there were increasing numbers of blacks in outlying townships: 30,529 in Washington, 14,632 in Lawrence, and 11,469 in Wayne.[2]

The movement outside the area's center continued during the eighties. By 1990 only 34 percent of the total black population remained in Center Township, while 23 percent lived in Washington Township, 16 percent in Lawrence, 11 percent in Wayne, and 2 percent in Pike and Warren. However, in the three townships along the southern border of Marion County (Decatur, Perry, and Franklin) the total number of blacks was only about one percent.[3]

The increase in black population in urban centers made African Americans more visible in politics, although the increase in numbers was not always reflected in increased power.

At the state level, there were a number of "firsts" in the appointment of black citizens to state offices. In 1973 Governor Otis Bowen named the realtor William T. Ray, a Republican and former president of the Indianapolis NAACP, as an administrative assistant to the governor, the highest state office held by an African American to that date. Bowen also appointed Beatrice Holland, a Richmond school teacher who was co-chairman of the Richmond Human Relations Commission, as the first African American to head the Indiana Civil Rights Commission, a position always held since then by a black appointee. Governor Robert Orr, Bowen's successor, named Halton Hayes director of the Indiana Employment Security Division, the first member of his race to hold that position. Governor Evan Bayh named Robert D. Rucker Jr., an East Chicago attorney, as the first black to serve on the Indiana Court of Appeal, and in 1995 Bayh appointed attorney Myra C. Selby of Indianapolis as the first African American and first woman Indiana Supreme Court justice.

Blacks were also elected to state offices. In 1992 Pamela Carter made news when she was elected Indiana attorney general, becoming the first African American and the first woman to hold that prestigious state office.[4] Dwayne M. Brown, a graduate of the Columbia School of Law, was elected clerk of the Indiana Supreme Court in 1990, the highest office to which an African American had been elected; he was convicted and removed from office in 1995 for using state employees to campaign for him.[5]

Blacks became more visible and more numerous in the General Assembly after that body finally passed a reapportionment law in 1972, which provided for single-member districts for most seats in the house of representatives. This broke the stranglehold that rural forces had held for generations and increased representation of urban districts, particularly in the counties where African Americans were concentrated. The consequences were particularly important in Indianapolis, where, instead of a slate of representatives elected at large from all of Marion County, the county was divided into districts, resulting in the creation of a number of districts in which blacks were in a majority or were the largest element in the population. This not only ensured increased numbers of black representatives but also gave members an opportunity to acquire experience and seniority, which had been impossible when the entire Marion County delegation shifted control between Republicans and Democrats. The new law also ended the charge, often made earlier, that black candidates were picked by white political bosses.[6]

The largest number of African American lawmakers have been from Indianapolis and Gary. Some of them are very able and have acquired power and influence.[7]

The one important exception to the pattern of black Democrats from predominantly black districts in urban centers was representative Hurley Goodall of Muncie. A Democrat, Goodall was first elected in 1978 and served continuously until 1993. African Americans are a minority of the population in Muncie and Delaware County. Goodall, who attended several colleges and universities, was a factory worker with strong union ties until 1958, when he was accepted as a member of the Muncie fire department. Since then he has held a number of civic positions, including serving on the Muncie Human Rights Commission and the Muncie School Board.[8]

The number and influence of African American members by 1979 had grown to

William T. Ray, Indianapolis realtor and civil rights leader, was the first
African American appointed to state office, serving as assistant to Governor Otis Bowen.
Indianapolis *Recorder* Collection, Indiana Historical Society.

the point that they formed a black legislative caucus to sponsor and lobby for legislation of special importance to racial minorities.

By the end of the 1960s, either the General Assembly or Congress had enacted all the important civil rights laws that had been the principal goals of African Americans. On paper, at least, the rights of equality and full citizenship had been won. During the seventies and more recently, new issues and new legislative goals have emerged, some of them responding to problems unique to African Americans, others of a broader nature, to solve or ameliorate problems faced by all underprivileged groups.

One unforeseen consequence of legislation outlawing discrimination and denial of access to public accommodations was the decline of businesses that catered especially to black patrons. This led to a movement to aid and promote minority-owned businesses. A bill sponsored by Carolyn Mosby and a white colleague in the senate and a similar measure sponsored by Goodall in the lower house provided for the creation of a commission to assist businesses owned by members of racial minorities. The goal of the commission was that at least 5 percent of state contracts be awarded to minority businesses. Another law established a pool of state funds to accelerate growth of minority businesses.[9]

Black lawmakers had a special interest in legislation to make the birthday of Martin Luther King Jr. a holiday, and after several legislative delays a bill was passed and signed by Governor Robert Orr in 1986.[10]

Other proposals affected white constituents as well as blacks. One that attracted widespread attention in the press was a proposal for casino gambling, which was opposed by many church groups. The strongest supporters of the measure were in Gary, where the decline of the steel mills caused widespread unemployment and poverty. The proposal was first sponsored in 1989 by state senator Mosby. After Mosby's death, Earline Rogers became the leading supporter in the upper house, while Charlie Brown led support in the house of representatives. The house bill also had support in other parts of the state from groups that saw gambling as a panacea for economic problems. The 1993 house bill legalized casino gambling in Gary, French Lick, and West Baden Springs and on excursion boats on the Ohio River. The bill was opposed by Democratic Governor Evan Bayh, a fact that Gary blacks regarded as a betrayal. Bayh vetoed the bill, but it was passed over his veto and became a law in 1993.[11]

By the 1990s there was a growing concern among thoughtful African Americans about the problems associated with young black males. Statistics showed that the rates of unemployment and of crime were higher for young black men than for any other segment of the population and that the killing of blacks by other blacks was a major cause of high mortality rates among them. As a partial remedy to this deplorable state of affairs, state representative Vernon Smith of Gary headed a legislative committee which recommended legislation to deal with the problem. After rejecting some of Smith's proposals, the General Assembly agreed to the creation of a commission on the social status of black males.[12]

Several of the most aggressive African American legislators were from Gary; and, particularly during the long tenure of Hatcher as mayor, Gary had a national reputation as a center of black power. Hatcher took the lead in organizing the Indiana black caucus, which sought the election of more black public officials. Gary was host to a meeting of the National Black Caucus in 1972. At the meeting Hatcher urged delegates not to work within the framework of the existing two-party system but "to make black political power a factor that could not be ignored in Washington, in state houses, or in court houses." However, at a later meeting of the National Black Caucus in Gary in 1975, many black elected officials were offended by those who used the rhetoric of class struggle and revolution and spoke of the need for a new political party. Hatcher expressed concern that the philosophy advocated by these speakers was in direct conflict with the beliefs of black politicians who sought to work within the existing political system. As a result, the Indiana organization voted to sever its ties with the national caucus.[13]

In 1975 Hatcher was still firmly in control of the office of mayor, in spite of the decline of Gary's economy that resulted from the collapse of the steel industry. Downtown banks, department stores, and hotels had closed, and crime, particularly drug-related crime, was increasing. Several powerful local black politicians were attempting to form an anti-Hatcher coalition. Hatcher's longtime rival Dozier T. Allen challenged him in the 1975 Democratic primary, but Hatcher won renomination by a comfortable margin. In November he defeated the Republican candidate, former police chief James Hilton, by more than 17,000 votes.[14]

In 1979, Hatcher won a fourth term and in 1983, a fifth. However, in the 1986 May primaries, the Hatcher organization suffered some humiliating defeats, and in June, Thomas Barnes, the Calumet Township assessor, announced that he would be a candidate for mayor in the May 1987 Democratic primary. Barnes had graduated from Roosevelt High School and Purdue and later earned a law degree. He had been endorsed by Hatcher when he ran for township assessor. In announcing his candidacy for mayor, Barnes did not entirely repudiate what Hatcher had accomplished, but he said that the city government was not working and that the time had come for Hatcher to move out and give new leadership a chance.[15]

Before the 1987 primary, Jesse Jackson had come to Gary to campaign for Hatcher, but a number of other former Hatcher supporters, among them Earline Rogers, declared their support for Barnes. Most of the media supported Barnes, who was victorious on the day of the primary. He won 24,450 votes, while Hatcher trailed with 18,400. In November, Barnes won 23,027 votes, while his Republican opponent received a mere 1,138 votes. In 1991, Barnes was elected to a second term without significant opposition.[16] He did not run for reelection in 1995.

Although by 1995 Gary began to get revenues from the city's riverboat gambling casinos, crime and unemployment rates were still high. Gary's political scene changed surprisingly when Scott L. King, a white defense attorney, won the Democratic primary and the November mayoral election, defeating black Republican Diane Boswell. Despite opposition from Barnes, who supported the Republican candidate on grounds that a white mayor would not "do," Gary's preponderantly black voters supported King by a large majority. King was credited with an improvement in city services (e.g., extending bus service into Merrillville to open job opportunities) and a vigorous attack on drug traffic. He ran again in 1999, winning the primary handily.[17]

In sharp contrast to Gary, black Democrats in Indianapolis have acquired little power in the city-county government created by the UniGov law, since Democrats have been outnumbered in the city-county council. Among the handful of black council members, Rozell Boyd has been consistently reelected and is recognized as the minority spokesman. In 1993 blacks held only 7 council seats out of a total of 29.[18]

As in other cities throughout the state, African Americans in Indianapolis remain solid supporters of the Democratic Party, although a small minority of blacks, out of principle or expediency, ally themselves with the Republican Party. Both Mayor Hudnut and his successor Stephen Goldsmith named black Republicans as their deputy mayors; Hudnut appointed Joseph Slash and Paula Parker-Sawyer, and Goldsmith named Robert L. Wood.

Desegregation of public schools and problems of resegregation have continued to be important issues in both the African American and white communities, and there have been significant changes in attitudes and goals among both groups.

In poverty-stricken Gary there were only 500 white and Asian students enrolled in the public schools by 1988, while there were more than 25,000 African Americans and about 900 Hispanics. Over 98 percent of the students were nonwhite.[19] It was obvious that racial integration had become impossible. "The mid-1980s Gary schools," writes Ronald Cohen, " were overwhelmingly black, plagued with economic problems, occasionally violent, and marked by sporadic academic, athletic, and social success." At the same time, the state government had established rules requiring more testing and had increased requirements for graduation, while the state legislature mandated budget cuts. Declining real estate values and shortages in tax collections caused the school board to cut more than $1.6 million from the budget. This led to dismissal of teachers, social workers, and other school employees.[20]

Indianapolis Public Schools, which continued to have the largest enrollment of any school system in the state, faced similar problems, though they were not as acute as those in Gary. The most pressing and publicized issues resulted from the mandate of the federal courts to bus IPS black students to township schools as a method of desegregation.

In July 1981, IPS submitted plans for busing about six thousand black students to six township school systems. (Washington and Pike Townships were exempt from the court order because their schools reflected significant residential integration.) A community Desegregation Advisory Council, which included a number of black clergymen, assumed responsibility for monitoring the treatment of black students bused to township schools. The council lacked enforcement powers but heard complaints from parents and other interested persons. There were reports of a few racial incidents in which African American students were openly attacked and harassed by whites, but much more numerous were parents' objections to the disproportionate numbers of black students who were disciplined and suspended. The unfriendly, sometimes hostile, attitude of white teachers and students was cited as the reason for the large number of dropouts among IPS students. Parents objected to a variety of conditions that isolated black students in the township schools and deprived black parents of a say in how the schools were run. For example, they pointed out that bus

schedules, as well as prejudice, prevented black students from participating in extracurricular activities after school hours. The scarcity of African Americans appointed
as teachers and other school personnel in the township schools meant that black students were forced to deal almost exclusively with white persons in positions of power.
Parents also complained that township school boards were made up entirely of white
suburban residents and that there was no provision for parents of the students from
IPS to participate in making school policies. Some townships responded by providing places on the school boards for representatives of the IPS students. However, in
spite of complaints, some surveys showed that black parents supported busing, saying their children were receiving better training than they would have received in the
Indianapolis schools.[21]

Although the township school corporations had consistently opposed plans to
bring pupils from IPS to their schools, paying large legal fees year after year to challenge the federal court's rulings, the township school systems benefited financially
from busing from IPS. Under court orders, the General Assembly appropriated special funds to cover costs of desegregation, including costs of transportation and programs for training teachers in human relations and counseling. In addition, since state
aid for tuition depended on student enrollment and attendance, the township schools
received increased state tuition payments. IPS, which lost both students and state tuition payments, was compensated for these losses for five years under orders from
the court.[22]

State aid to IPS for desegregation came to an end in 1985, while township systems
continued to receive state funds. The Indianapolis school system was faced with increasing problems as the result of a declining tax base and fewer students; enrollments
in IPS have declined from more than 100,000 students to fewer than 50,000. One consequence was a reduction in teachers' salaries, which IPS claimed caused Indianapolis teachers to take positions in the township schools and prevented IPS from hiring
more black teachers and administrators. As a result of these inequities, the Indianapolis
school board decided in 1989 to attempt to reopen the desegregation case in Judge
Dillin's court. They asked the court to order the state to pay funds to solve continuing problems related to desegregation in the Indianapolis schools. "We simply do not
have the funds to continue to support the desegregation effort we have under way,"
Indianapolis superintendent James Adams testified, "or to initiate new desegregation
programs, without undercutting education for all students in our district."[23]

However, Judge Dillin dashed hopes of additional funding by refusing to reopen
the case. After this rejection, Adams resigned as superintendent, and the school board
began a national search for his successor. In January 1991 the board, now consisting
of three African Americans and three white members, voted to appoint Shirl E. Gilbert,
already a deputy superintendent, as the first black superintendent of the Indianapolis schools.[24]

School issues, already complicated, were complicated further during the mayoralty
campaign of 1991. Stephen Goldsmith, the Republican who won the election, announced that he favored plans to stop the busing of IPS students to the townships
and return them to IPS. This proposal brought protests from all of the six township

systems to which IPS students were bused. Attorneys for the schools cited problems with enrollments, finances, staffing, and use of school buildings which would result if the mayor's plan were adopted. The superintendent of Wayne Township Schools said, "Things are working out well" under the court order and added, "Why tamper with something that is not broken?"[25]

The future of Indianapolis schools became increasingly gloomy after 1991 as the result of budgetary problems and looming deficits. Superintendent Gilbert attempted to reinvigorate the school system by promoting decentralization of administration and innovation, but his efforts were hampered by financial limitations. His Select Schools plan was intended to give parents limited choices in deciding which schools their children would attend. The reshuffling of school districts required the approval of Judge Dillin, who upheld the plan because it required that enrollments maintain a racial ratio between white and black students of between 35 and 65 percent.[26]

Select Schools went into operation at the beginning of 1993 school year. However, contrary to the expectations that the system would reduce busing, few parents or pupils chose to attend their neighborhood schools. At least 80 percent chose schools outside their district. In 1992 about 45 percent of IPS students were transported by bus; in 1993 about 80 percent of the 45,000 students rode buses. Analysis of enrollments at the beginning of the school year seemed to show that the new plan had not reduced problems of racial imbalance, but at the beginning of the second semester, Gilbert claimed that only 14 percent of the schools had failed to meet the goal of racial balance.[27]

Gilbert's disputes with the school board led to his leaving the post in 1994, but Select Schools continued until 1997 under the first woman and first Hispanic IPS superintendent, Esperanza Zendejas. Zendejas's vigorous focus on school accountability, coupled with the continuing loss of students and funding, was said by some to undermine teacher morale.[28] These problems were heightened when the board's attempt to solve IPS's problems by reclaiming the students being bused to township schools failed in 1997. Judge Dillin denied IPS's request to lift his order for interdistrict busing and explained, "It was this Court's intent that the order would be continuing and permanent."[29] In a surprising reversal of this view in June 1998, Dillin approved an agreement among IPS, the townships, and the Justice Department that busing would be phased out and court supervision of IPS would end after an eighteen-year transition period.[30]

The decision to end busing came in spite of broad support for it from the persons most directly involved: the children bused from Indianapolis to the township schools and those who taught and administered them there. Whatever the judgment of history about the wisdom of busing students to achieve integrated schools, Indianapolis was the only large American city that showed a large drop in school segregation between 1980 and 1996. Whether the schools would resegregate when busing ended was a question for the new century.[31]

State universities as well as city school systems faced increasing budgetary constraints in the 1980s, but they continued efforts to recruit African American students. However, the number of African Americans remains small in comparison with the number of white students. Enrollment of black students at state institutions in 1992 reached almost 20,000—the largest figure up to that time—but it was just a small fraction of the number of white enrollees.[32] The principal reasons for the small number of African Americans were probably lack of money, inadequate preparation in high school, and lack of motivation. In order to attend college, many blacks needed to have part-time or full-time jobs. This was undoubtedly the reason for the relatively high numbers of African American students at the urban regional campuses of Indiana and Purdue Universities, particularly Indiana University–Purdue University in Indianapolis (IUPUI) and the regional campuses in South Bend, Fort Wayne, and Gary.

Efforts to attract black professors and administrators were also more successful in urban centers than in Bloomington and West Lafayette. The School of Social Work at IUPUI has been particularly successful in attracting highly qualified minority faculty. In 1993, 27 percent of the tenure-track professors at the Indianapolis campus were members of racial minorities. In the university as a whole, only 12.8 percent of tenure-track faculty were members of minorities.[33]

The proportion of African American administrators at urban regional campuses was also quite large. When the IUPUI campus opened in Indianapolis in 1967, Dr. Joseph Taylor, a sociology professor and former head of Flanner House, was named dean of the School of Liberal Arts, and the number of black administrators has continued to grow. In 1993, Hilda Richards was named chancellor of the IU Northwest campus at Gary. She became the first woman chancellor at any Indiana University campus. In 1990, Leo Bryant was named vice chancellor at the Purdue campus at Hammond.

Private institutions also continued efforts to recruit black students, sometimes by offering them special scholarships. These institutions also made efforts to attract African American professors and administrators, with varying degrees of success.

A unique private institution in which nearly all students as well as teachers and administrators are African Americans is Martin University in Indianapolis. It was founded as Martin Center in 1969 and named in memory of Martin Luther King Jr. and Saint Martin de Porres, the first mulatto saint. The moving spirit behind the founding of the center was Father Boniface Hardin, a Benedictine. Sister Jane Schilling also played an important part in the success of the institution. Begun as a center to address racial problems, particularly those posed by sickle-cell anemia, its services and functions grew. In 1977 Martin Center became Martin College, a nondenominational institution, intended to fill the needs of minorities and other underprivileged persons who could not afford the costs of other institutions. The college was accredited in 1987, and in 1990 it was given the status of a university accredited by the North Central Association of Colleges and Schools. The college had an enrollment of seven students in 1977, and by 1990 it had 1,100 students, most of them adults.[34]

Probably the most visible and the most paradoxical development in African American society in recent years is the widening gap between a prosperous middle class and a poverty-stricken "underclass" in the forlorn inner cities. Members of the middle class, with education and incomes comparable to their white counterparts, have moved into comfortable older residential urban areas that are racially mixed, like But-ler Tarkington in Indianapolis, or into new houses in the suburbs. A recent survey shows that in Marion County, most African Americans with annual incomes of $25,000 to $50,000 live outside Center Township. African Americans in the inner city huddle in overcrowded, often dilapidated, rental housing. Black males in these areas are often school dropouts who have never had a job and have no prospect of finding one. They are not prepared to cope with the demands of the new technological era, in which there is little place for common laborers. Many black women in the inner city, also school dropouts and often mothers of small children, exist on welfare and food stamps. Unemployed males, often members of gangs, turn increasingly to drugs and crime as a way of existence. There is a pervasive atmosphere of hopelessness.[35]

In sharp contrast to these conditions, a growing number of African Americans head their own businesses or have attained managerial positions in businesses or institu-tions owned by whites. An early example is Dr. Frank Lloyd, appointed to head In-dianapolis's Methodist Hospital in the 1960s, becoming the first of a number of blacks in managerial positions at the hospital. Eli Lilly Pharmaceutical Company now has a number of African Americans in managerial positions, as do most Indianapolis banks. There are also African Americans on the boards of these institutions. Nevertheless, black managers are the exception rather than the rule. In Indianapolis in 1993, al-though blacks held more than five thousand positions classified as managerial, they made up only about 5 percent of the total pool of managers. Oftentimes these blacks feel that their positions give them responsibilities not shared by their white counter-parts. As one black manager observed, they "were expected to be black, act white, over-come stereotypes and cope with discrimination." He added, "you can't just think about the business. You have to deal with the cultural side too."[36]

In 1967 there had been only two notable African American manufacturing busi-nesses in Indianapolis: Madam Walker, Incorporated, and Summit Laboratories, In-corporated, both in the cosmetics business. By the 1990s there were a number of no-table manufacturing corporations and other black-owned businesses. Perhaps the preeminent example of a successful African American businessman is Henry G. Mays, owner of Mays Chemical Company. A graduate of Indiana University with a bache-lor's degree in chemistry and a master's in business administration, Mays worked for Cummins Engine Company in Columbus and Eli Lilly Company in Indianapolis be-fore becoming president of a small chemical distribution company in Indianapolis. In 1980 he founded his own company, a highly successful venture that soon made its owner one of the wealthiest and most influential citizens of Indianapolis. He has been president of the Indianapolis Chamber of Commerce, often regarded as a bastion of white conservatives. In addition to performing a long list of community services, Mays also owned the Indianapolis *Recorder*.[37]

Mays Chemical and other successful enterprises owned by African Americans in Indiana cities are in a sense "minority businesses," but they do not fit the definition used by those who demand special legislation and subsidies to encourage develop-ment and businesses owned by ethnic minorities.[38]

Minority businessmen joined together in 1991 to form the Hoosier Minority Chamber of Commerce. The new organization was headed by Harry Alford, a former state employee, who said that the group was begun primarily because black business owners were tired of promises that were never fulfilled. As noted, the state legislature had enacted a program intended to help minority businesses and created an Enterprise Development Fund to implement the legislation. Thereafter, Governor Robert Orr promised that in the future the state would place 5 percent of its contracts with minority businesses. While the state sometimes reached this goal for a few months, it regularly failed to meet it throughout an entire year. A frequent excuse was that it was impossible to find minority-owned businesses equipped to fulfill requirements of some contracts. The federal government had also appropriated $200 million for "set asides" for minority-owned companies in defense department contracts. However, there were frequent waivers because, it was claimed, it was impossible to find minority companies equipped to fulfill contract requirements.[39]

The 1980s, a period of recession in which most businesses showed a decline, was not a good period for minority-owned businesses in Indiana. According to the U.S. census the number of minority-owned enterprises in the United States grew almost 38 percent from 1982 to 1987, but in Indiana the rate of growth was only about 17 percent—less than half the national average.[40]

The Indianapolis Chamber of Commerce led several attempts to encourage investments in minority-owned businesses. The most ambitious of these was LYNX Capital Corporation, founded in 1991 with the support of Eli Lilly Company and most of the city's banks and utilities. William Mays headed the board of directors of LYNX. The purpose of the program was to make loans available to businesses that were too risky to get regular bank loans. LYNX did not make loans of less than $75,000 and required that companies applying for loans have at least five employees. At the outset LYNX was inundated with applications for loans, but it is too early to assess its success or failure. However, Harry Alford of the Hoosier Minority Chamber of Commerce expressed skepticism about an effort dominated by the white power structure. What was needed, he said, was to convince the city's large businesses to do more business with minority suppliers.[41]

Some minority-owned businesses have thrived without doing much business with whites; one example was the architectural firm Blackburn Associates owned by Walter Blackburn, son of Cleo Blackburn, longtime head of Flanner House. After earning degrees at Purdue and Howard University, Walter Blackburn returned to Indianapolis to begin his career as an architect. He established his own firm and eventually employed a staff of sixteen. Most of his work has been in the inner city, designing low-income housing as well as churches and schools. One of Blackburn's most publicized designs was a large office and parking building at 500 Indiana Avenue, long the center of black business and entertainment. This project was an example of white financial support for a black-designed and executed structure. Construction was financed in part by state funds and by a grant from Lilly Endowment, while the contract for construction was awarded to African American Oscar Robertson of Attucks High School and national basketball fame, who heads Oscar Robertson and Associates. The Madam Walker Urban Life Center was one of the owners of the new building.[42]

In Gary and other cities in the northern part of the state, minority businesses faced problems similar to those in Indianapolis. The Gary Human Relations Council concluded that banks in Gary, East Chicago, and Hammond consistently showed a pattern of making little capital available for minorities. Partly to combat this situation, a nonprofit organization, Venture Association of Northwest Indiana (VANI), was created to help entrepreneurs present their needs to potential investors. But prospects for businesses of all kinds were darkened by the decline of the steel industry in the Calumet area and the resulting unemployment.[43]

While minority businesses struggled, African American members of the professions—physicians, dentists, lawyers—made some gains as racial barriers fell. The white community recognized some of their members as civic leaders, but for the most part their patients and clients continued to be members of their own race.

Among physicians in Indianapolis Dr. Frank Lloyd, mentioned above as manager of Methodist Hospital, long maintained a preeminent position. He was a founder of Midwest National Bank and WTLC radio station, which for many years has been the focal point of news broadcasts of particular interest to the black community.

In 1990 Dr. George Rawls became the first black president of the Indiana State Medical Association. He was elected at a time when the profession faced such problems as the high rate of infant mortality among Indianapolis blacks. But gratifying as the recognition of men like Lloyd and Rawls was to the African American community, the hard fact is that the pool of black physicians appears to be declining. In 1990 it was estimated that African Americans made up only about 2 percent of Indiana's physicians, and the number of African Americans in medical schools is declining, probably because of the cost and length of required training.[44]

Most racial barriers in the legal profession have fallen. Black lawyers are freely admitted to the American Bar Association and its local affiliates, but many African Americans also maintain their membership in the National Bar Association. The number of black lawyers increases slowly, and most of them are concentrated in the Indianapolis and Gary areas. It was estimated in 1991 that approximately 132 African American attorneys belonged to the Marion County Bar Association and the Kimbrough Bar Association in Gary. As we have seen, a fairly large number of black lawyers from these areas have made careers in politics and government. A few black lawyers joined prestigious white law firms, but most members of the profession continued to serve a largely black clientele. However, more and more of them were forming partnerships and moving into specialized areas of law.[45]

Although a few African Americans were self-employed or work in minority-owned businesses, the vast majority worked as employees of white-owned businesses and corporations. During the eighties, unemployment among both whites and blacks increased and incomes fell. In Gary, in particular, changes in the steel industry, long the principal employer in the city, led to widespread unemployment. The steelworkers' union in Gary accepted a substantial cut in wages and benefits in 1984, with the understanding that the savings would be used to rebuild and modernize old mills, but layoffs continued. By 1986 fewer than 3,000 jobs remained among the members of Steelworkers Local 1014 in Gary, which had 8,500 workers among its members in

1983. In 1987 the Gary *Post Tribune* reported that the national rate of unemployment of members of all races was about 6 percent, but that in Gary and the Calumet area it was about 13 percent.[46]

Nationally it was estimated that almost half of routine steelmaking jobs disappeared between 1974 and 1988 (from 480,000 to 260,000) as the steel industry installed robot machinery. Computer-regulated robots increased productivity and drastically reduced the number of workers. Inland Steel closed two of its old cold-rolling mills, laying off hundreds of routine workers. Inland Steel and Nippon Steel joined together to build a cold-rolling mill fifty miles west of Gary. The new mill reduced the time needed to produce a coil of steel to one hour, and the entire plant was run by a small band of trained technicians. Such plants had no need for traditional blue-collar workers.[47]

Gary's employment opportunities rebounded somewhat in the 1990s with the opening of new casinos, the expansion of city bus service to nearby Merrillville, and the improvement of Gary's airport to provide passenger service. By May 1997 unemployment in Gary had dwindled from 13.5 percent the previous year to 8.5 percent.[48]

In Indianapolis, which had a much more diversified economy than Gary's, there was also growing unemployment during the eighties. Decreases in federal aid to states and cities also led to further loss of jobs. The rate of unemployment among blacks was significantly higher than among white workers. The average rate of unemployment among African Americans in 1991 was more than 10 percent, compared to 5.4 percent for whites.[49] By the end of the decade, Indianapolis, like the rest of the state, experienced significant recovery in employment opportunities, based on a widespread business expansion. Downtown Indianapolis became a lively center of shopping and nightlife in the 1990s for the first time in decades, and manufacturing and construction jobs also grew. The overall jobless rate in Marion County was 2.5 percent in May 1999, forcing employers to train unskilled workers and to pay higher wages. Observers believed black unemployment was dwindling as well.[50]

Both whites and blacks dismissed from jobs in industry in the 1980s were forced to take service jobs—in hospitals, fast-food eating-places, and supermarkets—at a fraction of the wages they had been paid in industry. Members of both races who were unable to get even these jobs were forced to turn to welfare, but the percentage of blacks in this position was higher than for whites.[51] Hence, the Welfare Reform Act of 1996, which sharply limited the federal commitment to help support families with dependent children, could be expected to affect Indiana's African Americans more than its whites. But the booming economy at the end of the century at least masked this impact.

As economic conditions worsened in the 1980s, the number of complaints of job discrimination before the Indiana Civil Rights Commission increased, and as well-paying jobs became more scarce, white workers who had been willing to accept affirmative action plans in employment began to complain of "reverse discrimination" and to denounce "quotas." Both Presidents Reagan and Bush vetoed civil rights laws, which they claimed established quotas.[52]

Fewer complaints about discrimination in housing were filed with the Civil Rights Commission and local agencies than about employment. Nevertheless, some discrimination and a pervasive pattern of residential segregation persisted. Almost complete residential segregation continued in Gary, one of the most segregated cities in the United States. While there were few instances of overt discrimination in Indianapolis, segregated housing patterns persisted in many areas. Some discrimination continued, particularly in rental property. When African Americans inquired about availability of apartments in a building in which most tenants were white, managers sometimes denied that there were any vacancies. There were few overt examples of outright refusal to rent to blacks, but once black tenants became a majority, white tenants moved away. The same pattern prevailed in individual houses, both rentals and those occupied by white owners.[53]

African Americans of all income levels were at a disadvantage if they tried to borrow money or renovate a home. The 1991 report of the Home Mortgage Disclosure Act found that only 328 African Americans in Indianapolis applied for home purchase loans, and that 25 percent of these were rejected. Whites applied for 11,646 mortgage loans and only 9.8 percent were rejected. Of 1,178 home improvement loan applications submitted by blacks, 50 percent were denied, while only 21 percent of white applicants were rejected. The report showed that income levels made little difference in denial of loans to African Americans.[54]

When better housing was available, blacks sometimes failed to take advantage of it. Federally subsidized programs such as the "set aside" program initiated by the Department of Housing and Urban Development (HUD) were intended to give persons with low incomes better housing, regardless of race. Under the HUD program, developers were given low-interest loans to build or renovate apartment complexes provided that they set aside 20 percent of the units for low-income tenants. But many of the subsidized apartments were in the suburbs, and African Americans were reluctant to move into the suburbs for a variety of reasons. One was lack of public transportation, which made it difficult or impossible for persons without cars to reach their workplace and which hampered access to hospitals. African Americans were also reluctant to move to a suburban area unless there were other members of their race nearby.[55]

In the inner city where African Americans were concentrated, various programs showed some progress in rehabilitating old houses for purchase by first-time homeowners. In 1990 in Gary, which had the highest percentage of abandoned and foreclosed homes per capita in the United States and the lowest urban property values, HUD began a program to sell houses on which mortgages had been foreclosed to nonprofit organizations at a discount. In response, a local church coalition raised funds to take advantage of the program.[56]

Several neighborhood associations in Indianapolis, with the cooperation of the city government, have also made some progress in rehabilitating repossessed abandoned houses in black neighborhoods and selling them to first-time homeowners. A few new homes are also being built in predominantly black neighborhoods with money from the Indiana Housing Authority. Tenants who rent them are given the option of buying the houses after fulfilling long-term leases.[57]

In both Indianapolis and Gary, such limited public housing as existed was always looked upon as primarily "black housing." All ten public housing projects in Indianapolis were in Center Township or in neighborhoods adjacent to it. In 1993, 96 percent of the residents were black. Most of the projects had been built in the sixties, and by the nineties they were in dire need of repairs and rehabilitation. Tenants complained about lack of heat, plumbing that did not work, broken windows, broken locks, and general disarray.[58]

Residents of these dilapidated structures had grievances besides the absence of repairs and maintenance. Police statistics showed that an average of 20 percent of rapes, robberies, vandalism, and vehicle-related crimes took place within five blocks of public housing projects. Police also made many drug-related arrests in these areas.[59]

Residents of the inner city lived in constant fear of crime against themselves or members of their families and neighbors. Blacks made up about 12 percent of the population of the United States according to the 1990 census, but they made up over half of the victims of murder. Homicide was the leading cause of death for African Americans between the ages of 25 and 34. Gary had one of the highest crime rates of any city in the United States. In Indianapolis, where African Americans made up about 21 percent of the population, they were responsible for 56 percent of the cases of homicide and homicide-related injuries as well as a large percentage of other violent crimes. Especially disturbing to African Americans was the increasing number of crimes committed by blacks against fellow blacks, particularly by young black males against other young black males. There were increasingly frequent reports of clashes between rival gangs of young black males, some of them related to rivalries over the control of sales of illegal drugs. This problem was linked to the high rate of unemployment among men in the inner city. Growing numbers of young blacks who had not finished high school, unable to find jobs, stopped looking for legitimate employment and turned to gangs and crime. Statistics gathered in Indianapolis in 1993 showed that African American male unemployment was almost three times as great as for white males. The number of violent incidents resulting in injuries and death for black males was seven times that for white males.[60]

Unemployment and crime among young black men received so much publicity that both the state legislature and the city government of Indianapolis created commissions to study the problem and make recommendations. Following the first meeting of the Indianapolis group, a member said, "We can no longer sit idly by as a significant number of African American males are turning to gangs for companionship and failing to find employment because they're not prepared or have not had an opportunity." He also pointed out that these young males contributed to a related problem of the black community by fathering a growing number of children born to unmarried teenage girls. He said that young males fathered children "with little or no intent to be fathers."[61]

As the commission member suggested, one of the problems of the inner city's black community was the increasing number of households headed by black females— almost a third of all black households according to the 1990 U.S. census. A large percentage of such households were headed by unmarried mothers who were unprepared to cope with the responsibilities of parenthood, as evidenced, for example, by the rate of infant mortality. The Children's Defense Fund, a national organization, reported that in the 1980s black babies in Indianapolis were dying at the highest rate in the United States in cities of more than 500,000 residents.[62]

When they learned that Mayor Hudnut had not included any funds for combating this shameful statistic in the proposed city budget, black ministers and other black leaders converged on a city-county meeting to protest. As the result of the protests, the city-county council appropriated $1.5 million to be used to combat infant mortality. The Indianapolis Campaign for Better Babies, a private organization, was also formed. Prenatal clinics financed by both public and private money began operations under the Marion County Health Department. The department also made small grants to such institutions as Flanner House and Martin University to encourage women to use the services of prenatal clinics. As a consequence of such efforts, infant mortality began to decline, and Indianapolis lost the undesirable distinction of having the highest infant mortality rate in the United States.[63]

A State Council on Black and Minority Health created in 1987 released a report and recommendations in 1991 that recognized that infant mortality was only one of the health problems faced by African Americans and that lack of medical care led to

Members of SCLC and supporters protest police brutality in Indianapolis in 1975.
Indianapolis *Recorder* Collection, Indiana Historical Society.

needless deaths among the poor. While its members were aware that authorities were reluctant to use public money, the council made a number of recommendations that would lead to better health among indigent blacks. They recommended that churches cooperate with local clinics to provide more sites for routine health care and screenings, and they encouraged more private physicians to accept indigent patients. The council also recommended incentives for employers to provide insurance for persons in low-paying jobs. These recommendations, which relied on voluntary efforts, were generally regarded as inadequate to meet the needs of the poor, but they and the Campaign for Better Babies increased public awareness of the health problems of the black community.[64]

Inadequate health care and high mortality rates were only two of the problems faced by residents of the inner city. A more immediate problem was crime. But while law-abiding citizens constantly faced threats of assaults and other crimes against themselves and members of their families, they also remained fearful of the police. Many believed that the system of criminal justice was not fair to members of their race. There were constant complaints that police use unnecessary force in dealing with blacks suspected of crimes. In 1990 a group of black ministers, while acknowledging that the black community was failing "to properly train our young people," insisted that this was no justification "for our youth—and our youth only—to be shot down by the police in senseless killings." The chief of police in Indianapolis insisted before an investigating committee from the NAACP's national office that relations between the police and the community had improved since the 1970s. During the term of Mayor Hudnut, he said, police shootings of suspected black criminals had declined. Stephen Goldsmith, Hudnut's successor, expressed hope that relations between police and the black community would improve in his administration. As one step toward this he appointed James D. Toler, a long-respected African American police officer, as chief of police. After appointing Toler, Goldsmith announced that, although members of the police had authority to use force in bringing suspected criminals under control, "Regardless of the circumstances, police officers are not justified in inflicting punishment on a citizen, however offensive their [sic] action has been."[65] However, whether the announced policy would be observed by all members of the police force remained to be seen.

Complaints of police brutality and arbitrary arrests were not limited to Indianapolis. In both large and small communities throughout the state, there were complaints about indignities suffered by African American males at the hands of police. A common bitter joke was that they were likely to be stopped and arrested for "driving while black."[66]

10

✣

The
Continuing
Search
for Identity

Lana Ruegamer

As difficult as it is to judge how the civil rights "revolution" of the 1960s and subsequent events affected relatively measurable conditions like employment, housing, and education for Indiana's African Americans, it is even more difficult to determine how those changes affected the way blacks saw themselves and were seen by others. What follows is a sketch based on as-yet fragmentary records.[1]

One of the earliest ways that the changes of the 1960s affected black identity was by prompting demands for a new name: in Indiana, as in other states, young men took the initiative in asserting a new racial identity by rejecting the name "Negro" in favor of "black" or "Afro-American." Although older "Negro" leaders had led the movements that ended the legal segregation of schools and broke the racial barriers to public accommodations in Indiana, the word "Negro" suggested to many younger blacks and whites a stereotype of patience and powerlessness in the face of injustice and insult. By contrast, "black" and "Afro-American" suggested less predictable and more assertive behaviors. Both new terms, however, were rejected by an overwhelming majority of Negroes as late as 1969. In a poll done for the Indianapolis *Star* in April, the only group that favored those names in significant numbers were males between the ages of eighteen and twenty-nine, 47 percent of whom preferred either "black" (29 percent) or "Afro-American" (18 percent). Only 25 percent of young women preferred them. There was also a very large generation gap in name preferences: over 70 percent of men over thirty preferred "Negro," followed by those who responded "don't care" (15–22 percent). But, as one older woman leader recalls ruefully, "'black' was rammed down our throats by the young people."[2]

For younger people, the militancy of the Black Panthers and other black-power movements offered an enormous psychic shift from the models of dignified patience identified with their parents' and grandparents' generations. The identity suggested by the name "black" was deeply empowering; one middle-aged African American academic remembers with a shake of his head his image as a graduate student in 1974, wearing the uniform of the black-power movement—an "Afro" and a beret, which evoked a big response from whites.[3]

And yet the new black militancy was made possible for most of those who adopted it because of changes in laws and attitudes of the white majority; only with federal support as a backup for equal rights and with the enforcement of state statutes outlawing discrimination could activists reasonably hope their demonstrations would lead to justice rather than to martyrdom or futility. While there was reason to hope that active protests against illegal or unjust policies would help achieve equality, many questions remained: how would the laws be interpreted (by mostly white judges, jurors, and police)? And how would whites respond unofficially to blacks' more assertive demands for equality? These were crucial questions in the late 1960s and through the 1970s, and they illustrate the constraints citizens formerly known as Negroes faced in reinventing themselves as persons with equal rights. The questions also imply that identity changes are inevitably mutual; if "whites" were in a position to limit blacks' self-definition, blacks were at the same time forcing white people, collectively and individually, to reconsider the meaning of being white.

After the 1970s, the experience of being black in Indiana became increasingly diverse. The conditions of life for most African Americans in Indiana in the 1980s and 1990s became more like those of most whites; in growing numbers, blacks worked, lived, and went to school with whites, though often their neighborhoods and their schools were mostly black. Inevitably they developed different notions of racial identity from those who remained behind in ghettos, where unemployment, inferior housing, the absence of whites, and high rates of crime made their lives increasingly unlike those of most other people. At the other end of the scale emerged an elite based on wealth, education, and family prestige, whose lives became more like those of other elites than like most whites or blacks. The differences among these three basic groups of African Americans—the majority "middle class," the large minority who were poor, and the elite—in many cases came to seem more significant than the things they had in common, with some notable exceptions.

This chapter offers an analysis of some of the elements that affected Negro/black/ African American identity(ies) in Indiana in the decades after the civil rights movement: revolt in the universities; the desegregation of middle-class blacks; the increasing isolation and deterioration of ghettos; the crisis in criminal justice; challenges to traditional black churches for community leadership; the presence of African Americans in popular media; and the emergence of black individuals as leaders in Hoosier and American culture.

Revolt in the Universities

One of the principal targets for change selected by the younger generation in the late 1960s and 1970s was the schools they attended, especially the institutions of higher learning, which identified valid subjects for study and also determined who was authorized to teach and research these subjects. "Black" students, as they named themselves, were part of a multiracial and national youth movement that charged universities with being accomplices in perpetuating racial injustice at home in the United States and abroad in Vietnam. Beginning in Berkeley with the Free Speech Movement in the early 1960s, college students, most of them white, used the tactics of the civil rights movement to assert their rights to participate in governing the universities. Black students in large eastern universities organized separately to demand changes in university policies toward African American students, especially to demand that universities add the study of black history and culture to the curriculum.

The only large student bodies in Indiana were in state universities located in small cities (Bloomington and West Lafayette) with very few African Americans as residents or students. Widespread political activism among students was virtually unknown in Indiana before 1966, when Bloomington's Progressive Reform Party—running on a platform of free speech, an end to curfews for women students, and support for a university employees union—won a university election with an unprecedented turnout of student voters. The "new breed of student politicians on the Bloomington campus" wanted to end the war in Vietnam and reform American society. They were potential allies of the black student group, which nevertheless viewed them with caution.

There were fewer than 500 African American students out of a campus student body of 26,000 at IU's main campus in the 1960s. A significant number were engaged in graduate studies; Indiana University had a larger black graduate student population than most other midwestern state universities because it had been one of the earliest to admit blacks to advanced degree programs.[4] Graduate student leadership was to make up in many ways for the size of the group. But black students were not only few in numbers; they also felt especially vulnerable because south central Indiana was notorious for "sunset" or "sundown" laws. When students elected a black student body president in 1960, crosses had been burned on the campus.[5]

The climate of student-university relations at IU heated up in 1967 when a group of demonstrators at the business school protested against recruiters for the Dow Chemical Company, notorious as manufacturers of napalm used in Vietnam. Local policemen wielding newly issued "riot sticks" arrested thirty-five demonstrators, including one African American graduate student, Bob Johnson, who was singled out by police for assault and by the court for more severe sentencing than the others. Johnson was an important figure in IU's student revolt—as a leader, an intellectual, and a personal bridge between black students and whites, with many of whom he was on good terms. Shortly after the Dow incident, Johnson became president of a new local organization, the Afro/Afro-American Student Association (AAASA), which rallied blacks to action. In the early spring of 1968, the AAASA began to demand that the university recruit more African American students and faculty members and institute a black studies program; they sat-in outside the president's campus residence in April for six hours, asserting their right to protest nonviolently against university policies.[6]

Martin Luther King Jr.'s assassination in Memphis a few days later sparked the creation of a new group of black students, the Ad Hoc Committee Against Racism (AHCAR), which staged a dramatic confrontation with the university in early May, on the eve of the Little 500 bicycle race. The race was the principal annual event of Bloomington's historically all-white fraternities. AHCAR announced that its members would sit-in on the stadium track where the race was to be run until the university forced the elimination of racist policies in the fraternities. They sat-in for thirty-eight hours, much of the time in the rain, with rumors of planned KKK violence circulating. A whirlwind of negotiating between the administration and fraternities resulted in the announcement that racial discrimination had been eliminated from the charters of IU's white fraternities, except one, which was not permitted to participate in the race held a week later.[7]

Student protest at Indiana University prompted various responses from trustees. The board ruled that the administration had the power to expel any student "who engages in conduct which unreasonably interferes with the freedom of movement of persons on any campus of the university." But the trustees also responded to black demands by authorizing a program to recruit and support promising lower-income undergraduates who did not meet standard admissions criteria; the Groups program, which has principally served African American students, began in the fall of 1968.[8]

Black students in Bloomington were able to draw upon an increasing radicalization of the white student body and faculty in 1969 and 1970 to achieve their goal of the creation of a black studies program at IU. Indeed, this goal was one of the few accomplished by student activists at IU.

In the fall of 1968, Rollo Turner, a black graduate student in sociology who had led earlier confrontations on campus, argued before a Joint Committee on Discriminatory Practices that beauty contests, which used a white standard of beauty and treated women as objects, were inherently racist and demeaning to all women. The committee was persuaded and ended the contests. Shortly afterward, in response to proposals that black student leaders and black faculty had submitted (drafted by Bob Johnson), the administration began to plan the creation of a new administrative position with responsibility for racial relations as well as a Black Studies Institute, with faculty member Orlando Taylor of the linguistics department as vice chancellor and institute head. In January, the faculty council approved a proposal to create a black studies department and to recruit black students and faculty.[9]

In the midst of these signs of victory for student activists, there were alarming episodes of white violence directed at blacks. In September 1968, a few miles up the road in Martinsville, a young black woman selling encyclopedias door-to-door was stabbed to death with a screwdriver by an assailant who was never brought to justice. A few months later the Black Market, a business run by Turner to give black and white students a place to hang out together, was firebombed by a KKK member. Some African American student leaders received death threats, and some began to carry weapons in self-defense.[10]

The issue that galvanized university students in Indiana, including the IU student body, into mass protests was the large tuition increase (70 percent) for the next academic year that was announced by the trustees of each of the state universities in the spring of 1969. The increases were not only burdensome in themselves—and for many students they could be prohibitive—they dramatized students' powerlessness within the university. Administrators put forward a budget to fund goals adopted without student consent or even consultation, and when the state legislature refused to appropriate enough funds to meet the budget, the trustees taxed students and their families for the shortfall. For several years, IU student leaders had been sharply criticizing the parental role the university insisted upon vis-à-vis students, i.e., requiring women students to be in their quarters by specific hours, denying students under twenty-one the right to live off-campus, and requiring a dress code for students at mealtimes in residence halls.[11] Treating college-age students and graduate students like children contrasted strikingly with the fate of their peers who served in Vietnam. And college-age students had no political voice; the amendment to lower the voting age to eighteen was not adopted until 1971.

At IU and Indiana State University in Terre Haute, black students took a leading part in student protests, and at IU their leadership drew national attention; but the first big response to the tuition increases came from Purdue students in West Lafayette, where nearly all the students were white. They boycotted classes for a week in April and camped-in at the student union, demanding that the increase be rescinded and that students be represented on the board of trustees. More than 250 persons were eventually arrested for refusing to end the demonstration, a building was fire-bombed, and 50 faculty members fasted for five days to protest the arrests.[12]

IU students joined the protest late in April. They boycotted classes for nine days early in May and attended almost daily rallies in the thousands, stunning organizers by the size of their turnout. Black student organizations joined the boycott, issuing separate demands at a rally on May 1 to exempt black students from tuition increases: the university's new plan to recruit more African Americans would be meaningless if students could not afford to come. Unfortunately one leader was quoted at that rally as threatening to "burn the university down" if their demands were not met within 24 hours; as he spoke, smoke appeared in the background from a fire in the university graduate library (a crime that was never solved).[13]

The same day at Indiana State University (ISU) a handful of students calling them-selves "Students for a Better University," at least some of whom apparently were black, barricaded themselves outside of the treasurer's office and asked for a ratification of a student constitution and bill of rights. They also wanted the establishment of a black studies department, controlled by black faculty members. They left when threatened with expulsion, and apparently this was the only demonstration at ISU in 1969.[14]

Back in Bloomington between 7,000 and 10,000 students voted to continue the boycott on May 5, while in sympathy the faculty council refused to urge them to end it. IU students constituted most of the 5,000 students from all four state universities who marched on the state capitol in Indianapolis on May 7 to protest the increase. That same day, 500 honor students walked out of the Founder's Day ceremony at IU in protest.[15]

At this point, black students at IU stepped forward to try to force a resolution. While student leaders, administrators, and faculty members were attempting to ne-gotiate an end to the class boycott on May 8, about 150 African American students, led by Rollo Turner and Professor Orlando Taylor, staged a "lock-in," blocking the doors of the faculty lounge in Ballantine Hall. Turner announced they would stay until "the Board of Trustees decides to talk to us." Around 2:30 A.M., when the po-lice threatened to move in unless the "lock-in" ended and after Chancellor John Sny-der promised that he would try to arrange a meeting with the trustees, the black stu-dents left the building. The student strike ended the next day. The Monroe County sheriff demanded a grand jury investigation of the events, which resulted in the in-dictment of Professor Taylor and eight students (including one white student) for "riotous conspiracy." (IU Northwest, in Gary, possibly inspired by black student ac-tivism in Bloomington, reported the day after the "lock-in" that 3,800 of its students boycotted classes to protest the increase.) Meeting with a delegation of Bloomington students on May 11, the IU trustees promised that no qualified student would be forced to drop out of school because of the increase, but the rise in tuition remained in place. Though black students had boldly tried to force a resolution to an issue that affected all students, they and the mass boycott failed.[16]

Black students' repeated demonstrations of willingness in 1968 and 1969 to ex-pose themselves to danger and to embarrass the administration kept pressure on IU to deliver the black studies program and administrative officer that had been planned,

Black students were in the forefront of the protest against fee increases at Indiana University in the spring of 1969; here students are conferring with Acting Chancellor John W. Snyder at a protest meeting attended by about five thousand students in Dunn Meadow. Unidentified *Indiana Daily Student* photographer, courtesy *Indiana Daily Student.*

but Orlando Taylor's arrest in May 1969 and his resignation delayed the implementation of the plan until the university found a replacement.

While IU was searching for a vice chancellor for Afro-American Affairs, black students at IU and ISU continued to challenge university policies; but in 1969–1970 more of the leaders at IU were now undergraduates. In November 1969 fourteen black IU football players, who were part of a team that had gone to the Rose Bowl two seasons before, charged the coaching staff with racial discrimination and protested by refusing to attend two practice sessions. While four of them soon returned to the team, ten players were eventually dropped for extending their protest; the conflict was costly both to the players involved, who lost their chance at an athletic career, and to the team. As they met with Coach John Pont, who denied the charges, their representative in the attempt to resolve the dispute was Professor Herman Hudson of Linguistics.[17]

Black undergraduates at ISU protested racial slurs posted on a residence hall bulletin board in late April 1970 by sitting-in, a demonstration that was followed by "a riot." The Black Student Union handed a list of demands to ISU trustees the next day that included more black advisers, student participation in orienting black students and running the dormitories, and "making decisions for the black studies program." The KKK responded by distributing racist leaflets throughout the campus.[18] A young white faculty member in English, who included writings by African American authors in her courses, challenged the power of the Klan by using their leaflets as a subject for literary analysis. She remembers that one student asked her whether she was not afraid. She also recalls that when black students sat in at a Board of Trustees meeting, members of a white fraternity came after them with guns and shot out windows.[19] The local press reported that white students who attended the meeting applauded trustees for rejecting black student demands. ISU eventually established a Center for African American Studies in 1972 and began granting degrees in African American Studies in 1979.[20]

Another example of black undergraduate leadership that year was provided by IU junior Keith Parker, a self-described Black Panther and Methodist from Indianapolis, who was elected student government president in March 1970. Parker, along with his vice president Mike King, who edited the *Spectator,* an alternative student newspaper, led the student body during the apex of activism on the Bloomington campus in the spring of 1970, following President Richard Nixon's sudden announcement on April 30 that he was widening the war in Vietnam by attacking Cambodia. College students all over the country erupted in protest, and several days later four students were killed at Kent State University by Ohio National Guardsmen brought in to quell the demonstrations. Instead of ending the unrest, these events prompted student protests that eventually shut down more than 270 colleges and universities.[21] Within a week it was reported that in Indiana nearly 60 percent of Notre Dame students were boycotting classes, and students were on strike at IU South Bend and ISU as well.[22] At DePauw University someone started a fire in the ROTC building.[23]

IU students gathered by the thousands in protest, but they did not force the university to close. They also remained nonviolent, in part because of Keith Parker's leadership. He and King responded effectively to the challenge of keeping large crowds of spontaneous protesters focused, peaceful, and away from the policemen the administration had deployed to protect their offices. As Parker told students on May 1 as he led them away from Bryan Hall, the main administrative building on campus,

Student body president Keith Parker led antiwar demonstrations at Indiana University in 1970. Unidentified *Indiana Daily Student* photographer, courtesy *Indiana Daily Student.*

"We can accomplish our purpose of presenting our demands without anyone getting ripped up."[24]

Parker also used his leadership to secure white student support for issues important to blacks: students who voted to support antiwar measures at the rally on May 1 also demanded that IU bring in black students to raise their representation in the university to equal their proportion of the state population and that IU contribute to the defense fund for Black Panther Bobby Seale, believed by many to be the target of government persecution for his radical beliefs.[25]

After the Kent State killings, Parker urged a class boycott and tried to organize pickets while students participated in a referendum on the war and other issues on his agenda. Nearly 18,000 students voted, and two-thirds opposed the invasion of Cambodia and wanted Congress to cut off support for the Vietnam War; about the same number backed a call for the IU Foundation to open its records to public inspection; more than half supported canceling classes to protest the Cambodian incursion and wanted the university to repudiate the war.[26]

In the wake of the referendum, several hundred students demonstrated outside Bryan Hall, asking President Joseph Sutton to respond personally to students and to promise to protect the rights of dissenters. Sutton called the police because the students were blocking the doors, and eight picketers were arrested. But Sutton and Chancellor Byrum Carter, after negotiating with Parker and other student leaders, agreed to a public meeting with students.[27] There were teach-ins to follow, but the protests were over. At IU there had been no violence, no destruction of property, and the Black Panther student body president, working with a white radical vice president, was as responsible as anyone for the nature of student protest in Bloomington.

Meanwhile, Herman Hudson accepted the position of vice chancellor for Afro-American Affairs in March 1970, after he was satisfied that black students approved the appointment; he then proceeded to build a new Afro-American Studies department to offer classes by the fall. Hudson brought considerable personal authority to the position. Trained in linguistics at the University of Michigan, he had spent six years as a Columbia University faculty member administering English-language instruction in Afghanistan at the secondary school level.[28] With his experience in administration and with his academic background, Hudson brought credibility to the project. Beyond this, Hudson was an inspiring person. He had lost most of his vision when he was a young child and had pursued his education and career with this added challenge.

Hudson believed it was important for the program to be an integral part of the university, a department with regular university funding and tenure-worthy faculty members to make it permanent. (He proposed this to Chancellor Carter in 1970, and the board of trustees approved it in April 1971.) Faced with a scarcity of well-prepared black academics, who were in demand for new black studies programs in universities around the country, Hudson nurtured talented black graduate students at IU and elsewhere. He also hired Phyllis Klotman, a white scholar who specialized in black literature.[29]

The creation of a department of Afro-American Studies at the state's flagship campus for liberal arts meant that the university had committed itself in a major way to a new field of knowledge. There was less commitment to recruiting black under-graduates to come to Bloomington; the Groups program, which focused on low-income students who, although promising in some way, did not meet standard admissions criteria, did virtually all the university's recruiting of black students.[30] Until Hudson proposed the Minority Achievers Program in 1987 there was no program to encourage well-qualified African American students to come to Bloomington—to come despite the very small number of black students on campus and the town's reputation as inhospitable to blacks. As a result, black students continued after 1970 to form a tiny minority of the student body, about 3 percent in a state in which blacks constitute about 8 percent of the whole population.[31]

But the development of African American studies programs at the state's colleges and universities represented the victory of black students in forcing white academics to acknowledge a place for black history and culture in the universe of knowledge.[32] And pressure to demonstrate that universities were not racist led to increased willingness to hire black faculty outside the field of Afro-American Studies. Hence, black scholars slowly began to change the face and the content of the state's universities, offering examples of African Americans as intellectual authority figures and models for students, both black and white. These scholars were almost always overworked, since they had not only to satisfy their university's demands for publication and teaching but also were expected to serve as the black or minority representative on an exhausting round of committees and as the unofficial mentors for virtually all black students.[33]

In the 1970s IU Bloomington's attractions for black students seeking graduate training were enhanced because the Afro-American Studies department and the Groups program offered opportunities for graduate student jobs. Bloomington thus became the setting—a seemingly unlikely one—for a pioneering group of midwestern African American intellectuals. Lacking the extensive resources available in cities with large black populations, Bloomington's black intelligentsia banded together to form a closely knit community; they constituted a small black island in a sea of white faces. Consequently, in the 1970s and early 1980s they had picnics, went to football games, and attended the local black church as a group. Most had grown up in larger urban settings with well-established African American communities. In Bloomington they had to reinvent themselves as members of the mainstream academy while in exile from "home."

This was true to some extent, of course, for much of the faculty in every university: university towns are filled with people in "exile" from New York and Chicago, from London and Paris, from Rome and Budapest, and a multitude of other places. But the black faculty and graduate students faced a heightened sense of isolation because of the tradition of racial prejudice, not only among the local townspeople but also among many white faculty members.[34] For some black scholars the friendships they formed with white students in graduate school were their first experience of interracial friendship, and this was undoubtedly true also for many of the white students whose friends they became. And the children of black faculty members were their hostages to fortune. Their children were often the only black students in their grades or even sometimes the only black students in their school. One African American administrator recalled that her daughter came home from nursery school and asked when *she* would be white. Later, when her parents had worked hard to give her a sure sense of her own identity as an African American, they discovered from her teacher that she was refusing to play with white children; and then they had to repair this misunderstanding of their teaching.[35]

The black undergraduates who came to residential colleges in Bloomington and elsewhere in the state were mostly from Indianapolis and Gary, where large African American communities insulated them to some extent from contact with whites. Some later remembered that they had their first personal encounters with racial prejudice in college dormitories. One girl reported to a faculty member in the 1970s that her roommate dressed and undressed under the covers to avoid being seen by a black person. Some experienced even more painful rejection: when their white roommates saw with whom they were to room, they just moved out.[36]

Students from moderate to low-income families were the principal residents of the large dormitories in Bloomington. Wealthier white students tended to live in fraternity and sorority houses or in off-campus housing. The Bloomington dorms became a laboratory for college-age integration. The pressures were sometimes great. The university created a special Racial Incidents Team in 1988 to help students who believed they had been the targets of prejudice. Composed of staff, students, and faculty members, the team heard grievances and attempted to resolve them. Usually the incidents involved the use of offensive terms and the offenders claimed to be "kidding." Many black students, perhaps most, felt more comfortable in mostly black settings such as the Afro-American Culture Center than in the Student Union. For a significant percentage of black freshmen every year, especially those who had not attended integrated high schools, the experience of alienation from the tens of thousands of white students and thousands of foreign students of various ethnicities in Bloomington was profound. Many dropped out. The shift from the all- or mostly African American schools and neighborhoods in which they had grown up to the overwhelmingly white-dominated campus in Bloomington was a "culture shock" that left painful memories.[37]

Despite these difficulties, the decade of the 1970s was a period in which more and more college-age blacks went to college. The 1980–1981 school year showed 20,711 black students enrolled in Indiana's public universities, which constituted 10.2 percent of the total student population in the state, about the same percentage that African Americans made up of the state's college-age population (eighteen-to-twenty-four-year-olds). Here was a first: only a decade after the civil rights revolution, an historically excluded and oppressed population in a state not usually described as progressive sent the same proportion of its children to college as the majority whites did. Whatever else it meant, clearly a significantly larger proportion of African American youth saw themselves as potential members of their state's elite of college-educated persons than had earlier generations of Indiana blacks.[38]

The percentage of black students enrolled in Indiana colleges and universities declined after 1981, while overall enrollment increased 21 percent. The trend was the same in other states. The Indiana Commission for Higher Education (ICHE), at the prompting of the Black Legislative Caucus and the Coalition of Blacks in Higher Education, began tracking black college enrollments in 1984. At first, ICHE's view was that the black student-age population was behaving the way Indiana's white youth behaved in not choosing to go to college.[39] Indiana's traditional economic reliance on durable goods industries with older technologies had meant that many of the state's youth had job opportunities that did not require higher education.[40] But that explanation overlooked the decline in the number and proportion of black students compared to whites enrolling in college after 1981. Clearly the relatively widespread optimism among Indiana's African Americans about their prospects in higher education had diminished by 1981, along with the comparative prosperity of the 1970s.

The economic recovery in the 1990s was reflected by a rebound in the number of black college students. ICHE reported that 6 percent of students enrolled in Indiana colleges and universities in 1993–1994 were black. More meaningful yet, perhaps, was the report that African Americans were staying in college longer. In Bloomington IU reported an increase in black students returning after the freshman year, from 68.1 percent in 1995–1996 to 87.3 percent in 1998–1999.[41]

Desegregation of Middle-Class and Elite Blacks

During the 1970s some younger entrepreneurs and community leaders adopted the new "black" identity. In Indianapolis they founded Indiana Black Expo in 1970, which created an annual event for African Americans to recognize the community's accomplishments and to hear national leaders speak; it also provided a marketplace for black business. Black Expo's principal activity, beginning in 1971, has been a weeklong fair held in July, with speakers, entertainers, cultural exhibits, and beauty contests. The fair offered to Indianapolis African Americans and out-of-towners who came for the event a chance to demonstrate black unity and prosperity in a public space. The African Americans who came to the Expo's programs in downtown Indianapolis enjoyed the relatively rare chance to revisit some of the positive elements of segregated black community as blacks left the old neighborhoods for other parts of Indianapolis.

As housing and some job barriers fell in the 1970s, Indianapolis's African Americans, like those in other parts of the state, were increasingly separated, both physically and psychologically, by economic and social class differences. Those who had good jobs and education left Center Township, the "bottoms," where blacks had been mostly confined in segregated housing before the 1960s and 1970s; they also left a segregated way of life. This move entailed a racially integrated business and social life. Earlier, black professionals had been confined to life in the ghetto, where they shared many of the disadvantages of poorer and less educated African Americans but where they exercised a leadership based on personal acquaintance with other members of the community. When opportunities opened, black professionals moved into new neighborhoods that were racially integrated and *economically* segregated.[42]

Indianapolis architect Walter Blackburn is an example of someone whose life fit this pattern. Blackburn lived as a child with his family above Flanner House, where his father Cleo headed the settlement for many decades to help provide services for other African Americans. Like many of his contemporaries, the younger Blackburn's career led him into a social and professional life that reached beyond racial boundaries.[43] Blackburn attended Shortridge, an integrated high school in the 1950s, where some of his fellow students became friends and business contacts in years to come. Inspired by the civil rights movement when he was studying architecture at Howard University, Blackburn expressed his racial identity in a strong desire to excel, to show that an African American could succeed as an architect, without being dependent on white partners. For many of Blackburn's generation, personal achievement was also perceived as a gift to the black community, a source of pride and encouragement, an element in a collective racial identity. Blackness, for them, meant tremendous strength and determination to overcome obstacles, a quality some described as "soul." It also meant both a sense of solidarity with other African Americans and a sense of racial competition with whites, in which blacks cheered for other blacks. And "for a black person not to speak to another black on the street—something is wrong."[44]

Blackburn described himself as a member of a transitional generation. His children grew up in a racially integrated and more prosperous world and redefined the meaning of their racial identity. Inevitably, perhaps, race played a smaller role in their lives than it did in his.[45]

It was not only the most prosperous African Americans who left Center Township in Indianapolis and other ghettos in the 1970s and 1980s; *most* former residents left the old neighborhoods. Usually they moved to areas where there was a sizable black population; for example, in the late 1990s only a third of Marion County blacks lived in majority white areas. In 1990 the average Indianapolis African American resided in a neighborhood that was two-thirds black. This was not the ideal "mix" that most preferred, since nearly 70 percent of black people polled about their housing preferences in Indianapolis in 1993 said that they would like to live in neighborhoods with an even mix of blacks and whites; only a quarter of those polled said they preferred mostly black neighborhoods. But far fewer whites polled at the same time said they wanted to live in racially mixed areas; 48 percent said they would prefer such neighborhoods, but interestingly whites said they thought that very few *other* whites (10.3 percent) preferred racially mixed areas.[46]

While the old black community of Indianapolis eroded in the decades after the civil rights revolution, and members moved to better housing in racially mixed areas, most were still choosing the relative psychological safety of largely African American neighbors. Some were dissuaded from mostly white neighborhoods by real estate agents and homeowners who evaded laws prohibiting discrimination; some were no doubt dissuaded by highly publicized instances of white hostility to blacks moving into "white" neighborhoods. Nevertheless, most were living in housing that was better in quality in neighborhoods with more racial mixture than in the period before 1970. One observer optimistically concluded that residential segregation in Indianapolis was "largely history" since the 1990 census showed that there were African Americans living in every area of the city. [47]

For some of the black newcomers to mostly white areas, the experience of living

Walter Blackburn,
Indianapolis architect.
Courtesy of Walter
Blackburn.

Below: David Hubbard and
Collins Ferguson, migrants
from the South to Lafayette
in the late 1940s, after their
retirement in the 1980s.
Courtesy of Dorothy
Ferguson.

with white neighbors proved disappointing; no matter how prosperous, educated, and refined the new black resident was, some blacks believed that white neighbors never saw beyond color. "You're always black first in their eyes, never a person." But when whites did seem to forget they were talking to a black person the result could also be painful: "She said to me, 'and there I was when this big black man came into this place,' as though I would understand her fear of a big black man."[48]

Racial prejudice no longer kept African Americans from access to housing and public accommodations in Indiana, but there were still common humiliations, reminders that many whites felt free to show prejudice. Undercover investigators for WRTV in Indianapolis in a 1993 television series, *Blacks and Whites: Can We All Get Along?*, documented with video cameras that on every occasion when white women students from Butler University shopped in Indianapolis mall stores they were treated courteously and quickly helped, while black Butler women were not greeted and not helped until they requested it. While the white student members of the investigating team were surprised, black students expected it. "It's just the way it is, and you can't let it bother you."[49]

Similarly, African Americans in integrated workplaces often believed they had to be stoical in withstanding workplace racism. Some were passed over for promotion for decades without explanations from supervisors about how their work should be improved. Those who acquired seniority sometimes found that white supervisors would change the rules to deprive them of seniority's traditional privileges. Minority members who were supervisors were also sometimes given "the blues" (harassed) by whites further up in the hierarchy. Black workers who were union members could earn wages and benefits that gave them a middle-class lifestyle and permitted them to educate their children, but the price was sometimes to tolerate harassment and humiliation. "People prefer to promote members of their own ethnic groups," observed one African American worker at a large manufacturing plant in Indianapolis. A college graduate, she was regularly passed over for promotion.[50]

Most probably tolerated the discrimination to keep the job, but some did not. One South Bend woman quit her job and sued the Kroger supermarket chain for illegally denying her employment opportunities after she was refused promotion for ten years, despite good work evaluations and despite her being asked to train the persons who were hired to supervise her. She won and received a modest damages settlement.[51]

A 1993 poll of Indianapolis blacks most likely reflected the belief of most African Americans in the state: when asked whether they agreed with the statement "Whites don't want blacks to get ahead," 62.1 percent said yes. Certainly most black business owners agreed. WRTV found it difficult to interview black businessmen because they did not want it known that their businesses were black-owned for fear that whites would avoid them if they knew.[52]

The Ghettos

If relatively prosperous blacks continued to experience prejudice as they left the ghetto to move on to better jobs and housing, those who remained in Indianapolis's Center Township and other "old neighborhoods" found their living conditions deteriorating significantly. Many lost the benefits of segregation without gaining the advantages of integration. Segregation had created many side-effects: the unity of the black community; the concerned leadership of that community by professionals; the relative insignificance of economic differences among African Americans and their consequent ambivalence about the majority society's emphasis on wealth as the standard of merit; and a tradition of black self-help. All of these factors dwindled as the lives of most African Americans became more like those of other Americans. For those who for one reason or another were unable or unwilling to leave, the message was clear. Their home became stigmatized as the place successful people left, the symbol of poverty and failure. And without the shield of middle-class blacks, those who were poorer were also more vulnerable to the hostility of the whites who provided city services, especially police and firefighters.[53]

Messages about the disintegration of traditional social structures in the old black neighborhoods, especially in Indianapolis and Gary, began to make headlines in Indiana by the mid-1980s. The enormous increase in teenage out-of-wedlock pregnancies and black-on-black crime was both profoundly disturbing in itself and disturbing because it reinforced old racial stereotypes. The message seemed to be that fairly large numbers of black young people growing up in poverty had abandoned the goals of education, work, and family formation in favor of violent crime and living on welfare. The self-destructiveness of such choices seemed dramatized by the news in 1987 that Marion County had the highest black infant mortality rate in the United States. Here was a shameful witness to the state's traditional weakness in public health and to the failure of the larger urban community to accept responsibility for helping poor people get along.[54]

For many older African Americans, especially those who had earlier considered themselves "Negroes" or "colored" persons, the unmarried teenaged mothers represented an outrage, a breakdown of traditional ethics of responsibility and hard work. Some blamed the welfare system; others pointed to schools in which too little was demanded and too little discipline imposed. One retired Indianapolis Public Schools teacher and longtime activist, for example, argued that real achievement required high standards and qualified teachers. For her, one key to reducing the number of teenage mothers was increasing the number of students who did their homework and were required to learn fundamental skills and knowledge. The mistake, from her point of view, was in giving up on children by *not* holding them to a high standard of achievement.[55]

Blacks and Criminal Justice

But in the early 1990s, the emergency of teenage mothers and dying babies was eclipsed by the related problems of young black men in Indiana, especially the increase in the numbers of those involved with the criminal justice system. While adult black males constituted about 8 percent of the male population of the state, they were nearly 40 percent of the state's prison population. African American prisoners were usually from the ghettos; they were poor, and they were school dropouts. Some prisoners from Indianapolis and Gary were gang members. The most alarming statistic was the rise in homicides: in 1989 in Indianapolis there were 68; in 1991 there were 109; by 1998 there were 160. While in 1991 half of the victims were black, by 1998, 64 percent were. In Fort Wayne, 80 percent of homicide victims in 1991 were African Americans. A special commission that studied homicides concluded 74.4 percent of the homicide victims knew the person who killed them.[56]

In 1991, the General Assembly appointed a special committee to study the problems of black males, which researched the "largest urban areas with significant Black populations" (Fort Wayne, Gary, South Bend, Indianapolis, and the Indiana State Prison). The group chastised the government for its failure to make a general plan to address the crisis and claimed, "The state is in a state of denial."[57]

While the committee agreed that "poverty, racism, [and] discrimination" were the root causes of the problems of black males, the report also reflected divisions among African Americans.[58] One group focused on character issues, stressing the need to change values, develop responsibility, and control anger, and another focused on injustice issues, urging "white government" to work harder to accommodate African American problems.[59] Among the former were those who saw slavery as the root cause of poor parenting, apathy, unemployment, and addictions; they also cited dependency as a result of too many handouts. Their solutions tended to be to expand self-help programs, such as volunteering in schools, supporting neighborhood associations, and "go[ing] back to the Lord," and encouraging greater congregational involvement with prisoners and ex-prisoners.[60] Those who saw the problems principally as failures of a white majority to provide justice and equality to African Americans stressed an expansion of social programs and a change in existing programs to accommodate black male needs. The emphasis in this group was twofold: hiring black males as role models in all areas and changing white behaviors to be more responsive to the special needs of black males.[61]

Observers from both perspectives agreed that the problems reflected a very broad range of issues, from unemployment to health care, education, criminal justice, and family structure; the list of causes was discouragingly long. And all African Americans in Indiana's larger urban areas agreed that young black males were specially targeted by police, who were mostly white.[62] WRTV's weeklong series on relationships between blacks and whites in Indianapolis in 1993 attracted a barrage of criticism from the Fraternal Order of Police and from a local newspaper when their undercover investigations showed that for two nights in a row policemen stopped black male college students driving expensive cars in the suburbs while white college students drove the same cars in the same places unimpeded. In two programs police officers speaking with disguised voices said that racism was common in the Indianapolis police department, that many policemen believed all black males are guilty until proven innocent, and that police officers who mistreated blacks were not punished.[63]

One of the relatively few issues that continued to inspire black unity in the increasingly diverse African American communities in Indiana's larger cities was resentment against police and distrust of the justice system. In part this response reflected the history of police using deadly force against African American suspects far more often than they did against whites. The most egregious cases in Indianapolis have caused an uproar in the black community. In 1981 an African American was shot and killed on Monument Circle in Indianapolis in a dispute over a parking ticket, while his wife and child looked on.[64] In 1989 a fourteen-year-old in police custody, hand-cuffed in the backseat of a police car, was said by police to have committed suicide. The prima facie implausibility of this explanation prompted an enormous public response. Some black leaders arranged to hire a retired policeman as an independent investigator; after a two-week investigation in which the city cooperated he concluded that there was no evidence the police killed the youth. A further investigation by the FBI, at the request of a local church leader, also ruled the boy's death a suicide.[65] But the perception that whites could harm blacks and not be punished was reinforced by the shooting of Vernon Jordan, then national president of the Urban League, when he visited Fort Wayne in June 1980. An all-white jury acquitted his assailant in 1982.[66]

The trial in Indianapolis of heavyweight boxer Mike Tyson dramatized the difference in perception of justice between blacks and whites. Tyson, accused of raping an eighteen-year-old beauty-pageant contestant at Indiana Black Expo in the summer of 1991, was convicted by a mostly white jury in February 1992, despite the belief of two-thirds of the black community that he was not guilty and had been unfairly judged.[67] The response seemingly reflected a widespread conviction that the justice system was regularly unfair to black males. Like African Americans all over the country, Indiana blacks responded similarly to the O. J. Simpson murder trial in 1995, cheering when the Los Angeles jury acquitted him, despite evidence of his guilt that the overwhelming majority of whites found conclusive. While the lives of most blacks have become more like those of most whites in the past thirty years, this acute sense of injustice in punishing crime continued to mark racial identity.

The black perception of chronic unfairness in the criminal justice system was part of a larger sense of relative powerlessness. African Americans in Indianapolis lost significant power when UniGov was adopted, finessing the Democratic majority within the old city boundaries by expanding city government to incorporate heavily Republican suburbs. The result was a regular Republican advantage in city politics and a concurrent disadvantage to Democrats, of whom black voters constitute a large percentage.[68] While blacks in Gary had political power, the city's dependency upon a single industry along with its chronic economic woes sharply undercut the impact of local politics. Elsewhere blacks were always badly outnumbered. Hence, while individual African American politicians could exercise considerable influence in the state on the basis of personal leadership abilities, as *African Americans* they exercised little political power.[69]

The Media and the Leaders

In many ways, of course, the changes since 1970 have expanded the power of Indiana's African Americans. The once-routine denial of jobs and housing to blacks became a federal crime—and consequently, significantly less routine. The opportunities for African Americans to compete on an equal basis for offices, prizes, and commissions have expanded considerably: black candidates have been elected to Congress and to statewide office; they have also been elected as presidents of statewide professional associations, as Indiana University trustee, and as Miss Indiana.[70] African Americans have been appointed to serve as Indianapolis school superintendent, chief of Indianapolis police, appellate court judge, and Indiana women's prison superintendent.[71] Indianapolis architect Walter Blackburn was chosen to design a major national museum, the National Underground Railroad Museum in Cincinnati.[72]

African American newscasters have also become among the most visible daily interpreters of local and state happenings. Few blacks appeared on local television stations in the 1970s. Barbara Boyd was consumer affairs reporter for Channel 6, and Alpha Blackburn broke new ground by hosting a regular program, "Indy Today," on Channel 8 in the mid-1970s.[73] In 1993 when WRTV produced "Blacks and Whites: Can We All Get Along?" the reporters called attention to the absence of black "anchors" on weekly television news. By 1995 WRTV had hired James Adams for its nightly evening news programs, and black women reporters appeared regularly on weekday news for three other stations.[74]

While African American reporters offered attractive images of blacks in the media, the news they reported often emphasized black crime and social disintegration. The regular increase in news stories showing African Americans accused of and victims of crime, compounded by entertainment programming that often reinforced stereotypes of black poverty and violence, inaccurately suggested to both blacks and whites that most blacks were poor.

Television and the print media were influential in presenting interpretations of Indiana's black history, which constituted another important element in the creation of racial identity in the period after 1970. There were Negro History weeks in Indianapolis in the late 1960s and Negro History months in 1969 and 1970, but in 1973 Black History Month was inaugurated as an annual event, triggering the publication of newspaper articles, the preparation of exhibits, and essay contests. Most public schools recognized February as a time to emphasize black historical accomplishments.[75] The civil rights movement also generated new interest on the part of professional historians in black history, and most of the history of blacks in Indiana has appeared since 1970.[76] But history was not left only to historians and schools. In 1975 an Indianapolis group formed a Black Bicentennial Committee to honor citizens in a special publication.[77] By the mid-1980s, several ambitious black history projects were underway in Indiana: Ophelia Umar's Freetown Village was proposed as a permanent exhibit to be located in the White River State Park, and at Purdue, Professor Darlene Clark Hine, spurred by Indianapolis public school teacher Shirley Herd, directed a drive to collect documents on black women in the Middle West. By 1988 IPS was working on a black history curriculum, which was incorporated into the classrooms that fall.[78]

The Indiana Historical Society established a Black History section for its members in 1979, began publishing a quarterly newsletter, *Black History News and Notes,* and collected materials for research. Some good local histories of African Americans in Indiana appeared, and some county histories were published.[79] By the mid-1980s there were a few film documentaries on aspects of Indiana black history: "Two Dollars and

Barbara Boyd, pioneer television reporter. Indianapolis *Recorder* Collection, Indiana Historical Society.

a Dream" examined the career of Madam C. J. Walker for PBS, while "Masters of Disaster" chronicled the triumph of a black chess team from an Indianapolis elementary school that won the national chess championship for that level in 1983.[80]

These efforts and the state's adoption of Martin Luther King Jr.'s birthday as a state holiday raised the consciousness of many Hoosiers, white and black, about earlier black experiences in the state. It is less clear how much they provided a "usable past" for either children or adults. For school children the story of black people's courageous resistance to oppression, service to their country in wartime, defeat of segregation in the 1950s and 1960s, and individual achievement offered a parable of black heroism and white guilt that some have found difficult to assimilate into a useful worldview. Some black children heard the history with anger, cynicism, and even despair: if, after all of the history of suffering and legal changes, African Americans were still the victims of poverty and injustice, what hope was there? Many young white children heard the history as a parable of conversion: the sacrifice of noble black heroes like King and Medgar Evers *saved* the white sinners by showing them their wickedness, and changing the law was the sign of whites' salvation. "Now," children reasoned, it was a good society, and blacks should be grateful. Some drew a more hostile conclusion: changing the laws had resulted in "reverse discrimination." Now, they concluded, blacks had unfair advantages and whites were victims.[81]

"Whites" and "blacks" were, of course, not the only groups in Indiana and the United States. Persons of Hispanic and Asian ethnicities were also present in increasing numbers, and for them black history had even more ambiguous significance. Like earlier groups of American immigrants—the nineteenth-century Irish, Italians, and Eastern European groups—some resented the notion that African Americans deserved any special attention or compensatory aid. Others, especially those educated in public schools, probably adopted the views of the majority of their fellow students.

A small number of blacks found the "official" versions of black history offered in the public schools and universities to be completely inadequate; they argued that this history (of which the present study is an example) reflected the prejudice that viewed culture from a European, i.e., white, perspective. For these critics, any Eurocentric history that stressed the priority of European "discoverers" and colonizers of nonwhites in interpreting history was racist. They frankly claimed a political agenda for educating black students and demanded an Afrocentric historical curriculum that asserted the superiority of African peoples, on the grounds that black students' self-esteem would be enhanced by interpretations that emphasized African cultural achievements. Critics of Afrocentrism rejected the implicit racism in the philosophy and also denied the assumption that blacks and whites could not share an historical perspective. They argued that, since African Americans' forebears had participated in a predominantly European culture in America for hundreds of years, blacks inherited *both* African and European history and should not be limited to one perspective. But the Afrocentric critique challenged mainstream historians to reexamine their implicit acceptance of European preeminence in all areas of history and culture.[82]

Popular culture wielded considerable power in shaping African American identity after 1970, when television executives and advertisers began to include black performers in commercials and entertainment programs. It is difficult to know how Hoosiers in particular interpreted television's version of African Americans, but no serious discussion of changes and continuities in racial identities can ignore the impact of a performer like Bill Cosby. A few blacks were "crossover" superstars, whose appeal had no racial boundaries: Bill Cosby, Eddie Murphy, Oprah Winfrey, Michael

Jackson, and Michael Jordan each in distinctive ways had extraordinary appeal. Jordan, especially, achieved an heroic stature based on his athletic prowess and enormous personal dignity and confidence. He may have established professional basketball as the favorite American sport. Some other black performers achieved "crossover" popularity, while yet others appealed more exclusively to a black audience. Each conveyed different messages about racial identity. The superstars clearly suggested that racial identity was a relatively secondary part of individual identity.

The 1980s and 1990s featured a long string of situation comedies set in "the ghetto," starring African Americans and replicating older stereotypes. The principal audience for these programs was composed of African Americans; researchers documented that the top-rated programs among blacks had little in common with the overall ratings. An Indianapolis *Star* editorial attributed the perpetuation of stereotypes to racist beliefs among white programmers, who create "sitcoms like Martin and The Wayans Bros., in which African Americans are mostly gigglin', shufflin', shuckin' and jivin' caricatures."[83] But the ratings analyses seem to suggest this is at best an incomplete analysis. By the end of the 1990s, there were few blacks appearing in prime-time programming on the major networks, though they continued to be important presences in athletic events, in daytime programming, and in commercials on the major networks.[84]

Black athletes captured the imaginations of many white Hoosier sports fans as well as blacks, and team loyalties have played a major role in "Americanizing" African Americans as they did with European immigrant athletes in earlier generations. While Oscar Robertson, one of the greatest athletes in the sport of basketball, inspired the passionate loyalty of black fans and won the admiration of many whites when he played for Crispus Attucks and for Cincinnati in the 1950s and 1960s, by the 1990s Indianapolis's Reggie Miller had become a hero to young fans, both black and white, in a way that Robertson had not been permitted to be. These new loyalties meant that it was not only African Americans in the 1990s but also a large body of white Purdue fans who were aggravated by the media attention given to white player Damon Bailey of IU during the years when a player of yet greater accomplishment, Glenn Robinson of Purdue, was active.[85]

Challenges to Churches

Many observers believed that black churches constituted the most powerful institutions in the lives of African Americans, and ministers continued to act as community spokesmen after 1970, especially speaking out against perceived inequalities in policing and the court system.[86]But the doctrinal differences that often divided Protestants reinforced other factors that increasingly separated groups of African Americans—how much they earned, where they lived, how they lived—and this made churches less likely to adopt common policies in addressing the problems of ghettos. Even if Baptists were willing to adopt economic programs to aid poorer blacks, Pentecostals were unlikely to agree. Moreover, black churches generally supported conservative theological views that emphasized individual salvation rather than social reform. While promoting basic civil rights had been a policy all could support, the problems of poverty and social disintegration suggested no equally obvious and un-controversial common policy. All blacks had shared the oppression of segregation before the civil rights revolution, but now the problems of the ghetto were more and more remote from the lives of most church members. The churches used the lan-guage of scripture and gospel music to focus strongly on personal moral behavior and family responsibility; but ghetto youths increasingly knew only the language of mass culture, especially commercial television, popular music, and films, which em-phasized self-gratification, sexuality, and material wealth. These cultural differences meant that mainstream black churches faced competition for members and author-ity from sects that proselytized more aggressively in inner cities: the fast-growing Pen-tecostal groups and the Islamic movement.[87]

Relatively few of the African Americans in Indiana who converted to Islam joined Louis Farrakhan's controversial Nation of Islam (NOI), which continued the racist policies that characterized Elijah Muhammad's black Muslims before his death in 1975. Though it attracted few adherents, NOI generated controversy with its leaders' flamboyant and provocative antiwhite rhetoric, which targeted Jews, in particular, as scapegoats for black problems. Many middle-class blacks and whites excused Far-rakhan's attacks on Jews because NOI brought an orderly and hardworking body of young black men into some of the most desolate and dangerous black areas ("neigh-borhoods" seems a euphemistic term) to proselytize and to organize programs to re-duce crime, help students with homework, and train young men in marketable skills. Their conservative appearance contrasted vividly with the garb of ghetto youths, which more often signaled the need to join a street gang than the hope or expectation of a job. African Americans who had moved up were impressed that NOI provided mis-sionaries to those who were left behind in the old neighborhoods.[88]

The Million Man March organized by Farrakhan in 1995 further enhanced NOI's reputation. The occasion appealed to many as an opportunity for African American men to "witness" for one another their atonement for failings and make pledges to accept responsibility for their own lives and commitment to their families and com-munities. Indianapolis sent about a thousand marchers, and Reverend Charles Williams, president of Indiana Black Expo, described the event as "a holy day." While the number of participants from Indiana was smaller than organizers had predicted, the experience was a moving one for those who went. Farrakhan's call for black men to organize to help their communities and to get involved in schools inspired some marchers to new activism. In South Bend, for example, they formed a Million Man March Committee; after a symbolic march of all the black male students around Dick-inson Middle School, the committee asked the boys to commit themselves to live re-sponsibly, avoiding alcohol, drugs, and sex. The experience prompted the marchers to mentor middle-school-age black youths for several years.[89]

It is noteworthy, however, that the substantial growth in congregations of Indi-ana's Muslims of African American descent in the 1980s and 1990s came, not in NOI, but in the mainstream of the Islamic movement, which rejected both racism and racial separation.[90]

While NOI and the 1995 march attracted national attention, local black churches worked with a lower profile through denominational projects, like the Baptists' SPIRIT movement, to engage young people in social and religious programs.[91] Despite all efforts by black religious leaders, gangs in large cities continued to appeal to many. They showed the power of the outlaw image for many young black males when their physical safety was not normally secure.

One consequence of the considerable changes in the lives of African Americans in Indiana since 1970 has been the emergence of "gaps" between generations whose experiences have been dissimilar. Most older Indiana blacks, people who were adults during World War II, tend to view the last third of the century as one of real progress. They tend to think of themselves as persons of color, but persons first. For example, Alice Brokenburr Ray pointed out that she had never felt so *visible* as a black person before the 1960s and 1970s, when race became a main topic of public discussion; for her, an important goal was for the perception of color difference to dwindle in importance. Collins Ferguson and David Hubbard, trained craftsmen who moved to Lafayette in the late 1940s after graduating from Tuskegee Institute in Alabama, expressed pride in their work and in their contributions as community members. For them, color was less significant than the quality of the work they performed and the quality of the individual relationships they formed. Frances Linthecome, without diminishing the level of injustice and prejudice she encountered in the years before segregation ended, expressed a pride in the United States. "I didn't feel this *was* my country before the 1960s. But after the civil rights movement and the laws changed, I was proud of America. It is hard for people to admit that they are wrong and to change, but that is what my country has done politically."[92]

Members of the generation that came of age in the decades after World War II are significantly more conscious of racial identity and more likely to feel both racial competition and resentment against inequality. For these now-middle-aged veterans of years of confronting inequality with the expectation that it would end, there is both pride in personal accomplishment and profound disappointment that instances of injustice and inequality persist. Kay Rowe, a recently retired IPS teacher active in school desegregation, expressed impatience with the seeming need of each white person to have a personal black acquaintance in order to perceive the injustice of racial stereotypes. "We're only 8 percent of the population. There just aren't enough of us to go around." It was time, she thought, for whites to "Get over it!" Others feared that older forms of exclusion would return or that a new disaster was on the horizon. One observer claimed that "the very future and survival of the Indianapolis African American community" depended upon improving the economic and social conditions of blacks.[93] This sense of urgency often drove members of this generation to leadership in organizations or movements to help other members of the community, and there was often a strong and positive sense of black identity. Some spoke nostalgically of the benefits of segregation in their childhoods.[94]

The generation born after the civil rights revolution is significantly more diverse in experience than the previous one. Most in Indiana have attended integrated schools, lived in integrated neighborhoods, and come from families that would describe themselves as "middle-class"—i.e., above the poverty line. But within this general description there is a wide variety of experience. There are very wealthy African Americans in this generation who have lived in exclusive, integrated neighborhoods, attended private schools, and experienced a life of social and economic privilege beyond the access of prosperous black families and most whites of earlier generations. Some of these young people no longer see racial identity as an important factor in their lives. The children of black professionals have also attended good schools and formed some friendships outside racial boundaries, as have perhaps most blacks of their generation. These middle-class younger people find it relatively easy to interact with whites in school and in the workplace. They may or may not attend a black church or date members of another race. For them, too, race has receded as a major part of their sense of personal identity.[95]

But the large minority of the younger generation that have lived in an almost exclusively black world, attended schools resegregated by the loss of black middle-class families, and are poorer and less likely to be raised by two-parent families have created a distinctive black identity that is both fascinating and repellent to middle-class blacks and whites.[96] Their street culture, with its distinctive patois (unintelligible to outsiders), its celebration of violence and sexuality, its contempt for work and school, like the street gang cultures of the immigrant Irish and the Italians of the early part of the century, represents the collapse of parental authority and the inability of its members to support themselves with legitimate work. Its wildness has a fascination for middle-class youths, both black and white, on the brink of accommodating themselves to the world of regular work, as gangsters have fascinated generations of Americans.[97]

But unlike earlier "gang" societies of immigrants, Indiana's ghetto gang members have few prospects for honest employment once they pass their youth. Even Indiana's relatively old-technology industries employ too few unskilled workers to accommodate many semiliterate black youths and single mothers. This group has fewer options than virtually any other segment of Indiana society. And without a major commitment to making the schools and streets in those neighborhoods safe for their residents, it is difficult to imagine how they will be able to equip themselves for self-support in the postwelfare, postindustrial Hoosier economy.

Perhaps the only safe conclusion to be drawn about black identity in Indiana at the end of the twentieth century is that race has dwindled in importance somewhat. Two instances illustrate the ways in which this has occurred. The first concerns the election in November 1998 of a highly qualified African American, retired FBI agent Oatess Archey, as Indiana's first black sheriff. What made this already interesting event striking was that it was the mostly white voters of Grant County who elected him, and Marion in Grant County was the site of Indiana's last lynching, in 1930. The scions of Marion's lynch mob of seventy years before chose a black man to be their chief law enforcement officer.

The second instance concerns an institution dedicated to the preservation of an important expression of African American culture, the Afro-American Choral Ensemble of Indiana University's School of Music. The group, led by director James

Oatess Archey, elected Grant County sheriff in 1998, was the first
African American sheriff in Indiana. Courtesy of Oatess Archey.

Indiana's Afro-American Choral Ensemble, led by Professor James Mumford.
Courtesy of African American Arts Institute, Indiana University.

Mumford, performs African American songs and spirituals and preserves traditional styles. In Mumford's most recent student auditions for new members, in the spring of 1999, nineteen of the twenty-seven singers who tried out were whites. Mumford was faced with the interesting quandary of trying to preserve and interpret black culture through white singers eager to learn folkways—black identity—that would permit them to sing "black." In contrast with the minstrel shows popular in the last century, in which whites wore "blackface" and perpetuated stereotypes that demeaned blacks, the Choral Ensemble expresses black musical culture with both respect and artistic veracity, and the whites who learn the style of the group "borrow" elements of black culture, in much the same way that W. E. B. DuBois learned the style of his white schoolmates in his Massachusetts hometown in the late nineteenth century. What is interesting is that at the end of the twentieth century "blackness" has become, for some whites at least, a desirable cultural style to be absorbed into a developing personal identity, as elements of "whiteness" have long been available to groups who Americanized themselves in part by adopting its styles.

Jesse Jackson reported in 1988 that the consensus of seventy-five black groups was that "blacks" preferred to be called "African Americans." It was an example of identity by fiat, as the black power movement's insistence on "black" rather than "Negro" had been in the late 1960s.[98] Indiana, like the rest of the country, was still absorbing the significance of "African American" as the designated identity for its formerly black and Negro (and colored) citizens. It seemed to confirm that for African Americans, as for many Americans of European and Asian backgrounds, ethnicity was a more attractive aspect of their personal and group identity than race. While the cultural meaning of African ethnicity in the Indiana heartland was still being negotiated, by the end of the century it had both expanded, to permit its exemplars places at the table, and contracted, so that it mattered less while they sat there.

Notes

1. The Age of Accommodation

1. Department of Commerce, Bureau of the Census, *Negro Population in the United States 1790–1915* (Washington, D.C., 1968), p. 207; Monroe Work (ed.), *Negro Yearbook; An Annual Encyclopedia of the Negro*, 1925–1926 (Tuskegee Institute, Alabama), p. 429. Prior to 1960, racial classifications were made by the enumerator on the basis of that person's perception. Since 1960, persons have been asked to identify their race on the printed census forms. U.S. Bureau of the Census, *1970 Census of Population: Negro Population*, p. ix.

2. The total born in Indiana was 25,224. Of the remainder, 20,756 were born in Kentucky, 5,073 in Tennessee. U.S. Census Bureau, *Negro Population, 1790–1915*, p. 31.

3. Ibid., p. 92. In 1910 only 41 percent of the white population was classified as urban. Ibid., p. 91.

4. Darrel Bigham, *We Ask Only a Fair Trial: A History of the Black Community in Evansville, Indiana* (Bloomington, Ind., 1987), pp. 171–72; "Lyles Station Then and Now" (pamphlet [n.p., n.d.], Indiana State Library), p. 7.

5. Indianapolis *World*, July 14, 1900; Emma Lou Thornbrough, *The Negro in Indiana before 1900: A Study of a Minority* (Indianapolis, 1957), pp. 225–27; Indianapolis *Recorder*, June 21, 1902. As recently as the 1960s the Indiana Civil Rights Commission was investigating the question of "Sunset Laws."

6. Thornbrough, *Negro in Indiana*, p. 225; U.S. Census Bureau, *Negro Population, 1790–1915*, pp. 74, 93, 97; Hurley Goodall and J. Paul Mitchell, *A History of Negroes in Muncie* (Muncie, Ind., 1976), pp. 9–10.

7. One of the largest was that of the Roberts family, which came from North Carolina and settled in Hamilton County. Other families gathered at Lyles Station in Gibson County, at Weaver in Grant County, and at various places in Wayne and Randolph Counties. One of the most enduring reunions was at the Beech Settlement in Rush County. Indianapolis *Recorder*, August 7, 1909; *Black History News and Notes*, No. 3 (October 1980), p. l.

8. Clifton J. Phillips, *Indiana in Transition: The Emergence of an Industrial Commonwealth, 1880–1920* (Indianapolis, 1968), p. 66; Elizabeth Balanoff, "A History of the Black Community of Gary, Indiana, 1906–1940" (Ph.D. dissertation, University of Chicago, 1974), pp. 8–10, 17; James B. Lane, *"City of the Century": A History of Gary, Indiana* (Bloomington, Ind., 1978), pp. 28–29. More than two-thirds of the population were foreign-born or the children of foreign-born parents. Balanoff, "History of the Black Community of Gary," pp. 13, 17.

9. Thornbrough, *Negro in Indiana*, pp. 259, 245, 329, 126.

10. Lincoln Hospital Association, Indianapolis, *First Annual Report* (pamphlet [n.d.], Indiana State Library), p. 5; L. M. Campbell Adams, "Investigation of Housing and Living Conditions in Three Districts in Indianapolis," No. 9, *Indiana University Studies*, Vol. 8, No. 8, Study No. 10 (September 1910), pp. 134–35.

11. Bigham, *We Ask Only a Fair Trial*, pp. 110–14.

12. Balanoff, "History of the Black Community of Gary," pp. 19, 21.

13. U.S. Census Bureau, *Negro Population, 1790–1915*, p. 518.

14. Indianapolis *Recorder*, February 13, 1915; Bigham, *We Ask Only a Fair Trial*, pp. 169–70;

Indianapolis *World,* January 27, 1900; Phillips, *Indiana in Transition,* pp. 343–47; U.S. Census Bureau, *Negro Population, 1790–1915,* pp. 518, 521.

15. Indiana *Laws* (1885), p. 76.

16. Indianapolis *Recorder,* February 17, 1900; Indianapolis *World,* February 17, 1900.

17. Lincoln Hospital Association, *First Annual Report,* p. 5.

18. Balanoff, "History of the Black Community of Gary," p. 129; Bigham, *We Ask Only a Fair Trial,* pp. 123–24; Indianapolis *Recorder,* January 4, 1913.

19. In Evansville the rate of conviction of blacks was higher than for whites. Indianapolis records do not show the number of convictions. Indianapolis Superintendent of Police, *Annual Reports,* in *Annual Reports of City Government, Indianapolis,* 1901–1915; Bigham, *We Ask Only a Fair Trial,* p. 133. The police did not publish reports specifying the numbers of white women and black women who were arrested; they specified only the numbers of male and female arrests and the numbers of black and white arrests. But the matron's report covers all women and boys under 15, and of this group, nearly half of the arrested persons were black.

20. "Negro No Accounts," Indianapolis *News,* December 12, 1912; Balanoff, "History of the Black Community of Gary," p. 20.

21. Thornbrough, *Negro in Indiana,* p. 323; Indiana *Laws* (1877), p. 124. This law remained in effect until the adoption of the 1949 law abolishing segregation in public education.

22. Thornbrough, *Negro in Indiana,* p. 329.

23. National Association for the Advancement of Colored People, *Sixth Annual Report* (1915), p. 9; Indianapolis *Freeman,* November 18, 1916; "Report of Director of Manual Training," in Indianapolis Public Schools, *Annual Report,* 1908–1909, p. 194.

24. Indianapolis *News,* June 16, 1916.

25. Bigham, *We Ask Only a Fair Trial,* pp. 40–46, 127.

26. Ibid., pp. 125–26.

27. Ibid., pp. 125, 127.

28. Indiana Superintendent of Public Instruction, *Report,* 1904, pp. 205, 238–40, 253–59, 263, 266–67.

29. Indiana Superintendent of Public Instruction, *Twenty-eighth Biennial Report,* 1916, pp. 863–64.

30. Goodall and Mitchell, *History of Negroes in Muncie,* p. 11.

31. Quoted in Ronald D. Cohen, *Children of the Mill: Schooling and Society in Gary, Indiana, 1906–1960* (Bloomington, Ind., 1990), p. 8.

32. Ibid., pp. 8, 36, 68; Balanoff, "History of the Black Community of Gary," pp. 44–45, 271–72. There were also efforts to create separate classes for blacks in the adult education classes. Cohen, *Children of the Mill,* p. 37.

33. U.S. Census Bureau, *Negro Population, 1790–1915,* pp. 415, 420; Department of Commerce, U.S. Census Bureau, *Negro Population in the United States, 1910–1930,* p. 214.

34. Indianapolis Public Schools, *Annual Report,1908–1909,* p. 218; Indianapolis *News,* June 11, 1914, June 16, 1916.

35. Eagleson was later the first black to receive a master's degree from the university. Frances V. Halsell Gilliam, *A Time to Speak: A Brief History of the Afro-Americans of Bloomington, Indiana, 1865–1965* (Bloomington, Ind., 1985), pp. 44–45.

36. Gilliam, *A Time to Speak,* pp. 73, 40; Rhett S. Jones, "The Story of Kappa Alpha Psi," *Black History News and Notes,* No. 12 (February 1983), pp. 5–6; Indianapolis *Star,* February 2, 1991.

37. Indianapolis *News,* Feb. 2, 1991; *Butler Collegian,* Feb. 28, 1990; *Negro Yearbook,* 1915–26, p. 458. There are four national black sororities: Alpha Kappa Alpha, Delta Sigma Theta, Sigma

Gamma Rho, and Zeta Phi Beta. There are four national fraternities: Alpha Phi Alpha, Kappa Alpha Psi, Phi Beta Sigma, and Omega Psi Phi. All of these organizations were founded in the first quarter of the twentieth century. Jones, "The Story of Kappa Alpha Psi," p. 5.

38. Bigham, *We Ask Only a Fair Trial*, p. 126.

39. Stanley Warren, "Percy Julian: The DePauw Years," *Black History News and Notes*, No. 40 (May 1990), pp. 3–4. Julian was awarded an honorary degree by DePauw in 1947.

40. Indianapolis *Freeman*, August 12, 1916. Another example was the case of a black man who was given the "third degree" and "roughed up" by a policeman. After the policeman was exonerated following an investigation, the *Freeman* said the finding was a surprise, but added: "Yet it is not up to us to revise its returns. Perhaps the decision was for the best in the interests of discipline, law and order." Ibid., April 18, 1916.

41. The Indianapolis papers were the only black newspapers in the state prior to the founding of the Gary *Sun* in 1917. John W. Miller, *Indiana Newspaper Bibliography: Historical Accounts of All Indiana Newspapers Published from 1804 to 1980* (Indianapolis, 1982), pp. 228–32. During most of its existence Alexander Manning, a Democrat, was publisher of the *World*, but from 1904 to 1912, Gurley Brewer, an active Republican, joined Manning in publishing the paper. *World*, April 12, 1919.

42. George L. Knox, *Slave and Freeman: The Autobiography of George L. Knox* (Lexington, Ky., 1979), passim.

43. [Wilma L. Gibbs], "George P. Stewart and the Indianapolis Recorder," *Black History News and Notes*, No. 42 (November 1990), pp. 1–3, 8. The *Recorder* is now owned by black businessman William Mays.

44. Indianapolis *Freeman*, October 4, 1908.

45. Indianapolis *Recorder*, December 21, 1901.

46. Ibid., August 7, 1909; Indianapolis *World*, March 29, 1919; Bigham, *We Ask Only a Fair Trial*, p. 166; *Negro Yearbook*, 1918–1919, p. 363; Knox, *Slave and Freeman*, p. 33.

47. Indianapolis *Recorder*, December 21, 1901, June 27, 1902; Bigham, *We Ask Only a Fair Trial*, p. 168.

48. Charles Latham Jr., "Madam C. J. Walker and Company," *Traces of Indiana and Midwestern History*, I (Summer 1989), 29–36.

49. Indianapolis *Recorder*, December 21, 1901; Thornbrough, *Negro in Indiana*, pp. 262, 309, 338, 387.

50. Clyde N. Bolden, "Indiana Avenue: Black Entertainment Boulevard" (Ph.D. dissertation, Boston University, 1981), p. 10.

51. Bigham, *We Ask Only a Fair Trial*, pp. 164–65, 168; Balanoff, "History of the Black Community of Gary," pp. 38–41; Goodall and Mitchell, *History of Negroes in Muncie*, p. 12; Indianapolis *Recorder*, June 21, 1901.

52. Indianapolis *Recorder*, December 21, 1901, March 9, 1940, August 9, 1947; Indianapolis *Times*, August 6, 1947; Indianapolis *News*, November 16, 1949, July 21, 1964, March 29, 1974; Stanley Warren, "Robert L. Bailey: A Great Man with a Thirst for Justice," *Black History News and Notes*, No. 55 (February 1994), pp. 6–7.

53. Bigham, *We Ask Only a Fair Trial*, p. 357; Balanoff, "History of the Black Community of Gary," p. 151.

54. Bigham, *We Ask Only a Fair Trial*, pp. 82–83, 168, 178, 184, 187; Indianapolis *Recorder*, January 24, 1953.

55. [Wilma L. Gibbs], "Henry L. Hummons Collection," *Black History News and Notes*, No. 30 (November 1987), p. 1.

56. Bigham, *We Ask Only a Fair Trial*, pp. 123, 128.

57. Indianapolis *Recorder,* September 23, 1944. Mary Cable was the wife of George W. Cable, a postal employee. For more on their son Theodore see below, chapter 3, note 50.

58. Darlene Clark Hine, *When the Truth Is Told: A History of Black Woman's Culture and Community in Indiana, 1875–1950* (Indianapolis, 1981), p. 46; *Negro Yearbook,* 1912, p.151; ibid., 1925–1926, pp. 414–15; Indianapolis *Recorder,* August 28, 1901; Indianapolis *Ledger,* October 31, 1914.

59. Otis Moss Jr., quoted in Lawrence M. Lindley, "American Baptist Policy and Racial Diversity" (typed manuscript, Indiana State Library), p. 6.

60. Thornbrough, *Negro in Indiana,* pp. 153–56, 370–71; Bigham, *We Ask Only a Fair Trial,* pp. 10, 76; Balanoff, "History of the Black Community of Gary," p. 52; Judge Kelley, "First History of Allen Chapel, AME" (pamphlet, Indiana State Library), pp. 23–28, 33, 35.

61. Balanoff, "History of the Black Community of Gary," p. 51; Bigham, *We Ask Only a Fair Trial,* p. 180; Indianapolis *News,* July 21, 1990; Indianapolis *World,* August 13, 1916; Indianapolis *Freeman,* September 4, 11, 1920.

62. Indianapolis *World,* February 11, 1911; "History of Second Christian Church, 1866 to 1966" (pamphlet, Indiana State Library), pp. 3, 7–8, and passim; *Negro Yearbook,* 1921, p. 207.

63. Morris E. Golder, *The Life and Works of Bishop Garfield Thomas Haywood, 1880–1931* ([Indianapolis?], 1977), pp. 1, 4–13, 27, 31–37, 48–49, 53; Morris Elder Golder, "A Doctrinal Study of the Pentecostal Assemblies of the World" (M.A. thesis, Butler University, 1959), pp. 5, 16, 29, 37, and passim; Tom Hall, "Bishop Garfield T. Haywood and Christ Temple," *Black History News and Notes,* No. 5 (May 1981), pp. 7–12; ibid., No. 6 (Aug. 1981), pp. 7–12.

64. Hine, *When the Truth Is Told,* pp. 21–27. For examples of women's church groups and their activities see Indianapolis *Recorder,* February 7, 1903, March 25, April 15, 1916.

65. Hine, *When the Truth Is Told,* pp. 21, 16.

66. Bigham, *We Ask Only a Fair Trial,* pp. 182–83; Balanoff, "History of the Black Community of Gary," pp. 62–65.

67. *Moore and Langen Printing Co.'s Terre Haute City Directory,* 1901–1902, p. 63.

68. Thornbrough, *Negro in Indiana,* pp. 147–48.

69. Like churches, buildings of fraternal orders represented one of the largest kinds of financial investment in black communities. In the United States there were more than sixty Negro fraternal organizations that were more or less national in scope, with about two million members. In 1918 it was estimated that buildings owned by the Knights of Pythias represented the largest investment, followed by the Colored Odd Fellows and the Masons. *Negro Yearbook,* 1918–1919, p. 457.

70. Bigham, *We Ask Only a Fair Trial,* pp. 183–84; Indianapolis *World,* January 20, 1900; Indianapolis *Recorder,* March 3, 1900.

71. Indianapolis *Star,* July 8, 1921.

72. Indianapolis *Recorder,* January 6, 1912.

73. Earline Rae Ferguson, "The Women's Improvement Club of Indianapolis: Black Women Pioneers in Tuberculosis Work, 1903–1938," *Indiana Magazine of History,* LXXXIV (September 1988), pp. 239–40, 245, 250–52.

74. Indianapolis *Recorder,* February 13, April 9, 30, 1904, July 6, October 8, 1916; Indianapolis *Ledger,* June 5, 1915.

75. Bigham, *We Ask Only a Fair Trial,* pp. 188–89; Hine, *When the Truth Is Told,* pp. 55–57, 62. Stewart also founded a day nursery, the Phyllis Wheatley Home, and the Association of College Women in Evansville.

76. Indianapolis *Recorder,* April 30, 1904.

77. Ibid., June 25, 1904, February 13, 1909, January 3, 1914; Indianapolis *Freeman,* December 27, 1919; Indianapolis *Ledger,* October 10, 24, 1914, January 16, June 5, 1915.

78. *The Crisis,* 2 (September 1912), p. 215; ibid., 3 (April 1913), p. 297; Indianapolis *Ledger,* September 26, October 17, 24, 1914; Indianapolis *Recorder,* September 28, 1912, April 29, June 17, 1916; Indianapolis *World,* August 26, 1916. Freeman Ransom was the most prominent black man associated with the suffrage movement in Indianapolis.

79. Ruth H. Crocker, "Sympathy and Science: The Settlement Movement in Gary and Indianapolis to 1930" (Ph.D. dissertation, Purdue University, 1988) p. 172, 191; Indianapolis *Recorder,* March 3, 1900.

80. Crocker, "Sympathy and Science," pp. 174, 183–87, 195; Indianapolis *Recorder,* October 3, 1903; Indianapolis *News,* October 1, 1915.

81. Ruth H. Crocker, "Christamore House: An Indiana Settlement House from Private to Public Agency," *Indiana Magazine of History,* LXXXIII (June 1987), p. 121.

82. Thornbrough, *Negro in Indiana,* pp. 380–81; [Gibbs], "Henry L. Hummons Collection," p. 1.

83. Indianapolis *Recorder,* January 2, 1909, August 3, October 19, 1912; *Negro Yearbook,* 1921–1922, p. 219.

84. Bertram Emerson Gardner, "The Negro Young Men's Christian Association in the Indianapolis Community" (M.A. thesis, sociology, Butler University, 1951), pp. 22–24, 52–53; Indianapolis *Freeman,* October 20, 1917; Indianapolis *World,* August 17, 1918; Indianapolis *Star,* September 25, 1964; Indianapolis *Recorder,* September 26, 1964.

85. Bigham, *We Ask Only a Fair Trial,* p. 187.

86. Madge Dishman, "Paving the Way," *Black History News and Notes,* No. 2 (August 1985), pp. 5–7; Indianapolis *Ledger,* November 7, 1914; Indianapolis *Recorder,* March 13, 1915; Indianapolis *News,* December 1, 1917.

87. Thornbrough, *Negro in Indiana,* p. 379; Indianapolis *Recorder,* August 29, 1903, April 23, 30, 1910, March 18, 1916.

88. Indianapolis *Ledger,* May 8, 1915.

89. Lincoln Hospital Association, *First Annual Report,* pp. 2, 5, 12; Indianapolis *World,* April 22, 1911; Indianapolis *Ledger,* October 11, 1913, January 11, March 21, April 25, 1914.

90. Hine, *When the Truth Is Told,* pp. 42–43; Indianapolis *Recorder,* September 10, 1904, July 15, 1905; Indianapolis *Ledger,* October 24, 1914.

91. Thornbrough, *Negro in Indiana,* pp. 315, 395; *Indiana Laws,* 1909, p. 341.

92. Knox, *Slave and Freeman,* p. 23–28. The *Freeman* was usually strongly partisan and reflected the accommodationist philosophy that won the confidence of the white community. However, Knox was not always subservient to Republican leaders. In 1904 he tried to run as an independent candidate for Congress against a Republican incumbent, whom he accused of betraying the interests of southern blacks. In 1916 he supported Democrat Tom Taggart for U.S. Senator because as mayor of Indianapolis he had a record of fair treatment of blacks.

93. See letter of Freeman Ransom to James Weldon Johnson, May 17, 1926, Records of the National Association for the Advancement of Colored People, hereafter NAACP Records (Library of Congress, Washington, D.C.).

94. Dallas Sprinkle, *The History of Evansville Blacks* (Evansville, 1994), pp. 45–53.

95. Indianapolis *Recorder,* November 2, 1912; Indianapolis *World,* March 14, 1916; Indianapolis *Freeman,* April 5, 1924.

96. Indianapolis *Ledger,* April 24, 1915.

97. *The Crisis,* 2 (July 1912), p. 124; Constitution of the Indianapolis branch with signatures of officers, May 24, 1913, NAACP Records.

98. *NAACP Fourth Annual Report,* 1913, pp. 27–28; *The Crisis,* 3 (February 1913), p. 244; ibid., 4 (September 1914), p. 237; ibid., 5 (April 1915), p. 303; Mary Cable to Miss Narney, January 23, 1914, NAACP Records; "Annual Report of Indianapolis Branch 1913–14," manuscript, ibid.; Robert Brokenburr to Mary White Ovington, January 14, 1918, ibid.

99. Balanoff, "History of the Black Community of Gary," p. 122; application for charter for Gary branch, June 28, 1916, NAACP Records; Elizabeth Lylle, secretary, Gary branch to Mr. Nash, May 10, 1917, ibid.; *The Crisis,* 7 (January 1917), p. 121.

100. Bigham, *We Ask Only a Fair Trial,* p. 123; *The Crisis,* 6 (March 1916), p. 258; ibid., 9 (April 1919), pp. 264–65.

101. *The Crisis* 9 (April 1919), pp. 264–65.

102. Indianapolis *Recorder,* June 15, 1912.

103. Indianapolis *Freeman,* January 7, May 26, 1917; Indianapolis *Recorder,* January 6, 1912.

104. Duncan P. Schiedt, *The Jazz State of Indiana* (Pittsboro, Ind., 1977), pp. 10–11.

105. Indianapolis *Recorder,* September 25, 1909, January 10, 1910, January 31, 1914.

106. Thornbrough, *Negro in Indiana,* p. 383; Bigham, *We Ask Only a Fair Trial,* p. 178; Gilliam, *A Time to Speak,* p. 40; Indianapolis *Freeman,* February 17, 1917, December 20, 1919.

107. Indianapolis *Recorder,* January 2, 1909, August 11, 1900, September 18, 1909; Bigham, *We Ask Only a Fair Trial,* p. 176.

2. The Great Migration and the First World War

1. U.S. Census Bureau, *Negro Population, 1790–1915,* pp. 31, 87

2. James R. Grossman, *Land of Hope: Chicago Black Southerners and the Great Migration* (Chicago, 1989), pp. 28–30; Carol Marks, *Farewell, We're Good and Gone: The Great Black Migration* (Bloomington, Ind., 1989), p. 16.

3. Grossman, *Land of Hope,* pp. 57, 64.

4. Marks, *Farewell,* p. 122.

5. Bigham, *We Ask Only a Fair Trial,* p. 108.

6. Marks, *Farewell,* p. 122; U.S. Bureau of the Census, *Negroes in the United States, 1920–1932,* pp. 55, 58.

7. U.S. Census Bureau, *Negroes in the United States, 1920–1932,* p. 58.

8. Ibid., pp. 34–36, 44.

9. Indianapolis *Freeman,* September 30, October 28, 1916, January 27, June 2, July 7, 1917; Indianapolis *Recorder,* November 18, 1916.

10. An Urban League was not established in Indianapolis until 1965.

11. R. L. Polk and Co., *Indianapolis City Directory,* 1910, passim; Crocker, "Sympathy and Science," p. 197.

12. Crocker, "Sympathy and Science," p. 199; Indianapolis *Freeman,* October 11, 1919.

13. Crocker, "Sympathy and Science," pp. 216–17; Flanner House, *Circular of Information Concerning Day Workers,* 1922, n.p., pamphlet (Indiana Division, Indiana State Library).

14. Indianapolis *Freeman,* February 16, 1924.

15. Ibid., June 29, August 31, 1918; Indianapolis *World,* October 5, 1918.

16. Crocker, "Sympathy and Science," pp. 202, 212; Indianapolis *News,* April 5, 1916.

17. Crocker, "Sympathy and Science," p. 197; Indianapolis *News,* June 5, 1914, April 5, 1916.

18. Emmett Jay Scott Jr., *Negro Migration during the War* (New York, 1920), pp. 109–10; Balanoff, "History of the Black Community of Gary," pp. 23, 152.

19. Balanoff, "History of the Black Community of Gary," pp. 151–54 and passim. In East

St. Louis at least 40 blacks had been killed in 1917 in a riot over employment of blacks in a factory with a government contract.

20. Ibid., pp. 21, 25, 102.

21. Crocker, "Sympathy and Science," p. 434.

22. B. F. Gordon, *The Negro in South Bend: A Social Study* (South Bend, Indiana, 1922), pp. 46–49, 55, 92.

23. National Urban League, *A Study of the Social and Economic Condition of the Negro Population of Fort Wayne, Indiana* (n.p., 1949), pp. 5–7; Bigham, *We Ask Only a Fair Trial*, pp. 138, 152–160, 169; U.S. Census Bureau, *Negroes in the United States 1920–1932*, p. 58.

24. Indianapolis *Freeman*, May 26, June 9, 16, 1917; John Hope Franklin, *From Slavery to Freedom: A History of Negro Americans* (5th ed., New York: Alfred Knopf, 1980), p. 327. In this instance the national office of the NAACP supported a separate officers' training camp on the grounds that it would give blacks a fair chance for promotion, while in a racially mixed camp white officers would certainly be prejudiced against them.

25. Indianapolis *Freeman*, May 18, 1918; Bigham, *We Ask Only a Fair Trial*, p. 136; Balanoff, "History of the Black Community of Gary," pp. 136, 141.

26. Elder Diggs, "Indianapolis YMCA during the World War," typed manuscript, n.p., n.d. (Indiana Division, Indiana State Library); Indianapolis *News*, April 19, 1918; Indianapolis *Freeman*, May 4, 1918.

27. Diggs, "Indianapolis YMCA"; Balanoff, "History of the Black Community of Gary," pp. 134–36; Bigham, *We Ask Only a Fair Trial*, pp. 136–37; Goodall and Mitchell, *History of Negroes in Muncie*, pp. 13–15.

28. Diggs, "Indianapolis YMCA"; Balanoff, "History of the Black Community of Gary," p. 135. Diggs, mentioned in chapter 1 as a student at Indiana University and founder of Kappa Alpha Mu fraternity, was commissioned a First Lieutenant and after the war served as chairman of a state committee that compiled a document, now in the Indiana Division of the Indiana State Library, entitled "Some Data Bearing Upon the Part Which the Colored Citizens of Indianapolis and Marion County Took in the World War." The compilation includes typewritten accounts of the role of the Senate Avenue YMCA and other groups, but there is no pagination. Franklin, *From Slavery to Freedom*, p. 327.

29. Indianapolis *Freeman*, Aug. 18, 1917; Marks, *Farewell*, p. 97.

30. Franklin, *From Slavery to Freedom*, p. 331; Orville Funk, "Lt. Aaron R. Fisher, Hoosier Hero," *Black History News and Notes*, No. 25 (May 1987), pp. 4–6.

31. Indiana World War Record, "Gold Star Honor Roll. A Record of Indiana Men and Women Who Died in the Service of the United States and the Allied Nations in the World War 1914–1918" (Indiana Historical Commission, Indianapolis, 1921, Indiana State Archives).

32. Elder Diggs, "Part Played by Colored Citizens of Indianapolis and Marion County."

33. Indianapolis *World*, April 6, October 12, 1918; Indianapolis *Freeman*, June 29, 1918.

34. Balanoff, "History of the Black Community of Gary," pp. 133, 137–38; Bigham, *We Ask Only a Fair Trial*, pp. 136–37; Goodall and Mitchell, *History of Negroes in Muncie*, pp. 13–15; Indianapolis *Freeman*, August 24, 1918.

35. Indianapolis *Freeman*, November 30, 1918.

3. The Twenties

1. Franklin, *From Slavery to Freedom*, pp. 330, 341.

2. *The Crisis* 15 (January 24, 1925), pp. 131–32; *The Fiery Cross*, December 6, 1922, January 19, 1923; Indianapolis *Recorder*, July 3, 24, 31, 1926.

3. Balanoff, "History of the Black Community of Gary," p. 128; Gordon, *Negro in South Bend,* pp. 1–2.

4. The revived Ku Klux Klan, which had no direct relationship with the Klan of the Reconstruction era, was organized in Atlanta in 1915 and moved into Indiana soon after the war. By the early 1920s there were klaverns in all parts of the state. Leonard J. Moore, *Citizen Klansmen: The Ku Klux Klan in Indiana, 1921–1928* (Chapel Hill, N.C., 1991).

5. Balanoff, "History of the Black Community of Gary," p. 9; Bigham, *We Ask Only a Fair Trial,* pp. 209–10; *Fiery Cross,* February 16, May 16, 1923.

6. Robert L. Brokenburr, mimeographed letter, 1921, NAACP Records; Report of Secretary, Indianapolis Branch, to National Convention, June 20, 1924, ibid.; Indianapolis *Freeman,* February 2, 1924. Frances Linthecome recalled a friend's telling her that in the 1920s, when she and her family moved onto Forty-first Street, beyond the traditional Fortieth Street boundary limiting African American settlement, the Klan paraded down Forty-first Street to drive them away. Telephone interview with Frances Linthecome, August 21, 1999.

7. Correspondence for Terre Haute, South Bend, Gary, NAACP Records; *The Crisis,* 15 (March 1925), p. 213.

8. Indianapolis *Freeman,* May 17, 1924; William W. Giffin, "The Political Realignment of Black Voters in Indianapolis, 1924," *Indiana Magazine of History,* LXXIX (June 1983), pp. 138–39. The Democratic nominee for governor, Carleton B. McCulloch, denied that he had ever been a member of the Klan, while the Republican candidate, Ed Jackson, did not disclaim his membership. The Democratic state platform, while not mentioning the Klan by name, said that the Republican Party had "been delivered into the hands of an organization which has no place in politics and which promulgates doctrines that tend to break down the safeguards which the Constitution throws around every citizen." The platform also condemned efforts to make political issues of race and religion.

9. Indianapolis *Freeman,* September 20, October 4, 25, 1924; Letter from Secretary, National Office, to Dr. O. W. Langston, September 25, 1924, NAACP Records.

10. Giffin, "The Political Realignment of Black Voters in Indianapolis, 1924," pp. 143, 146; Indianapolis *News,* November 4, 1924; Indianapolis *Star,* November 5, 1924.

11. Indianapolis *Freeman,* August 16, September 20, 1924; Ernest Tidrington to Hon. J. H. Tinsley, July 5, 1924, George Stewart Papers (Indiana Historical Society Library); Bigham, *We Ask Only a Fair Trial,* p. 211; Balanoff, "History of the Black Community of Gary," pp. 322, 327.

12. Emma Lou Thornbrough, "Segregation in Indiana during the Klan Era of the 1920's," *Mississippi Valley Historical Review,* XLVII (March 1961), p. 165.

13. Ibid., p. 616; James H. Madison, *Indiana through Tradition and Change: A History of the Hoosier State and Its People, 1920–1945* (Indianapolis, 1982), pp. 68–69.

14. Indianapolis *News,* November 2, 5, 1925; Indianapolis *Star,* November 4, 1925.

15. Indianapolis *Freeman,* February 26, March 4, 18, April 16, May 13, 1916, July 17, 1920.

16. Indianapolis *Freeman,* July 7, 1920; Indianapolis *Recorder,* March 1, 1924.

17. Indianapolis *World,* May 6, 1921; *Groom* v. *Meriweather et al.* and *Slutzky et al.* v. *Meriweather,* 79 *Indiana Appellate* 274–76 (1922). For other efforts by whites to prevent African Americans from acquiring homes in white neighborhoods see Thornbrough, "Segregation in Indiana during the Klan Era," pp. 597–98.

18. Indianapolis *Freeman,* July 24, 1924; Indianapolis *News,* March 16, 1926.

19. Indianapolis Common Council, *Journal,* 1924, pp. 54, 82. Persons of a minority race who had already acquired property in the block were allowed to retain and reside in it but could not sell it to a member of a minority race without the consent of the majority. Violators were subject to fifty-dollar fines and imprisonment for thirty days.

20. Indianapolis *News,* March 16, 1926; Indianapolis *Recorder,* March 6, 1926.

21. Indianapolis *Recorder,* March 6, 1924, May 15, 1926; typed news release, March 19, 1926, NAACP Records; *The Crisis,* 16 (May 1926), p. 24.

22. The case was *Edward S. Gaillard* v. *Dr. Guy L. Grant.* Indianapolis *News,* November 24, 1926; Indianapolis *Recorder,* June 5, 12, November 27, 1926; Copy of Judge Chamberlin's opinion, NAACP Records; NAACP, *Annual Report,* 1926, p. 10; *The Crisis,* 17 (January 1927), p. 142. City Attorney Allen Rucker, who was allowed to intervene in the case, tried to have the suit dismissed on the grounds that there had been collusion between Grant and Gaillard.

23. Indianapolis *Recorder,* December 11, 1926; *Harmon* v. *Tyler,* 273 *US* 668 (1927).

24. Balanoff, "History of the Black Community of Gary," pp. 161–68, 177.

25. Terms of school board members were staggered so that two members did not take office until two years after they were elected.

26. Indianapolis *Daily Times,* November 9, 1921; Indianapolis *News,* June 15, 1918, May 13, 1919, October 25, 1921.

27. Indianapolis Board of School Commissioners, Minutes, Book Y, September 25, 1923, pp. 22, 85, 159, 192, 304–305; ibid., Book X, December 12, 1923, p. 64; Indianapolis *Freeman,* March 1, 1924.

28. Indianapolis Board of School Commissioners, Minutes, Book W, June 13, 1922, pp. 226–27, 396–97; Indianapolis *Daily Times,* May 27, 1922.

29. Indianapolis Board of School Commissioners, Minutes, Book BXX November 14, 1922–September 11, 1923, pp. 29–30 (November 22, 1922); Indianapolis *News,* December 13, 1922.

30. Indianapolis Board of School Commissioners, Minutes, Book X, December 23, 1922, pp. 63–64; ibid., Book AA, May 12, 1925, p. 14; Indianapolis *News,* December 12, 1922; Indianapolis *Freeman,* May 24, 1924; *The Crisis,* 15 (May 1925), p. 36. See also letters of Assistant Secretary to Mrs. Albert S. Dent, Indianapolis, December 7, 1922, Louis Harry Barry to Walter White, December 14, 1922, Director of Branches to Harry D. Evans, president of the Indianapolis Branch, January 13, 1923, NAACP Records.

31. Indianapolis *Freeman,* January 19, 1924; Indianapolis *Recorder,* April 3, June 19, 1926; *Greathouse* v. *Board of School Commissioners of City of Indianapolis,* 198 *Ind.* 95 (1926).

32. Indianapolis *News,* October 23, 30, 1925; Indianapolis *Times,* October 10, 25, November 2, 5, 1925.

33. Indianapolis Board of School Commissioners, Minutes, Book FF, September 10, 1929, pp. 238–39; *Directory of Indianapolis Public Schools,* 1929–1930; Indianapolis *Recorder,* October 5, 1925, March 27, 1926; Madison, *Indiana through Tradition and Change,* pp. 70–75.

34. For examples of the charges against the "Klan board" in 1929 see editorial in Indianapolis *Times,* October 29, 1929; Indianapolis *Star,* October 22, 1929; Indianapolis *News,* November 2, 1929. The most recent study of the Indiana Klan suggests that "establishment" opposition to the "Klan" school board by the Chamber of Commerce and business and financial interests was motivated primarily by opposition to higher taxes that the building program initiated by the "Klan board" would entail. See Moore, *Citizen Klansmen,* pp. 147–50, 182. The Citizens Committee, victorious in 1929, continued to control the Indianapolis Public School System with little opposition for almost half a century. See below, chapter 7.

35. Cohen, *Children of the Mill,* pp. 84, 92, 94; Balanoff, "History of the Black Community of Gary," p. 271; Thornbrough, "Segregation in Indiana during the Klan Era" p. 607.

36. Lane, *"City of the Century,"* p. 144; Balanoff, "History of the Black Community of Gary," p. 285, 290–92; Cohen, *Children of the Mill,* p. 97; Thornbrough, "Segregation in Indiana during the Klan Era," p. 607; Correspondence between J. R. Garrett of Gary and J. W. Johnson of the New York office, October 9, 13, 1928, NAACP Records.

37. Balanoff, "History of the Black Community of Gary," pp. 286–87, 290–91; Cohen, *Children of the Mill,* pp. 148–49; *State, ex rel Cheeks* v. *Wirt, Superintendent of Gary Schools et al.,* 203 *Ind.* 121 (1932).

38. Cohen, *Children of the Mill,* p. 151; Balanoff, "History of the Black Community of Gary," p. 304; Goodall and Mitchell, *Negro Community in Muncie,* p. 11; Indianapolis *Recorder,* September 13, 1930; Indianapolis *Freeman,* May 31, 1924.

39. Bigham, *We Ask Only a Fair Trial,* pp. 143–44; Stanley Warren, "The Other Side of Hoosier Hysteria: Segregation, Sports, and the IHSAA," *Black History News and Notes,* No. 54 (November 1993).

40. Dave DeJernet, from Washington High School in Davies County, and Jack Mann of the Bearcats of Muncie Central High made basketball history as the star players in state tourneys. Raymond Dukes, who played football as a student at Noblesville High School, became captain of the Howard University football team. Goodall and Mitchell, *Negro Community in Muncie,* p. 27; Indianapolis *Freeman,* January 26, 1924; Indianapolis *Recorder,* March 22, 1930, March 28, 1931.

41. Typed program, 1929 Indiana State Conference, NAACP Records; Indianapolis *Recorder,* November 9, 30, 1929.

42. Indianapolis *Freeman,* August 29, 1924; [*Editor's note:* Thornbrough's notes indicate that she intended a more extensive reference to Garvey. For Garvey see Edmund David Cronon, *Black Moses: The Story of Marcus Garvey and the Universal Negro Improvement Association* (Madison, Wis., 1955); Judith Stein, *The World of Marcus Garvey* (Baton Rouge, La., 1986); and Lawrence W. Levine, "Marcus Garvey and the Politics of Revitalization," in *Black Leaders of the Twentieth Century,* ed. John Hope Franklin and August Meier (Urbana, Ill., 1982).].

43. Balanoff, "History of the Black Community of Gary," pp. 298–300, 412–13; Cohen, *Children of the Mill,* pp. 93, 99, 148. Born in the Virgin Islands, educated in Denmark and at Columbia University, McFarlane had come to Gary in 1927 as principal of the old Roosevelt annex. Although his academic credentials were impeccable, integrationists opposed him for his separatist views. In speeches to the white members of the Rotary and Lions Clubs he urged separate schools as a means of developing pride and self-respect. His remarks led the black Gary *American,* a strong supporter of the NAACP, to say it was "pitiable" to see an educated Negro "accept segregation with a lover's kiss."

44. Indianapolis *World,* August 3, 1918, July 18, 1921; Indianapolis *Freeman,* August 9, 1924; Indianapolis *Recorder,* July 24, 1926; Thornbrough, "Segregation in Indiana during the Klan Era" p. 609.

45. J. W. Johnson, Assistant Secretary, to Mrs. H. L. Cromwell Lewis, President Gary Branch, May 26, 1926, NAACP Records; Balanoff, "History of the Black Community of Gary," pp. 459–60.

46. William H. Walsh, *The Hospitals of Indianapolis* (Indianapolis, 1930), pp. 89, 92.

47. Indianapolis *Recorder,* April 22, May 21, 1927, April 6, 13, 20, 1929, February 15, 1930.

48. Walsh, *Hospitals of Indianapolis,* pp. 90–91, 95; Indianapolis *Star,* December 12, 1932; Indianapolis *News,* December 12, 1932.

49. Balanoff, "History of the Black Community of Gary," pp. 440–42.

50. U.S. Census Bureau, *Negroes in the United States, 1920–1932,* pp. 374, 454.

51. Crocker, "Sympathy and Science," pp. 201, 203, 205, 207; Ferguson, "Women's Improvement Club," pp. 248–49. Beginning in February 1919, the Marion County Tuberculosis Society opened a branch clinic in Flanner House, but City Hospital did not admit black tuberculosis patients until 1938. Crocker, "Sympathy and Science," p. 208.

52. "YWCA First Annual Report," Indianapolis *Freeman,* February 23, 1924; Dishman, "Paving the Way," p. 5.

53. Crocker, "Sympathy and Science," pp. 299, 442–43, 446–47; Balanoff, "History of the Black Community of Gary," pp. 446–49. Trinity Church was renamed Delaney Church after the minister's death, and a public housing project that opened in 1940 was named after him.

54. Indianapolis *Recorder,* August 6, 1927. Attucks High School opened with a staff of forty-eight experienced teachers, all of them with at least a baccalaureate degree, several with advanced degrees. Some came from the faculties of Negro colleges. By 1934, of a faculty of sixty-two, nineteen held master's degrees, two held Ph.D. degrees. Frederick H. Gale, "First Twenty-five Years of Crispus Attucks High School, Indianapolis, Indiana" (master's thesis, Ball State University, 1955); Indianapolis *Recorder,* April 30, May 14, September 10, 1927; Indianapolis *News,* April 18, 1934; *Attucks Beacon,* passim.

55. Balanoff, "History of the Black Community of Gary," p. 301; Cohen, *Children of the Mill,* pp. 78–79.

56. Bigham, *We Ask Only a Fair Trial,* p. 128.

57. Paul De Bono, "Black Ball: Negro Leagues Locals Etched Their Names in Baseball History," Indianapolis *New Times,* 7 (April 1991), pp. 6–7; Indianapolis *Freeman,* July 21, August 2, 1924; Indianapolis *Recorder,* June 25, 1927.

58. The Walker Building was constructed at the direction of Madam Walker's daughter and sole heir, A'Lelia Walker. Gloria J. Gibson-Hudson, "'To all classes; to all races; this house is dedicated': The Walker Theater Revisited," *Black History News and Notes,* No. 35 (February 1989), pp. 4–5. The theater's opening film was *The Magic Flame,* starring Ronald Coleman and Vilma Banky.

59. Some local players later became famous nationally. For example, Noble Sissle began his career at Hills Indiana Theater. In 1927 he returned to Indianapolis with Eubie Blake to give a benefit performance at Tomlinson Hall to the accompaniment of "Dippy" Miller and his jazz band. Indianapolis *Recorder,* March 12, 1927. Although during the heyday of jazz and blues in the twenties Indiana Avenue was famous as a center of black entertainment, records about local singers and musicians are meager. Duncan Schiedt, *The Jazz State of Indiana* (Pittsboro, Ind., 1977), pp. 15, 94–100, and passim; Bolden, "Indiana Avenue," pp. 30–31.

60. Indianapolis *Recorder,* May 1, 1926; Bolden, "Indiana Avenue," pp. 16, 31; Schiedt, *Jazz State of Indiana,* p. 183.

61. U.S. Census Bureau, *Negroes in the United States, 1920–1932,* Table 11, p. 58; William Pickens, "Aftermath of a Lynching," *The Nation,* April 15, 1931.

62. Deeter was later reported to have told his aunt, as he was dying, that the girl had not been molested. Mrs. F. K. Bailey to Walter White, August 11, 1930, NAACP Records. Contemporary newspaper accounts give Cameron's name as Herbert, but in his memoirs, published many years later, his name is James.

63. Marion *Chronicle,* August 7, 8, 1930; Indianapolis *Star,* August 8, 9, 1930; NAACP, *Annual Report,* 1931, pp. 35–36; New York *Times,* August 8, 1930; Indianapolis *News,* August 9, 1930.

64. Indianapolis *Star,* August 9, 1930; Indiana *Laws* (1901), pp. 311–12; Emma Lou Thornbrough, *Since Emancipation: A Short History of Indiana Negroes, 1863–1963* ([Indianapolis, 1963]), p. 38; Copy of petition presented to Gov. Harry G. Leslie, August 20, 1930, NAACP Records; G. N. T. Gray to Walter White, August 22, 1930, ibid.; Indianapolis *Recorder,* October 18, 1930, March 21, 1931.

65. NAACP, *Annual Report,* 1930, p. 35; White to James H. Ogden, attorney general, August 22, 1930, NAACP Records; Indianapolis *Recorder,* January 3, 10, 1931; Pickens, "Aftermath of a Lynching."

66. "Given Short Prison Term," news release, July 17, 1931, NAACP Records; James Cameron, *A Time of Terror* (Milwaukee, 1982), pp. 181–82.

67. Indiana *Laws* (1931), pp. 245–47; Indiana *Laws* (Special Session, 1932), p. 271; Indianapolis *Recorder*, January 31, March 7, 14, 1931, August 6, 1932; NAACP, *Annual Report*, 1931, p. 31.

4. Depression, the New Deal, and Political Realignment

1. Indianapolis *Recorder*, February 22, September 27, 1930, August 20, 1932. Freeman Ransom estimated the number of unemployed blacks in Indianapolis at about 75 percent. Freeman Ransom to William Pickens, March 10, 1933, NAACP Records. For a similar estimate in Muncie see Goodall and Mitchell, *History of Negroes in Muncie*, p. 24.

2. Guichard Parris and Lester Brooks, *Blacks in the City: A History of the National Urban League* (Boston, 1971), p. 26; Horace R. Cayton and George S. Mitchell, *Black Workers and the New Unions* (Westport, Conn., 1970), pp. 32–33.

3. Indianapolis *Recorder*, October 3, 1931; "The Employment Department," in Flanner House program, October 6, 1929, mimeographed pamphlet (Indiana Division, Indiana State Library).

4. Indianapolis *Recorder*, August 20, 1932, May 6, 1933, January 13, 1934; Balanoff, "History of the Black Community of Gary," p. 476.

5. National Urban League, *A Study of the Social and Economic Conditions of the Negro Population of Gary, Indiana* (New York, 1944), p. 41; U.S. National Youth Administration, Indiana, *Juvenile Delinquency in Marion County* (Indianapolis, 1936), pp. 6–7, 16, 42–44.

6. Cohen, *Children of the Mill*, pp. 132–33; Balanoff, "History of the Black Community of Gary," p. 311–12.

7. Cohen, *Children of the Mill*, p. 147.

8. Indianapolis *Recorder*, October 1, November 9, 1932, June 10, 1933, October 6, 20, 27, 1934, May 4, 1935. The Monday Luncheon Club said there was evidence that yearly salaries of Attucks teachers were $300 to $1,000 less than those of teachers at Washington High School (opened the same year as Attucks) although Attucks teachers had higher academic qualifications. Ibid., October 6, 1934.

9. Madison, *Indiana through Tradition and Change*, p. 105; Indianapolis *Star*, February 5, December 21, 1930; Robert S. Lynd and Helen Merrell Lynd, *Middletown in Transition: A Study in Cultural Conflicts* (New York, 1937), p. 111; Indianapolis *Recorder*, September 26, 1931.

10. Madison, *Indiana through Tradition and Change*, p. 105.

11. Arthur M. Schlesinger Jr., *The Crisis of the Old Order* (Boston, 1957), p. 169; Indianapolis *Star*, October 24, 1930. As conditions grew worse, Hoover approved legislation that authorized loans from the Reconstruction Finance Corporation to state and local governments for relief and for public works that were self-liquidating.

12. Indianapolis *Star*, October 30, November 7, 1930; Indianapolis *Times*, November 6, 1930; Madison, *Indiana through Tradition and Change*, pp. 106–107; Indianapolis *News*, November 30, 1931; Indianapolis *Recorder*, December 19, 1931.

13. Indianapolis *Recorder*, February 1, 8, 1930, September 19, October 11, 1930, January 17, October 3, 1931.

14. Balanoff, "History of the Black Community of Gary," pp. 200–204; Lane, *"City of the Century,"* p. 198; Indianapolis *Recorder*, May 16, 1931; undated clipping from Gary *American*, NAACP Records; "Activities of Gary Youth Council of NAACP," typed manuscript, ibid. Efforts in Chicago and cities in the East to boycott stores that did not employ blacks spread to Indiana. *The Crisis*, 20 (March 30, 1930), p. 102.

15. Indianapolis *Recorder,* February 22, April 5, 12, 19, 1930, March 7, October 3, 1931, February 10, June 2, December 2, 1934.

16. Gary *American,* July 25, 1931, quoted in Balanoff, "History of the Black Community of Gary," p. 418; ibid., p. 420; Indianapolis *Recorder,* January 26, April 20, May 4, 1935, February 22, March 7, 1936.

17. Balanoff, "History of the Black Community of Gary," pp. 208–12; Lane, *"City of the Century,"* pp. 186–87. Reddix left Gary to accept a position with the Farm Security Administration, a New Deal agency. He later became president of Jackson State College.

18. Indianapolis *News,* August 31, 1986; Indianapolis *Star,* September 1, 1986; Indianapolis *Recorder,* September 30, October 7, December 6, 1933. Osborne was one of the early black leaders in the Democratic Party in Indianapolis. He was appointed to several minor offices and elected trustee of Center Township in 1966, a post that he held until his death in 1986. For a typical letter by Osborne see ibid., November 15, 1935. Similar letters urging economic independence appeared almost every week. Leaders of Consumers Unit hoped to acquire land south of Indianapolis near the town of Franklin. When they were unable to do this, they turned their hopes to land about 15 miles west of Indianapolis.

19. Indianapolis *Recorder,* March 2, 1935. It was also reported that the federal agency had taken an option on a tract of land for the project. Ibid., August 17, 1935.

20. Ibid., March 30, May 11, June 1, August 11, 1935.

21. Cayton and Mitchell, *Black Worker and the New Unions,* p. 113; Indianapolis *Recorder,* November 15, 1930, October 17, 1931, June 4, 18, October 15, 1932.

22. Raymond Wolters, *Negroes and the Great Depression: The Problem of Economic Recovery* (Westport, Conn., 1970), pp. 352–83, passim, quotation from Bunche, p. 362; Indianapolis *Recorder,* February 22, March 14, October 10, 1936.

23. Indianapolis *Recorder,* January 14, 1933; Madison, *Indiana through Tradition and Change,* p. 105.

24. Madison, *Indiana through Tradition and Change,* pp. 107–31; Frank Freidel, *Franklin D. Roosevelt: A Rendezvous with Destiny* (Boston, 1990), pp. 100–102, 135; Indianapolis *Recorder,* July 29, August 31, December 2, 1933; Balanoff, "History of the Black Community of Gary," p. 215; Bigham, *We Ask Only a Fair Trial,* p. 278.

25. Indianapolis *Recorder,* June 2, October 27, 1934. Figures provided by the U.S. Census Bureau early in 1934 showed that more than one-third of the black population in Indianapolis was receiving some sort of public relief. Ibid., March 1, 1934. The percentage was about the same in Evansville and perhaps even higher in Gary. Bigham, *We Ask Only a Fair Trial,* p. 218; Balanoff, "History of the Black Community of Gary," p. 233.

26. Madison, *Indiana through Tradition and Change,* p. 127; Indianapolis *Recorder,* December 2, 1933, July 14, September 8, 1934, April 11, June 20, July 25, September 5, October 17, 1936; James Warren Bailey, *A Brief History of the Negro in Anderson* (n.p., 1938), pp. 31–32; Bigham, *We Ask Only a Fair Trial,* p. 218; Gary *American,* January 22, 1937. See also George T. Blakey, "Battling the Great Depression on Stage in Indiana," *Indiana Magazine of History,* XC (March 1994), pp. 1–25.

27. Indianapolis *News,* August 20, 30, 1939; Indianapolis *Star,* August 20, 1939; Gary *American,* February 11, 1938.

28. Indianapolis *Recorder,* February 24, 1934, June 29, September 21, 1935. The recently created Marion County Welfare Department, which principally served indigent elderly persons, had a staff of thirty-seven members, all of them white, although probably one-third of their clients were black. After complaints, five black women were added to the staff of investigators. Ibid., May 23, June 20, 1936.

29. Ibid., March 2, 1929, September 16, 30, October 7, December 16, 25, 1933, March 17, 1934.

30. Ibid., March 17, April 28, July 21, August 25, September 16, November 24, 1934.

31. Ibid., July 27, November 9, 1929, November 24, December 1, 1934.

32. Ibid., September 23, November 24, December 22, 1934, January 25, February 8, May 4, 18, July 6, August 3, 1935. It was reported that some union locals offered to admit blacks if they paid an initiation fee of $75, although white members paid only $10. Ibid., January 25, 1935.

33. Ibid., February 18, April 18, 1936; Indianapolis *News,* April 30, 1937; Indianapolis *Star,* February 16, 1938.

34. "Lockefield Garden Apartments," 1937, brochure (Indiana Division, Indiana State Library); *Lockefield News,* October 1, November 29, December 24, 1938, October 31, December 1940, ibid.

35. Indianapolis *News,* June 10, 1938; Gary *American,* October 4, 1940.

36. Gary *American,* September 15, 29, 1939, October 4, 11, November 3, December 13, 20, 1940, January 3, March 21, 1941.

37. Bigham, *We Ask Only a Fair Trial,* p. 219; Indianapolis *Recorder,* November 2, December 14, 1935.

38. Indiana House of Representatives, *Journal* [hereafter, *Indiana House Journal*] (1939), p. 866; Indianapolis *Recorder,* February 25, March 4, 11, 1939.

39. Indianapolis *News,* April 28, 1939; Indianapolis *Star,* September 15, 16, 23, 1939.

40. Among the interns admitted was Dr. Francis Hummons, son of Dr. H. L. Hummons. A graduate of Attucks, DePauw University, and Indiana University School of Medicine, Francis Hummons completed his internship in 1942. Indianapolis *Recorder,* July 27, August 3, 1940, July 18, 1942; Indianapolis *News,* September 12, 1990.

41. Indianapolis *Recorder,* February 7, 10, 1942, March 27, 1943. The first African American nurse employed by City Hospital was Elizabeth Fisher Scott, who had been required to transfer from Shortridge High School to Attucks when it opened in 1927. She had gone to Chicago for her training as a nurse. She later became the first black supervisor for the Morgan Health Center in Indianapolis. Indianapolis *Star,* February 18, 1970.

42. Indianapolis *Recorder,* February 6, 1943. Batties, the son of Dr. Mark Batties, who earlier had been the principal figure in the private Community Hospital for blacks, graduated from the University of Chicago Medical School. Dr. Middleton, a native of South Carolina, was a graduate of Meharry Medical School and did postgraduate work at several universities. He later was on the staffs of St. Vincent and Winona hospitals and was an assistant professor at Indiana University School of Medicine. Indianapolis *News,* February 11, 1991; "Civic Leaders and Their Letters," *Black History News and Notes,* No. 40 (May 1990), pp. 1–8.

43. Indianapolis *Freeman,* September 11, 1920; Bigham, *We Ask Only a Fair Trial,* p. 211. In 1930 at the height of his career Tidrington was shot to death by a political rival. Ibid., p. 212; Dallas W. Sprinkle, *The History of Evansville Blacks* (Evansville, Ind., 1974), p. 253.

44. Balanoff, "History of the Black Community of Gary," pp. 334, 351; Indianapolis *Recorder,* August 8, 1926, November 3, 10, 1928. In the 1929 city elections in Indianapolis, when the Democrats won a sweeping victory following the scandals of the Duvall administration, a larger number of blacks than usual voted for Democrats, but the two predominantly black wards in the city remained in the Republican column. Ibid., November 9, 1927.

45. Indianapolis *Recorder,* April 5, 12, 19, November 1, 1930; Freeman Ransom to Walter White, October 4, 1930, NAACP Records.

46. Indianapolis *Star,* November 5, 1930; Bigham, *We Ask Only a Fair Trial,* p. 213; Indianapolis *Recorder,* November 8, 1930.

47. Indianapolis *Recorder,* May 21, June 18, 25, 1932. This system, in which a single black representative from each party was endorsed, prevailed in Marion County until the 1970s, when the state legislature was reapportioned.

48. Ibid., October 22, 29, November 5, 1932. Privately Freeman Ransom predicted that 75 percent of black voters in Indianapolis would cast their votes for Democrats. F. B. Ransom to Walter White, October 18, 1932, NAACP Records.

49. Alan F. January and Justin E. Walsh, *A Century of Achievement: Black Hoosiers in the Indiana General Assembly* (Indianapolis, 1986), pp. 23–24.

50. Indianapolis *Recorder,* May 12, November 3, 10, 1934; January and Walsh, *Century of Achievement,* p. 27. Theodore Cable, the son of George and Mary Cable, the noted educator and clubwoman and first president of the Indianapolis NAACP, graduated from Shortridge High School and Harvard College, where he won fame as an athlete. He was a graduate of Indiana University School of Dentistry. According to the *Recorder,* a Republican paper, Brokenburr barely "squeezed" into the list of candidates endorsed by the Republican organization; all other black aspirants, including Bailey, were "cut out" by white Republicans, the paper claimed. In some precincts, it charged, Republicans circulated "100 percent American Slates," containing the names of white candidates only. This treatment, the *Recorder* predicted, would cause some black Republicans to vote for Democrats in November. Ibid., May 13, 1934.

51. *Indiana House Journal* (regular session 1933), pp. 494, 588, 660, 711, 827, 1052; Indiana *Laws* (1933), p. 1228.

52. Emma Lou Thornbrough, "Breaking Racial Barriers to Public Accommodations in Indiana, 1935 to 1963," *Indiana Magazine of History,* LXXXIII (December 1987), pp. 305–306; *Indiana House Journal,* 1935, pp. 154, 187, 228, 262, 716–17, 785–86; Indianapolis *Recorder,* February 2, 9, 1935.

53. James Philip Fadely, "Editors, Whistle Stops, and Elephants: The Presidential Campaign of 1936 in Indiana," *Indiana Magazine of History,* LXXXV (June 1989), pp. 101–37; Indianapolis *Recorder,* April 11, 18, May 2, 9, October 31, 1936; Thornbrough, "Breaking Racial Barriers," p. 306.

54. Indianapolis *Recorder,* September 5, 19, 26, 1936.

55. Ibid., November 7, 1936; Balanoff, "History of the Black Community of Gary," pp. 365–66; Bigham, *We Ask Only a Fair Trial,* p. 225. During his single term in the General Assembly, Talley was unobtrusive, sponsoring no controversial bills. Thornbrough, "Breaking Racial Barriers," p. 306; January and Walsh, *Century of Achievement,* p. 25.

56. Madison, *Indiana through Tradition and Change,* pp. 147–48; Indianapolis *Recorder,* May 7, November 12, 1938. Chester Allen, a native of Rhode Island, received a Ph.B. degree from Brown University and LL.B. from Boston University before moving to South Bend in 1930. January and Walsh, *Century of Achievement,* p. 26.

57. *Indiana House Journal* (1939), pp. 556, 765, 849, 878, 1043; Indiana *Laws* (1939), pp. 474, 658; Indianapolis *Recorder,* March 4, May 11, 1939.

58. Indianapolis *Recorder,* April 11, November 7, 1942, November 11, 1944; January and Walsh, *Century of Achievement,* p. 30, 31. Grant was inducted into the army in 1942 and had to be furloughed to attend legislative sessions. After two terms as representative, Grant served as a deputy prosecuting attorney and in 1958 was appointed by President Eisenhower to the state advisory committee of the U.S. Civil Rights Commission. Jesse Dickinson had a varied career. Born in rural Oklahoma, he managed to graduate as a voice student by working his way through Bethel College in that state. In 1928 he moved with his family to South Bend, where he continued his career as a singer and organizer of vocal groups and held a number of other jobs, including a position as social worker and recreational director under the WPA and work

in a defense factory during the Second World War. He also continued his education, enrolling in extension courses in various local colleges over a long period of time. Biographical notes on Jesse Dickinson in Manuscript Guide, Indiana Historical Society Library.

59. Indianapolis *Recorder,* October 25, 1944.

5. The Second World War

1. Gary *American,* September 15, 1939; Indianapolis *Recorder,* October 19, 1940, January 1, 4, 1941.

2. Gary *American,* December 12, 1941, January 2, 1942; Bigham, *We Ask Only a Fair Trial,* p. 226; Indianapolis *Recorder,* December 13, 1941, January 3, 17, 25, 1942; Thornbrough, "Breaking Racial Barriers," pp. 306–307.

3. Franklin, *From Slavery to Freedom,* pp. 428–29, 434.

4. Ibid., pp. 429, 434.

5. Indianapolis *News,* July 5, 1943; Indianapolis *Recorder,* June 10, 1944.

6. Dorothy L. Riker, *Hoosier Training Ground: A History of Army and Navy Training Centers, Camps, Forts, Depots, and Other Military Installations within the State Boundaries during World War II* (Bloomington, Ind., 1952), pp. 11, 30–31, 83, 85, 97, 124, 143, 151, 165, 272. Indianapolis *Recorder,* August 21, 1943, September 2, 1944. Atterbury later also served as a camp for Italian prisoners of war.

7. Indianapolis *Recorder,* August 1, 1942, January 1, 15, 1944; Max Parvin Cavnes, *The Hoosier Community at War* (Bloomington, Ind., 1961), pp. 148–50; Lynn W. Turner and Heber P. Walker (comps.), *Indiana at War: A Directory of Hoosier Civilians Who Had Positions of Responsibility in Official, Volunteer, and Cooperative War-time Organizations* (Bloomington, Ind., 1951), pp. 363, 381–82; Indianapolis *Star,* August 15, 1942. Nettie Ransom was Freeman Ransom's wife.

8. Indianapolis *Recorder,* April 24, 1943; Gary *American,* February 18, March 3, 1944.

9. Cavnes, *Hoosier Community at War,* pp. 155–56; Turner and Walker, *Indiana at War,* p. 352; Bigham, *We Ask Only a Fair Trial,* pp. 230–31.

10. Cavnes, *Hoosier Community at War,* pp. 151–53; Turner and Walker, *Indiana at War,* p. 355.

11. Indianapolis *Recorder,* December 9, 1944, March 17, April 14, 21, May 5, July 7, 14, 1945; Riker, *Hoosier Training Ground,* pp. 160–61; Franklin, *From Slavery to Freedom,* p. 436.

12. Indianapolis *Recorder,* December 2, 1942, May 8, 1943, May 27, 1944.

13. Ibid., September 12, 1942.

14. U.S. Department of Commerce, Bureau of the Census, 1950 Census of Population, *Indiana: General Characteristics,* Table 34, pp. 59–60; Indianapolis *Star,* September 15, 1951.

15. Cavnes, *Hoosier Community at War,* pp. 138–39.

16. "Housing in Indianapolis, Report of the Citizens Housing Committee," 1940, p. 1, mimeographed document (Indiana Division, Indiana State Library).

17. "Governor's Housing Commission Findings," 1941, pp. 7, 9, Indiana State Library; Indianapolis *Recorder,* August 23, 30, 1941.

18. Indianapolis *Recorder,* May 23, 1943, January 29, April 15, 1944.

19. Ibid., October 25, 1941; *Lockefield News,* March 30, June 30, 1942, June 30, 1943.

20. Indianapolis *Recorder,* November 20, 1943, July 29, 1944.

21. The Indiana General Assembly passed a state housing law in 1937 that enabled local housing authorities to borrow money for construction from the U.S. Housing Authority, but the state law did not become operative in any city until the city council authorized the creation of a local housing authority.

22. National Urban League, *Study of the Negro Population of Gary,* pp. 16–21.

23. Cavnes, *Hoosier Community at War,* pp. 141–43; Indianapolis *Recorder,* April 8, 1944.

24. National Urban League, *Study of the Negro Population of Fort Wayne,* p. 27; Indianapolis *Recorder,* February 23, 1940, March 17, 1945.

25. Cavnes, *Hoosier Community at War,* p. 141; Bigham, *We Ask Only a Fair Trial,* p. 226.

26. U.S. Bureau of the Census, *Census of the United States (1940): Population,* vol. 2, p. 696.

27. National Urban League, *Study of the Negro Population of Gary,* p. 6; Cavnes, *Hoosier Community at War,* p. 111.

28. Cavnes, *Hoosier Community at War,* pp. 110, 146–47; Ralph H. Turner, *A Preliminary Survey of Integration of Negroes into Employment in Indianapolis* (n.p., 1948), p. 12; Bigham, *We Ask Only a Fair Trial,* p. 230; Gary *American,* September 4, 1942; Indianapolis *Recorder,* June 8, 1940.

29. Indianapolis *Recorder,* August 17, October 26, November 16, 1940, January 11, 1941.

30. Ibid., March 22, 1941.

31. Madison, *Indiana through Tradition and Change,* pp. 386–87; Cavnes, *Hoosier Community at War,* pp. 114–18; Indiana State Defense Council, *The Problem in May 1941: The Story of H.B. 445, A Bill that Failed and the Problem of the Negro* (Indianapolis, 1941); Indianapolis *Recorder,* March 8, 15, 1941. The American Legion opposed H.B. 445 on the grounds that it was inspired by Communists. Ibid., March 22, 1941.

32. Madison, *Indiana through Tradition and Change,* p. 385; Cavnes, *Hoosier Community at War,* p. 115.

33. Indianapolis *Recorder,* June 14, 1941; Franklin, *From Slavery to Freedom,* pp. 426–27.

34. Madison, *Indiana through Tradition and Change,* p. 386; Cavnes, *Hoosier Community at War,* p. 130.

35. Cavnes, *Hoosier Community at War,* p. 118; Indianapolis *Recorder,* May 23, 1942.

36. Turner and Walker, *Indiana at War,* p. 500; Turner, *Preliminary Survey of Integration,* pp. 19, 23. In Gary black bus drivers were hired for the first time as the result of a campaign by the black Ministerial Alliance. Gary *American,* February 4, 1944.

37. Madison, *Indiana through Tradition and Change,* p. 388; Indianapolis *Recorder,* October 20, 1942; ibid., *Victory Progress Edition,* July 5, 1945.

38. National Urban League, *Study of the Negro Population of Gary,* p. 8; Bigham, *We Ask Only a Fair Trial,* pp. 229–30; Cavnes, *Hoosier Community at War,* pp. 128–29.

39. Cavnes, *Hoosier Community at War,* pp. 131–32; Goodall and Mitchell, *History of Negroes in Muncie,* p. 231.

40. Turner, *Preliminary Survey of Integration,* p. 24; Indianapolis *Recorder,* March 28, April 18, October 17, 1942, February 5, 1944; ibid., *Victory Progress Edition;* Cavnes, *Hoosier Community at War,* p. 121; National Urban League, *Study of the Negro Population of Fort Wayne,* p. 22; Bigham, *We Ask Only a Fair Trial,* p. 230.

41. Turner, *Preliminary Survey of Integration,* pp. 27–28; Cavnes, *Hoosier Community at War,* p. 121, 123, 134; Indianapolis *Recorder,* May 1, 8, October 9, 1943; Bigham, *We Ask Only a Fair Trial,* p. 229. Some of the blacks who were put on the machines had been Allison employees longer than the white strikers, many of whom were recent arrivals in the city.

42. Madison, *Indiana through Tradition and Change,* p. 383.

43. Indianapolis *Recorder,* March 23, 1935; Balanoff, "History of the Black Community of Gary," pp. 221–22. The frustrations experienced by Indianapolis blacks in the construction of Lockefield Gardens probably contributed to antiunion attitudes. In 1936 John L. Lewis, President of the United Mine Workers, one of the few industrial unions in the American Federation of Labor, was given authority to organize a Committee for Industrial Organizations (CIO).

The CIO later voted to become independent from the AFL and became the Congress of Industrial Organizations. After the war, the two labor organizations frequently acted jointly as the AFL/CIO.

44. Balanoff, "History of the Black Community of Gary," pp. 223–25, 231; Turner, *Preliminary Survey of Integration,* p. 33.

45. Madison, *Indiana through Tradition and Change,* pp. 247–48, 252–56.

46. Committee of Industrial Organizations, *Yearbook of Indiana State Industrial Union Council,* 1942, p. 50.

47. Gary *American,* April 27, 1945; National Urban League, *Study of the Negro Population of Gary,* p. 11; Goodall and Mitchell, *History of Negroes in Muncie,* p. 36.

48. Gary *American,* March 3, 1944; National Urban League, *Study of the Negro Population of Gary,* p. 11; Indianapolis *Recorder,* June 17, October 21, 1944, March 16, 1945; Cavnes, *Hoosier Community at War,* p. 124. At the P. R. Mallory Company in Indianapolis a dispute arose over whether a dance should be racially mixed or whether there should be a separate dance for black members, and similar disputes occurred in other factories.

49. Gary *American,* October 24, 1941; Indiana State Defense Council, *The Indiana Plan of Bi-racial Cooperation,* Pamphlet 3 (April 1942, Indianapolis) p. 16; Cavnes, *Hoosier Community at War,* p. 117.

50. National Urban League, *Study of the Negro Population of Gary,* p. 10.

51. Indianapolis *Times,* September 9, 1943; Indianapolis *Recorder,* March 11, 1944; Gary *American,* January 12, 1945. Similar "Hold Your Job" campaigns were launched in other Indiana cities and all across the country.

52. Indiana *Laws* (1945), pp. 1499–1503; Indianapolis *Recorder,* January 27, February 3, 24, March 3, 10, 1945, February 19, 1949; *Federation News,* April 1945, p. 1; Gary *American,* April 6, 1945.

53. Indianapolis *Recorder,* July 17, 24, 1943; Bigham, *We Ask Only a Fair Trial,* p. 232. There were widespread suspicions that rumors were spread by such nativist groups as the League for White Supremacy. *Indiana CIO Yearbook,* 1943, pp. 80–83.

54. Indianapolis *Recorder,* July 24, 1943.

55. Bigham, *We Ask Only a Fair Trial,* p. 232–33; Indianapolis *Recorder,* June 3, 10, August 12, 1944. Catholic schools in the northern part of the state had always admitted black students.

56. Indianapolis *Star,* August 2, 1943; Indianapolis *Recorder,* August 7, 1943, June 9, August 25, 1945; Henry J. Richardson and Howard J. Baumgartel, "History of the 1949 Indiana School Desegregation Law," Box 20, Henry J. Richardson Papers (Indiana Historical Society Library).

57. Office of Community War Services, Federal Security Agency, Chicago, "Report on Racial Situation in Gary, Indiana," mimeographed document labeled "confidential," ISL, pp. 1–5.

58. Indianapolis *Recorder,* August 12, September 2, 1944.

59. Ibid., June 23, 1945; Gary *American,* June 29, 1945.

60. Indianapolis *Recorder,* October 25, 1945.

6. Postwar Years

1. Indianapolis *News,* January 4, 1963.

2. According to the United States census of 1970 in Indianapolis, although the number of blacks increased between 1960 and 1970, their percentage of the total population had declined to 16.7 percent as the result of the so-called UniGov law of 1968, which incorporated all of Marion County into the city. In Gary in 1970 the percentage of blacks was 53.5; in Fort Wayne, 11.1; in South Bend, 8.7; in Evansville, 7.5; in East Chicago, 28.4. U.S. Census Bureau, *1970*

Census of Population: General Population Characteristics, Indiana, pp. 55–56. The 1968 UniGov law is discussed in chapter 8.

3. Indiana Civil Rights Commission, "Facts and Figures," 1960, p. 1 (mimeographed document, Indiana State Library); *Indiana Civil Rights Commission Bulletin* (March 1965), p. 9.

4. United States Commission on Civil Rights, Indiana Advisory Committee, *Gary Midtown West Families on AFDC: A Report of a Public Meeting Concerning the Aid to Families with Dependent Children Program in Gary, Indiana* ([Washington, D.C.], 1966), pp. 1–2.

5. Community Service Council of Metropolitan Indianapolis, *The Negro in Indianapolis: A Summary of Local Data* (Indianapolis, 1967), p. 19; Indianapolis *News,* May 13, 1971.

6. Indianapolis *News,* May 19, June 2, 1960.

7. Quoted in James H. Madison, *The Indiana Way: A State History* (Bloomington and Indianapolis, 1986), pp. 313–14.

8. Indianapolis *Recorder,* May 18, November 9, 1946. Decker, the only black representative ever elected from Vanderburgh County, was active in the United Automobile Workers. Ibid., December 21, 1946; January and Walsh, *Century of Achievement,* p. 33.

9. Indianapolis *Recorder,* May 8, November 6, 1948, January 1, 1949.

10. Ibid., January 17, February 21, April 3, June 12, 19, 26, July 10, 31, 1948. There are numerous letters in NAACP Records from members of the NAACP denouncing Ransom's ties with the Progressive Party. See, for example, Henry J. Richardson to Thurgood Marshall, May 5, 1948, NAACP Records. These criticisms, however, did not prevent Ransom from being repeatedly elected as president of the state conference of the NAACP.

11. Indianapolis *Recorder,* November 11, 1950.

12. Ibid., November 1, 8, 1952.

13. Ibid., November 6, 1954, November 10, 1956, January 30, 1957.

14. Ibid., March 12, 1955.

15. Ibid., May 7, 1955, May 3, 17, 1958.

16. Ibid., October 27, 1951, June 21, 1952.

17. Franklin, *From Slavery to Freedom,* p. 451.

18. Thornbrough, "Breaking Racial Barriers," p. 312.

19. Ibid., p. 311.

20. Indianapolis *Recorder,* November 27, 1948; Lane, *"City of the Century,"* p. 270.

21. Thornbrough, "Breaking Racial Barriers," pp. 312–14.

22. Indianapolis *Recorder,* December 15, 1945; Thornbrough, "Breaking Racial Barriers," p. 314.

23. Indianapolis *Recorder,* January 8, 1949.

24. Indianapolis *Star,* February 3, March 14, 1953; Indianapolis *Times,* December 21, 1952; Indianapolis *News,* October 10, 1955; Indianapolis *Recorder,* August 30, 1958. A copy of the 1953 ordinance is in the Urban League Papers (Indiana Historical Society), Box 1.

25. "Indiana State Conference of NAACP Branches, October 25 and 26, 1947, Fort Wayne, Indiana," NAACP Records.

26. Indianapolis *Recorder,* December 15, 1953.

27. Ibid., March 27, 1943.

28. January and Walsh, *Century of Achievement,* pp. 10–11; Goodall and Mitchell, *History of Negroes in Muncie,* p. 34; Indianapolis *Recorder,* February 15, 1947; Thornbrough, "Breaking Racial Barriers," p. 316.

29. Thornbrough, "Breaking Racial Barriers," p. 314.

30. Ibid., pp. 316–17.

31. Ibid., p. 317.

32. Ibid., p. 318.

33. Ibid., pp. 318–19.

34. Gilliam, *A Time to Speak,* p. 88; Thornbrough, "Breaking Racial Barriers," pp. 320–21.

35. National Urban League, *Study of the Negro Population of Gary,* pp. 4, 35.

36. Thornbrough, "Breaking Racial Barriers," pp. 322–23; Indianapolis *Recorder,* September 8, 15, 1945.

37. Lane, *"City of the Century,"* pp. 274–75; Indianapolis *Recorder,* September 8, 15, 1945, June 13, 1946.

38. Thornbrough, "Breaking Racial Barriers," pp. 323–24; Indianapolis *News,* June 30, July 25, 1956.

39. Indianapolis *Recorder,* August 2, 1947, January 29, 1949, January 17, 1953; ibid., *Victory Progress Edition.*

40. Turner and Walker, *Indiana at War,* p. 25; Indianapolis *News,* November 11, 1949.

41. Turner and Walker, *Indiana at War,* pp. 30, 35; Indianapolis *News,* November 12, 1949. Failure of the Indianapolis Street Railway Company to employ black operators on trolleys and buses was attributed to the strength of the AFL union to which white operators belonged. The business manager of the company told members of the state FEPC that if blacks were hired, white union members would start a massive strike that would paralyze public transportation. Indianapolis *Recorder,* April 5, 1952.

42. Indianapolis *Recorder,* June 29, 1946.

43. Ibid., January 22, 29, February 19, 1949.

44. Ibid., February 10, 17, March 3, 1951.

45. Ibid., February 12, 1949, January 29, February 5, 26, 1955, January 26, 1957, December 20, 27, 1958, January 31, 1959; Indianapolis *Times,* January 22, 1957.

46. Indianapolis *Recorder,* June 22, July 6, 1946.

47. Indianapolis Common Council, *Proceedings,* 1946, pp. 879–81, 932, 944–45; Indianapolis *Recorder,* October 12, 26, November 2, 1946.

48. Indianapolis *Recorder,* September 23, October 14, November 25, December 30, 1950; Indianapolis *News,* June 21, 1957.

49. James H. Madison, *Eli Lilly: A Life, 1885–1977* (Indianapolis, 1989), p. 100; Indianapolis *Recorder,* March 10, 1951.

50. Indianapolis *Times,* August 4, 1959; Lane, *"City of the Century,"* pp. 272–73; Indianapolis *Recorder,* September 27, 1952; Merit Employment Papers, Box 1, Indianapolis Urban League Papers (Indiana Historical Society Library).

51. It received no public money but was partially funded by the United Way. Information about Merit Employment Association in manuscript "Historical Background to Urban League" and other papers in Box 1, Indianapolis Urban League Papers.

52. *Report of State Advisory Committee to the U.S. Commission on Civil Rights, 1959* (U.S. Government Printing Office, 1960), p. 12.

53. Indianapolis *Recorder,* July 7, 1945; "Race Relations Clinic June 5–6, 1945," typescript (Indiana State Library).

54. Indianapolis *Star,* September 13, 1944; Indianapolis *Recorder,* September 16, 1944.

55. Indianapolis *News,* November 9, 1949.

56. Indianapolis *Star,* September 13, 1944; Indianapolis *News,* November 22, 1949.

57. "Post War Plans for Indianapolis," p. 16, pamphlet (Indiana State Library).

58. Cavnes, *Hoosier Community at War,* p. 139–40; Indianapolis *Recorder,* July 21, 1945. The area selected to be condemned and cleared was a short distance north of Attucks High School. Cleo Blackburn was born in Mississippi and moved to Indianapolis in 1928. A graduate of But-

ler with a master's degree from Fisk University, Blackburn was a Disciples of Christ minister and director of Flanner House for nearly thirty years. *Survey Graphic* praised Flanner Homes. Roger William Riis and Webb Waldron, "Fortunate City: Story of Flanner House Negro Neighborhood Settlement in Indianapolis," *Survey Graphic*, XXXIV (August 1945), pp. 339–42.

59. Michelle Hale, "Self Help Moves from the Neighborhood to the Nation: Flanner House, 1936–1953," *Black History News and Notes*, No. 46 (November 1991), pp. 6–8.

60. Indianapolis *News*, September 13, 1950; *Indiana House Journal*, 1949, pp. 12, 412–14; *Indiana Senate Journal*, 1949, pp. 427, 778.

61. Indianapolis *Recorder*, January 27, 1945; Indianapolis *Times*, June 18, July 7, 1953. Judge Steckler was probably influenced by a 1948 decision of the U.S. Supreme Court in which the justices ruled that a restrictive covenant could not be enforced by a state because it would violate the Fourteenth Amendment, which prohibited a state from denying any person "equal protection under the laws." *Shelley* v. *Kraemer*, 334 *US* 1.

62. Indianapolis *News*, February 7, 1950; Indianapolis *Recorder*, October 14, 1950. The two were Lockefield Gardens and Barrington Heights.

63. Indianapolis *News*, November 27, 1951; Indianapolis *Star*, March 2, 3, 1952.

64. Indianapolis *Star*, March 4, 1952; Indianapolis *Recorder*, March 8, 1952.

65. Indianapolis *Times*, August 9, 1959. These percentages published in the *Times* were not official U.S. census figures.

66. Ibid., July 31, 1960. By the middle 1960s the Mapleton Fall Creek Association and the Meridian-Kessler Association in areas adjacent to the Butler Tarkington area were discouraging white flight and working to maintain racial balance.

67. Indianapolis *News*, November 25, 1956, February 25, 1960, July 28, 1965; Indianapolis *Times*, August 7, 1959. For the Grandview community in Washington Township and the Fox Lake community of summer homes see chapter 8.

7. School Desegregation

1. Indiana *Laws* (1877), p. 124.

2. NAACP, *Annual Report*, 1941, p. 19; Indianapolis *Recorder*, March 8, June 7, December 8, 1941; correspondence between Thurgood Marshall and Prentice Thomas, February 26, March 20, 30, April 12, July 15, September 6, 1941, NAACP Records. There were no black lawyers in Jeffersonville.

3. Cohen, *Children of the Mill*, p. 184.

4. Ibid., pp. 177–86; Lane, *"City of the Century,"* pp. 234–38.

5. Lane, *"City of the Century,"* pp. 238–39; Cohen, *Children of the Mill*, pp. 189–92.

6. Indianapolis *Recorder*, December 20, 1947, March 6, 1948.

7. Ibid., September 13, 1947, July 24, 1948; Marion Perry Wynn to Earl Dryer, President Elkhart NAACP Branch, September 3, 1947, NAACP Records; Earl Dryer to Marion Perry Wynn, October 11, 1947, August 18, 1948, ibid.

8. Because Attucks and other Negro high schools in the state were not permitted to join the Indiana High School Athletic Association, they could not compete in the state basketball tournaments. In 1941 state Senator Brokenburr introduced a bill in the General Assembly to admit black high schools to the association. The bill was not adopted, but in 1942 IHSAA admitted Attucks and other black high schools. In the 1950s under coach Ray Crowe the Attucks teams dominated the state tournaments, and players like Oscar Robertson and Hallie Brant became heroes, both in the black community and among white basketball fans. Indianapolis *Recorder*, February 15, March 1, 15, 1941, May 23, 1942; Herbert Schwomeyer, *Hoosier*

Hysteria: A History of Indiana High School Basketball (Greenfield, Ind., 1985. 6th ed.), pp. 236, 240.

9. The Monday Luncheon Club included a broad spectrum of leaders, including members of the NAACP, some Garveyites, ministers, and educators. Benjamin Osborne served as one of the presidents. Indianapolis *Recorder,* April 20, May 6, 13, 1933.

10. Ibid., May 12, June 9, 16, July 7, August 11, 1934.

11. A bill adopted by the General Assembly and endorsed by black leaders provided that in "cities of the first class" (i.e., Indianapolis) the school board should provide free transportation for pupils required to attend segregated schools if they traveled more than one-half mile to the school. Ironically, free transportation brought more students to Attucks and increased overcrowding. Indiana *Laws* (1935), pp. 1457–58; Indianapolis *Recorder,* February 23, March 4, 1935.

12. Indianapolis *Recorder,* December 7, 1935, January 11, March 7, 14, July 4, 1936. The new white high school was named the Thomas Carr Howe School.

13. Indianapolis School Board, Minutes, January 29, February 12, 1946, Book OO, pp. 1517, 1524; Indianapolis *Recorder,* January 26, February 2, 16, 1946.

14. Indianapolis School Board, Minutes, December 30, 1946, Book OO, pp. 1740–42; Indianapolis *Recorder,* December 31, 1946; Indianapolis *Times,* December 31, 1946.

15. *Indiana House Journal,* 1947, pp. 151, 302–303; Indianapolis *Star,* January 30, February 21, 1947; Indianapolis *Times,* February 21, 1947; Henry J. Richardson to Thurgood Marshall, January 30, 1947, NAACP Records. A copy of the statement by the Indianapolis Board of School Commissioners is in the NAACP Records.

16. *Indiana House Journal,* 1947, pp. 672–73; Indianapolis *Times* February 21, 1947; Indianapolis *News,* February 28, 1947; Indianapolis *Recorder,* March 1, 1947.

17. Indianapolis *Star,* April 19, 1947; Indianapolis *Recorder,* June 28, 1947; Indianapolis *Times,* July 16, 1947.

18. Report of Education Committee, Indianapolis branch of NAACP to national office, October 8, 1947, NAACP Records; Indianapolis School Board, Minutes, Book PP, September 30, 1947, p. 1917; Indianapolis *Star,* October 1, 1947; Indianapolis *Recorder,* October 4, 1947.

19. Willard Ransom to Thurgood Marshall, April 8, 1948, NAACP Records; Indianapolis *News,* September 29, 1948; Baumgartel and Richardson, "History of the 1949 Indiana School Desegregation Law," p. 7.

20. Henry J. Richardson and Willard Ransom to Thurgood Marshall, October 6, 1946, NAACP Records; Henry J. Richardson to Franklin H. Williams, Assistant Special Counsel, November 5, 1947, ibid.; Willard Ransom to Thurgood Marshall, April 8, 1948, ibid.; Indianapolis *Recorder,* October 11, 1947.

21. Indianapolis *Recorder,* January 9, 1949; Indianapolis *Star,* February 20, 1949.

22. Forty-five of the votes in favor were cast by Democrats, thirteen by Republicans. *Indiana House Journal,* 1949, pp. 221, 466, 628–29; Indianapolis *Star,* February 18, 1949.

23. The CIO, the Federation of Churches, the Indianapolis Jewish Community Relations Council, the Indianapolis Congress of Parents and Teachers, the League of Women Voters, and the Marion County Bar Association endorsed the bill, and most of them lobbied actively for its adoption. Indianapolis *Star,* February 22, 1949; Indianapolis *Times,* February 21, 1949; Indianapolis *Recorder,* February 26, March 19, 1949.

24. *Indiana Senate Journal,* 1949, pp. 506, 508, 711–12, 814; Indianapolis *Times,* February 23, 24, 1949; Indianapolis *Star,* February 23, 24, March 2, 1949; Indianapolis *Recorder,* March 5, 1949; press release, March 17, 1949, NAACP Records.

25. Indiana *Laws* (1949), pp. 604–607.

26. Willard Ransom to Gloster Current, April 14, 1949, NAACP Records; Indianapolis *Recorder,* July 1, 1950. In June 1950, Ransom, who had been stigmatized by both Democrats and Republicans for his support of Wallace and the Progressive Party in 1948, went to the NAACP national convention in Boston to receive an award for the Indiana Conference for its part in the adoption of the school law.

27. Indianapolis School Commissioners, Minutes, Book QQ, April 12, 1949, p. 169; Indianapolis *Recorder,* April 16, 23, June 1, 1949. Under the school board plan, pupils from one Negro elementary school, Number 10, on the south side were assigned to Manual High School. Pupils from all other Negro schools were assigned to Attucks.

28. Indianapolis *Recorder,* September 3, 1949; Indianapolis *News,* November 25, 1953.

29. Indianapolis *News,* November 25, 30, 1953; Indianapolis *Times,* August 8, 1953, October 10, 1954.

30. Indianapolis *Times,* September 15, 1965.

31. Indianapolis *Recorder,* June 5, 1965, April 8, November 4, 1967.

32. Ibid., July 15, 1950. Faced with increasing opposition, the Citizen's Committee did endorse Grant Hawkins in 1955. Hawkins, the first African American to be elected to the Indianapolis school board, was a graduate of Indiana University and owned a janitorial supply house. He was a Democrat. Ibid., July 3, 1955; Indianapolis *Times,* November 3, 1955. In 1959 the Citizens Committee endorsed and elected Jessie Jacobs, an NAACP activist.

33. Indianapolis *Recorder,* May 21, 1949, September 16, 1950, August 4, 1951; Indianapolis *News,* September 21, 22, 1954.

34. *Christian Science Monitor,* December 16, 1957; *Wayne Martin et al.* v. *Evansville-Vanderburgh School Corporation.*

35. Indianapolis *Star,* August 16, 1981; Indiana Department of Public Instruction, *Indiana School Desegregation: A Brief Historical Overview* (Indianapolis, 1979), p. 3. Dillin's order did not require two white elementary schools in remote parts of the county to participate in the two-way busing.

36. *Christian Science Monitor,* December 16, 1957. Despite the woeful inadequacies of the school buildings, teachers in these schools were often able and dedicated and were remembered with respect and affection after the schools were closed. For information about the Summit Street School in Corydon, which was closed in the 1950s and is being restored as a museum and cultural center, see Indianapolis *Star,* December 14, 1992.

37. Indianapolis *Recorder,* May 14, 1949, September 16, 1950.

38. Goodall and Mitchell, *History of Negroes in Muncie,* p. 42; "Elkhart Racial Study" folder, Box 4, Fair Employment Practices Commission papers (Indiana State Archives).

39. Cohen, *Children of the Mill,* pp. 229–31.

40. In Gary, as in all Indiana cities except Indianapolis, the mayor appointed members of the school board, and several blacks had served on the Gary board. In Indianapolis, where board members were elected, not a single African American was chosen until 1955. See n. 32 above. *Bell* v. *School City of Gary,* 213 F Supp 819; 324 F 2d 209; Ronald D. Cohen, "The Dilemma of School Integration in the North: Gary, Indiana, 1945–1960," *Indiana Magazine of History,* 82 (June 1986), pp. 169, 181–82.

41. Indianapolis *Star,* May 5, November 20, 1964.

42. Indianapolis *Recorder,* May 26, 1951.

43. Andrew Ramsey to June Shagaloff, Education specialist, NAACP National Office, March 8, 1965, NAACP Records. Ramsey, a teacher at Attucks, held a bachelors degree from Butler University and an M.A. from Indiana University. He taught both Spanish and French, was active in scholarly professional organizations, and was a leader in the American Federation of

Teachers as well as the NAACP. Urbane and soft-spoken, always courteous, he was also un-compromising in asserting the rights of members of his race. His insistence on teacher inte-gration finally led to his transfer to Howe High School. Indianapolis *Recorder,* May 15, July 10, 1965, April 18, 1967; Indianapolis *News,* April 15, 20, 1967.

44. *Civil Rights Act of 1964, U.S. Code* 2000-6 (a) and (b); Emma Lou Thornbrough, "The Indianapolis School Busing Case," in Patrick J. Furlong et al., *We the People: Indiana and the United States Constitution* (Indianapolis, 1987), p. 73.

45. *U.S.* v. *Board of School Commissioners, Indianapolis, Indiana,* 332 F Supp 655.

46. Indiana *Laws* (1965), p. 149; Indianapolis *Star,* November 21, 1964, January 21, 26, Feb-ruary 3, 1965; Indianapolis *Recorder,* January 15, 1965.

47. Indianapolis *News,* June 20, 1968.

48. Indianapolis *Star,* December 28, 29, 1968.

49. Ibid., November 22, 1968, July 18, 1972; Indianapolis *News,* August 27, 1969, February 3, March 30, 1970.

50. Dillin, a native of Petersburg, a county seat in southwest Indiana, was the son of a lawyer and early became interested in the law. After graduating from Indiana University and Indiana University law school, he served as a Democratic member in the state house of representatives before entering the army during the Second World War. In 1949, when the General Assembly passed the law abolishing segregation in public education, he was serving as legislative advisor to Governor Schricker. In 1951 Dillin returned to the state legislature as Democratic floor leader in the house of representatives. He was elected to the senate in 1959 and served as majority leader. He was regarded as a partisan Democrat but was admired for his skills, particularly by newspaper men, who voted him the "most valuable member" of the lower house in 1951 and as majority leader of the senate in 1961. Indianapolis *News,* June 14, 1956, September 22, Oc-tober 7, 1961; Indianapolis *Star,* November 11, 1960, March 16, May 5, 1961, July 9, 1976.

51. Indianapolis *News,* August 6, 1971.

52. *Swann* v. *Charlotte-Mecklenburg Board of Education,* 402 *US* 1 (1971).

53. *United States* v. *Board of School Commissioners, Indianapolis, Indiana,* 332 D Supp 655–60, 680.

54. Ibid., p. 678.

55. The politics of UniGov and the changes in government that resulted will be dealt with in chapter 8, but since the law was crucial to the school desegregation suit, its relationship to the schools in Marion County will be dealt with in this context. Thornbrough, "The Indianapolis School Busing Case," p. 79.

56. Ibid., pp. 79–80.

57. Ibid., p. 80.

58. Ibid.

59. Ibid., p. 82.

60. Ibid., pp. 82–83.

61. Ibid., p. 83.

62. Indiana *Laws* (1974), p. 3345.

63. Thornbrough, "The Indianapolis School Busing Case," p. 86.

64. Ibid., p. 87. The pro-integration CHOICE board also asked Judge Dillin for permission to change the status of the school board from that of defendant to that of plaintiff. Dillin re-fused this request but granted them permission to present alternatives to one-way busing.

65. See Emma Lou Thornbrough, "The Indianapolis Story: School Segregation and Deseg-regation in a Northern City," unpublished typescript, c. 1990, chapter 11, Emma Lou Thorn-brough papers (Indiana Historical Society Library).

66. Thornbrough, "The Indianapolis School Busing Case," p. 80.

67. Ibid., p. 88.

68. Thornbrough, "The Indianapolis Story," chapter 12.

69. Ibid., chapter 11; Thornbrough, "The Indianapolis School Busing Case," p. 80.

70. See chapter 8 below for a further account of desegregation in Indianapolis and the townships.

71. Indianapolis *Star*, August 16, 1981; Indiana Department of Public Instruction, *Indiana School Desegregation*, p. 17.

72. U.S. Commission on Civil Rights, "Report on Southside High School in Muncie, Indiana," mimeographed press release, 1968 (Indiana State Library); Indiana Department of Public Instruction, *Indiana School Desegregation*, p. 16.

73. "Equal Opportunity in Fort Wayne Schools," pamphlet (Indiana State Library); Indiana Department of Public Instruction, *Indiana School Desegregation*, p. 4.

74. Indiana Department of Public Instruction, *Indiana School Desegregation*, p. 17; Indianapolis *Star*, August 16, 1981.

75. Frank Orman Beck, *Some Aspects of Race Relations at Indiana University, My Alma Mater* ([Bloomington, Ind.], 1959), pp. 36–37, 46–47.

76. Indianapolis *Recorder*, September 9, 1944, February 10, October 6, 1945; Beck, *Some Aspects of Race Relations at Indiana University*, p. 56; Thornbrough, "Breaking Racial Barriers," pp. 342 and passim.

77. See A. Leon Higginbotham, *In the Matter of Color: Race and the American Legal Process* (New York, 1978), pp. vii, viii, and ix, for an account of treatment of African American students before the Second World War. Higginbotham was a student at Purdue in 1944.

78. Indiana Civil Rights Commission, *Indiana Civil Rights Commission: The First 25 Years, 1961–1986* ([Indianapolis, 1986]).

8. The Turbulent Sixties

1. Indianapolis *News*, December 13, 1959, April 28, May 2, 1960; Indianapolis *Recorder*, January 13, 1968. The Indianapolis Breadbasket members included black and white ministers of all faiths, and it also included nonsectarian community organizations and businessmen. Its goals were fair employment, development of Negro businesses, consumer programs, and career guidance for young people.

2. Indianapolis *News*, August 12, 1964. CORE, which had originated as an outgrowth of the Fellowship for Reconciliation and emphasized brotherhood of whites and African Americans under the leadership of James Farmer, later changed character and philosophy and became an all-black organization.

3. Indianapolis *News*, February 20, 21, 1961; Indianapolis *Times*, March 1, 8, 1964.

4. Indianapolis *News*, January 22, 24, 1969; Indianapolis *Recorder*, November 2, 1968.

5. Indianapolis *Times*, November 15, 1963, March 15, 1964.

6. Indianapolis *News*, August 10, 1964.

7. Ibid., August 3, 13, 1964; author's interview with Thomas Binford, August 16, 1989. Ransom criticized Blackburn for failing to "serve as a catalyst in breaking down barriers of discrimination." Blackburn, however, told the Indianapolis *News* that he did not oppose an Indianapolis Urban League. Ibid., July 30, 1964.

8. Paul Brockman, "Indianapolis Urban League," *Black History News and Notes*, No. 44 (May 1991); Indianapolis *News*, December 2, 1965; Indianapolis *Recorder*, December 19, 1964. The Association for Merit Employment became affiliated with the Indianapolis Urban League. The

Urban League also inherited the functions of the earlier Indianapolis Human Relations Council, which was dissolved.

9. Matthew E. Welsh, *View From the Statehouse; Recollections and Reflections, 1961–1965* (Indianapolis, 1981), pp. 62–63.

10. Indianapolis *Times*, December 18, 1960. Rufus Kuykendall, a black Republican lawyer who had served on the staff of the U.S. Civil Rights Commission, was elected chairman of the coalition while John Preston Ward, the lawyer who later served as one of the attorneys in the Indianapolis School Desegregation suit, served as legal counsel. Thornbrough, "Breaking Racial Barriers," pp. 331–32.

11. Thornbrough, "Breaking Racial Barriers," p. 332.

12. The vote was almost entirely along party lines. Twenty-nine Democrats and one Republican voted in favor of the minority report. Ibid., p. 334–35.

13. Ibid., p. 335.

14. Ibid. Hatcher, previously mentioned as director of Merit Employment, was a white Quaker from Kentucky; he had graduated from Indiana University and held a divinity degree from the University of Chicago.

15. *Indiana Laws,* 1963, pp. 216–22; Thornbrough, "Breaking Racial Barriers," pp. 336–37.

16. Indianapolis *Times*, March 29, 1963. A few months after the hearing, the National Association for Real Estate Brokers adopted a statement on minority housing. The Indianapolis Real Estate Board then adopted a similar statement that said realtors had no right to determine "the racial, creedal or ethnic composition of any area," and that realtors should feel free to enter into a broker-client relationship with persons of any race. Indianapolis *News*, October 21, 1963.

17. Lane, *"City of the Century,"* pp. 279–82.

18. Indianapolis *News*, July 21, 28, 1964; Indianapolis *Times*, March 1, 1964.

19. Indianapolis *Times*, February 9, 1965.

20. Indianapolis *Recorder*, February 13, 1965; Indianapolis *Star*, January 19, 1965; *Indiana Laws*, 1965, pp. 482–85.

21. Indianapolis *Times*, February 9, 1965.

22. Indiana *Laws* (1967), pp. 881–82; ibid., 1969, p. 1795; Indiana Civil Rights Commission, *Report for 1969*, pp. 3–4.

23. In 1965 the Indiana General Assembly wiped out the last vestige of laws that made distinctions based on race when it repealed the antimiscegenation law that prohibited racially mixed marriages. Indiana *Laws* (1965), p. 106; Indianapolis *Recorder*, January 16, 1965.

24. Welsh, *View From the Statehouse*, p. 196.

25. Indianapolis *Recorder*, July 6, 1963; Indianapolis *Times*, June 17, September 27, 1963; Indianapolis *News*, August 13, 1963.

26. Indianapolis *News*, July 28, 1964. Cummings, pastor of Trinity Christian M.E. Church, had moved to Indianapolis in 1941 and graduated from Attucks in 1944. Republican Rufus Kuykendall was also elected to the city council.

27. Indianapolis *Times*, June 27, 29, 1965.

28. Indianapolis *Star*, August 19, 1965.

29. Lane, *"City of the Century,"* pp. 292, 297; Matthew E. Welsh, "Civil Rights and the Primary Election of 1964 in Indiana: The Wallace Challenge," *Indiana Magazine of History*, LXXV (March 1979), pp. 26–27. In Glen Park opposition to the prospect of public housing led the white population to circulate petitions seeking disannexation from Gary. The Wallace victory in Lake County had little effect on the state as a whole. Lyndon B. Johnson won the electoral votes of Indiana in November.

30. Lane, *"City of the Century,"* pp. 282–84; William E. Nelson and Philip J. Meranto, *Electing Black Mayors: Political Action in the Black Community* (Columbus, Ohio, 1977), pp. 197–99; James Haskins, *A Piece of the Power: Four Black Mayors* (New York, 1972), pp. 55–60.

31. Lane, *"City of the Century,"* p. 287.

32. Ibid., 289–90; Nelson and Meranto, *Electing Black Mayors,* pp. 301–302.

33. Nelson and Meranto, *Electing Black Mayors,* p. 263; Indianapolis *Recorder,* January 6, 1968.

34. Lane, *"City of the Century,"* p. 293.

35. Ibid., p. 295.

36. Nelson and Meranto, *Electing Black Mayors,* p. 377.

37. Indianapolis *Recorder,* October 21, 1967.

38. James C. Owen and York Willbern, *Governing Metropolitan Indianapolis: The Politics of Unigov* (Berkeley, Cal., 1985), pp. 90–91.

39. *Indiana Laws,* 1969, pp. 357–448.

40. Indianapolis *Recorder,* January 4, 18, 25, 1969. The U.S. Census of 1970 showed that blacks made up about 27 percent of the population of the old city of Indianapolis but only 17 percent of Marion County.

41. By 1965, twelve commissions had been created by acts of city councils and eight more had been created by mayors without council action. Indiana Civil Rights Commission, *Bulletin,* March 1965, p. 5. In 1963 a Human Relations Council was organized in Crawfordsville, where the total number of blacks was only 183. The action came about as a result of instigation by a group of Wabash College students. Before the creation of the council, blacks had never ventured into local hotels, restaurants, or barbershops. Indianapolis *News,* April 8, 1963.

42. Thornbrough, "Breaking Racial Barriers," pp. 342–43; Indiana Civil Rights Commission, *Civil Rights Bulletin,* July 1963, pp. 8–10; Indiana Civil Rights Commission, *Report,* 1966, p. 10; ibid., 1968, part 1, p. 6.

43. Indianapolis *Star,* March 31, 1963.

44. Ibid., August 11, 1963.

45. Indianapolis *News,* December 14, 1961.

46. U.S. Advisory Commission on Civil Rights, *Fifty State Reports,* 1961, pp. 143–45.

47. Indianapolis *Recorder,* September 21, 1963; Indiana Civil Rights Commission, *Civil Rights Bulletin,* October 1963, pp. 1–5; ibid., August 31, 1968. The Indianapolis *Recorder* found it newsworthy when the William H. Block Company, one of the largest department stores in Indianapolis, accepted a Negro in its training program for salespersons. A "selective buying" campaign by SCLC had some success in persuading A & P supermarkets to employ more blacks.

48. Indianapolis *Star,* October 1, 1967.

49. Indianapolis *News,* December 10, 1965.

50. Ibid., March 4, 1970.

51. Indianapolis *Star,* March 15, 1962.

52. Ibid., August 14, 1963.

53. Indianapolis *Star Magazine,* April 21, 1957, p. 6; Indianapolis *Times,* August 4, 1959.

54. U. S. Bureau of the Census, *1970 Census, Negroes,* Table 13, pp. 182, 186; Indianapolis *News,* October 30, 1968.

55. "Elkhart Racial Study," Box 4, Fair Employment Practices Commission Records (Indiana State Archives).

56. State Advisory Committee, U.S. Civil Rights Commission, *Report,* 1959, pp. 117–18; Indianapolis *News,* February 5, 1960.

57. Indianapolis *Times,* August 6, 1959; Advance Mortgage Corporation, "Midwestern Minority Housing Markets: A Special Report" (n.p., 1962), pp. 6, 18; testimony of William T.

Ray, in *United States of America Plaintiff* v. *Board of School Commissioners of Indianapolis,* July 12–21, 1971, pp. 38–39.

58. Indiana Civil Rights Commission, *Bulletin,* October 1964, p. 11; ibid., March 1965, p. 7.

59. Indianapolis *News,* August 5, 1965, August 9, 1972.

60. Ibid., August 7, 1972.

61. Indianapolis *Star,* May 28, 1967; Indianapolis *News,* August 7, 1972.

62. Indianapolis *News,* February 25, 1960, May 30, 1968, May 12, 1969. The country club was built and owned by African Americans, but whites were eligible for membership. The club was not a financial success, and the building was later sold to a black congregation as a church.

63. "History of Fox Lake Resort 1925–1965," Spears Papers (Indiana Historical Society Library); Fox Lake newsletters from 1965 to 1971, clipping from Fort Wayne *Journal Gazette,* June 27, 1982, ibid.

64. Arthur Whitman, "The Indianapolis Formula for Racial Peace," Indianapolis *Sunday Star Magazine,* December 8, 1968, pp. 4–7.

65. Indianapolis *News,* April 12, 1965.

66. Ibid., April 5, 10, 1968; Indianapolis *Star,* April 10, 1968.

67. Indianapolis *News,* April 17, 1993. It is worth noting that the assassination of Malcolm X in February 1965 attracted little attention in Indianapolis's black community. African American leaders interviewed by the Indianapolis *Star* expressed shock at his killing but insisted that they deplored his "extremism" and said that he would not have been killed if he had followed the precepts of King. However, Andrew Ramsey of the NAACP pointed out that Malcolm had been able to reach Negroes whom no one else could reach—"groups outside the pale of the regular civil rights movement"—and that the existence of extremist groups was evidence that "something is wrong." Indianapolis *Star,* February 22, 1965.

68. Indianapolis *Recorder,* April 13, 20, 1968.

69. Indianapolis *News,* July 12, 29, 1966.

70. Indianapolis *Times,* August 10, 1959, September 27, 1963, March 2, 4, 8, 1964; Indianapolis *News,* February 24, 1961; Indianapolis *Recorder,* May 18, 1968. Lugar later suspended one of the officers.

71. Indianapolis *Recorder,* June 29, 1968, March 22, 1969. The Panthers were sentenced to terms of two to fourteen years in prison and fined $2500 each.

72. Indianapolis *News,* June 6, 1969; Indianapolis *Recorder,* June 14, 1969.

73. Indianapolis *Recorder,* June 14, 1969.

74. Ibid., July 5, 19, 26, 1969.

75. Indianapolis *Star,* July 17, 1967, August 25, 1968.

76. Ibid., July 17, 1966, July 29, 1968; Indianapolis *News,* June 9, 1969.

9. Since 1970

1. U.S. Census Bureau, *Negro Population,* 1970, p. 10; Morton J. Marcus, "Indiana Minorities, 1980," *Indiana Business History Review,* 56 (April 1981), pp. 2–6; Indianapolis *Star,* February 6, 1991; Population Studies Division, Indiana Business Research Center, Indiana University School of Business and U.S. Bureau of Census, n.p. It is possible that the 1980 census finding that there were no blacks in some counties reflected the carelessness of the census taker. The 1990 census showed at least a few blacks in every county. For example, in the 1990 census Martin County showed a total of 12 blacks, although no blacks were counted in the 1980 census.

2. Figures compiled from 1980 U.S. Census (Tape File 4) by Indiana Research Center, Indiana University Graduate School of Business, Indiana State Library, and Indiana Department of Commerce.

3. Indianapolis *Star,* February 23, 1993.

4. Indianapolis *Star,* November 5, 1992, August 21, 1997, December 31, 1998; Indianapolis *News,* November 4, 1992. Carter did not run for reelection in 1996.

5. Indianapolis *Recorder,* January 13, 1973, January 3, 1981; Indianapolis *News,* September 24, 1990; Indianapolis *Star,* November 8, 1990.

6. Indiana *Laws* (1972), Public Law 14, pp. 210ff; ibid., Public Law 15, pp. 336f.

7. The senior member of the Indianapolis delegation is William Crawford, first elected in 1972 and serving continuously since that time. A native of Indianapolis, Crawford first acquired prominence as a leader in the local affiliate of the Southern Christian Leadership Conference. January and Walsh, *Century of Achievement,* p. 47. Also elected in 1972 was Julia Carson, a former employee of the United Auto Workers and a member of the staff of Congressman Andrew Jacobs. She resigned from the lower chamber in 1976 to become a candidate for the state senate where she served until 1990, when she resigned to be elected Trustee of Center Township. Ibid., p. 45. Carson was elected to Congress in 1996 and reelected in 1998. Joseph W. Summers, a prominent funeral director long active in the Democratic Party and the NAACP, was elected a representative in 1978. He served continuously until his death and has been succeeded by his daughter, Vanessa Summers Barnes. Ibid., p. 52. More recently Glenn Howard, a longtime member of the city-county council, was elected to the house of representatives. Billie Breaux, a public schoolteacher and a leader in the Indianapolis Education Association, was elected to succeed Julia Carson.

Among prominent and influential members of the house of representatives from Gary is Charlie Brown, a former teacher who has held a number of public positions in Gary. He was first elected in 1982 and has served continuously since then. Ibid., p. 56. Also prominent in recent years is Vernon Smith, mentioned below as an advocate of legislation dealing with problems of young black males.

The Gary delegation has included a number of able women. Among them is Katie Hall, a social studies teacher. Long prominent in civic affairs and a supporter of Mayor Hatcher, she was elected to the lower house in 1974, and after one term was elected to the senate. She resigned from that body after she was elected to the U.S. House of Representatives to fill the unexpired term of Representative Ray Madden, becoming the first African American from Indiana to serve in Congress. However, she was defeated in the Democratic primary in 1984. Ibid., p. 50. Hall was succeeded in the senate by Carolyn Mosby, who had been elected to the house of representatives in 1978. A graduate of Roosevelt High School, Mosby had attended several universities and had served as an administrative assistant in one of the offices at the University of Chicago as well as chairing the Gary Human Relations Commission and serving in numerous other civic organizations. Ibid., p. 54. When Carolyn Mosby died, she was succeeded in the senate by Earline Rogers, who had been elected to the house of representatives in 1982. Rogers holds a master's degree in education from Indiana University and has taught in the Gary schools for more than twenty years. Both as a representative and senator, she is recognized as one of the most articulate and persuasive members of the legislature, particularly in recent years as an advocate of casino gambling as a means of solving Gary's economic problems. Ibid., p. 58.

8. Ibid., p. 53. Goodall is also the author of *A History of Negroes in Muncie, Indiana,* published in 1976.

9. January and Walsh, *Century of Achievement,* p. 14.

10. Ibid., 16.

11. Indianapolis *News,* March 7, 1991, March 23, 1993; Indiana *Laws* (1993 Special Session), vol. 5, Public Law 247, p. 4821. Under the Indiana Constitution a simple majority can override a governor's veto.

12. Indianapolis *Star,* October 3, 1992, March 24, 1993; Indiana *Laws* (1993), vol. 4, Public Law 143, p. 3741.

13. Indianapolis *News,* March 7, 23, 1972, August 13, 1975.

14. Lane, *"City of the Century,"* p. 304.

15. Gary *Crusader,* May 18, June 21, 1986; Gary *Post Tribune,* May 6, 1987.

16. Gary *Post Tribune,* April 1, 16, 17, May 1, 2, June 6, November 4, 1987.

17. Indianapolis *Star,* April 27, November 8, 1995; Minneapolis *Star Tribune,* July 31, 1996; Chicago *Sun-Times,* May 1997; South Bend *Tribune,* February 19, 1998; Indianapolis *News,* May 31, 1999.

18. Indianapolis *Star,* February 27, 1993.

19. Cohen, *Children of the Mill,* p. 241.

20. Ibid.; Gary *Crusader,* February 1, 15, March 1, April 6, June 21, 1986.

21. Indianapolis *News,* November 22, 1982; Thornbrough, "The Indianapolis Story," chapter 12.

22. Thornbrough, "The Indianapolis Story," chapter 11, passim.

23. Indianapolis *Star,* May 16, 1989, June 9, 1989.

24. Indianapolis *News,* September 11, 1990; Indianapolis *Star,* January 16, 1991.

25. Indianapolis *Star,* September 4, 1992. Judge Dillin denied Goldsmith's plea that the city be a party to the Select Schools case described below.

26. Indianapolis *News,* July 10, 1992, February 10, 1993.

27. Ibid., July 30, 1993; Indianapolis *Star,* February 21, 1994.

28. Indianapolis *Star,* February 28, August 19, 1997.

29. Ibid., December 24, 1997.

30. Ibid., June 24, 1998.

31. Ibid., February 18, 1997; Gary Orfield and John T. Yun, *Resegregation in American Schools* (Cambridge, Mass., 1999 <www.law.harvard.edu/groups/civilrights>).

32. Indianapolis *News,* April 10, 1993.

33. Ibid., January 18, 1993.

34. Ibid., December 5, 1990.

35. Indianapolis *Star,* February 23, 1993.

36. Ibid.

37. Ibid., January 24, 1981, December 11, 1992; Indianapolis *News,* June 9, 1992.

38. As used in this context, "minorities" include African Americans, Hispanics, and women.

39. Indianapolis *Star,* January 25, September 10, 1991, February 23, 1993; Indianapolis *News,* February 23, 1993.

40. Indianapolis *Star,* December 1, 1991.

41. Ibid., September 6, December 1, 1991.

42. Ibid., February 21, November 22, 1992, February 21, 1993. Blackburn's favorite among the buildings he has designed is Grace Apostolic Church, a spectacular white building for the Pentecostal sect in an impoverished area on College Avenue. Blackburn died in August 2000.

43. Gary *Crusader,* January 4, September 6, October 11, 1986.

44. Indianapolis *News,* January 2, 1990.

45. *Indiana Lawyer,* II (July 17–30, 1991), p. 1; Indianapolis *News,* April 22, 1975.

46. Gary *Crusader,* August 9, 1986; Gary *Post Tribune,* April 4, 1987.

47. Robert B. Reich, *The Work of Nations: Preparing Ourselves for Twenty-first-Century Capitalism* (New York, 1991), pp. 213–15.

48. Chicago *Sun-Times,* May 1997.

49. Indianapolis *Star,* February 23, 1993.

50. Ibid., February 4, 8, 1995, April 17, 1998; Indianapolis *Business Journal,* May 31, 1999.

51. Reich, *Work of Nations,* p. 216.

52. Indiana Civil Rights Commission, *Annual Report,* 1975–1976; ibid., 1977–1980; Indianapolis *Recorder,* May 28, 1988; Indianapolis *Star,* February 23, 26, 1993.

53. Indianapolis *Star,* February 26, 1993.

54. Ibid., November 5, 1992.

55. Ibid., December 17, 1989.

56. Ibid., July 14, 1990.

57. Indianapolis *News,* November 5, 1992, December 17, 1993.

58. Indianapolis *Star,* August 8, 1993.

59. Ibid., December 17, 1989.

60. David Hatchet, "Black and Blue; Relations between Blacks and Police Continue to Stagnate," *The Crisis,* 98 (December 1991), p. 13; Indianapolis *Star,* August 10, 1986; Gary *Crusader,* January 4, 1986; Indianapolis *News,* August 30, 1993.

61. Indianapolis *News,* October 1, 1992.

62. Indianapolis *Star,* July 2, August 6, 1989; Indianapolis *Recorder,* February 17, March 19, 1988.

63. Indianapolis *Star,* August 6, 1989, April 28, 1990; Indianapolis *News,* February 22, 1994, March 4, 1991.

64. Indianapolis *News,* November 29, 1991.

65. Ibid., December 17, 1991; Indianapolis *Star,* May 2, 1992.

66. Indianapolis *Star,* February 27, 1993.

10. The Continuing Search for Identity

1. Professor Thornbrough's manuscript included only the title for this chapter and the indication that it would cover the period since 1970. The author would like to thank Frances Linthecome, Kay Rowe, Martin Ridge, Suellen Hoy, George Juergens, James H. Madison, Alice Brokenburr Ray, Phyllis Klotman, Paul Eisenberg, Janice Wiggins, James Mumford, and Pam Freeman for reading and commenting on the manuscript. I alone, of course, am responsible for its contents.

2. Indianapolis *Star,* September 19, 1969, reporting on a poll done in April; interviews with Frances Linthecome, Indianapolis, fall and winter 1998–1999.

3. Interview with Prof. Fred McElroy, Bloomington, Ind., March 11, 1999.

4. Interview with Janice Wiggins, director of Groups Program, Indiana University, Bloomington, March 9, 1999; Mary Ann Wynkoop, "Dissent in the Heartland: The Student Protest Movement at Indiana University, Bloomington, Indiana, 1965–1970" (Ph.D. dissertation, Indiana University, Bloomington, 1992), pp. 85–92.

5. Indianapolis *Star,* April 8, 1960; Indianapolis *News,* April 9, 1960. Thomas I. Atkins was the student body president elected in April 1960.

6. Wynkoop, "Dissent in the Heartland," pp. 120, 122–23.

7. Ibid., pp. 124–28. The fraternity that did not change its charter immediately was Phi Delta Theta, whose national leaders would not accept the changes the local president urged.

8. Ibid., p. 145; interview with Wiggins.

9. Interview with Professor emeritus Herman Hudson, Bloomington, Indiana, August 17, 1999; Wynkoop, "Dissent in the Heartland," pp. 136–37, 156.

10. Wynkoop, "Dissent in the Heartland," pp. 139, 157–59; Bloomington *Herald-Telephone,* September 17, 29, 1968; interview with Professor emeritus George Juergens, August 26, 1999.

11. Wynkoop, "Dissent in the Heartland," pp. 59–62.

12. Terre Haute *Star,* April 17, 23, May 3, 7, 22, 1969; Bloomington *Herald-Telephone,* May 6, 7, 1969.

13. Wynkoop, "Dissent in the Heartland," pp. 167–74; Bloomington *Herald-Telephone,* May 1, 3, 4, 5, 6, 8, 9, 1969; Terre Haute *Star,* April 25, 29, May 1, 2, 3, 6, 9, 1969; interview with Juergens, 1999.

14. Terre Haute *Star,* May 2, 5, 1969.

15. Ibid., May 6, 8, 1969; Bloomington *Herald-Telephone,* May 4, 5, 6, 8, 1969; Wynkoop, "Dissent in the Heartland," pp. 172–73.

16. Wynkoop, "Dissent in the Heartland," pp. 174–79; Indianapolis *News,* May 10, 1969; Terre Haute *Star,* May 12, 1969.

17. Interview with Hudson; interview with Juergens, 1999; Wynkoop, "Dissent in the Heartland," pp. 197–99.

18. Terre Haute *Star,* April 24, 25, 29, 1970.

19. Interview with Professor emeritus Phyllis Klotman, Bloomington, Ind., February 8, 1999.

20. Ibid.; Terre Haute *Star,* April 30, May 1, 2, 1970; Indianapolis *Recorder,* May 9, 1970; ISU website <http://wweb.indstate.edu/afri/>, May 1999.

21. Wynkoop, "Dissent in the Heartland," pp. 209–11, 217, 221; Bloomington *Herald-Telephone,* May 8, 9, 1970.

22. Bloomington *Herald-Telephone,* May 8, 9, 1970.

23. Terre Haute *Star,* May 7, 1970.

24. Quoted in Wynkoop, "Dissent in the Heartland," p. 217.

25. Bloomington *Herald-Telephone,* May 4, 1970.

26. Ibid., May 8, 1970; Wynkoop, "Dissent in the Heartland," p. 224. On other issues that Parker and King urged, most students who voted were unconvinced: most wanted ROTC to continue, and less than a fifth favored giving university money to Seale's defense fund.

27. Bloomington *Herald-Telephone,* May 13, 1970; Wynkoop, "Dissent in the Heartland," pp. 225–26.

28. Interview with Hudson.

29. Interview with Hudson. William Wiggins and Fred McElroy were IU graduate students in folklore and English when Hudson hired them, and Portia Maultsby was doing graduate work in music at the University of Wisconsin. All became tenured IU faculty members.

30. Interview with Klotman; interview with Wiggins; interview with McElroy.

31. Interview with Hudson. Joseph Hartley, who was an administrator at IU in the late 1960s and early 1970s, recalled that he and other faculty members "went about offering special scholarships to attract quality black students at Bloomington campus." Interview with Joseph R. Hartley by Jean Freedman, April 25, 1992 (91–98), typescript, Oral History Research Center, hereafter cited as OHRC, Indiana University, Bloomington.

32. Many of the state's colleges and universities offer programs in African American studies: Purdue University offers an undergraduate major in the field, e.g., while Ball State, DePauw, and Notre Dame offer undergraduate minors.

33. Herman C. Hudson, *The Black Faculty at Indiana University, Bloomington, 1970–93* (Bloomington, Ind., c. 1994), pp. 4–5. It is perhaps worth noting that faculty members rep-

resenting other minority groups and all women faculty also carry a similar extra burden of responsibility.

34. Interview with McElroy; interview with Juergens, 1999.

35. Interview with Wiggins; interview with McElroy.

36. Interview with Klotman; interview with Shirley Palmer, Indianapolis, March 18, 1999.

37. Interview with Pam Freeman, Assistant Dean of Students and head of the Racial Incidents Team, Indiana University, Bloomington, Ind., December 14, 1998; interview with Wiggins.

38. Indianapolis *News,* April 13, 1985; Indianapolis *Star,* February 14, 1987.

39. United Press International, July 11, 1984; Indianapolis *Star,* February 14, 1987.

40. James H. Madison, *The Indiana Way: A State History* (Bloomington and Indianapolis, 1986), pp. 276–81.

41. Indianapolis *Star,* May 26, 1996; South Bend *Tribune,* January 10, 1999.

42. *Final Report of the Interim Study Committee on the Problems of Black Males* (Indianapolis, 1992), p. 3.

43. Interview with Walter Blackburn, Indianapolis, February 17, 1999.

44. Ibid.

45. Ibid.

46. Monroe Little, "Black Indianapolis and Housing," in Monroe Little, ed., *The State of Black Indianapolis* (Indianapolis, 1992), p. 155; poll in *Blacks and Whites: Can We All Get Along?* (videotape, WRTV Indianapolis, 1992).

47. Monroe Little, "History," in Little, *State of Black Indianapolis,* p. 18; Amos Brown, *A Profile of the Indianapolis Black Community* (Indianapolis, 1992); Little, "Black Indianapolis and Housing," p. 156; Indianapolis *Star,* December 3, 1993.

48. Interview with Alice Brokenburr Ray and William Ray, Indianapolis, November 1998.

49. *Blacks and Whites.*

50. Interview with Palmer.

51. South Bend *Tribune,* July 17, 1994.

52. *Blacks and Whites.*

53. *Final Report . . . on Problems of Black Males,* p. 4.

54. Eric J. Bailey, "The Health Care Status of Black Indianapolis," in Little, *State of Black Indianapolis,* pp. 64–65.

55. Interviews with Linthecome.

56. *Final Report . . . on the Problems of Black Males,* pp. 27–28; Monroe H. Little, "Black Indianapolis, Crime and the Court System," in Little, *State of Black Indianapolis,* pp. 108–10; Indianapolis *Star,* February 8, 1998.

57. *Final Report . . . on the Problems of Black Males,* p. 2.

58. Ibid.

59. Ibid., p. 3.

60. Ibid., pp. 4–5.

61. See for example ibid., pp. 3, 5, 24–25.

62. Ibid., 25; Little, "Crime and the Court System," pp. 111–12, 119.

63. *Blacks and Whites.*

64. Indianapolis *News,* November 20, 25, December 21, 1981; Indianapolis *Star,* November 21, December 23, 1981, February 17, March 16, 1982.

65. Indianapolis *Star,* September 25, 26, 29, 30, October 1, 2, 3, 4, 7, 9, 11, 13, 14, 18, November 1, 17, 1987.

66. Washington *Post,* June 5, September 5, 1980; New York *Times,* August 14, 1982.

67. Little, "Crime and the Court System," p. 119.

68. William A. Blomquist, "Black Indianapolis, Unigov, and Politics," in Little, *State of Black Indianapolis,* pp. 70–97.

69. Part of the objection many blacks in Indianapolis expressed with regard to the extensive busing of IPS students to township schools was that it was ordered by a federal judge, who was not answerable to them, and that it removed their children from local schools, which parents could influence, to township schools where they had no say.

70. For African Americans elected to Congress and statewide office see above, pp. 191, 265n. For the first black Indianapolis school superintendent see above, p. 196. The first black president of the Indiana State Teachers Association was elected in 1983. Indianapolis *Star,* April 29, 1983. Cora Smith Breckinridge of Elkhart was the first African American elected to serve as Indiana University alumni trustee. South Bend *Tribune,* July 1, 1997. Robert J. Taylor had been appointed trustee of Purdue University in 1990. Indianapolis *News,* September 21, 1990. Pat Patterson of Gary was Miss Indiana in 1971. Indianapolis *Star,* June 28, 1982.

71. James Toler was the first African American appointed Indianapolis police chief and served December 1991–September 1995. Indianapolis *Star,* September 13, 1996. The first black appellate court judge in Indiana was East Chicago attorney Robert D. Rucker Jr.; ibid., September 23, 1990. Clarence Trigg was the first black superintendent of the Indiana Women's Prison. Indianapolis *News,* April 11, 1977.

72. Indianapolis *Star,* September 4, 1998.

73. Indianapolis *Recorder,* 1969; Indianapolis *Star,* August 20, 1974. Alpha Blackburn is married to Walter Blackburn.

74. *Blacks and Whites;* Indianapolis *Star,* December 14, 1995.

75. Indianapolis *Star,* February 13, 1966, February 12, 1967, January 16, 1969, February 4, 1973, January 12, 1978, January 30, 1979.

76. A brief look at the sources cited for this book makes this abundantly clear. Except for the books and articles Thornbrough herself published on Indiana black history, there was very little before 1970.

77. Indianapolis *News,* December 1, 1975; Indianapolis *Star,* May 24, 1976.

78. Indianapolis *Star,* February 3, 1984, August 23, 1988; Indianapolis *News,* September 28, 1984; Darlene Clark Hine, Patrick Kay Bidelman, and Shirley M. Herd, eds., *The Black Women in the Middle West Project: A Comprehensive Resource Guide* (Indianapolis, 1986).

79. Wilma Gibbs, "Connecting the Dots: The Quest to Gather the History of African-Americans in Indiana—A Question and Answer Approach," *Black History News and Notes,* No. 48 (May 1992), pp. 5–7.

80. New York *Times,* February 19, 1986; Washington *Post,* February 21, 1988.

81. Note, for example, the comments of whites on the call-in line to Channel 6 WRTV in Indianapolis after the airing of its series *Black and Whites.* Interview with Freeman. It is interesting that Benjamin Smith, the racist and former IU student who killed an African American and a Korean in a two-state rampage in July 1999, claimed that he turned to race hatred after studying black history in school.

82. See, for example, an article on Afrocentrism in public schools that focuses on Indianapolis; Suzanne Daley, "Inspirational Black History Draws Academics' Fire," New York *Times,* October 10, 1990.

83. Lynn Ford, "Stereotypes of Minorities Still Promoted on Television," Indianapolis *Star,* January 20, 1996.

84. The subject of black musical performers and racial identity is beyond the scope of this essay; but any complete treatment of the meaning of racial identity in Indiana and the nation must acknowledge the enormous influence of African American musical innovations and per-

formers in shaping American national character. From Gary's Michael Jackson to the latest versions of "hip-hop," black musical culture has long been the principal driving force in American popular music.

85. In mid-twentieth-century America, Joe DiMaggio, son of Sicilian immigrants, who dropped out of school because he scarcely could read, represented for many an ideal of American grace and manhood as a baseball superstar. At the end of the century, 140 years after the end of slavery and nearly 400 years after African Americans first came to what is now the United States, Michael Jordan reinvented an ideal of American manhood—but this ideal was a college graduate, a highly articulate analyst of his game, a multimillionaire, and black. Similarly, Oprah Winfrey emerged as a new icon of American womanhood—highly articulate and well informed, a multimillionaire, a major force in establishing reading clubs among women, and black.

86. Lilly Endowment, *The Black Church in America* (Indianapolis, 1992); Indianapolis *News*, February 6, 1982; Indianapolis *Star*, February 14, 1999.

87. *Black Church in America;* Christopher Slone, "Black Churches Pursue Unity, Not Uniformity," *Christianity Today*, 41 (July 14, 1997), pp. 64–67; L. C. Rudolph, *Hoosier Faiths: A History of Indiana Churches and Religious Groups* (Bloomington, Ind., 1995), pp. 442, 463–64, 634–40.

88. Indianapolis *Star*, November 6, 1995; "Battling for Souls," *Newsweek*, October 30, 1995.

89. Indianapolis *Star*, October 13, 15, 16, 1995; South Bend *Tribune*, October 27, 1995, October 17, 31, 1996; Louisville *Courier-Journal*, December 10, 1995.

90. Rudolph, *Hoosier Faiths*, pp. 635–38; Indianapolis *Star*, August 25, 1998.

91. South Bend *Tribune*, June 2, 1995.

92. Interview with Alice Brokenburr Ray; interview with Collins Ferguson and David Hubbard, Lafayette, Indiana, March 20, 1999; interview with Linthecome.

93. Interview with Kay Anderson Rowe, Bloomington, November 1998; interview with McElroy; Little, "History of Black Indianapolis," p. 21.

94. Interview with Blackburn.

95. Interview with Rays; interview with Blackburn; interview with Wiggins; interview with Palmer.

96. Interview with Freeman; interview with Wiggins.

97. Irish and Italian gangs offered a major subject for Hollywood films during the Depression; see *Public Enemy*, dir. William Wellman (1931), and *Little Caesar*, dir. Mervyn Leroy (1930). Literary works also explored these phenomena: see, for example, James T. Farrell, *Studs Lonegan* trilogy (1932–1935), and Mario Puzo, *The Godfather* (1969). Progressive era social workers reported juvenile delinquency among immigrants as a sign of parental breakdown of authority. Sophonisba P. Breckinridge and Edith Abbott, *The Delinquent Child and the Home: A Study of the Delinquent Wards of the Juvenile Court of Chicago* (New York, 1917), chapter III and passim. For an historical analysis of the view that the poor are more highly sexed and less moral than others see, e.g., Edmund Morgan, *American Slavery, American Freedom* (New York, 1975).

98. B. L. Martin, "From Negro to Black to African American: The Power of Names and Naming," *Political Science Quarterly*, 106 (Spring 1991), pp. 83–108.

Index

Page numbers in *italics* refer to illustrations.

Index

Page numbers in *italics* refer to illustrations.

EMMA LOU THORNBROUGH
(1913–1994)

Emma Lou Thornbrough was the acknowledged expert on Indiana black history. She was author of *The Negro in Indiana before 1900: A Study of a Minority* (1957, reprinted 1993) and *Since Emancipation: A Short History of Indiana Negroes, 1863–1963* (1964), and she edited *This Far by Faith: Black Hoosier Heritage* (1982). Professor of History at Butler University from 1946 to 1983, Thornbrough held the McGregor Chair in History and received the university's highest award, the Butler Medal, in 1981. She completed a draft of all but the last chapter of this book before her death in 1994.

LANA RUEGAMER

Lana Ruegamer, editor for the Indiana Historical Society from 1975 to 1984, is the author of *A History of the Indiana Historical Society, 1830–1980.* She taught at Indiana University from 1986 to 1998 and is presently Associate Editor of the *Indiana Magazine of History.* Her article "Dorothy Lois Riker, 1904–1994: Reflections on Indiana History, Historical Editing, and Women in the Historical Profession" won the 1995 Thornbrough Prize for best article published in the *Indiana Magazine of History.*